Microsoft® Access
Data Analysis

Microsoft® Access
Data Analysis
Unleashing the Analytical
Power of Access

Michael Alexander

Wiley Publishing, Inc.

Microsoft® Access Data Analysis: Unleashing the Analytical Power of Access

Published by
Wiley Publishing, Inc.
10475 Crosspoint Boulevard
Indianapolis, IN 46256
www.wiley.com

Copyright © 2006 by Wiley Publishing, Inc., Indianapolis, Indiana
Published simultaneously in Canada

ISBN 13: 978-0-7645-9978-1
ISBN 10: 0-7645-9978-X

Manufactured in the United States of America

10 9 8 7 6 5 4 3

1B/SQ/RS/QV/IN

For Mary, Ethan, and Emma

About the Author

Michael Alexander is a Microsoft Certified Application Developer (MCAD) with more than 13 years experience consulting and developing office solutions. Michael started his career in consulting and development at the White House Communications Agency in Washington DC where he spearheaded the development of a standalone HRIS system for the White House's Military Office. He parlayed his experience with VBA and VB into a successful consulting practice in the private sector, developing middleware and reporting solutions for a wide variety of industries. He currently lives in Plano, TX where he serves as the director of an analytical services department of a $700 million company. In his spare time, he runs a free tutorial site, `www.datapig technologies.com`, where he shares basic Access and Excel tips with intermediate users.

Credits

Acquisitions Editor
Katie Mohr

Development Editors
Gabrielle Nabi
John Sleeva

Technical Editor
Mike Stowe

Production Editor
Angela Smith

Copy Editor
Kim Cofer

Editorial Manager
Mary Beth Wakefield

Vice President & Executive Group Publisher
Richard Swadley

Vice President and Publisher
Joseph B. Wikert

Project Coordinator
Ryan Steffen

Graphics and Layout
Carrie Foster
Jennifer Heleine
Melanee Prendergast

Quality Control Technicians
Brian H. Walls
John Greenough

Proofreading and Indexing
TECHBOOKS Production Services

Contents

Acknowledgments

Thank you to Robert Zey for his work on Chapter 1. Thank you to Martin Green, who runs one of the best Access tutorials sites around, for allowing me to include some of his examples in this book. Thanks to Darren Evans for all the input during the writing process. A big thank you to Mike Stowe, a superb technical editor who kept me honest and sparked some great ideas. A special thanks to Katie Mohr for taking a chance on this project and being such a wonderful project manager. Finally, many thanks to Gabrielle Nabi, John Sleeva, and the brilliant team of professionals who helped bring this book to fruition.

Introduction

Defining Data Analysis

If you were to ask a random sampling of people what data analysis is, most would say that it is the process of calculating and summarizing data to get an answer to a question. In one sense, they are correct. However, the actions they are describing represent only a small part of the process known as data analysis.

For example, if you were asked to analyze how much revenue in sales your company made last month, what would you have to do in order to complete that analysis? You would just calculate and summarize the sales for the month, right? Well, where would you get the sales data? Where would you store the data? Would you have to clean up the data when you got it? How would you present your analysis: by week, by day, by location? The point is that the process of data analysis is made up of more than just calculating and summarizing data.

A more representative definition of data analysis is the process of systematically collecting, transforming, and analyzing data in order to present meaningful conclusions. To better understand this concept, think of data analysis as a process that encapsulates four fundamental actions: collection, transformation, analysis, and presentation.

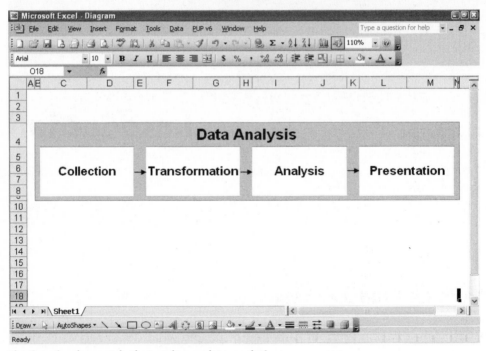

The four fundamentals that make up data analysis.

- **Collection** encompasses the gathering and storing of data—that is, where you obtain your data, how you will receive your data, how you will store your data, and how you will access your data when it comes time to perform some analysis.

- **Transformation** is the process of ensuring your data is uniform in structure, free from redundancy, and stable. This generally entails things like establishing a table structure, cleaning text, removing blanks, and standardizing data fields.

- **Analysis** is the investigation of the component parts of your data and their relationships to your data source as a whole. You are analyzing your data when you are calculating, summarizing, categorizing, comparing, contrasting, examining, or testing your data.

- **Presentation** deals with how you make the content of your analysis available to a certain audience—that is, how you choose to display your results. Some considerations that go along with presentation of your analysis include the platform you will use, the levels of visibility you will provide, and the freedom you will give your audience to change their view.

Keeping these four fundamentals in mind as you move through this book will help you recognize what is being accomplished in each chapter and how using Access can enhance your data analysis.

Why Use Microsoft Access for Data Analysis?

When you ask most people which software tool they use for their daily data analysis, the answer you most often get is Excel. Indeed, if you were to enter "data analysis" in an Amazon.com search, you would get a plethora of books on how to analyze your data with Excel. Well, if so many people seem to agree that using Excel to analyze data is the way to go, why bother using Access for data analysis? The honest answer: To avoid the limitations and issues that plague Excel.

Where data analysis with Excel can go wrong

Your humble author must confess that he has used Excel for years and continues to use it every day. It is considered the premier platform for performing and presenting data analysis. Anyone who does not understand Excel in today's business world is undoubtedly hiding that shameful fact. The interactive, impromptu analysis that can be performed with Excel makes it truly unique in the industry. However, years of consulting experience have brought your capable author face-to-face with managers, accountants, and analysts alike who have had to accept one simple fact: their analytical needs had outgrown Excel. They all met with fundamental issues that stemmed from one or more of Excel's three problem areas: scalability, transparency of analytical processes, and separation of data and presentation.

Scalability

Scalability is one of Excel's immediate drawbacks. As of Office 2003, 65,536 rows of data are all that can neatly be placed into a single Excel tab. Why is this problematic? Imagine that you are working in a small company and you are using Excel to analyze your monthly transactions. As time goes on, you build a robust process complete with all the formulas, pivot tables, and macros you need to analyze the data that is stored in your neatly maintained tab. What happens when you reach the 65,536 limit? Do you start a new tab? How do you analyze two datasets on two different tabs as one entity? Are your formulas still good? Will you have to write new macros? These are all issues that need to be dealt with.

Of course, you will have the Excel power-users, who will find various clever ways to work around this limitation. In the end, though, they will always be just workarounds. Eventually, even power-users will begin to think less about the most effective way to perform and present analysis of their data and more about how to make something "fit" into Excel without breaking their formulas and functions. I do concede that Excel is flexible enough that a proficient user can make most things "fit" into Excel just fine. However, when users think only in terms of Excel, they are undoubtedly limiting themselves, albeit in an incredibly functional way!

In addition, this limitation often forces Excel users to have the data prepared for them. That is, someone else extracts large chunks of data from a large database, and then aggregates and shapes the data for use in Excel. Should the serious analyst always be dependent on someone else for his or her data needs? What if an analyst could be given the tools to "access" vast quantities of data without relying on someone else to give him the data he needs? Could that person become more valuable to the organization? Could that person focus on the accuracy of the analysis and the quality of the presentation instead routing Excel data maintenance?

Access is an excellent—many would say logical—next step for the analyst who faces an ever-increasing data pool. Because an Access table has no predetermined row limitations, an analyst will be able to handle larger datasets without requiring the data to be summarized or prepared to fit into Excel. And because many tasks can be duplicated in both Excel and Access, an analyst that is proficient at both will be prepared for any situation. The alternative is telling everyone, "Sorry, it is not in Excel."

Another important advantage of using Access is that if the process, which is currently being tracked in Excel, ever becomes more crucial to the organization and needs to be tracked in a more "enterprise-acceptable" environment, it will be easier to upgrade and scale up if it is already in Access.

NOTE An Access table is limited to 256 columns but has no row limitation. This is not to say that Access has unlimited data storage capabilities. Every bit of data causes the Access database to grow in file size. To that end, an Access database has a file size limitation of 2 GB.

Transparency of analytical processes

One of Excel's most attractive features is its flexibility. Each individual cell can contain text, a number, a formula, or practically anything else the user defines. Indeed, this is one of the fundamental reasons Excel is such an effective tool for data analysis. Users can use named ranges, formulas, and macros to create an intricate system of interlocking calculations, linked cells, and formatted summaries that work together to create a final analysis.

So what is the problem with that? The problem is that there is no transparency of analytical processes. In other words, it is extremely difficult to determine what is actually going on in a spreadsheet. Anyone who has had to work with a spreadsheet created by someone else knows all too well the frustration that comes with deciphering the various gyrations of calculations and links being used to perform some analysis. Small spreadsheets that are performing modest analysis are painful to decipher, whereas large, elaborate, multi-tab workbooks are virtually impossible to decode, often leaving you to start from scratch.

Even auditing tools that are available with most Excel add-in packages provide little relief. The following figure shows the results of a formula auditing tool run on an actual workbook used by a real company. This is a list of all the formulas in this workbook. The idea is to use this list to find and make sense of existing formulas. Notice that line 2 shows that there are 156 formulas. Yeah, this list helps; good luck.

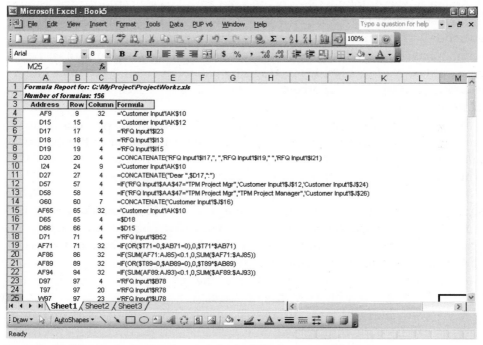

Formula auditing tools don't help much in deciphering spreadsheets.

Compared to Excel, Access seems rigid, strict, and unwavering in its rules. No, you can't put formulas directly into data fields. No, you can't link a data field to another table. To many, Excel is the cool gym teacher that lets you do anything, while Access is the cantankerous librarian that has nothing but error messages for you. However, all this rigidity comes with a benefit.

Because only certain actions are allowable, you can more easily come to understand what is being done with a set of data in Access. If a dataset is being edited, a number is being calculated, or any portion of the dataset is being affected as a part of an analytical process, you will readily see that action, whether in a query or a procedure that is being explicitly called in a macro or an event. This is not to say that users can't do foolish and confusing things in Access. However, you definitely will not encounter hidden steps in an analytical process such as hidden formulas, hidden cells, or named ranges in dead tabs.

Separation of data and presentation

The general concept is that data should be separate from presentation; you do not want the data to become too tied into any one particular way of presenting that data. For example, when you receive an invoice from a company, you don't assume that the financial data on that invoice is the true source of your data. It is a presentation of your data. It can be presented to you in other manners and styles on charts or on Web sites. But the data on these items is never the actual copy of the data itself. This sounds obvious, but it becomes important when you study an approach of using Access and Excel together for data analysis.

What exactly does this concept have to do with Excel? People that perform data analysis with Excel, more often than not, tend to fuse the data, the analysis, and the presentation together. For example, you will often see an Excel Workbook that has 12 tabs, each representing a month. On each tab, data for that month is listed, along with formulas, pivot tables, and summaries. What happens when you are asked to provide a summary by quarter? Do you add more formulas and tabs to consolidate the data on each of the month tabs? The fundamental problem in this scenario is that the tabs actually represent data values that are fused into the presentation of your analysis. The point is that data should not be tied to a particular presentation, no matter how apparently logical or useful it may be. However, in Excel, it happens all the time.

In addition, as previously discussed, because all manners and phases of analysis can be done directly within a spreadsheet, Excel cannot effectively provide adequate transparency to the analysis. Each cell has the potential of holding formulas, being hidden, or containing links to other cells. In other words, there is a fine line between analysis and data that makes it difficult to determine exactly what is going on in a spreadsheet. Moreover, it takes a great deal of effort in the way of manual maintenance to ensure that edits and unforeseen changes don't affect previous analyses.

Access inherently separates its analytical components into tables, queries, and reports. By separating these elements, Access makes data less sensitive to changes and creates a data analysis environment where you can easily respond to new requests for analysis without destroying previous analyses.

Many who use Excel will find themselves manipulating its functionalities to approximate this database behavior. If you find yourself in this situation, you must ask yourself if you are using Excel's functionality to make it behave like a database application, perhaps the real thing just might have something to offer. Utilizing Access for data storage and analytical needs would enhance overall data analysis and would allow Excel power-users to focus on the presentation in their spreadsheets.

In the future, there will be more data, not less—and more demands for complex data analysis, not fewer. Power-users are going to need to add some tools to their repertoire in order to get away from being simply "spreadsheet mechanics." Excel can be stretched to do just about anything, but maintaining such "creative" solutions can be a tedious, manual task. You can be sure that the sexy part of data analysis is not in routine data management within Excel. Rather, it is in the creating of slick processes and utilities that will provide your clients with the best solution for any situation.

Deciding whether to use Access or Excel

After such a critical view of Excel, it is important to say that the key to your success in the sphere of data analysis will not come from discarding Excel altogether and exclusively using Access. Your success will come from proficiency with both applications, and the ability to evaluate a project and determine the best platform to use for your analytical needs. Are there hard and fast rules that you can follow to make this determination? The answer is no, but there are some key indicators in every project that you can consider as guidelines to determine whether to use Access or Excel. These indicators are the size of the data, the data's structure, the potential for data evolution, the functional complexity of the analysis, and the potential for shared processing.

Data size

The size of your dataset is the most obvious consideration you will have to take into account. Although Excel can handle a little more than 65,000 rows, it is generally a good rule to start considering Access if your dataset reaches 50,000 rows. The reason for this is the fundamental way in which Access and Excel handle data. When you open an Excel file, the entire file is loaded into

RAM to ensure quick data processing and access. The drawback to this behavior is that Excel requires a great deal of RAM to process even the smallest change in your spreadsheet. You may have noticed that when you try to perform an AutoFilter on a large formula-intensive dataset, Excel is slow to respond, giving you a "Calculating" indicator in the status bar. The larger your dataset, the less efficient the data crunching in Excel will be. Access, on the other hand, does not follow the same behavior as Excel. When you open an Access table, it may seem as though the whole table is opening for you, but in reality Access reads only small portions of data at a time. This minimizes the RAM needed to open the dataset, ensures the cost-effective use of memory, and allows for more efficient data crunching on larger datasets. In addition, Access allows you to make use of indexes that enable you to search, sort, filter, and query extremely large datasets very quickly.

Data structure

If you are analyzing data that resides in one table that has no relationships with other tables, Excel is a fine choice for your analytical needs. However, if you have a series of tables that interact with each other, such as a Customers table, an Orders table, and an Invoices table, then consider using Access. Access is a relational database, which means that it is designed to handle the intricacies of interacting datasets. Some of these are data integrity, the prevention of redundancy, and the efficient comparison and querying between the datasets. You learn more about the concept of table relationships in Chapter 1.

Data evolution

Excel is an ideal choice for quickly analyzing data that is being used as a means to an end—that is, a temporary dataset that is being crunched to obtain a more valuable subset of data. The result of a pivot table is a perfect example of this kind of one-time data crunching. However, if you are building a long-term analytical process with data that has the potential of evolving and growing, Access is a better choice. Many analytical processes that start in Excel begin small and run fine in Excel, but as time goes on, these processes grow in both size and complexity until they reach the limits of Excel. The message here is that you should use some foresight and consider future needs when determining which platform is best for your scenario.

Functional complexity

There are far too many real-life examples of analytical projects where processes are brute-forced into Excel even when Excel's limitations have been reached. How many times have you seen a workbook that contains an analytical process encapsulating multiple tabs, macros, pivot tables, and formulas that add, average, count, look up, and link to other workbooks? The fact is that when Excel-based analytical processes become overly complex, they are difficult to manage, difficult to maintain, and difficult to translate to others. Consider using Access for projects that have complex, multiple-step analytical processes.

Shared processing

Although it is possible to have multiple users work on one central Excel spreadsheet located on a network, ask anyone who has tried to coordinate and manage a central spreadsheet how difficult and restrictive it is. Data conflicts, loss of data, locked-out users, and poor data integrity are just a few examples of some of the problems you will encounter if you try to build a multiple-user process with Excel. Consider using Access for your shared processes. Access is better suited for a shared environment for many reasons. Some of these are the ability for users to concurrently enter and update data, inherent protections against data conflicts, prevention of data redundancy, and protection against data entry errors.

A Gentle Introduction to Access

Many seasoned managers, accountants, and analysts come to realize that just because something can be done in Excel does not necessarily mean Excel is the best way to do it. This is the point when they decide to open Access for the first time. When they do open Access, the first object that looks familiar to them is the Access table. In fact, Access tables look so similar to Excel spreadsheets that most Excel users try to use tables just like a spreadsheet. However, when they realize that they can't type formulas directly into the table or duplicate most of Excel's behavior and functionality, they start to wonder just what exactly is the point of using Access?

In truth, when many Excel experts find out that Access does not behave or look like Excel, many write Access off as being too difficult to learn or "taking too much time" to learn. However, the fact is that many of the concepts behind how data is stored and managed in Access are concepts with which the user is already familiar. Any Excel user needs to learn such concepts in order to perform and present complex analysis. Investing a little time upfront to see just how Access can be made to work for you can save a great deal of time later in automating routine data processes.

Through the course of this book, you learn various techniques in which you can use Access to perform much of the data analysis you are now performing exclusively in Excel. This section is a brief introduction to Access from an Excel expert's point of view. Here, you will focus on the "big picture" items in Access.

If some of the Access terms mentioned here are new or not terribly familiar, be patient. They will be covered in more depth as the book progresses.

Tables

What will undoubtedly look most familiar to you are Access tables. Tables appear almost identical to spreadsheets with the familiar cells, rows, and columns. However, the first time you attempt to type a formula in one of the "cells," you will see that Access tables do not possess Excel's flexible, multi-purpose nature, which allows any cell to take on almost any responsibility or function. The Access table is simply a place to store data.

All the analysis and number crunching happens somewhere else; here in tables, the numbers and text are simply stored. This way, data will never be tied to any particular analysis or presentation. The data is in its raw form, leaving it up to users to determine how they want to analyze it or display it. If an Excel user begins to use nothing else of Access except tables, she can still immensely increase her effectiveness and productivity.

Queries

You may have heard of Access queries but have never been able to relate to them. Consider this: in Excel, when you use AutoFilter, or a VLookup formula, or Subtotals, you are essentially running a query against some set of data to achieve an answer. A query is a question you pose to get an answer. The answer to a query of your data can be a single item, a Yes/No answer, or many rows of data. In Excel, the concept of querying data is a bit nebulous, because it can take the form of the different functionalities in Excel, such as formulas, AutoFilters, and pivot tables.

In Access, a query is an actual object that has its own functionalities. A query is separate from a table in order to ensure that data is never tied to any particular analysis. Your success in using Microsoft Access to enhance your data analysis will, in no small part, depend on your ability to create all manner of both simple and complex queries.

Reports

Reports, an incredibly powerful component of Microsoft Access, allow data to be presented in a variety of styles. Access reports, in and of themselves, provide an excellent illustration of one of the main points of this book: data should be separate from the analysis and presentation. A report is the shell of how a particular set of data should be analyzed and presented; it is not the data itself, nor is it necessarily tied to how the data is represented. As long as the report receives the data it requires in order to accurately and cleanly present its information, it will not care where the information came from.

Access reports can have mixed reputations. On the one hand, they can provide clean-looking PDF-esque reports that are ideal for invoices and form letters. On the other hand, Access reports are not ideal for showing the one-shot displays of data that Excel can provide. However, Access reports can easily be configured to prepare all manner of report styles.

Macros and VBA

Just as Excel has macro and VBA functionality, Microsoft Access has its equivalents. This is where the true power and flexibility of Microsoft Access data analysis resides. Whether you are using them in custom functions, batch analysis, or automation, macros and VBA can add a customized flexibility that is hard to match using any other means.

What You Will Learn from This Book

If you have picked up this book, you are likely working in a data-intensive environment where data analysis is an integral part of your responsibilities, and you have a sense that there are powerful functionalities in Access that you have been missing out on. If this is true, you should trust your instincts more often. Indeed, using Access for your data analysis needs can help you streamline your analytical processes, increase your productivity, and analyze the larger datasets that have reached Excel's limitations.

Throughout this book, you will come to realize that Access is not the dry database program used only for storing data and building departmental applications. Access possesses strong data analysis functionalities that are easy to learn and certainly applicable to many types of organizations and data systems.

Within the first three chapters, you will be able to demonstrate proficiency in Access, executing powerful analysis on large datasets that have long since reached Excel's limitations. Within the first nine chapters, you will be able to add depth and dimension to your analysis with advanced Access functions, building complex analytical processes with ease. By the end of the book, you will be able to create your own custom functions, perform batch analysis, and develop automated procedures that essentially run on their own.

What this book does and does not cover

- **Will this book teach me all about Access?** Many books on the market go into every aspect of Access in detail, but this is not one of them. Although this book does cover the fundamentals of Access, it is always in the light of data analysis and it is written from a data analyst's point of view. This is not meant to be an all-encompassing book on Access.

That being said, if you are a first-time user of Access, you can feel confident that this book will provide you with a solid introduction to Access that will leave you with valuable skills you can use in your daily operations.

■ **Will this book cover data management theory and best practices?** This book is neither meant to be a book on data management theory and best practices, nor to expound on high-level business intelligence concepts. This is more of a "technician's" book, providing hands-on instruction that introduces Access as an analytical tool that can provide powerful solutions to common analytical scenarios and issues. After reading this book, you will be able to analyze large amounts of data in a meaningful way, quickly slice data into various views on-the-fly, automate redundant analysis, save time, and increase productivity.

■ **Will this book teach me statistical analysis?** Although this book does contain a chapter that demonstrates various techniques to perform a whole range of statistical analysis, it is important to note that this book does not cover statistics theory, methodology, or best practices.

How this book is organized

Part I: Fundamentals of Data Analysis in Access

Part I provides a condensed introduction to Access. You will learn some of the basic fundamentals of Access, along with the essential query skills required throughout the rest of the book. Topics covered in this section include relational database concepts, query basics, and aggregate, action, and crosstab queries.

Part II: Basic Analysis Techniques

Part II introduces you to some of the basic analytical tools and techniques available to you in Access. Chapter 3 covers data transformation, providing examples of how to clean and shape raw data to fit your needs. Chapter 4 provides in-depth instruction on how to create and utilize custom calculations in your analysis. Chapter 4 also shows you how to work with dates, using them in simple date calculations or performing advanced time analysis. Chapter 5 discusses some conditional analysis techniques that enable you to add logic to your analytical processes.

Part III: Advanced Analysis Techniques

Part III demonstrates many of the advanced techniques that truly bring your data analysis to the next level. Chapter 6 covers the fundamental SQL statements and introduces you to subqueries and domain aggregate functions. Chapter 7 picks up from there and demonstrates many of the advanced statistical analyses you can perform using subqueries and domain aggregate functions. Chapter 8 provides you with an in-depth look at using pivot tables and pivot charts in Access.

Part IV: Automating Data Analysis

Part IV takes you beyond manual analysis with queries and introduces you to the world of automation. Chapter 9 gives you an in-depth view of how macros can help increase your productivity by running batch analysis. Chapter 10 introduces you to Visual Basic for Applications (VBA) and shows you how it can help improve your data analysis. Chapter 11 shows you some of the techniques behind automating Excel. Chapter 12 describes best practices for building and maintaining your database, as well as ways to get help in Access when you need a push in the right direction.

About the companion database

You can find the examples demonstrated throughout this book in the companion database, which is located at www.wiley.com/go/accessdataanalysis.

Fundamentals of Data Analysis in Access

Access Basics

When working with Access for the first time, it is tempting to start filling tables right away and querying data to get fast results, but it is important to understand the basics of the relational database concept before pounding away at data. A good understanding of how a relational database works will help you take full advantage of Access as a powerful data analysis solution. This chapter covers the fundamentals of Access and methods to bring data into the program.

Access Table Basics

Upon opening Access, you notice that the Database window, shown in Figure 1-1, has seven sections. Each section represents one of the seven database objects: tables, queries, forms, reports, pages, macros, and modules. The "Tables" selection is at the top of the list, because it is the precise location where your data will be stored. All other database objects will refer to the Access tables for data, whether asking questions of the data or creating reports based on the data. This section covers the basics to get you working with Access tables immediately.

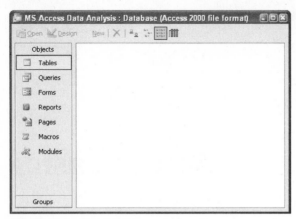

Figure 1-1   The Database window has seven main sections you can work with: Tables, Queries, Forms, Reports, Pages, Macros, and Modules.

What is a table?

One way to think of a table is as a collection of data concerning a specific entity (for example, customers, branches, transactions, products, and so on). You want each of these entities to have its own unique table. Among the many advantages to storing your data using this approach is eliminating or significantly decreasing duplicate information. Later in the chapter, you learn about the dangers inherent in storing data with excessive duplications.

Opening a table in Datasheet view

Open your sample database, click the Tables section (highlighted in Figure 1-1), and then double-click the CustomerMaster table. When the table opens, it is in the Datasheet view. In this view, you are able to directly view and edit the contents of the table. As you can see in Figure 1-2, the names of the columns are at the top.

Identifying important table elements

Access tables consist of rows, with each row representing a single instance of the table name or entity. In CustomerMaster, each row represents a single distinct customer with which the firm does business. In proper database terminology, a row is called a *record*.

The table also comprises columns, with each column representing a particular piece of information common to all instances of the table's entity. In CustomerMaster, each column represents some attribute of the customer that you want to record. In proper database terminology, a column is known as a *field*.

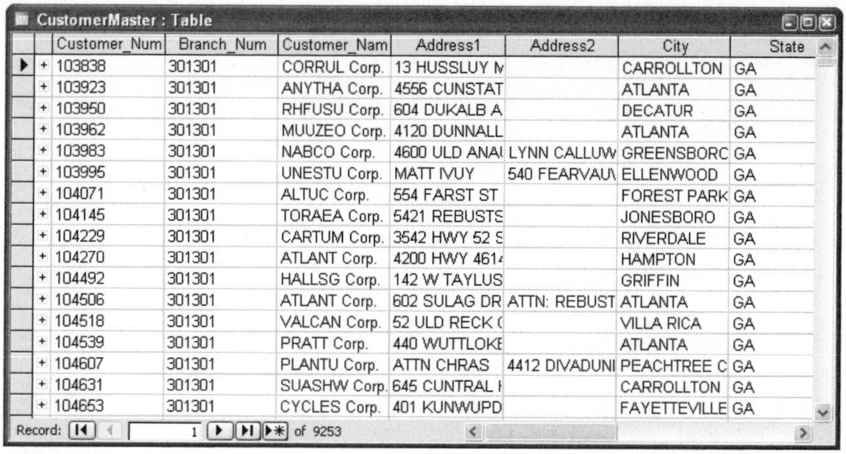

CustomerMaster : Table

Customer_Num	Branch_Num	Customer_Nam	Address1	Address2	City	State
103838	301301	CORRUL Corp.	13 HUSSLUY M		CARROLLTON	GA
103923	301301	ANYTHA Corp.	4556 CUNSTAT		ATLANTA	GA
103950	301301	RHFUSU Corp.	604 DUKALB A		DECATUR	GA
103962	301301	MUUZEO Corp.	4120 DUNNALL		ATLANTA	GA
103983	301301	NABCO Corp.	4600 ULD ANAI	LYNN CALLUW	GREENSBORC	GA
103995	301301	UNESTU Corp.	MATT IVUY	540 FEARVAU\	ELLENWOOD	GA
104071	301301	ALTUC Corp.	554 FARST ST		FOREST PARK	GA
104145	301301	TORAEA Corp.	5421 REBUSTS		JONESBORO	GA
104229	301301	CARTUM Corp.	3542 HWY 52 S		RIVERDALE	GA
104270	301301	ATLANT Corp.	4200 HWY 461		HAMPTON	GA
104492	301301	HALLSG Corp.	142 W TAYLUS		GRIFFIN	GA
104506	301301	ATLANT Corp.	602 SULAG DR	ATTN: REBUST	ATLANTA	GA
104518	301301	VALCAN Corp.	52 ULD RECK (		VILLA RICA	GA
104539	301301	PRATT Corp.	440 WUTTLOKE		ATLANTA	GA
104607	301301	PLANTU Corp.	ATTN CHRAS	4412 DIVADUNI	PEACHTREE C	GA
104631	301301	SUASHW Corp.	645 CUNTRAL I		CARROLLTON	GA
104653	301301	CYCLES Corp.	401 KUNWUPD		FAYETTEVILLE	GA

Record: 1 of 9253

Figure 1-2 Opening the table in Datasheet view allows you to view and edit the data stored in the table.

TIP **The number of records in a table is visible at the bottom left of the Datasheet view, next to the record selectors.**

Opening a table in Design view

Through the Design view of a table, you are able to set the field names and data types. To get to the Design view of the CustomerMaster table, right-click the CustomerMaster table and select Design View. As you can see in Figure 1-3, the Design view shows you the fields that comprise the CustomerMaster table in an easy-to-manage view. Note how each field has a field name and a data type. Data types are discussed later in this chapter.

The *field name* is the descriptive text string given to a particular column of a table. It is what appears at the top of the table when it is in the Datasheet view. Follow these guidelines when naming your fields:

- The maximum length of a field name is 64 characters.
- Your field name cannot include a period (.), an exclamation point (!), an accent grave (`), or brackets ([ ]).
- You can begin your field name with leading spaces.

TIP **It is good practice not to put any spaces in your field names. When constructing queries or referring to tables in VBA code, spaces in the field names can lead to problems. If you need to indicate a space in your field name, use the underscore character.**

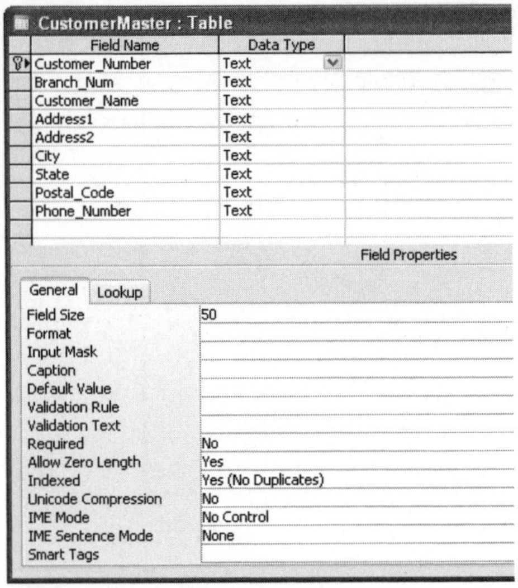

Figure 1-3   Opening the table in Design view allows you to add field names or change existing ones.

Exploring data types

The field's data type ensures that only a certain type of data is allowed in the field. If a data type is tagged as a number, Access will not allow any text to be entered into that field. By setting the data type of each column, you go a long way toward ensuring the integrity and consistency of the data. The concept of the data type is crucial to not only understanding Access, but also to unlocking the power of the programming language behind Access, VBA. Quite simply, computers process and store data and that data is categorized by its type.

With the CustomerMaster table left open in Design view, place your cursor in the Data Type section of the first field and click the drop-down arrow shown in Figure 1-3. A list of predefined data type choices becomes visible. These data types are Text, Memo, Number, Date/Time, Currency, AutoNumber, Yes/No, OLE Object, and Hyperlink. The following sections describe these data types in more detail.

Text

Any combination of letters, numbers, spaces, and characters is considered Text. This is by far the most common data type. Although Text can be a number, it should not be a number used in a calculation. Examples of the Text data type are customer names, customer numbers (using customer numbers in calculations would have no meaning), and addresses. The maximum number of characters allowed in a Text field is 255.

Memo

If you need to store text data that exceeds the 255-character limit of the Text field, you should use the Memo field. Long descriptions or notes about the record can be stored in fields of this type.

Number

The Number type is used for all numerical data that will be used in calculations, except money or currency (which has its own data type). Actually, Number is several data types under one heading. When Number has been selected as a data type in the Design view of the table, go to the Field Size field at the top of the General tab. When you select the down arrow, you get the following options: Byte, Integer, Long Integer, Single, Double, Replication ID, and Decimal. Probably the most common field sizes of the Number data type are Long Integer and Double. Long Integer should be selected if the numbers are whole numbers that do not have any non-zeros to the right of the decimal point. Double should be selected if decimal numbers need to be stored in that field.

Date/Time

Another data type often used in calculations is Date/Time. Recording the time that certain events occurred is among the more important uses of this data type. Recording dates and times allows you to compare data by time durations, be it months, years, or whatever. In the business world, the Date field can be crucial to analysis, especially when identifying seasonal trends or making year over year comparisons.

Currency

Currency is a special calculation data type, ideal for storing all data that represents amounts of money.

AutoNumber

This data type is actually a Long Integer that is automatically and sequentially created for each new record added to a table. The AutoNumber can be one mechanism by which you can uniquely identify each individual record in a table. You will not enter data into this field.

Yes/No

In some situations, the data that needs to be represented is in a simple Yes/No format. Although you could use the Text data type for creating a True/False field, it is much more intuitive to use Access's native data type for this purpose.

OLE Object

This data type is not encountered very often in data analysis. It is used when the field must store a binary file, such as a picture or sound file.

Hyperlink

When you need to store an address to a Web site, this is the preferred data type.

Preparing to create a table

Before you start creating a table, you need to answer the following questions:

- What is the name of the table? What is the entity for which you would like to collect and store data?
- What are the names and types of columns or fields? Which attributes of this particular entity do you need to record/store? What are the appropriate data types of these fields?
- How can you identify each instance of the entity uniquely?

Keep in mind that to take full advantage of Access, you may have to split data that was previously stored in one large dataset into separate tables. For example, think of a flat-file list of invoice details in Excel. Typically, this list would repeat Invoice Header information for each individual detail of that invoice. In order to eliminate as much of the duplicate data as possible, you would divide the single list into two logical parts: InvoiceHeaders and InvoiceDetails. Each unique Invoice will be listed only once in the Invoice-Headers table. All of the details for that invoice will be in the InvoiceDetails table. Given this structure, Access will be able to recognize a relationship between the two tables.

Different methods for creating a table

Access provides different methods for creating a table. You can, for example, use the Datasheet view, the Design view, or the Table Wizard. For users new to Access, the Table Wizard provides an excellent opportunity to walk through the process. Tables are also created automatically when you import data from an outside source, such as an Excel spreadsheet. An Access table can also be a link to a table outside of the database. Importing and linking are covered later in this chapter.

If you are neither importing nor linking data, the ideal way to create a table in Access is with the Design view. You looked at the Design view previously and saw that it is essentially a list of columns and data types in the table. Here you can enter the names of every column and its matching data type.

Creating a table with Design view

Imagine that a company's human resources department asks you to create a simple list of employees in Access. To create a table in Design view, select Insert → Table. This opens the New Table dialog box shown in Figure 1-4.

You must now create a list of attributes, or fields, that describe each employee in a particular way. Among the more common attributes in this situation are the following: EmployeeNumber, FirstName, LastName, Address, City, State, Zip, and HourlyWage. You begin by entering the names of the columns going down the list.

Default data type

As you enter the field names, you may notice that the data type defaulted to the most common data type, Text. You now want to set the data types for each field, or at least change the data type of each non-text field. Choosing the correct data type for the first field, EmployeeNumber, may be initially confusing. With the word "Number" in the field, you might think that Number would be the logical choice for the data type. Actually, the rule of thumb is that if the field will not be used in a calculation, it is best to set its data type to Text. There is no logical meaning to performing calculations on the EmployeeNumber field. It is highly unlikely that adding two values from this column would give you information of any significance. Another reason for using the Text data type in the EmployeeNumber field is that there could be alpha characters or letters in the field.

Data types for calculations

The field names for this particular table should make it fairly obvious that you will want to set all of the fields to Text, except when it comes to HourlyWage. This field will almost certainly be used in calculations. For example, multiplying an employee's hourly wage by 40 will get you his or her weekly salary. So, because this field will certainly be used in calculations, and because it will represent a monetary value, you should change the data type to Currency. At this point, your Design view should look similar to the screen shown in Figure 1-5.

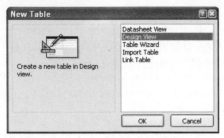

Figure 1-4   Open the New Table dialog box and double-click Design View.

Now you can save and name your table by selecting File → Save. Give the table an appropriate name, such as "Employees" or "EmployeeMaster." Keep in mind that at this point, this table contains no data. You can start entering employee information directly into the table through the Datasheet view. If you have a table with a small number of records, you can enter your records manually. However, most sets of data are quite large, so other techniques of bringing data into Access are covered later in the chapter.

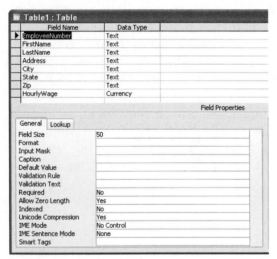

Figure 1-5   After entering the field name, the data type defaults to Text.

Tricks of the Trade: Working with the Field Builder

A great tool for beginning Access users is the Field Builder. It works as a wizard to help you build your table and also gives you practice selecting data types. In the Design view, select the column for which you would like to build a field and click the Build button on the toolbar. In Figure 1-6, you can see what the Field Builder looks like.

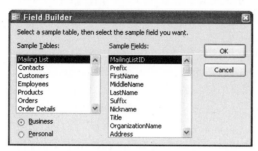

Figure 1-6 The Field Builder utility can help you build your table with just a few clicks of the mouse.

The Field Builder provides a collection of sample tables, each with their own sample fields. It is very likely that you will find a field equivalent to what you would like to create in this list. When you select a field, not only will the name of the field be added to the Design view of the table, but the suggested data type will be added for you as well. This can be a great way to teach yourself about data types. Simply create a dummy table and choose the fields that interest you or that you might potentially need in the future. Then, after selecting each item, check to see what data type was automatically populated in the list. Look at different Number fields and pay attention to different settings for the Field Size in the Number data type.

Advanced Table Concepts

Now that you can create a table and manually enter data into it, this section turns to more advanced table concepts. When working with data in tables, you may encounter situations in which you want to restrict or default data that is entered in particular columns. There is also the question of being able to uniquely identify each record in any given table.

Field properties

After entering field names, data types, and descriptions, you can set individual field properties for each column, which will affect how the data is stored and presented, among other things. The list of field properties is dependent on the data type chosen for that field. Some field properties are specific to Text fields, and others are specific to Number fields. The field properties are located in the Design view of a table on the General tab at the lower left. The following sections cover the more important ones.

NOTE Note that the properties shown on the General tab change to reflect the data type you choose.

Field Size

You encountered Field Size before, when working with the Number data type. This property also exists for the common Text data type. This property allows you to set a maximum size limit on data entered in that column. For the Text data type, size refers to the length (number of characters and spaces) of the Text data in that column. For example, if you look at the Employees table, you see a field for State. Your company tells you that the names of states should be recorded using their two-letter designation. If you therefore set the field size to "2" for the State column, the user will be unable to type any text longer than two characters. So with Access, you are not only able to force a certain data type in a particular column, but you can also customize that individual column to accept data only in the rigid format that you specify.

Format

The Format property enables you to customize the way numbers, dates, times, and text are displayed and printed. As with the Field Size property, the format available for selection will depend on the data type of that column. For example, with a Currency field, you can display the data in a form that uses a dollar sign, or a Euro sign, or no sign at all. The data itself will not be changed with these settings, just how the data is displayed. Format is especially useful when it comes to Date/Time data types. Whether you want to display data in the long format or short format, this property allows you to set that option.

USING THE INPUT MASK WIZARD

There is an extremely helpful tool called the Input Mask Wizard. To call this wizard, place your cursor inside the field for which you need an input mask. This will make visible a button with the ellipsis dots (...). Click the newly visible button to activate the Input Mask Wizard. The wizard provides the most common examples of Input Masks and even allows you to test their behavior. Figure 1-7 shows the Input Mask Wizard.

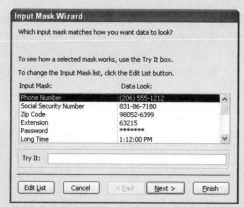

Figure 1-7 The Input Mask Wizard enables you to specify the structure of data being entered into a field.

Input Mask

The Input Mask property can be useful in data entry situations. Whereas Format controls how data is displayed, Input Mask controls how data is entered into a particular field. Input Mask is available for the following data types: Text, Number, Date/Time, and Currency. For example, if a user needs to enter a telephone number, Input Mask can create the characters and structure with which everyone is familiar. As the user types, the number automatically assumes a phone number format: (###) ###-####.

Decimal Places

In number fields, you can set the number of decimal places that will be recorded to the right of the decimal point. There is an Auto setting, which will defer to the Format setting to determine the correct number of places. Apart from Auto, you are able to select 0 to 15 for the number of decimal places.

Default Value

An important database concept, Default Value can help save time in the data entry process. The default value is automatically placed in a column every time a new record is added. Defaults can be overridden, so your column is not forced to have only that particular value.

Required

Another important property, Required simply forces a user to enter some value, using the proper data type, in the designated field. A new record will not be added if the Required field is not properly filled. As with Input Mask, this property is an excellent mechanism for asserting more control over the data entry process.

Primary key

You will recall that earlier in the chapter, you needed to ask yourself three questions to determine just how a new table was to be created. The third question specified that you need a way to identify or reference every record. In other words, there needs to be some unique text or number column that will have no duplicate values, in much the same way that Social Security numbers uniquely identify individuals. Each person has one and only one Social Security number. By definition, you cannot have a Social Security number that represents two people. This unique column is known as a *primary key* and it is the mechanism by which you relate different tables to each other.

To set the primary key, right-click the field that could be a primary key candidate and select Primary Key.

At this point, Access will automatically determine if that particular field contains duplicate data—that is, data items that exist in more than one row.

If there are duplicates, Access informs you with an error message. You must remove any duplicates if that column is indeed to become the primary key for the table.

> **TIP** Access provides its own automatic primary key with the AutoNumber data type. The AutoNumber simply increments one for each record added, so there will be no duplicates. However, it is preferable to use actual data for a primary key and not just some number that indicates the record's position in a table.
>
> If every employee has a unique employee number, that field would be an ideal primary key. If you have a situation where there is no unique single column, consider using a combination of columns that together make up a unique record. You can set multiple columns to be the primary key; this is called a *Compound Key*. It has the effect of combining separate columns to represent a single, unique value.

Tricks of the Trade: Sorting and Filtering for On-the-fly Analysis

---

There is inherent functionality within Access that can assist you in performing quick, impromptu data analysis.

SORTING

It is significantly safer to sort data in an Access table than in an Excel spreadsheet. One of the potential problems with sorting data in Excel has to do with the free-form nature of a spreadsheet, which allows you to inadvertently sort only one column in your dataset. With Access, you do not have to worry about the impact on presentation when you sort. The data is separate from the presentation.

Open up a table in the Datasheet view and select the column you want to sort. That is, click the gray box with the column name once. This action should highlight the entire column. Once your column is highlighted, right-click and then select Sort Ascending or Sort Descending from the popup menu shown in Figure 1-8.

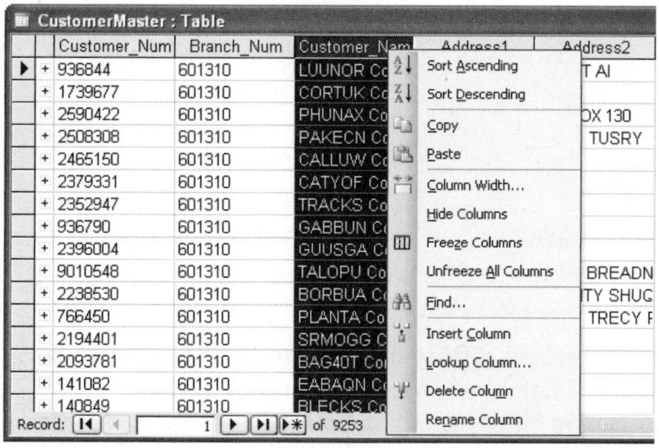

Figure 1-8 From the right-click menu, you can choose to sort a column in ascending or descending order.

FILTERING

Another extremely useful table function is Filter By Selection and Filter Excluding Selection. The idea behind these filters is that you will click a single data value in a record. Choosing Filter By Selection then hides all records that do not have that particular value in that particular column. This can be an excellent method to perform fast analysis.

Suppose you have a list of employees and you want to quickly know how many are in California. Find a record—any record—whose state is California, then click in the State column of that record. After filtering by selection, only records with California as the state will be visible. The non-California records are not deleted; they are just temporarily hidden by the filter.

continues

To demonstrate this functionality in action, open the CustomerMaster table and right-click in the State column. The popup menu shown in Figure 1-9 activates. Type CA in the Filter For text field to filter only those customers based in California.

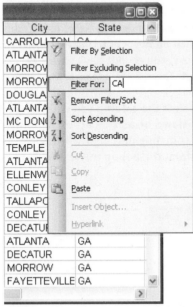

Figure 1-9 The Filter For functionality allows you to filter your data on-the-fly.

You can easily remove the filter and restore the table to its natural state by clicking the following: Records → Remove Filter/Sort. Another useful filter works in the opposite manner. The Filter Excluding Selection hides all records that have the same value in the column that you clicked. Going back to our example, if a user selects a record with California as its state, the Filter Excluding Selection hides all records where the state is California. All records with that data value have been temporarily hidden from view.

Getting Data into Access

Now that you have learned basic and advanced table concepts, you are ready to bring data from outside sources into Access. Apart from creating a table from scratch and manually entering the data, the two main methods for bringing data into Access are importing and linking.

Importing

With importing, you are making a copy of the data and filling a newly created table with the copied data. After importing, the data is disconnected from the source from which it was imported. If any future changes are made to the outside source, they will not be reflected in the Access data. This is true in the other direction, in that changes to your Access data will not affect the original source. After importing a table, it is common to treat that Access data as the true data source. Any updating, appending, or deleting will be done to the Access data. Then, when it is time to analyze the data, you can be sure it reflects the latest, most accurate version of that data.

Linking

When you link a table to Access, you are creating a pointer to another data source. When the Access database is opened, it establishes links to its outside data source and displays the data as if it were a regular local Access table. However, there is no data residing in Access. The data is physically located on another computer, server, or source. If you change the data in the Access table, the true data source will reflect that change. If you change the original data source, those changes will be reflected when you reopen the linked table.

Things to remember about importing data

Your decision whether to import or link data depends on the situation. When you import data, it resides directly in the Access file, so operations on that data perform much faster. With linked tables, you may be dependent on the speed of the connection with the data source or the speed of the database engine at the other end.

One important point to remember is that when importing data, you can select to create a new table or import your data into an existing table. If you choose to create a new table, Access makes a copy of the data to import, then attempts to determine the column names and field data types. Access may make an incorrect assumption about the data type, but you can go back and make the necessary changes. If you choose to import data to an existing table, you must make sure that the data types of the fields are compatible. If you attempt to import a text string into a number field, for example, an error will occur.

WARNING It is important to remember that Access does not let go of disk space on its own. This means that as time goes on, all the file space taken up by the data you imported will be held by your Access file, regardless of whether or not the data is still there. With that in mind, it is critical that you "compact and repair" your Access database regularly to ensure that your database does not grow to an unmanageable size, or even worse, become corrupted. To compact and repair your database, simply select Tools → Database Utilities → Compact and Repair Database.

Importing data from Excel spreadsheets

You can import data from a wide variety of sources into Access tables: Excel spreadsheets, text files, or another database table. Access provides a set of easy-to-use Import wizards, such as the one illustrated in Figure 1-10, that guide you through the process of importing data.

If you are importing a properly formatted Excel flat file, the wizard prompts you to ask if the top line is the location of the column names. Another extremely useful feature of this wizard is that it lets you select a column to serve as the primary key of the table or it will add an AutoNumber primary key. If you select a column to serve as the primary key, the wizard performs a test on the column to ensure against duplicate values. If duplicate values exist in that column, the wizard informs you that it cannot set that column as the primary key and the table is imported anyway.

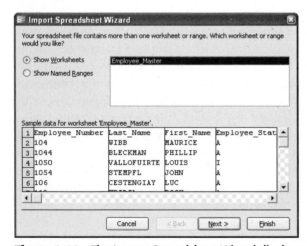

Figure 1-10 The Import Spreadsheet Wizard displays sample data from the worksheet selected in the display.

TIP The Import Spreadsheet Wizard attempts to make an educated guess as to what data type to set for each column. Still, it is a good idea to check the data type of each column after importing the data, because you may need to make some changes.

Importing data from text files

Similar to importing data from spreadsheets, the data in text files must be in a consistent format in order for the wizard to extract the information correctly. Typically, the data in text files is delimited (separated) by commas. Access will properly interpret this and separate the data located between the commas into their appropriate fields. Usually someone in I.T. will prepare a text file of data for the analyst, or it can be an output of a mainframe application.

The Relational Database Concept

A *relational database* is a database that is structured around shared attributes between two or more datasets. In a relational database, data is stored in tables based on logical characteristics to minimize redundancy and to improve data integrity. Access is a relational database. If you want to understand just how Access works, you need to understand the relational database concept.

Excel and the flat-file format

The term *flat file* is used to describe a single table that has a two-dimensional structure consisting of rows and columns. Although flat files are generally easy to use and understand, they contain lots of redundant data and virtually no inherent mechanisms to protect data integrity. When you are working with data in an Excel file, you are working with a flat file.

Some data analysis scenarios are not terribly complex, which means that a flat-file representation of the data to be analyzed is adequate. However, most data-analysis scenarios require analyzing data that is much more multi-dimensional. One of the main reasons the flat file can prove inadequate is that it is two-dimensional. Real-world business data rarely falls into a convenient, two-dimensional format. Of course, it can be forced into that format by the Excel guru who wants all analysis to fit into the spreadsheet. Take a look at a typical example of a flat file. Figure 1-11 shows a typical flat-file list of invoices.

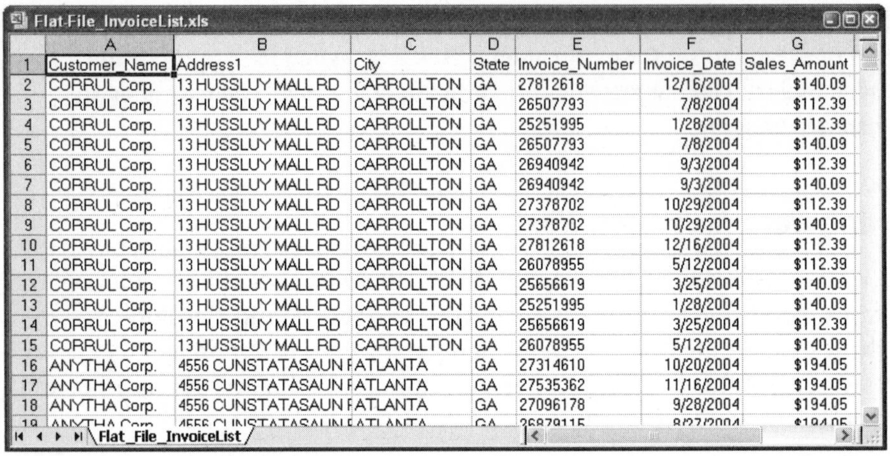

Figure 1-11   Data is usually stored in an Excel spreadsheet using the flat-file format.

In order to get the customer information for each invoice, several fields exist for customer-specific information: customer name, address, city, and so on. Because most firms sell to customers more than once, you can see that customer information is often repeated. Duplicate information is one of the main drawbacks of the flat-file format.

What is wrong with duplicate data? Initially, the duplicate data may not appear to be a potential source of future problems, but upon further examination, you discover the shortcomings. First is file size. Duplicate data wastes space, both on the computer hard drive, where the file is stored, and in the computer's memory, where the data resides when it is being operated on. Although the enormous amounts of memory that are standard with today's machines go a long way toward handling excessive demands, having duplicate data wastes valuable computer space and resources. The duplicate information is not valuable to us. In fact, it leads to problems, particularly when data needs to be updated. As you can see in Figure 1-11, a number of different invoices have been recorded for CORRUL Corp. You can also see that the information for CORRUL Corp. is repeated for every invoice. What if CORRUL Corp.'s customer information changes, though? What if it acquires new office space and you want to reflect this change of location in your data? You would have to update the change in several different places, ensuring that every invoice correctly maps back to its relevant customer information.

Although excellent functions are available that can find and replace data in Excel, there is still a danger that you might not make all of the updates correctly. Whenever you are changing the same, duplicate information, the risk of introducing unintentional errors is always present. This could significantly affect your data analysis. For example, suppose that CORRUL Corp. moved to a different city. Figure 1-12 demonstrates how easy it is to incorrectly update the data.

	A	B	C	D	E	F	G
1	Customer_Name	Address1	City	State	Invoice_Number	Invoice_Date	Sales_Amount
2	CORRUL Corp.	4120 DUNNALLY AVE S\	ATLANTA	GA	27812618	12/16/2004	$140.09
3	CORRUL Corp.	4121 DUNNALLY AVE S\	ATLANTA	GA	26507793	7/8/2004	$112.39
4	CORRUL Corp.	4122 DUNNALLY AVE S\	ATLANTA	GA	25251995	1/28/2004	$112.39
5	CORRUL Corp.	4123 DUNNALLY AVE S\	ATLANTA	GA	26507793	7/8/2004	$140.09
6	CORRUL Corp.	4124 DUNNALLY AVE S\	ATLANTA	GA	26940942	9/3/2004	$112.39
7	CORRUL Corp.	4125 DUNNALLY AVE S\	ATLANTA	GA	26940942	9/3/2004	$140.09
8	CORRUL Corp.	4126 DUNNALLY AVE S\	ATLANTA	GA	27378702	10/29/2004	$112.39
9	CORRUL Corp.	4127 DUNNALLY AVE S\	ATLANTA	GA	27378702	10/29/2004	$140.09
10	CORRUL Corp.	4128 DUNNALLY AVE S\	ATLANTA	GA	27812618	12/16/2004	$112.39
11	CORRUL Corp.	4129 DUNNALLY AVE S\	ATLANTA	GA	26078955	5/12/2004	$112.39
12	CORRUL Corp.	4130 DUNNALLY AVE S\	ATLANTA	GA	25656619	3/25/2004	$140.09
13	CORRUL Corp.	4131 DUNNALLY AVE S\	ATLANTA	GA	25251995	1/28/2004	$140.09
14	CORRUL Corp.	4132 DUNNALLY AVE S\	ATLANTA	GA	25656619	3/25/2004	$112.39
15	CORRUL Corp.	13 HUSSLUY MALL RD	CARROLLTON	GA	26078955	5/12/2004	$140.09
16	ANYTHA Corp.	4556 CUNSTATASAUN F	ATLANTA	GA	27314610	10/20/2004	$194.05
17	ANYTHA Corp.	4556 CUNSTATASAUN F	ATLANTA	GA	27535362	11/16/2004	$194.05
18	ANYTHA Corp.	4556 CUNSTATASAUN F	ATLANTA	GA	27096178	9/28/2004	$194.05

Figure 1-12 The last record of CORRUL Corp. was not correctly updated to the new address.

If the City data is not properly updated everywhere, when you attempt a by city filter/analysis, you will not get accurate results. Some of the invoice records could reflect the incorrect state locations of the customer. The attributes of data can and often do change, and if these changes are not accurately recorded, your data analysis will provide an incorrect picture of the actual situation.

Splitting data into separate tables

Data must be consistent if analysis is to have any true value in the decision-making process. Duplicate data is the bane of consistent data. If an entity is changed in one place, it must be changed everywhere. Wouldn't it be more logical and efficient to record the name and information of a customer only once? Instead of recording the same customer information repeatedly, you could simply have some form of customer reference number, which could then send you to another list where the information is unique and written once.

This brings us back to the relational database concept, which enables you to have separate, carefully designed unique lists of data that are related to one another by their unique identifiers (primary key).

Many Excel users, in fact, without realizing it, make great efforts to make the data on their spreadsheets "relational." For example, the use (or overuse) of the VLOOKUP or HLOOKUP helps you match data from separate lists that have some data field or key in common. Although much is possible with these functions, they do have their limitations. Furthermore, the functions are not very intuitive. They attempt to solve a problem that Access was designed from the ground up to address. When Excel users use these functions to bring data from separate lists onto a single row, they are in essence creating a relationship of that data. The problem is that the data has not really been related; it has simply been shown how it could relate to each other on a particular spreadsheet tab. A different tab may choose to "relate" the data in a completely different way.

The problem for the analyst is that if there were relationships between the data that were consistent or even permanent, it would be easier to somehow reflect them in a behind-the-scenes representation of the data. Some of the data relationships can be quite complex, and if the analyst is forced to remember and manually enforce all of them, analysis is detracted from and the possibility of mistakes increased.

Foreign key

To set relationships between tables, you take a primary key field from one table and use it to relate that entity to records in another table. When the primary key is used in a different table in order to establish relationships, it is called a *foreign key*. In the TransactionMaster table, for example, you see a Customer_Number field. This is the same primary key field from the CustomerMaster table.

Relationship types

Three types of relationships can be set in a relational database:

- **One-to-one relationship.** For each record in one table, there is one and only one matching record in a different table. It is as if two tables have the exact same primary key. Typically, data from different tables in a one-to-one relationship will be combined into one table.

- **One-to-many relationship.** For each record in a table, there may be zero, one, or many records matching in a separate table. For example, if you have an invoice header table related to an invoice detail table, and the invoice header table uses Invoice Number as the primary key, the invoice detail will use the Invoice Number for every record representing a detail of that particular invoice. This is certainly the most common type of relationship you will encounter.

- **Many-to-many relationship.** Used decidedly less often, this type of relationship cannot be defined in Access without the use of a mapping table. This relationship states that records in both tables can have any number of matching records in the other table.

In the sample database, relationships have already been established between the tables. Take a look at some of these relationships in order to get a better idea of how they can be set and changed. In the Tools menu, select Relationships so you can view the relationships that have already been set. As shown in Figure 1-13, the lines between the tables signify the relationships.

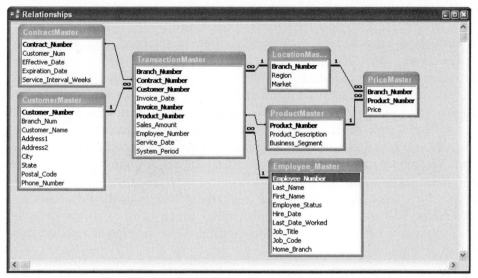

Figure 1-13   A one-to-many relationship between tables can be identified by the infinity symbol on the line connecting the tables.

Creating and editing relationships

In the Relationships window, you can add tables by right-clicking the display and selecting Show Table. Once your tables have been added, relationships can be established by dragging one field from one table to a field in another table. Figure 1-14 shows the Edit Relationships dialog box that then appears.

You can also edit an existing relationship by right-clicking the line connecting the two tables.

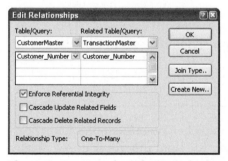

Figure 1-14   Based on the use of primary keys and foreign keys, the Edit Relationships dialog box attempts to guess the kind of relationship you want to establish.

Referential integrity

In addition to establishing relationships between tables, you are able to enforce certain rules that guide these relationships. For example, if you have an Invoice table with a Customer_Number foreign key, you will not be able to add an invoice for a customer number that does not exist in the other table. You must add the new customer to the customer table before the new foreign key can be placed in the invoice table. Also, if you attempt to delete a customer from a table when there are matching invoices for that customer, an error will occur. Referential integrity allows you to use Access to maintain the relationships that you have created.

By clicking the Enforce Referential Integrity checkbox in the Edit Relationships dialog box, you tell Access to first verify that a valid relationship exists between the two tables. Here are some conditions that need to be met to establish referential integrity:

- The field that is used to match the two tables must be a primary key in one of those tables.

- The field that is used to match the two tables must be of the same data type.

Once the validity of the relationship has been established, referential integrity will be continuously enforced until switched off.

Cascading updates and deletes

The main purpose of referential integrity is two-fold: first, to prevent changing a primary key value for which there are matching foreign key values in a second table, and second, to prevent the deletion of a primary key value for which there are matching foreign key values. These two rules of referential integrity can be overridden by clicking either Cascade Update Related Fields or Cascade Delete Related Records. This topic is touched on again in Chapter 2.

Query Basics

Once the data is in Access and the relationships between the tables have been established, you are ready to start analyzing the data. As you can see on the Database window, "Queries" is the next main database object. This section focuses on perhaps the most common type of query: the select query. It also discusses the basic concept of the query and provides a few examples to illustrate just how easy they are to create in Access.

What is a query?

By definition, a query is a question. For our purposes, it is a question about data, which is stored in tables. Queries can be exceedingly simple, like asking what all of the data in a table is. Queries can also be quite complex, testing for different criteria, sorting in certain orders, and performing calculations. In Access, two main types of queries exist: select and action queries. Select queries are perhaps the most common type. This query simply asks a question of the data and returns the results. No changes are made to the data whatsoever. You can always run select queries and never worry that the actual data is being altered. Action queries actually manipulate and change the data in a table. The action query can add records, delete records, or change information in existing records (updating). This type of query is discussed more fully in Chapter 2.

NOTE Keep in mind that the results of a query are separate from the query itself. The query is simply the question, not the results of the question. If the data in the table is changed and the query is run again, you could get different results. The results of a query are not located in a separate table that exists in Access. The results come directly from the table that is being queried. You have separated the raw data from the questions that you would like to ask of it.

Creating a select query

Quite often, when you are working with or analyzing data, it is preferable to work with smaller sections of the data at a time. The tables contain all the records pertaining to a particular entity, but perhaps for your purposes you need to examine a subset of that data. Typically, the subsets are defined by categories or criteria. The select query enables you to determine exactly which records will be returned to you.

If you thought that creating queries required learning a programming language or some other technological hurdle, that is not entirely accurate. Although it is possible to create queries using the programming language of databases—SQL—it is much more easy and intuitive to use the Query By Design (QBD). The Query By Design is a graphic user interface where the tables and columns are visually represented, making it easy to visualize the "question" you would like to ask of the data.

The Query By Design interface

Go to your sample database and select the Queries tab. At the top, double-click "Create query in Design view." The Show Table dialog box opens, sitting on top of a blank Query By Design (QBD) interface, as shown in Figure 1-15. Some also call this the query grid or design grid.

When creating your "question" of the data, the first thing you must determine is from which tables you need to retrieve data. The Show Table dialog box allows the user to select one or more tables. As you can see in Figure 1-15, there are also tabs for Queries and Both. One of the wonderful features of queries is that you are not limited to just querying directly off the table. You can create queries of other queries.

For this first query, select the CustomerMaster table, either by selecting the table in the list and clicking Add or by double-clicking the table in the list. Now that you have selected the table from which you want to retrieve data, you must select the fields of that table that you would like to retrieve.

The QBD is divided into two sections. The top half shows the tables or queries from which the query will retrieve data. The bottom half shows the fields from which the query will retrieve data. You can also add your own "calculation" fields that perform operations on other fields, and output the result.

You will notice in Figure 1-16 that the CustomerMaster table at the top half of the QBD lists all the fields, but has an asterisk at the top of the list. The asterisk is the traditional database symbol, which means that all fields from that table will be in the output.

Figure 1-15   The Show Table dialog allows you to select the tables or queries to which to add the Query By Design.

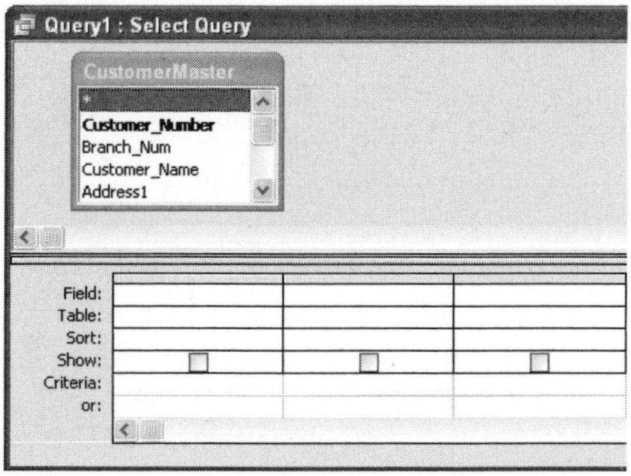

Figure 1-16 The Query By Design interface.

For this example, select the following three fields: Branch_Num, Customer_Name, and State. To select fields from the top half of the QBD, you can either double-click the field or click it once and drag it down to the bottom half. Now that field will be included in the output of the query. Figure 1-17 shows you how the Query By Design should look after selecting the output fields.

Running a query

At this point, you have all you need to run the query. You can run a query from the QBE in two ways. Either select Query/Run or click the red exclamation point in the toolbar. As you can see from Figure 1-18, the output from a query looks similar to a regular table after it is open.

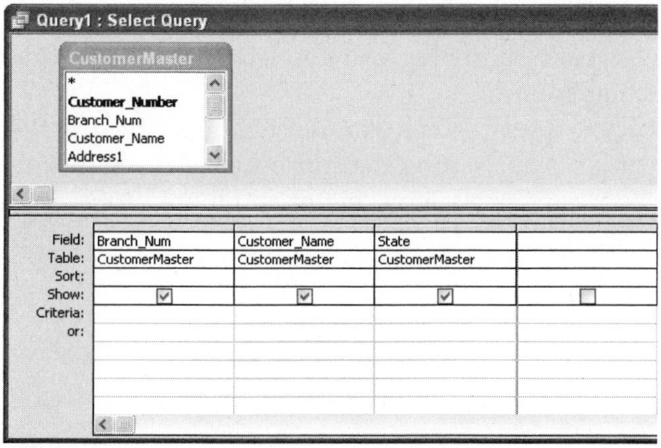

Figure 1-17 The lower half of the Query By Design interface shows the output fields of the select query.

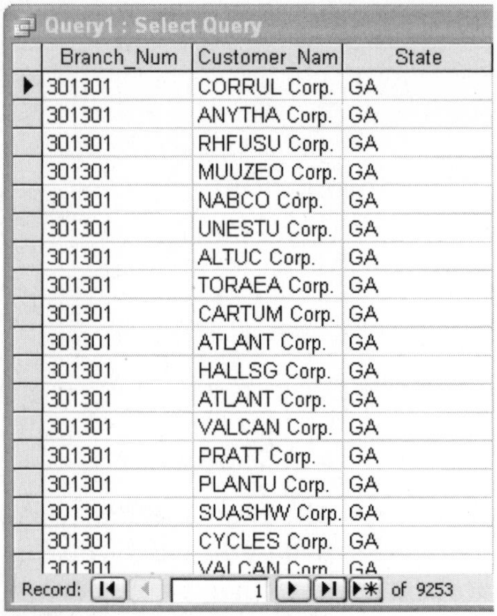

Query1 : Select Query

Branch_Num	Customer_Nam	State
301301	CORRUL Corp.	GA
301301	ANYTHA Corp.	GA
301301	RHFUSU Corp.	GA
301301	MUUZEO Corp.	GA
301301	NABCO Corp.	GA
301301	UNESTU Corp.	GA
301301	ALTUC Corp.	GA
301301	TORAEA Corp.	GA
301301	CARTUM Corp.	GA
301301	ATLANT Corp.	GA
301301	HALLSG Corp.	GA
301301	ATLANT Corp.	GA
301301	VALCAN Corp.	GA
301301	PRATT Corp.	GA
301301	PLANTU Corp.	GA
301301	SUASHW Corp.	GA
301301	CYCLES Corp.	GA
301301	VALCAN Corp.	GA

Record: 1 of 9253

Figure 1-18 The Datasheet view of query shows the results of the query.

Sorting query results

Here, you examine how you can sort the results of this query. Just as you sorted in Excel, you are going to select a column and choose between ascending sort and descending sort. In the bottom half of the QBD, you'll notice the Sort row on the grid. This is where you can select either one or multiple sort columns. If you select multiple sort columns, the query sorts the results in order of left to right.

Go to the State column and click your mouse on the Sort section. As shown in Figure 1-19, a down arrow appears, allowing you to select either Ascending or Descending for that particular column.

Select Ascending and rerun the query. When you ran the query before, the states were in no particular order. After setting the sort order of the State column to ascending, the query output simply looks better and more professionally formatted, as shown in Figure 1-20.

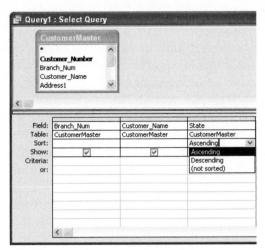

Figure 1-19 The sort order options for a column are provided by the Query By Design interface.

Branch_Num	Customer_Nam	State
601310	LUUNOR Corp.	AL
601310	CORTUK Corp.	AL
601310	PHUNAX Corp.	AL
601310	PAKECN Corp.	AL
601310	CALLUW Corp.	AL
601310	CATYOF Corp.	AL
601310	TRACKS Corp.	AL
601310	GABBUN Corp.	AL
601310	GUUSGA Corp.	AL
601310	TALOPU Corp.	AL
601310	BORBUA Corp.	AL
601310	PLANTA Corp.	AL
601310	SRMOGG Corp	AL
601310	BAG40T Corp.	AL
601310	EABAQN Corp.	AL
601310	BLECKS Corp.	AL
601310	UDSPU Corp.	AL
601310	WAYNUT Corp.	AL

Record: I◄ ◄ 1 ► ►I ►* of 9253

Figure 1-20 The results of the query are now sorted in ascending order by the State field.

Filtering query results

Next, you examine how you can filter the query output so that you retrieve only specific records to analyze. In Access, this filter is also called Criteria. You can see the Criteria section for each column added in your QBD. This is where you will enter the value, or values, for which you would like to query. When entering a value in the Criteria section, all records that match it are returned in the query output. When entering text, you must enclose the text string with quotation marks. You could either place them there yourself or type your text and click another part of the QBD to have the quotation marks placed automatically for you.

Suppose, for example, your manager wants to see the list of customers from California. Because California is designated by the abbreviation "CA" in the table, that is exactly what you will type in the Criteria section of the "State" column, as shown in Figure 1-21.

Now click the exclamation icon to rerun the query. You will notice first off that fewer records are returned. This is obvious from looking at the Record Selector at the bottom of the query output window. A quick scan of the results verifies that, indeed, only records with "CA" in the State column were returned, as shown in Figure 1-22.

TIP You can sort and filter query results just as if they were a table. Simply right-click the query results cell or column and the same options that appeared for tables will also appear.

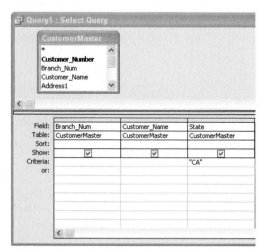

Figure 1-21   The Criteria section is where you will type in the value for which you want to filter the data.

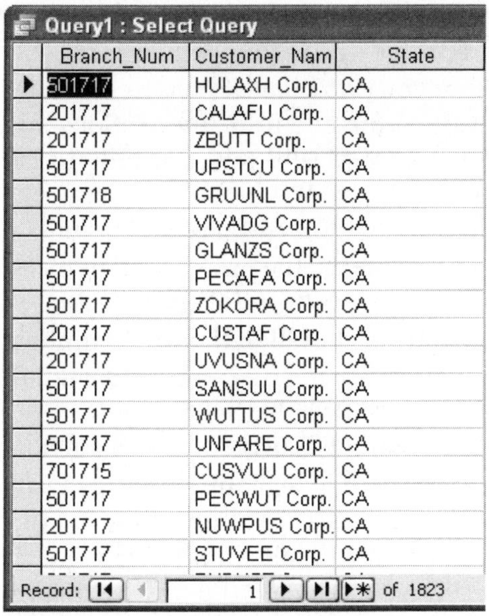

Query1 : Select Query

Branch_Num	Customer_Nam	State
501717	HULAXH Corp.	CA
201717	CALAFU Corp.	CA
201717	ZBUTT Corp.	CA
501717	UPSTCU Corp.	CA
501718	GRUUNL Corp.	CA
501717	VIVADG Corp.	CA
501717	GLANZS Corp.	CA
501717	PECAFA Corp.	CA
501717	ZOKORA Corp.	CA
201717	CUSTAF Corp.	CA
201717	UVUSNA Corp.	CA
501717	SANSUU Corp.	CA
501717	WUTTUS Corp.	CA
501717	UNFARE Corp.	CA
701715	CUSVUU Corp.	CA
501717	PECWUT Corp.	CA
201717	NUWPUS Corp.	CA
501717	STUVEE Corp.	CA

Record: 1 of 1823

Figure 1-22 The results of the query will be all records that match the criteria.

Querying multiple tables

This section explores how you can perform a query on multiple tables. Remember that you split the data into separate tables. You used Relationships to define the logical relationships between the data. Now you will query from the tables, based on the relationships that were established.

Suppose you want to see the customer transactions from Colorado. A quick examination of the TransactionMaster reveals that there is no State field on which you can filter. However, you see that there is a CustomerNumber field. In your Access relationships, you defined a one-to-many relationship between the CustomerNumber primary key in CustomerMaster and the Customer-Number foreign key in TransactionMaster. Another way to think of it is filtering the TransactionMaster indirectly by filtering a table that is related to it and using those results to determine which TransactionMaster records to return.

In the query that you already have open, add the TransactionMaster table so you can add some fields from that table to your query output. Two methods exist for adding a table to a query, which have already been created. The first method is to right-click the top half of the QBD (Query By Design) and select Add Table. The second method is to select the Add Table button in the toolbar. Either way, you will bring up the Add Table dialog box.

Once the TransactionMaster has been added to the QBD, you will notice that the previously established relationship is represented, as shown in Figure 1-23. A line connecting the two tables indicates that you don't have to set the relationship in the QBD; it is already there. You can see the one-to-many relationship, indicating possible multiple records in TransactionMaster for each individual customer in the CustomerMaster table.

You must now select the fields from your newly added table, which you need to have appear in the query output. Examine the individual invoices and invoice amounts that were issued to customers from California. Select the following three fields from the TransactionMaster table: Invoice_Number, Invoice_Date, and Sales_Amount. As shown in Figure 1-24, the field names from different tables are brought together in the bottom half of the QBD.

As you can see from Figure 1-25, you now have the invoice data matched with its appropriate customer data. Although there is repeating data, as with the flat-file examples, there is a significant difference. The repeating data is being read from a single source, the CustomerMaster table. If a value were to change in the CustomerMaster table, that changed value would be repeated in your query results. You have overcome potential update errors inherent with duplicate data.

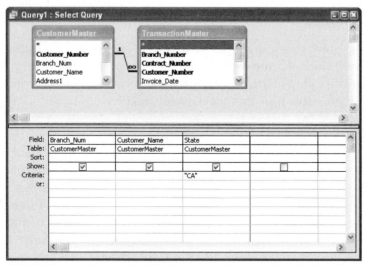

Figure 1-23   The relationship between the two tables is visually represented in the top half of the QBD.

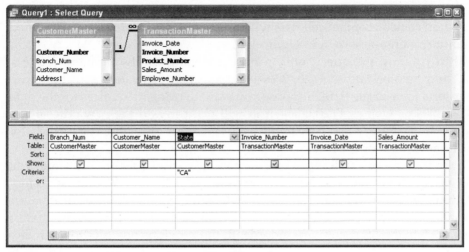

Figure 1-24   Run this query to examine the results.

Refining the query further

You can narrow down your results even further by filtering the query results according to a certain date. As you can see, there are several rows of criteria cells. These allow you to enter multiple criteria from which to filter. One thing to keep in mind is that each separate criteria row functions as its own separate set of criteria. Take a look at how this works.

Branch_Num	Customer_Nam	State	Invoice_Number	Invoice_Date	Sales_Amount
501717	HULAXH Corp.	CA	25474050	2/18/2004	$157.92
501717	HULAXH Corp.	CA	26099378	5/19/2004	$157.92
501717	HULAXH Corp.	CA	26799356	8/12/2004	$157.92
501717	HULAXH Corp.	CA	27454447	11/3/2004	$157.92
201717	CALAFU Corp.	CA	25473787	2/18/2004	$168.82
201717	CALAFU Corp.	CA	25886676	4/14/2004	$168.82
201717	CALAFU Corp.	CA	26480529	6/11/2004	$168.82
201717	CALAFU Corp.	CA	26744732	8/4/2004	$168.82
201717	CALAFU Corp.	CA	27179802	9/30/2004	$168.82
201717	CALAFU Corp.	CA	27616993	11/24/2004	$168.82
201717	ZBUTT Corp.	CA	2422259	10/20/2004	$168.82
201717	ZBUTT Corp.	CA	25320902	1/29/2004	$168.82
201717	ZBUTT Corp.	CA	25624624	3/5/2004	$168.82
201717	ZBUTT Corp.	CA	25938530	4/22/2004	$168.82
201717	ZBUTT Corp.	CA	26259822	6/4/2004	$168.82
201717	ZBUTT Corp.	CA	26582801	7/16/2004	$168.82
201717	ZBUTT Corp.	CA	27127412	8/31/2004	$168.82
201717	ZBUTT Corp.	CA	27670063	12/1/2004	$168.82
501717	UPSTCU Corp.	CA	25522369	2/24/2004	$124.43

Record: I◄ ◄ [1] ► ►I ►* of 13551

Figure 1-25   The results of the query have successfully brought together and matched data from two separate tables.

Click the Criteria cell in the Invoice_Date column and type **"4/20/2004"**. When you click out of that cell, you will notice that the date is now surrounded by number signs, as shown in Figure 1-26.

When running the query, only results matching the two criteria (State = "CA" and InvoiceDate = "4/20/2004") are returned. Now look at using multiple criteria for a single field. Suppose you want to bring in invoices for the data 11/19/2004 as well as 4/20/2004. You will want to add the new criteria line below the existing criteria. This will have the effect of testing the records for either one criteria or the other.

Because you want to limit your query to only results from California, you must retype "CA" on your new Criteria line. If you don't do that, the query will think that you want all invoices from California on 4/20/2004 or invoices from all states on 11/19/2004. The criteria lines will be evaluated individually. Add **"CA"** to the State column underneath the previous one, as shown in Figure 1-27.

After running the query, you can see that your results have been refined even further. You have only those invoices from California that were issued on November 19, 2004 and April 20, 2004. To use multiple criteria in a query, you are not limited to using the separate criteria lines. By using operators, you can place your multiple criteria on the same line.

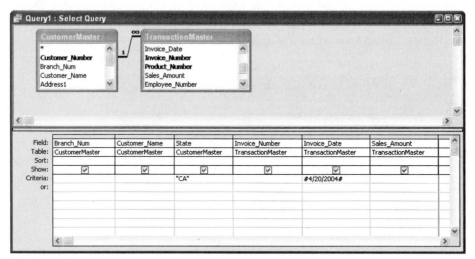

Figure 1-26   The number signs surrounding the date identify the criteria as being a Date/Time data type.

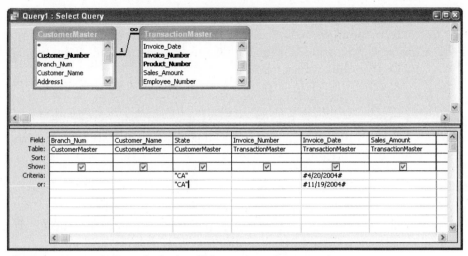

Figure 1-27 Each line of criteria will be evaluated separately.

Using operators in queries

You can filter for multiple criteria on any given field by using operators. The following operators allow you to combine multiple values in different logical contexts so that you can create complex queries.

Or

Either condition can be true. Multiple criteria values for one field can either be separated by a criteria line or combined in one cell with the use of the Or operator. For example, using your query, you can filter for both California and Colorado by typing **"CA" or "CO"** in the criteria field.

Between

Tests for a range of values. For example, using your query, you can filter for all invoices between 4/20/2004 and 11/19/2004 by typing **"Between #4/20/2004# and #11/19/2004#"** in the criteria field.

Like

Tests for string expression matching a pattern. For example, you can filter for all records with a customer number that begins with the number "147" by typing **"Like "147*"** in the criteria field. The asterisk is the wildcard character that can signify any character or combination of characters.

In

Similar to Or. Tests for all records that have values that are contained in parentheses. For example, you can filter for both California and Colorado by typing **"In ("CA", "CO")"** in the criteria field.

Not

Opposite of writing a value in criteria. All records not matching that value will be returned. For example, you can filter for all states except California by typing **"Not "CA""** in the criteria field.

Is Null

Filters all records that have the database value Null in that field.

The traditional mathematical operators allow you to construct complex criteria for fields, which are used in calculations: =, <, >, <=, >=, and <>.

For example, if you want to further refine your query so that only invoice amounts over $200 will be returned in the results, use the greater-than operator to filter the Sales_Amount, as shown in Figure 1-28.

After running the query, you can see that you narrowed down the results to just six records. These are the only records that match the multiple criteria, which were designated in the QBD. Figure 1-29 shows the query results.

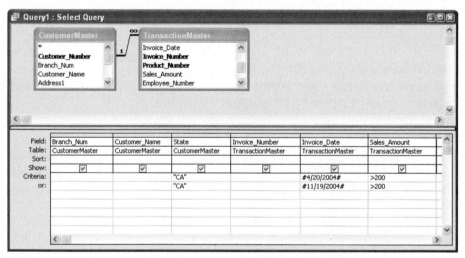

Figure 1-28   You can use operators to test for ranges of values.

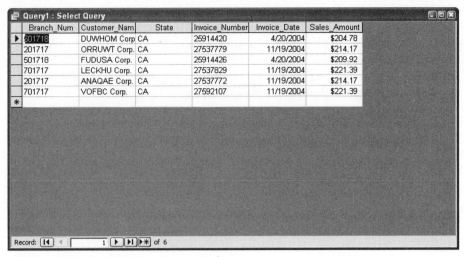

Figure 1-29   Here are your query results.

Exporting query results

Now that you have learned the basics of creating queries, you need to be able to export these results back to Excel or another format. The simplest way to do this in Access is to right-click the query after it has been saved. Select Export and choose the appropriate file type. The query will take a snapshot of the data at that moment in time and save the results in the requested format.

Tricks of the Trade: Outputting to Excel without Saving Anywhere

Open up the TransactionMaster table and highlight the first 10 rows, as shown in Figure 1-30.

Branch_Number	Contract_Numb	Customer_Num	Invoice_Date
101313	1134864	147616	5/13/2004
101313	1134864	147616	2/20/2004
101313	1134864	147616	8/12/2004
101313	1134864	147616	11/1/2004
101313	1134865	147634	1/16/2004
101313	1134865	147634	3/15/2004
101313	1134865	147634	5/5/2004
101313	1134865	147634	6/28/2004
101313	1134865	147634	8/23/2004
101313	1134865	147634	10/20/2004

Figure 1-30   Highlight the data you want to output to Excel.

continues

Go up to the application menu and select Tools → Office Links → Analyze It with Microsoft Office Excel. In just a few seconds, Excel will open up and only the data you selected will be output to a spreadsheet with labels. Figure 1-31 demonstrates how this looks.

This allows you to do some on-the-fly analysis between Access and Excel without saving a gaggle of temporary files.

	A	B	C	D
1	Branch_Number	Contract_Number	Customer_Number	Invoice_Date
2	101313	1134864	147616	13-May-04
3	101313	1134864	147616	20-Feb-04
4	101313	1134864	147616	12-Aug-04
5	101313	1134864	147616	01-Nov-04
6	101313	1134865	147634	16-Jan-04
7	101313	1134865	147634	15-Mar-04
8	101313	1134865	147634	05-May-04
9	101313	1134865	147634	28-Jun-04
10	101313	1134865	147634	23-Aug-04
11	101313	1134865	147634	20-Oct-04

Figure 1-31   Your data has been output to Excel.

CHAPTER 2

Beyond Select Queries

Retrieving and displaying specific records with a select query is a fundamental task in analyzing data. However, it's just a small portion of what makes up data analysis. The scope of data analysis is broad and includes grouping and comparing data, updating and deleting data, performing calculations on data, and shaping and reporting data. Access has built-in tools and functionality designed specifically to handle each one of these tasks.

This chapter takes an in-depth look at the various tools available in Access and how they can help you go beyond select queries.

Aggregate Queries

An *aggregate query*, sometimes referred to as a *group-by query*, is a type of query you can build to help you quickly group and summarize your data. With a select query, you can only retrieve records as they appear in your data source. With an aggregate query, however, you can retrieve a summary snapshot of your data that will show you totals, averages, counts, and more.

Creating an aggregate query

To get a firm understanding of what an aggregate query does, take the following scenario as an example. You have just been asked to provide the sum of total revenue by period. In response to this request, start a query in Design view and bring in the System_Period and Sales_Amount fields as shown in Figure 2-1. If you run this query as is, you will get every record in your dataset instead of the summary you need.

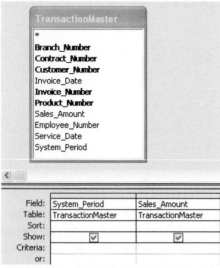

Figure 2-1 Running this query returns all the records in your dataset, not the summary you need.

In order to get a summary of revenue by period, you will need to activate Totals in your design grid. To do this, go up to the application toolbar and select View → Totals. As you can see in Figure 2-2, after you have activated Totals in your design grid, you will see a new row in your grid, called "Totals." The Totals row tells Access which aggregate function to use when performing aggregation on the specified fields.

Notice that the Totals row contains the words "Group By" under each field in your grid. This means that all similar records in a field will be grouped to provide you with a unique data item. The different aggregate functions are covered in depth later in this chapter.

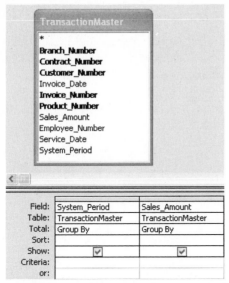

Figure 2-2 Activating Totals in your design grid adds a Totals row to your query grid that defaults to "Group By."

TIP You can also activate Totals by right-clicking anywhere inside the white area of the design grid and selecting Totals.

The idea here is to adjust the aggregate functions in the Totals row to correspond with the analysis you are trying to perform. In this scenario, you need to group all the periods in your dataset, and then sum the revenue in each period. Therefore, you will need to use the Group By aggregate function for the System_Period field, and the Sum aggregate function for the Sales_Amount field.

Because the default selection for Totals is the Group By function, no change is needed for the System_Period field. However, you will need to change the aggregate function for the Sales_Amount field from Group By to Sum. This tells Access that you want to sum the revenue figures in the Sales_Amount field, not group them. To change the aggregate function, simply click the Totals dropdown under the Sales_Amount field, shown in Figure 2-3, and select Sum. At this point, you can run your query.

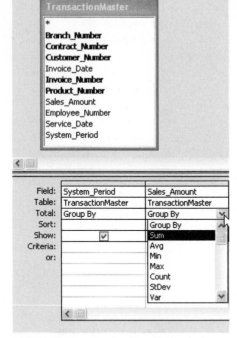

Figure 2-3 Change the aggregate function under the Sales_Amount field to Sum.

As you can see in Figure 2-4, the resulting table gives a summary of your dataset, showing total revenue by period.

System_Period	SumOfSales_Amount
200401	$651,344.58
200402	$1,157,448.14
200403	$631,891.28
200404	$847,452.44
200405	$962,700.12
200406	$861,433.00
200407	$614,902.35
200408	$1,225,471.18
200409	$580,914.19
200410	$880,726.44
200411	$997,995.44
200412	$884,122.17
200413	$477,788.16

Figure 2-4 After you run your query, you have a summary showing you total revenue by period.

Tricks of the Trade: Creating Aliases for Your Column Names

Notice that in Figure 2-4 Access automatically changed the name of the Sales_Amount field to SumOfSales_Amount. This is a normal courtesy extended by Access to let you know that the figures you see here are a result of summing the Sales_Amount field. This may be convenient in some cases, but if you need to distribute these results to other people, you may want to give this field a more seemly name. This is where aliases come in handy.

An alias is an alternate name you can give to a field in order to make it easier to read the field's name in the query results. Two methods exist to create an alias for your field:

◆ The first method is to preface the field with the text you would like to see as the field name, followed by a colon. Figure 2-5 demonstrates how you would create aliases to ensure that your query results have user-friendly column names. Running this query results in a table with a column called Period and column called Total Revenue.

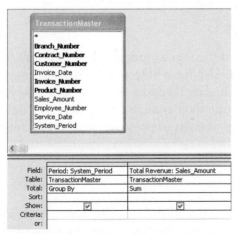

Figure 2-5   In this example, you are creating two aliases: Period and Total Revenue.

◆ The second method is to right-click the field name and select Properties. This activates the Field Properties dialog box. In this dialog box, simply enter the desired alias into the Caption input, as shown in Figure 2-6.

continues

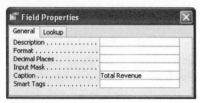

Figure 2-6 Using the Field Properties dialog box
is an alternative way of defining an alias for your field.

WARNING Be aware that if you do use the Field Properties dialog box to
define your alias, there will be no clear indication in your query's Design view,
or in your query's SQL string, that you are using an alias. This may lead to some
confusion for anyone using your queries. For this reason, it is generally better
to use the first method to define an alias.

Exploring aggregate functions

In the example in Figure 2-3, you selected the Sum aggregate function from the
Totals drop-down list. Obviously, you could have selected any one of the 12
functions available. Indeed, you will undoubtedly come across analyses where
you will have to use a few of the other functions available to you. In this light,
it is important to know the implications of each of these aggregate functions
for your data analysis.

Group By

The Group By aggregate function aggregates all the records in the specified
field into unique groups. Here are a few things to keep in mind when using the
Group By aggregate function:

- **Access will perform the** Group By **function in your aggregate query
  before any other aggregation.** If you are performing a Group By along
  with another aggregate function, the Group By function will be performed first. The example shown in Figure 2-4 illustrates this concept.
  Access groups the System_Period field before summing the
  Sales_Amount field.

- **Access treats multiple Group By fields as one unique item.** To illustrate this point, create a query that looks similar to the one shown in
  Figure 2-7. As you can see after running the query, Access counts all the
  transactions that were logged in the "200401" System_Period.

Field:	System_Period	System_Period
Table:	TransactionMaster	TransactionMaster
Total:	Group By	Count
Sort:		
Show:	☑	☑
Criteria:	"200401"	
or:		

⚠ Run the query to see the results.

Zalexcorp Integrated Facility Services -

System_Period	CountOfSystem_Period
▶ 200401	4164

Figure 2-7 After you run this query, you will have a summary showing you that there are 4,164 records in System_Period 200401.

Now return to Query Design view and add Product_Number, as shown in Figure 2-8. This time, Access treats each combination of System_Period and Product Number as a unique item. Each combination is grouped before the records in each group are counted. The benefit here is that you have added a dimension to your analysis. Not only do you know how many transactions per Product_Number were logged in 200401, but if you add up all the transactions, you will get an accurate count of the total number of transactions logged in 200401.

Field:	System_Period	Product_Number	System_Period
Table:	TransactionMaster	TransactionMaster	TransactionMaster
Total:	Group By	Group By	Count
Sort:			
Show:	☑	☑	☑
Criteria:	"200401"		
or:			

⚠ Run the query to see the results.

Zalexcorp Integrated Facility Services - [Query1 : Select Q

System_Period	Product_Number	CountOfSystem_Period
▶ 200401	16000	1087
200401	30300	1052
200401	70700	879
200401	81150	178
200401	87000	472
200401	90830	496

Figure 2-8 This query results in a few more records, but if you add up the counts in each group, they will total 4,164.

- **Access will sort each Group By field in ascending order.** Unless otherwise specified, any field tagged as a Group By field will be sorted in ascending order. If your query has multiple Group By fields, each field will be sorted in ascending order starting with the left-most field.

Sum, Avg, Count, StDev, Var

These aggregate functions all perform mathematical calculations against the records in your selected field. It is important to note that these functions exclude any records that are set to Null. In other words, these aggregate functions ignore any empty cells.

Sum

Sum calculates the total value of all the records in the designated field or grouping. This function works only with the following data types: AutoNumber, Currency, Date/Time, and Number.

Avg

Avg calculates the average of all the records in the designated field or grouping. This function works only with the following data types: AutoNumber, Currency, Date/Time, and Number.

Count

Count simply counts the number of entries within the designated field or grouping. This function works with all data types.

StDev

StDev calculates the standard deviation across all records within the designated field or grouping. This function works only with the following data types: AutoNumber, Currency, Date/Time, and Number.

Var

Var calculates the amount by which all the values within the designated field or grouping vary from the average value of the group. This function works only with the following data types: AutoNumber, Currency, Date/Time, and Number.

Min, Max, First, Last

Unlike other aggregate functions, these functions evaluate all the records in the designated field or grouping and return a single value from the group.

Min

Min returns the value of the record with the lowest value in the designated field or grouping. This function works only with the following data types: AutoNumber, Currency, Date/Time, Number, and Text.

Max

Max returns the value of the record with the highest value in the designated field or grouping. This function works only with the following data types: AutoNumber, Currency, Date/Time, Number, and Text.

First

First returns the value of the first record in the designated field or grouping. This function works with all data types.

Last

Last returns the value of the last record in the designated field or grouping. This function works with all data types

Expression, Where

One of the steadfast rules of aggregate queries is that every field must have an aggregation performed against it. However, there will be situations where you will have to use a field as a utility. That is, use a field to simply perform a calculation or apply a filter. These fields are a means to get to the final analysis you are looking for, rather than part of the final analysis. In these situations, you use the Expression function or the Where clause. The Expression function and the Where clause are unique in that they don't perform any grouping action per se.

Expression

The Expression aggregate function is generally applied when you are using custom calculations or other functions in an aggregate query. Expression tells Access to perform the designated custom calculation on each individual record or group separately.

Create a query in Design view that looks like the one shown in Figure 2-9. Note that you are using two aliases in this query: "Revenue" for the Sales_Amount field and "Cost" for the custom calculation defined here. Using an alias of "Revenue" gives the sum of Sales_Amount a user-friendly name.

Now you can use "[Revenue]" to represent the sum of Sales_Amount in your custom calculation. The Expression aggregate function ties it all together by telling Access that "[Revenue]*.33" will be performed against the resulting sum of Sales_Amount for each individual System_Period group. Running this query returns the total revenue and cost for each System_Period group.

Where

The Where clause allows you to apply a criterion to a field that is not included in your aggregate query, effectively applying a filter to your analysis. To see the Where clause in action, create a query in Design view that looks like the one shown in Figure 2-10.

As you can see in the Total row, you are grouping Product_Number and summing Sales_Amount. However, System_Period has no aggregation selected because you only want to use it to filter out one specific period. You have entered "200401" in the criteria for System_Period. If you run this query as is, you get the following error message: "You tried to execute a query that does not include the specified expression 'System_Period' as part of an aggregate function."

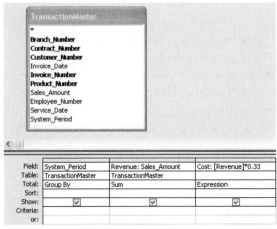

Figure 2-9   The Expression aggregate function allows you to perform the designated custom calculation on each System_Period group separately.

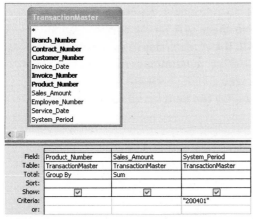

Figure 2-10   Running this query causes an error message
because you have no aggregation defined for System_Period.

To run this query successfully, click the Totals dropdown for the
System_Period field and select "Where" from the selection list. At this point,
your query should look similar to the one shown in Figure 2-11. With the
Where clause specified, you can successfully run this query.

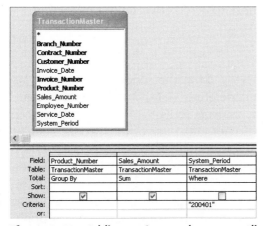

Figure 2-11   Adding a Where clause remedies
the error and allows you to run the query.

NOTE Here is one final note about the `Where` clause. Notice in Figure 2-11 that the checkbox in the Show row has no check in it for the System_Period. This is because fields that are tagged with the `Where` clause cannot be shown in an aggregate query. Therefore, this checkbox must remain empty. If you place a check in the Show checkbox of a field with a `Where` clause, you will get an error message stating that you cannot display the field for which you entered `Where` in the Total row.

Action Queries

You can think of an action query the same way you think of a select query. Like a select query, an action query extracts a dataset from a data source based on the definitions and criteria you pass to the query. The difference is that when an action query returns results, it does not display a dataset; instead, it performs some action on those results. The action it performs depends on its type.

NOTE Unlike select queries, you cannot use action queries as a data source for a form or a report, because they do not return a dataset that can be read.

Four types of action queries exist: make-table, delete, append, and update. Each query type performs a unique action, which is covered in this section.

Why use action queries?

As mentioned before, along with querying data, the scope of data analysis includes shaping data, changing data, deleting data, and updating data. Access provides action queries as data analysis tools to help you with these tasks. Unfortunately, too many people do not make use of these tools, instead opting to export small chunks of data to Excel in order to perform these tasks.

This may be fine if you are performing these tasks as a one-time analysis with a small dataset. However, what do you do when you have to carry out the same analysis on a weekly basis, or if the dataset you need to manipulate exceeds Excel's limits? In these situations, it would be impractical to routinely export data into Excel, manipulate the data, and then re-import the data back into Access. Using action queries, you can increase your productivity and reduce the chance of errors by carrying out all your analytical processes within Access.

Make-table queries

A *make-table* query creates a new table consisting of data from an existing table. The table that is created consists of records that have met the definitions and criteria of the make-table query.

Why use a make-table query?

In simple terms, if you create a query and would like to capture the results of your query in its own table, you can use a make-table query to create a hard table with your query results. You can then use your new table in some other analytical process.

What are the hazards of make-table queries?

When you build a make-table query, you have to specify the name of the table that will be made when the make-table query is run. If you give the new table the same name as an existing table, the existing table will be overwritten. If you accidentally write over another table with a make-table query, you will not be able to recover the old table. Be sure that you name the tables created by your make-table queries carefully to avoid overwriting existing information.

The data in a table made by a make-table query is not in any way linked to its source data. This means that the data in your new table will not be updated when data in the original table is changed.

Creating a make-table query

You have been asked to provide the company's marketing department with a list of customers, along with information about each customer's service interval. To meet this task, create a query in the Query Design view that looks similar to the one shown in Figure 2-12.

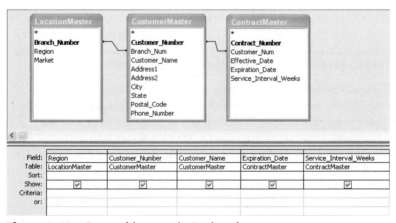

Figure 2-12 Create this query in Design view.

Select Query → Make-Table Query to activate the Make Table dialog box shown in Figure 2-13. Enter the name you would like to give to your new table in the Table Name input box. In this example, enter **Customer Intervals** as the table name. Be sure not to enter the name of a table that already exists in your database, because it will be overwritten.

Once you have entered the name, click the OK button to close the dialog box and then run your query. At this point, Access throws up the warning message shown in Figure 2-14 in order to make you aware that you will not be able to undo this action. Click Yes to confirm and create your new table.

When your query has completed running, you will find a new table called Customer Intervals in your Table objects.

Figure 2-13   Enter the name of your new table.

Figure 2-14   Click Yes to run your query.

Tricks of the Trade: Turning Aggregate Query Results into Hard Data

---

The results of aggregate queries are inherently not updatable. This means you will not be able to edit any of the records returned from an aggregate query. This is because there is no relationship between the aggregated data and the underlying data. However, you can change your aggregate query into a make-table query and create a hard table with your aggregate query's results. With your new hard table, you will be able to edit to your heart's content.

To illustrate how this works, create the query shown in Figure 2-15 in Design view. Then change the query into a make-table query, enter a name for your new table, and run it.

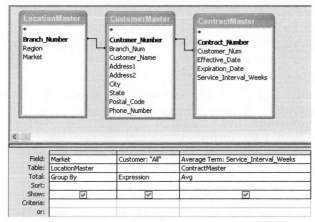

Figure 2-15 Running this query as a make-table allows you to edit the aggregate query's results.

TIP Notice that in Figure 2-15 you defined a column with an alias of "Customer." After the alias, you simply entered All in quotes. When you run the query, you will notice that your new table has a column named Customer in which the value for every record is All. This example illustrates that when running a make-table query, you can create your own columns on-the-fly by simply creating an alias for the column and defining its contents after the colon.

Delete queries

A *delete query* deletes records from a table based on the definitions and criteria you specify. That is, a delete query affects a group of records that meet a specified criterion that you apply.

Why use a delete query?

Although you can delete records by hand, in some situations using a delete query is more efficient. For example, if you have a very large dataset, a delete query will delete your records faster that a manual delete. In addition, if you want to delete certain records based on several complex criteria, you will want to use a delete query. Finally, if you need to delete records from one table based on a comparison to another table, a delete query is the way to go.

What are the hazards of delete queries?

Like all other action queries, you will not be able to undo the effects of a delete query. However, a delete query is much more dangerous than the other action queries because there is no way to remedy accidentally deleted data.

Given the fact that deleted data cannot be recovered, you should get in the habit of taking one of the following actions in order to avoid a fatal error:

- Run a select query to display the records you are about to delete. Review the records to confirm that these records are indeed the ones you want to delete, and then run the query as a delete query.

- Run a select query to display the records you are about to delete, then change the query into a make-table query. Run the make-table query to make a backup of the data you are about to delete. Finally, run the query again as a delete query to delete the records.

- Make a backup of your database before running your delete query.

Creating a delete query

Suppose the marketing department has informed you that the Customer Intervals table you gave them includes records that they do not need. They want you to delete all the customers that have an Expiration_Date earlier than January 1, 2006. In order to meet this task, design a query based on the Customer Intervals table you created a moment ago. Bring in the Expiration_Date field and enter **<#1/1/2006#** in the Criteria row. Your design grid should look like the one shown in Figure 2-16.

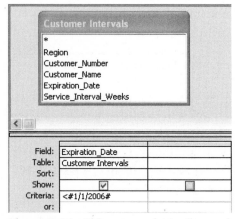

Figure 2-16   This query selects all records with an expiration date earlier than January 1, 2006.

Perform a test by running the query. Review the records that are returned, and take note that 567 records meet your criteria. You now know that 567 records will be deleted if you run a delete query based on these query definitions.

Return to the Design view. Go up to the application menu, select Query, and then select Delete Query. Run your query.

At this point, Access throws up a message, as shown in Figure 2-17, telling you that you are about to delete 567 rows of data and warning you that you will not be able to undo this action. This is the number you were expecting to see, because the test you ran earlier returned 567 records. Since everything checks out, click Yes to confirm and delete the records.

NOTE If you are working with a very large dataset, Access may throw up a message telling you that the "undo command won't be available because the operation is too large or there isn't enough free memory."

Many people mistakenly interpret this message as meaning that this operation can't be done because there is not enough memory. This message is simply telling you that Access will not be able to give the option of undoing this change if you choose to continue with the action.

This is applicable to delete queries, append queries, and update queries.

Figure 2-17   Click Yes to continue with your delete action.

Tricks of the Trade: Delete Records from One Table Based on the Records from Another

You will encounter many analyses where you will have to delete records from one table based on the records from another. This is relatively easy to do. However, many users get stuck on this because of one simple mistake.

The query in Figure 2-18 looks simple enough. It is telling Access to delete all records from the Customer Intervals table if the region in the Region field is found in the LocationMaster table.

continues

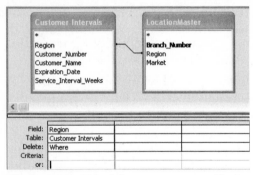

Figure 2-18   This delete query seems like it should run fine, but there is something wrong.

If you run this query, Access throws up the message shown in Figure 2-19. This message is asking you to specify which table contains the records you want to delete.

Figure 2-19   Access does not know which table from which you want the records deleted.

This message stumps many Access users because it doesn't clearly state what you need to do in order to remedy the mistake. Nevertheless, the remedy is a simple one.

First, clear the query grid by deleting the Region field. Next, double-click the asterisk (*) in the Customer Intervals table. This explicitly tells Access that the Customer Intervals table contains the records you want to delete. Figure 2-20 demonstrates the correct way to build this query.

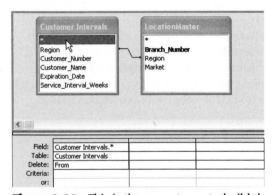

Figure 2-20   This is the correct way to build the query.

A Word on Cascade Deletes

If you are using relationships that enforce referential integrity, Access will not allow you to delete records in the joined field of one table if those records exist in a related table. In other words, you would not be able to delete a record from your Customers table if there are records in your Orders table that have matching Customer IDs because of the enforced one-to-many join on the Customer ID field. However, if you use cascading deletes, you negate this security feature altogether.

To see this concept in action, follow these steps:

1. Find the Northwind database in C:\Program Files\Microsoft Office\OFFICExx\SAMPLES (where xx is your version of Office). Make a copy of Northwind and paste the copy on your desktop.

2. Open the Northwind database you just pasted onto your desktop and open the Orders table. Note that there are 830 records there.

3. Open up the Customers table and try to delete the first customer record (Customer Id: AFKLI). Note that you get the following message: "The record cannot be deleted or changed because table 'Orders' includes related records." Close the Customers table.

4. Go up to the toolbar and select Tools → Relationships.

5. Double-click the join between the Orders table and the Customers table.

6. At this point, the Edit Relationships dialog box, shown in Figure 2-21, activates. Place a check in the checkbox next to "Cascade Delete Related Records" and click the OK button. Save the relationships when asked.

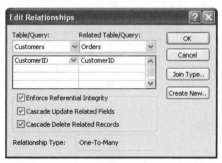

Figure 2-21 Activate cascade deletes by checking the checkbox.

7. Open up the Customers table and try to delete the first customer record (Customer Id: AFKLI). Note that you now get a message warning you that you are about to delete one record. Click the Yes button to confirm the delete.

8. Open the Orders table. Note that there are 824 records there.

You lost six records in the Orders table by deleting one record in the Customers table. Because referential integrity is enforced between Customers and Orders, Access will not allow any orders to exist that have a customer number that does not exist in the Customers table. The scary thing is that Access deleted these records without ever warning you that you were about to delete six records from the Orders table.

The bottom line is that although cascade deletes may be useful in some situations, they are extremely dangerous and should rarely be activated. If you are using relationships that enforce referential integrity in your database, be sure that all your enforced relationships have the Cascade Delete Related Records checkbox unchecked.

Append queries

An append query appends records to a table based on the definitions and criteria you specify in your query. In other words, with an append query, you can add the results of your query to the end of a table, effectively adding rows to the table.

Why use an append query?

With an append query, you are essentially copying records from one table or query and adding them to the end of another table. With that in mind, append queries come in handy when you need to transfer large datasets from an existing table to another. For example, if you have a table called Old Transactions where you archive your transaction records, you can add the latest batch of transactions from the New Transactions table by simply using an append query.

What are the hazards of append queries?

The primary hazard of an append query is losing records during the append process. That is, not all of the records you think you are appending to a table actually may make it to your table. Generally, records can get lost during an append process for two reasons:

- **Type conversion failure.** This failure occurs when the character type of the source data does not match that of the destination table column. For example, imagine that you have a table with a field called Cost. Your Cost field is set as a TEXT character type because you have some entries that are tagged as "TBD" (to be determined), because you don't know the cost yet. If you try to append that field to another table whose Cost field is set as a NUMBER character type, all the entries that have "TBD" will be changed to Null, effectively deleting your TBD tag.

- **Key violation.** This violation occurs when you are trying to append duplicate records to a field in the destination table that is set as a primary key or is indexed as No Duplicates. In other words, when you have a field that prohibits duplicates, Access will not allow you to append any record that is a duplicate of an existing record in that field.

Another hazard of an append query is that the query will simply fail to run. An append query can fail for two reasons:

- **Lock violation.** This violation occurs when the destination table is open in Design view or is open by another user on the network.

- **Validation rule violation.** This violation occurs when a field in the destination table has one of the following properties settings:

  - Required Field is set to Yes: If a field in the destination table has been set to Required Yes and you do not append data to this field, your append query will fail.

  - Allow Zero Length is set to No: If a field in the destination table has been set to Zero Length No and you do not append data to this field, your append query will fail.

  - Validation Rule set to anything: If a field in the destination table has a validation rule and you break the rule with your append query, your append query will fail. For example, if you have a validation rule for the Cost field in your destination table set to >0, you cannot append records with a quantity less than or equal to zero.

Luckily, Access will clearly warn you if you are about to cause any of the above-mentioned errors. Figure 2-22 demonstrates this warning message.

As you can see, this warning message tells you that you cannot append all the records due to errors. It goes on to tell you exactly how many records will not be appended because of each error. In this case, two records will not be appended: one because of a type conversion failure and another because of a key violation. You have the option of clicking Yes or No. Clicking the Yes button will ignore the warning and append all records minus the two with the errors. Clicking the No button will cancel the query, which means that no records will be appended.

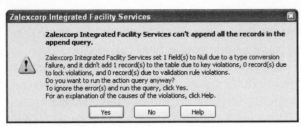

Figure 2-22 Warning message telling you that you will lose two records during the append process.

Keep in mind that like all other action queries, you will not be able to undo your append query once you have pulled the trigger.

TIP If you can identify the records you recently appended in your destination table, you could technically undo your append action by simply deleting the newly appended records. This would obviously be contingent upon you providing yourself a method of identifying appended records. For example, you could create a field that contains some code or tag that identifies the appended records. This code can be anything from a date to a simple character.

Creating an append query

Suppose the Marketing department contacts you and tells you that they made a mistake. They actually do need the customers that have an Expiration_Date earlier than January 1, 2006. They want you to add back the records you deleted. To do this, you will have to append the customers that have an Expiration_Date earlier than January 1, 2006 back to the Customer Intervals table.

In order to meet this task, create a query in the Query Design view that looks similar to the one shown in Figure 2-23.

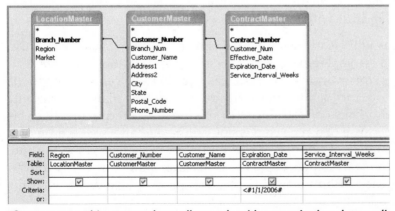

Figure 2-23 This query selects all records with an expiration date earlier than January 1, 2006.

Select Query → Append Query to activate the Append dialog box, as shown in Figure 2-24. In the Table Name input box, enter the name of the table to which you would like to append your query results.

Once you have entered your destination table's name, click the OK button. You will notice that your query grid has a new row called "Append To" under the Sort row. Figure 2-25 shows this new row.

The idea is to select the name of the field in your destination table where you would like to append the information resulting from your query. For example, the Region field in the Append To row shows the word "Region." This means that the data in the Region field of this query will be appended to the Region field in the Customer Intervals table.

Now you can run your query. After doing so, Access throws up a message like the one shown in Figure 2-26 telling you that you are about to append 567 rows of data and warning you that you will not be able to undo this action. Click Yes to confirm and append the records.

Figure 2-24 Enter the name of the table to which you would like to append your query results.

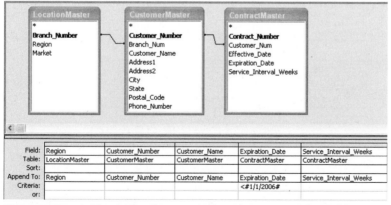

Figure 2-25 In the Append To row, select the name of the field in your destination table where you would like to append the information resulting from your query.

Figure 2-26   Click Yes to continue with your append action.

Tricks of the Trade: Adding a Totals Row to Your Dataset

Suppose your manager wants you to create a revenue summary report that shows the total revenue for all the employees in each market. He also wants to see the total revenue for each market. Instead of giving your manager two separate reports, you can provide one table that has employee details and market totals. This is an easy, two-step process:

1. **Make an Employees Summary.** Create a query in the Query Design view that looks similar to the one shown in Figure 2-27. Note that you are creating an alias for both the Last_Name field and the Sales_Amount Field. Change the query into a make-table query and name your table Revenue Summary. Run this query.

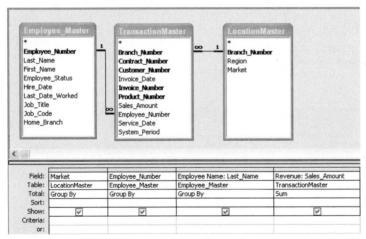

Figure 2-27   Run this query as a make-table query to make a table called Revenue Summary.

2. **Append the Market Totals.** Now use the Revenue Summary table you just created to summarize revenue by Market. To do this, create a query in the Query Design view that looks similar to the one shown in Figure 2-28.

Take a moment and look at the query in Figure 2-28. You will notice that you are making two custom fields: Total Tag1 and Total Tag2. You are filling these fields with the word "Total." This will ensure that the summary lines you append to the Revenue Summary table will be clearly identifiable, because they will have the word "Total" in the Employee_Number field and the Employee Name field.

Change the query into an append query and append these results to the Revenue Summary table.

Field:	Market	Total Tag1: "Total"	Total Tag2: "Total"	Revenue
Table:	Revenue Summary			Revenue Summary
Total:	Group By	Expression	Expression	Sum
Sort:				
Append To:	Market	Employee_Number	Employee Name	Revenue
Criteria:				
or:				

Figure 2-28 Run this market summary query as an append query and append it to the Revenue Summary table.

Now you can open the Revenue Summary table and sort by Market and Employee_Number. As you can see in Figure 2-29, you have successfully created a table that has a total revenue line for every employee and a total revenue line for each market, all in one table.

Market	Employee_Number	Employee Name	Revenue
BUFFALO	1416	CERMACHEIL	$959.70
BUFFALO	160133	MALISKI	$6,431.70
BUFFALO	160234	FOX	$109.00
BUFFALO	160235	STOFFERD	$373.60
BUFFALO	164550	TEMADY	$8,642.91
BUFFALO	2053	SMATH	$12,941.38
BUFFALO	3224	BEACE	$622.25
BUFFALO	4401	DIAST	$65,714.85
BUFFALO	4455	PIDLANIR	$2,680.65
BUFFALO	45641	EIGILLO	$30,388.14
BUFFALO	52311	SLAVIN	$4,005.01
BUFFALO	52562	CYGANAK	$32,042.99
BUFFALO	55051	SELINSKY	$145.15
BUFFALO	5601	WHATFAILD	$15,663.19
BUFFALO	56102	WANEGREDZKI	$69,034.80
BUFFALO	56405	BICKIR	$81,100.53
BUFFALO	6064	STANSEN	$60,337.57
BUFFALO	6146	BEWMAN	$752.85
BUFFALO	64100	CELIS	$33,770.34
BUFFALO	6442	KIASACK	$319.50
BUFFALO	6462	BIQGISS	$24,172.83
BUFFALO	6644	COX	$269.79
BUFFALO	Total	Total	$450,478.73
CALIFORNIA	1054	STEMPFL	$50,579.25

Figure 2-29 Sort by market and employee number to see each employee in a market, and the market total.

Update queries

When you build a make-table query, you will have to specify the name of the table that will be made when the make-table query is run. If you give the new table the same name as an existing table, the existing table will be overwritten. If you accidentally write over another table with a make-table query, you will not be able to recover the old table. Be sure that you name the tables created by your make-table queries carefully to avoid overwriting existing information.

The data in a table made by a make-table query is not, in any way, linked to its source data. This means that the data in your new table will not be updated when data in the original table is changed.

Why use an update query?

The primary reason to use update queries is to save time. There is no easier way to edit large amounts of data at one time than with an update query. For example, suppose you have a Customers table that includes the customer's zip code. If the zip code 32750 has been changed to 32751, you can easily update your Customers table to replace 32750 with 32751.

What are the hazards of update queries?

Like all other action queries, you will not be able to undo the effects of an update query. With that in mind, you should get into the habit of taking one of the following actions in order to give yourself a way back to the original data in the event of a misstep:

- Run a select query to display, then change the query into a make-table query. Run the make-table query to make a backup of the data you are about to update. Finally, run the query again as an update query to delete the records.
- Make a backup of your database before running your update query.

Creating an update query

You have just received word that the zip code for all customers in the 32750 zip code has been changed to 32751. In order to keep your database accurate, you will have to update all the 32750 zip codes in your CustomerMaster table to 32751. Create a query in the Query Design view that looks similar to the one shown in Figure 2-30.

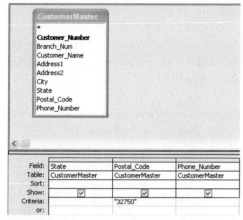

Figure 2-30 This query selects all customers that are in the 32750 zip code.

Perform a test by running the query. Review the records that are returned, and take note that 13 records meet your criteria. You now know that 13 records will be updated if you run an update query based on these query definitions.

Return to the Design view. Go up to the application menu, select Query, and then select Update Query. You will notice that your query grid has a new row called "Update To." The idea is to enter the value to which you would like to update the current data. In this scenario, shown in Figure 2-31, you want to update the zip code for the records you are selecting to 32751.

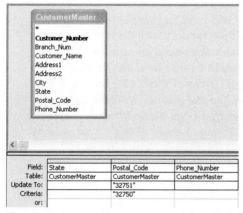

Figure 2-31 In this query, you are updating the zip code for all customers that have a code of 32750 to 32571.

Run the query. Access throws up the message shown in Figure 2-32, telling you that you are about to update 13 rows of data and warning you that you will not be able to undo this action. This is the number you were expecting to see, because the test you ran earlier returned 13 records. Since everything checks out, click Yes to confirm and update the records.

WARNING Bear in mind that cascading updates work the same way as cascading deletes. If you are using relationships that enforce referential integrity, Access will not allow you to update records in the joined field of one table if those records exist in a related table. However, if you place a check in the "Cascade Update Related Fields" checkbox in the Edit Relationships dialog box shown in Figure 2-21, you will negate this security feature altogether. For example, if you activate Cascading Updates and change a customer's ID in the Customers table, the CustomerID field in the Orders table is automatically updated for every one of that customer's orders.

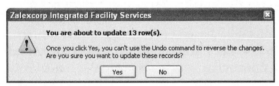

Figure 2-32   Click Yes to continue with your update action.

Tricks of the Trade: Using Expressions in Your Update Queries

You will come across situations where you will have to execute record-specific updates. That is, you are not updating multiple records with one specific value; instead, you are updating each record individually based on an expression.

To demonstrate this concept, start a query in Design view based on the Revenue Summary table you created during "Tricks of the Trade: Adding a Totals Row to Your Dataset." Build your query like the one shown in Figure 2-33.

This query is telling Access to update the Employee Name for each employee in the Revenue Summary table to the concatenated value of their [Last_Name] in the EmployeeMaster table, a comma, and their [First_Name] in the EmployeeMaster table.

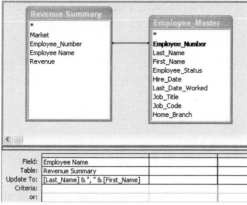

Figure 2-33 This update query is using an expression to make record-specific updates.

After you run this query, each employee will have their full name in the Employee Name field of the Revenue Summary table. For example, the name of employee number 104 in the Revenue Summary table will be updated from WIBB to WIBB, MAURICE.

Remember, this is just one example of an expression you can use to update your records. You can use almost any expression with an update query, ranging from mathematical functions to string operations.

A word on updatable datasets

Not all datasets are updatable. That is, you may have a dataset that Access cannot update for one reason or another. If your update query fails, you will get one of these messages: "Operation must use an updatable query" or "This recordset is not updatable."

Your update query will fail if any one of the following applies:

- **Your query is using a join to another query.** To work around this issue, create a temporary table that you can use instead of the joined query.

- **Your query is based on a crosstab query, an aggregate query, a union query, or a subquery that contains aggregate functions.** To work around this issue, create a temporary table that you can use instead of the query.

- **Your query is based on three or more tables and there is a many-to-one-to-many relationship.** To work around this issue, create a temporary table that you can use without the relationship.

- **Your query is based on a table where the Unique Values property is set to Yes.** To work around this issue, set the Unique Values property of the table to No.

- **Your query is based on a table on which you do not have Update Data permissions, or is locked by another user.** To work around this issue, ensure that you have permissions to update the table, and that the table is not in Design view or locked by another user.

- **Your query is based on a table in a database that is open as read-only or is located on a read-only drive.** To work around this issue, obtain write access to the database or drive.

- **Your query is based on a linked ODBC table with no unique index or a Paradox table without a primary key.** To work around this issue, add a primary key or a unique index to the linked table.

- **Your query is based on a SQL pass-through query.** To work around this issue, create a temporary table that you can use instead of the query.

Crosstab Queries

A *crosstab query* is a special kind of aggregate query that summarizes values from a specified field and groups them in a matrix layout by two sets of dimensions, one set down the left side of the matrix and the other set listed across the top of the matrix. Crosstab queries are perfect for analyzing trends over time or providing a method for quickly identifying anomalies in your dataset.

The anatomy of a crosstab query is simple. You need a minimum of three fields in order to create the matrix structure that will become your crosstab: the first field makes up the row headings, the second field makes up the column headings, and the third field makes up the aggregated data in the center of the matrix. The data in the center can represent a sum, count, average, or any other aggregate function. Figure 2-34 demonstrates the basic structure of a crosstab query.

Region Name	QTR1	QTR2	QTR3	QTR4
Region A	data	data	data	data
Region B	data	data	data	data
Region C	data	data	data	data

Figure 2-34   The basic structure of a crosstab query.

Two methods exist to create a crosstab query: using the Crosstab Query Wizard and creating a crosstab query manually using the Query Design grid.

Using the Crosstab Query Wizard

To activate the Crosstab Query Wizard, select Insert → Query. This brings up the New Query dialog box shown in Figure 2-35. Select Crosstab Query Wizard from the selection list and click the OK button.

The first step in the Crosstab Query Wizard is to identify the data source you will be using. As you can see in Figure 2-36, you can choose either a query or a table as your data source. In this example, you will be using the Transaction-Master table as your data source. Select TransactionMaster and click the Next button.

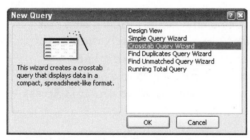

Figure 2-35 Select Crosstab Query Wizard from the New Query dialog box.

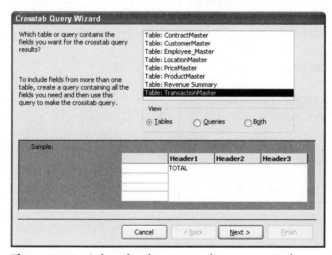

Figure 2-36 Select the data source for your crosstab query.

The next step is to identify the fields you would like to use as the row headings. Select the Product_Number field and click the button with the > symbol on it to move it to the Selected Items list. At this point, your dialog box should look like that shown in Figure 2-37. Notice that the Product_Number field is shown in the sample diagram at the bottom of the dialog box.

You can select up to three fields to include in your crosstab query as row headings. Remember that Access treats each combination of headings as a unique item. That is, each combination is grouped before the records in each group are aggregated.

The next step is to identify the field you would like to use as the column heading for your crosstab query. Keep in mind that there can be only one column heading in your crosstab. Select the Invoice_Date field from the field list. Again, notice in Figure 2-38 that the sample diagram at the bottom of the dialog box updates to show the Invoice_Date.

NOTE If the field that is being used as a column heading includes data that contains a period (.), an exclamation mark (!), or a bracket ([or]), those characters will be changed to an underscore character (_) in the column heading. This does not happen if the same data is used as a row heading. This behavior is by design, because the naming convention for field names in Access prohibits use of these characters.

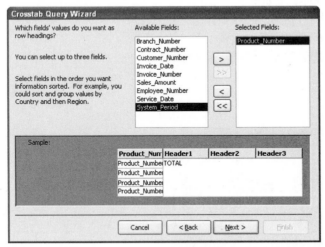

Figure 2-37   Select the Product_Number field and click the Next button.

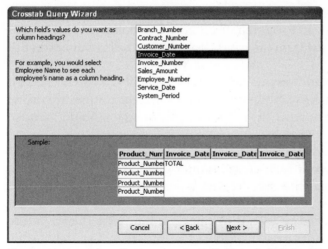

Figure 2-38 Select the Invoice_Date field and click the Next button.

If your column heading is a date field, as the Invoice_Date is in this example, you will see the step shown in Figure 2-39. In this step, you will have the option of specifying an interval to group your dates by. Select Quarter here and notice that the sample diagram at the bottom of the dialog box updates accordingly.

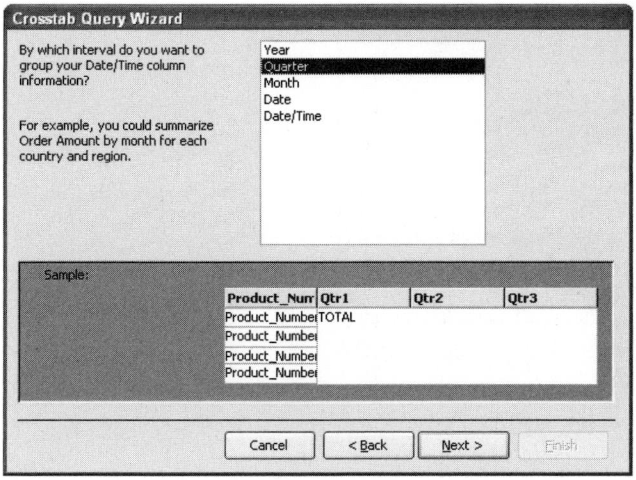

Figure 2-39 Select Quarter and click the Next button.

You're almost done. In the second-to-last step, shown in Figure 2-40, you will identify the field you want to aggregate and the function you want to use. Select the Sales_Amount field from the Fields list and then select Sum from the Functions list.

Notice the checkbox next to "Yes, include row sums." This box is checked by default to ensure that your crosstab query includes a Total column that contains the sum total for each row. If you do not want this column, simply remove the check from the checkbox.

If you look at the sample diagram at the bottom of the dialog box, you will get a good sense of what your final crosstab query will do. In this example, your crosstab will calculate the sum of the Sales_Amount field for each Product_Number by quarter.

The final step, shown in Figure 2-41, is to name your crosstab query. In this example, you are naming your crosstab "Product Summary by Quarter." After you name your query, you have the option of viewing your query or modifying the design. In this case, you want to view your query results, so simply click the Finish button.

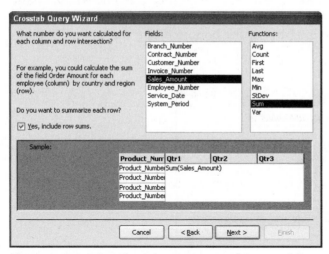

Figure 2-40 Select the Sales_Amount and Sum and then click the Next button.

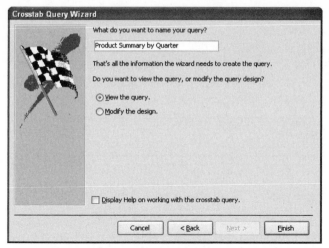

Figure 2-41 Click Finish to see your query results.

In just a few clicks, you have created a powerful look at the revenue performance of each product by quarter, as shown in Figure 2-42.

Product_Number	Total Of Sales_Amount	Qtr 1	Qtr 2	Qtr 3	Qtr 4
16000	$2,361,161.41	$563,800.21	$621,715.87	$600,810.41	$574,834.92
30300	$2,627,798.02	$612,496.21	$691,440.40	$674,592.20	$649,269.21
70700	$2,178,932.11	$533,128.55	$567,392.96	$552,382.16	$526,028.44
81150	$1,138,595.78	$257,218.54	$290,074.98	$297,252.21	$294,050.05
87000	$1,190,911.60	$288,795.91	$310,668.86	$303,084.76	$288,362.07
90830	$1,276,790.55	$293,195.50	$325,277.88	$329,788.62	$328,528.56

Figure 2-42 A powerful analysis in just a few clicks.

Tricks of the Trade: Turning Your Crosstab Query into Hard Data

You will undoubtedly encounter scenarios where you will have to convert your crosstab query into hard data in order to use the results on other analyses. A simple trick for doing this is to use your saved crosstab query in a make-table query to create a new table with your crosstab results.

Start by creating a new select query in Design view and add your saved crosstab query. In Figure 2-43, you will notice that you are using the "Product Summary by Quarter" crosstab you just created. Bring in the fields you will want to include in your new table.

continues

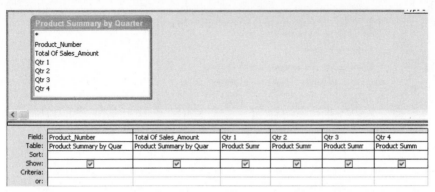

Figure 2-43   Create a select query using the crosstab query as your source data.

At this point, simply convert your query into a make-table query and run it.
After you run your make-table, you will have a hard table that contains the
results of your crosstab.

Creating a crosstab query manually

Although the Crosstab Query Wizard makes it easy to create a crosstab in just
a few clicks, it does come with its own set of limitations that may inhibit your
data analysis efforts. These are the limitations you will encounter when using
the Crosstab Query Wizard:

- You can only select one data source on which to base your crosstab.
  This means that if you need to "crosstab" data residing across multiple
  tables, you will need to take extra steps to create a temporary query in
  order to use as your data source.

- There is no way to filter or limit your crosstab query with criteria.

- You are limited to only three row headings.

- You cannot explicitly define the order of your column headings.

The good news is that you can create a crosstab query manually through the
Query Design grid. As you learn in the sections that follow, creating your
crosstab manually allows you greater flexibility in your analysis.

Using the Query Design grid to create your crosstab query

Create the aggregate query shown in Figure 2-44. Notice that you are using
multiple tables to get the fields you need. One of the benefits of creating a
crosstab query manually is that you don't have to use just one data source. You
can use as many sources as you need in order to define the fields in your query.

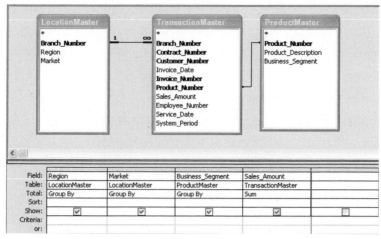

Figure 2-44 Create an aggregate query as shown here.

Next, select Query → Crosstab Query. At this point, you will notice that a row has been added to your query grid called "Crosstab," as shown in Figure 2-45. The idea is to define what role each field will play in your crosstab query. Under each field in the Crosstab row, you will select where the field will be a row heading, a column heading, or a value. Run the query to see your crosstab in action.

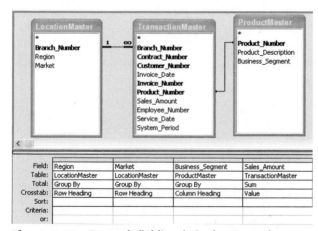

Figure 2-45 Set each field's role in the Crosstab row.

When building your crosstab in the query grid, keep the following in mind:

- You must have a minimum of one row heading, one column heading, and one value field.
- You cannot define more than one column heading.
- You cannot define more than one value heading.
- You are *not* limited to only three row headings.

Tricks of the Trade: Creating a Crosstab View with Multiple Value Fields

---

One of the rules of a crosstab query is that you cannot have more than one Value field. However, there is a trick to work around this limitation and analyze more than one metric with the same data groups. To help demonstrate how this works, create a crosstab query as shown in Figure 2-46 and save it as "Crosstab-1". Notice that your column heading is a custom field that will give you the region name and the word "Revenue" next to it.

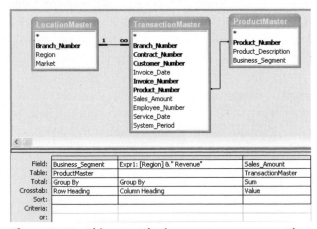

Figure 2-46   This crosstab gives you a revenue metric.

Next, create another crosstab query, as shown in Figure 2-47, and save it as "Crosstab-2". Again, your column heading is a custom field that will give you the region name and the word "Transactions" next to it.

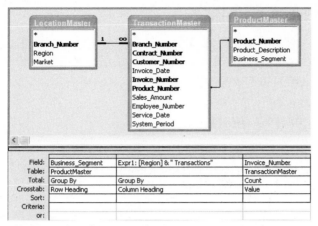

Figure 2-47 This crosstab gives you a transaction count metric.

Finally, create a select query that will join the two crosstab queries on the row heading. In the example shown in Figure 2-48, the row heading is the Business_Segment field. Bring in all the fields in the appropriate order. When you run this query, the result will be an analysis that incorporates both crosstab queries, effectively giving you multiple value fields.

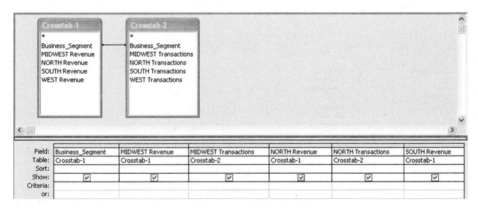

Figure 2-48 This crosstab gives you a transaction count metric.

NOTE Keep in mind that if you have more than one row heading, you will have to create a join on each row heading.

Customizing your crosstab queries

Creating a crosstab query manually allows you to customize your crosstabs in ways that are not possible through the Crosstab Query Wizard. You can apply a filter, prompt users for criteria, or even apply your own sort order.

Defining criteria in a crosstab query

The ability to filter or limit your crosstab query is another benefit of creating a crosstab query manually. To define a filter for your crosstab, simply enter the criteria as you normally would for any other aggregate query. Figure 2-49 demonstrates this concept.

Prompting users for criteria in a crosstab query

You can prompt your users for criteria in a crosstab query just as you would in a parameter query. To do this, simply create your crosstab query in the Query Design grid, and then select Query → Parameters. This activates the Query Parameters dialog box, shown in Figure 2-50, where you will define the required parameter. In this example, you will ask the user to enter the period they would to include in the crosstab.

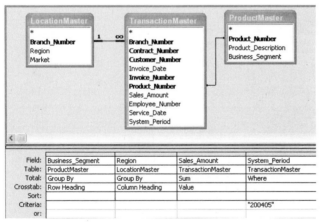

Figure 2-49   You can define a criterion to filter your crosstab queries.

Figure 2-50 Define your parameter in the Query Parameters dialog box.

NOTE Parameter queries are covered in depth in Chapter 8.

Now you can use your parameter in your crosstab query. As you can see in Figure 2-51, you will use your parameter to filter out a specific System_Period.

When you run this query, you will be asked to enter a period. If you enter 200405, you will receive the crosstab results of all records that fall into that period.

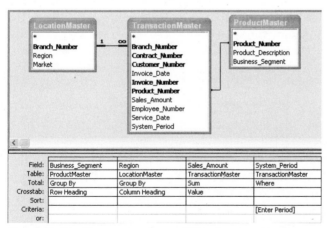

Figure 2-51 You can use your defined parameter in your query.

WARNING The parameter you use in your crosstab query must be identical to the parameter you defined in the Query Parameters dialog box. For example, if you define [Enter Period] as a valid parameter in the Query Parameters dialog box, then use [Enter the Period] in your crosstab query, you will get an error message stating that [Enter the Period] is not a valid field name or expression.

In addition, if you use [Enter Period] as a parameter in your crosstab query without first defining it in the Query Parameters dialog, you will get an error message.

Changing the sort order of your crosstab column headings

By default, crosstab queries sort their column headings in alphabetical order. For example, the crosstab query in Figure 2-52 produces a dataset where the column headings read in this order: Midwest, North, South, West.

This may be fine in most situations, but if your company headquarters is in California, the executive management may naturally want to see the West region first. You can explicitly specify the column order of a crosstab query by changing the Column Headings attribute in the Query Properties.

To get to the Column Headings attribute, open the query in Design view. Next, right-click in the gray area above the white query grid and select Properties. This activates the Query Properties dialog box shown in Figure 2-53. Here you can enter the order you would like to see the column headings by changing the Column Headings attribute.

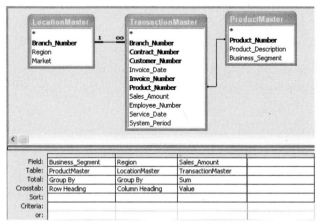

Figure 2-52   This crosstab displays all regions as columns in alphabetical order.

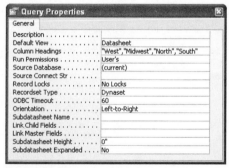

Figure 2-53   The Column Headings attribute is set to have the column headings read in this order: West, Midwest, North, South.

TIP   **Adjusting the Column Headings attribute comes in handy when you are struggling with showing months in month order instead of alphabetical order. Simply enter the month columns in the order you would like to see them. For example: "Jan","Feb","Mar","Apr","May","Jun","Jul","Aug","Sep","Oct","Nov","Dec".**

When working with the Column Headings attribute keep the following in mind:

- You must enter each column name in quotes and separate each column with commas.

- Accidentally misspelling a column name will result in that column being excluded from the crosstab results and a dummy column with the misspelled name being included with no data in it.

- You must enter every column you want to include in your crosstab report. Excluding a column from the Column Headings attribute will exclude that column from the crosstab results.

- Clearing the Column Headings attribute will ensure that all columns are displayed in alphabetical order.

Basic Analysis Techniques

CHAPTER 3

Transforming Your Data with Access

Data transformation generally entails certain actions that are meant to "clean" your data—actions such as establishing a table structure, removing duplicates, cleaning text, removing blanks, and standardizing data fields.

You will often receive data that is unpolished or "raw." That is to say, the data may have duplicates, there may be blank fields, there may be inconsistent text, and so on. Before you can perform any kind of meaningful analysis on data in this state, it's important to go through a process of data transformation, or data cleanup.

Although many people store their data in Access, few use it for data transformation purposes, oftentimes preferring instead to export the data to Excel, perform any necessary cleanup there, and then import the data back to Access. The obvious motive for this behavior is familiarity with the flexible Excel environment. However, exporting and importing data simply to perform such easy tasks can be quite inefficient, especially if you are working with large datasets.

This chapter introduces you to some of the tools and techniques in Access that make it easy for you to clean and massage your data without turning to Excel.

Finding and Removing Duplicate Records

Duplicate records are absolute analysis killers. The effect duplicate records have on your analysis can be far-reaching, corrupting almost every metric, summary, and analytical assessment you produce. It is for this reason that finding and removing duplicate records should be your first priority when you receive a new dataset.

Defining duplicate records

Before you jump into your dataset to find and remove duplicate records, it's important to consider how you define a duplicate record. To demonstrate this point, look at the table shown in Figure 3-1, where you see 11 records. Out of the 11 records, how many are duplicates?

If you were to define a duplicate record in Figure 3-1 as a duplication of just the SicCode, you would find 10 duplicate records. That is, out of the 11 records shown, 1 record has a unique SicCode whereas the other 10 are duplications. Now, if you were to expand your definition of a duplicate record to a duplication of both SicCode and PostalCode, you would find only two duplicates: the duplication of PostalCodes 77032 and 77040. Finally, if you were to define a duplicate record as a duplication of the unique value of SicCode, PostalCode, and CompanyNumber, you would find no duplicates.

SicCode	PostalCode	CompanyNumber
1389	77032	11147848
1389	77032	11147805
1389	77040	13399102
1389	77040	13398882
1389	77042	11160116
1389	77049	11218412
1389	77051	11165400
1389	77057	11173241
1389	77060	11178227
1389	77073	11190514
1389	77077	13535097

Figure 3-1   Are there duplicate records in this table? It depends on how you define one.

This example shows that having two records with the same value in a column does not necessarily mean you have a duplicate record. It's up to you to determine which field or combination of fields will best define a unique record in your dataset.

Once you have a clear idea what field, or fields, best make up a unique record in your table, you can easily test your table for duplicate records by attempting to set them as a primary or combination key. To demonstrate this test, open the LeadList table in Design view, then tag the CompanyNumber field as a primary key. If you try to save this change, you will get the error message shown in Figure 3-2. This message means there is some duplication of records in your dataset that needs to be dealt with.

Finding duplicate records

If you have determined that your dataset does indeed contain duplicates, it's generally a good idea to find and review the duplicate records before removing them. Giving your records a thorough review will ensure you don't mistake a record as a duplicate and remove it from your analysis. You may find that you are mistakenly identifying valid records as duplications, in which case you will need to include another field in your definition of what makes up a unique record.

The easiest way to find the duplicate records in your dataset is to run the Find Duplicates Query Wizard. To start this wizard, select Insert → Query. This activates the New Query dialog box, as shown in Figure 3-3. From there, you can select Find Duplicates Query Wizard and click the OK button.

Figure 3-2   If you get this error message when trying to set a primary key, you have duplicate records in your dataset.

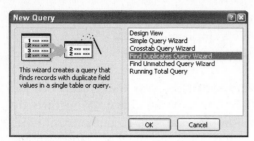

Figure 3-3   Select the Find Duplicates Query Wizard and click the OK button.

At this point, you must select the particular dataset you will use in your Find Duplicate query. Notice you can use queries as well as tables. Select the LeadList table, as shown in Figure 3-4.

Next, you must identify which field, or combination of fields, best defines a unique record in your dataset. In the example shown in Figure 3-5, the CompanyNumber field alone defines a unique record. Click Next.

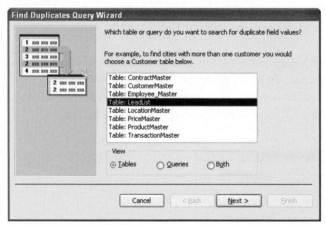

Figure 3-4   Select the dataset in which you want to find duplicates and click Next.

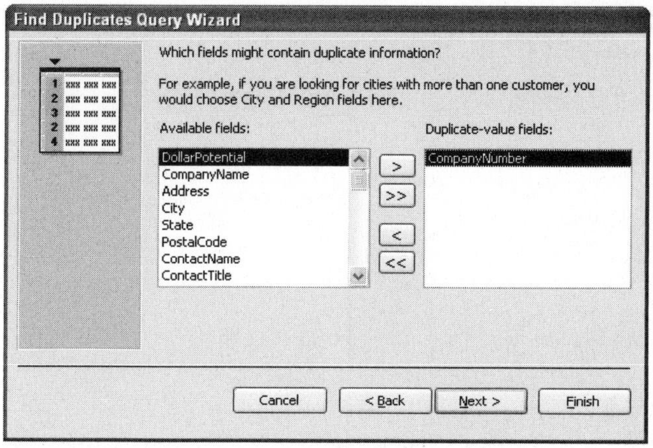

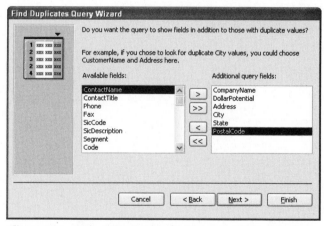

Figure 3-5   Select the field or fields that make up a unique record in your dataset.

The next step, shown in Figure 3-6, is to identify any additional fields you would like to see in your query. Click the Next button.

In the final step, shown in Figure 3-7, finish off the wizard by naming your query and clicking the Finish button.

Figure 3-6   Select the field or fields you want to see in your query.

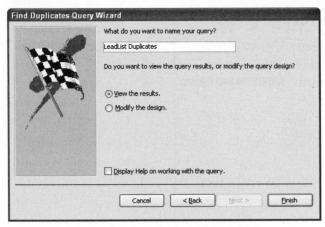

Figure 3-7   Name your query and click Finish.

Once you click Finish, your new Find Duplicates query immediately opens for your review. Figure 3-8 shows the resulting query.

NOTE The records shown in your Find Duplicates query are not only the duplications. They include one unique record plus the duplication. For example, in Figure 3-8, you will notice that eight records are tagged with the CompanyNumber 0974. Seven of the eight are duplicates that can be removed, whereas one should remain as a unique record.

CompanyNumber	CompanyName
0974	k s cinteco ltd
0974	k s cinteco ltd
0974	k s cinteco ltd
0974	k s cinteco ltd
0974	k s cinteco ltd
0974	k s cinteco ltd
0974	k s cinteco ltd
0974	k s cinteco ltd
▶ 10625840	nerth peant lanceln mirciqy
10625840	nerth peant lanceln mirciqy
11145186	stiwert & stivinsen sirvacis anc
11145186	stiwert & stivinsen sirvacis anc
11145186	stiwert & stivinsen sirvacis anc
11145186	stiwert & stivinsen sirvacis anc
11166089	alcen manifectiqang
11166089	alcen manifectiqang

Figure 3-8   Your Find Duplicates query.

Removing duplicate records

If you are working with a small dataset, removing the duplicates can be as easy as manually deleting records from your Find Duplicates query. However, if you are working with a large dataset, your Find Duplicates query may result in more records than you care to manually delete. Believe it when someone tells you that manually deleting records from a 5,000 row–Find Duplicates query is an eyeball-burning experience. Fortunately, there is an alternative to burning out your eyeballs.

The idea is to remove duplicates in mass by taking advantage of Access's built-in protections against duplicate primary keys. To demonstrate this technique, right-click the LeadList table and select Copy. Next, go up to the application menu and select Edit → Paste. At this point, the Paste Table As dialog box, shown in Figure 3-9, activates.

Name your new table "LeadList_NoDups" and select "Structure Only" from the Paste Options. This creates a new empty table that has the same structure as your original.

Next, open your new "LeadList_NoDups" table in Design view and set the appropriate field or combination of fields as primary keys. Again, it's up to you to determine which field or combination of fields will best define a unique record in your dataset. As you can see in Figure 3-10, the CompanyNumber field alone defines a unique record; therefore, only the CompanyNumber field will be set as a primary key.

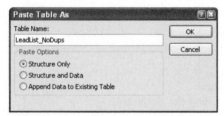

Figure 3-9   Activate the Paste Table As dialog box to copy your table's structure into a new table called "LeadList_NoDups."

Field Name	Data Type
CompanyNumber	Text
DollarPotential	Currency
CompanyName	Text
Address	Text
City	Text
State	Text
PostalCode	Text
ContactName	Text

Figure 3-10   Set as a primary key the field
or fields that best define a unique record.

Pause here a moment and review what you have so far. At this point, you
should have a table called LeadList and a table called LeadList_NoDups. The
LeadList_NoDups table is empty and has the CompanyNumber field set as a
primary key.

The last step is to create an append query that appends all records from the
LeadList table to the LeadList_NoDups table. When you run the append
query, you will get the message shown in Figure 3-11.

Because the CustomerNumber field in the LeadList_NoDups table is set as
the primary key, Access will not allow duplicate customer numbers to be
appended. In just a few clicks, you have effectively created a table free from
duplicates. You can now use this duplicate-free table as the source for any subsequent analysis.

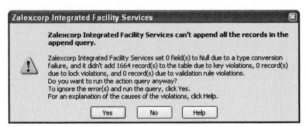

Figure 3-11   Now you can append all records excluding the duplicates.

Tricks of the Trade: Removing Duplicates with One Make-Table Query

Start a make-table query in Design view using, as the data source, the dataset
that contains the duplicates. Right-click the gray area above the white query
grid and select Properties. This activates the Query Properties dialog box shown
in Figure 3-12.

All you have to do here is change the Unique Values property to Yes. Close the Query Properties dialog box and run the query.

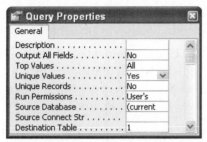

Figure 3-12 Running a make-table query with the Unique Values property set to Yes ensures that your resulting table contains no duplicates.

Common Transformation Tasks

You will find that many of the unpolished datasets that come to you will require the same transformation actions. In that light, this section covers some of the most common transformation tasks you will have to perform.

Filling in blank fields

Oftentimes, you will have fields that contain empty values. These values are considered "Null"—a value of nothing. Nulls are not necessarily a bad thing. In fact, if used properly, they can be an important part of a well-designed relational database. That being said, it is important to note that an excessive amount of Null values in your data can lead to an unruly database environment. Too many Nulls in a database make querying and coding for your data more difficult because you will have to test for Nulls in almost every action you take.

Your job is to decide whether to leave the Nulls in your dataset or fill them in with an actual value. When deciding this, you should consider the following general guidelines:

•

- **Use Nulls sparingly.** Working with, and coding for, a database is a much less daunting task when you don't have to test for Null values constantly.

- **Use alternatives when possible.** A good practice is to represent missing values with some logical missing value code whenever possible.

- **Never use Null values in number fields.** Use zeros instead of Nulls in a currency or a number field that will be used in calculations. Any mathematical operation that is performed using a field containing even one Null value will result in a Null answer (the wrong answer).

Filling in the Null fields in your dataset is as simple as running an update query. In the example shown in Figure 3-13, you are updating the Null values in the DollarPotential field to zero.

It's important to note that there are actually two kinds of blank values: Null and empty string (""). When filling in the blank values of a text field, include the empty string as a criterion in your update query to ensure that you don't miss any fields. In the example shown in Figure 3-14, you are updating the blank values in the Segment field to "Other."

Concatenating

It's always amazing to see anyone export data out of Access and into Excel, only to concatenate (join two or more character strings end to end) and then re-import the data back into Access. You can easily concatenate any number of ways in Access with a simple update query.

Figure 3-13 This query updates the Null values
in the DollarPotential field to a value of 0.

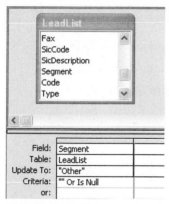

Figure 3-14   This query updates blank values in the Segment field to a value of "Other."

Concatenating fields

Look at the update query shown in Figure 3-15. In this query, you are updating the MyTest field with the concatenated row values of the Type field and the Code field.

> **TIP**   It's a good idea to create a test field in order to test the effects of your data transformation actions before applying changes to the real data.

Figure 3-15   This query concatenates the row values of the Type field and the Code field.

Take a moment to analyze the following query breakdown.

QUERY BREAKDOWN

♦ [Type]. **This tells Access to use the row values of the Type field.**

♦ &. **The ampersand is a character operator that joins strings together.**

* [Code]. **This tells Access to use the row values of the Code field.**

Figure 3-16 shows the results of this query.

Code	Type	MyTest
100199	DB	DB100199
200	DB	DB200
100199	DB	DB100199
100199	DB	DB100199
100199	DB	DB100199
100199	DB	DB100199
100199	DB	DB100199
100199	DB	DB100199
100199	DB	DB100199
100199	DB	DB100199
200	DB	DB200
100199	DB	DB100199

Figure 3-16 The MyTest field now contains the concatenated values of the Type field and the Code field.

WARNING When running update queries that perform concatenations, make sure the field you are updating is large enough to accept the concatenated string. For example, if the length of your concatenated string is 100 characters long, and the Field Size of the field you are updating is 50 characters, your concatenated string will be cut short without warning.

Augmenting field values with your own text

You can augment the values in your fields by adding your own text. For example, you may want to concatenate the row values of the Type field and the Code field, but separate them with a colon. The query in Figure 3-17 does just that.

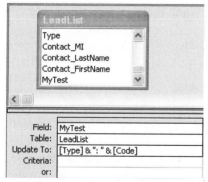

Figure 3-17   This query concatenates the row values of the Type field and the Code field and separates them with a colon.

Take a moment to analyze the following query breakdown:

QUERY BREAKDOWN

◆ [Type]. **This tells Access to use the row values of the Type field.**

◆ &. **The ampersand is a character operator that joins strings together.**

◆ " : ". **This text adds a colon and a space to the concatenated string.**

* [Code]. **This tells Access to use the row values of the Code field.**

Figure 3-18 shows the results of this query.

Code	Type	MyTest
100199	DB	DB: 100199
200	DB	DB: 200
100199	DB	DB: 100199
100199	DB	DB: 100199
100199	DB	DB: 100199
100199	DB	DB: 100199
100199	DB	DB: 100199
100199	DB	DB: 100199
100199	DB	DB: 100199
100199	DB	DB: 100199
200	DB	DB: 200
100199	DB	DB: 100199

Figure 3-18   The MyTest field now contains the concatenated values of the Type field and the Code field, separated by a colon.

NOTE When specifying your own text in a query, you must enclose the text in quotes.

Changing case

Making sure the text in your database has the correct capitalization may sound trivial, but it's important. Imagine you receive a customer table that has an address field where all the addresses are lowercase. How is that going to look on labels, form letters, or invoices? Fortunately, if you are working with tables containing thousands of records, Access has a few built-in functions that make changing the case of your text a snap.

Use the StrConv function to quickly change case

The LeadList table shown in Figure 3-19 contains an Address field that is in all lowercase letters.

To fix the values in the Address field, you can use the StrConv function, which is a function that converts a string to a specified case.

Address
▶ 46 gin criaghten w ebrems dr
426 bewlis rd
651 sheimekir ln
44 almgrin dr
35 mall ln
460 fillir rd
320 mimeraal dr ste 4
4010 shiradan st
5046 wistevir rd
40 meple st
242 biich st

Figure 3-19   The address field is in all lowercase letters.

ABOUT THE STRCONV FUNCTION

```
StrConv(string to be converted, conversion type)
```

To use the `StrConv` **function, you must provide two required arguments: the string to be converted and the conversion type.**

The string to be converted is simply the text you are working with. In a query environment, you can use the name of a field to specify that you are converting all the row values of that field.

The conversion type tells Access whether you want to convert the specified text to all uppercase, all lowercase, or proper case. A set of constants identify the conversion type:

- ◆ **Conversion type 1: Converts the specified text to uppercase characters.**

- ◆ **Conversion type 2: Converts the specified text to lowercase characters.**

- * **Conversion type 3: Converts the specified text to proper case. That is, the first letter of every word is uppercase.**

```
Examples:
```

> `StrConv("My Text",1)` **would be converted to "MY TEXT."**

> `StrConv("MY TEXT",2)` **would be converted to "my text."**

> `StrConv("my text",3)` **would be converted to "My Text."**

The update query shown in Figure 3-20 converts the values of the Address field to proper case.

Figure 3-20   The address field is in all uppercase letters.

NOTE   You can also use the `Ucase` and `Lcase` functions to convert your text to upper- and lowercase text. These functions are highlighted in Appendix A of this book.

Tricks of the Trade: Sorting by Capitalization

Ever needed to sort on the capitalization of the values in a field? The query in Figure 3-21 demonstrates a trick that sorts a query where all the values whose first letter is lowercase are shown first.

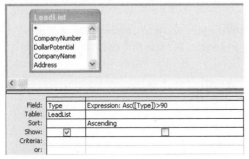

Figure 3-21   This query returns a dataset where all the values beginning with a lowercase letter are shown first.

How does this work? The Asc **function is used to convert a string to its ASCII code. For example,** Asc ("A") **would return 65 because 65 is the ASCII code for the uppercase letter *A*.**

If you pass a whole word to the Asc **function, it will return only the ASCII code for the first letter. Now in ASCII codes, uppercase letters A–Z are respectively represented by codes 65–90, and the lowercase letters a–z are respectively represented by codes 97–122.**

The function Asc ([Type]) >90 **is asking the question, "Is the ASCII code returned by the string greater than 90?" The answer will be either True or False (–1 or 0). If the answer is true, the first letter of the string is lowercase; otherwise, the first letter is uppercase.**

Figure 3-22 shows the results of the query with the Expression field displayed.

Type	Expression
db	-1
db	-1
db	-1
DB	0
DB	0
DB	0

Figure 3-22   This query is sorted in ascending order on the Expression field. Sorting this field in descending order displays values starting with uppercase letters first.

Removing leading and trailing spaces from a string

When you receive a dataset from a mainframe system, a data warehouse, or even a text file, it is not uncommon to have field values that contain leading and trailing spaces. These spaces can cause some abnormal results, especially when you are appending values with leading and trailing spaces to other values that are clean. To demonstrate this, look at the dataset in Figure 3-23.

This is intended to be an aggregate query that displays the sum of the dollar potential for California, New York, and Texas. However, the leading spaces are causing Access to group each state into two sets, preventing you from discerning the accurate totals.

You can easily remove leading and trailing spaces by using the Trim function. Figure 3-24 demonstrates how you would update a field to remove the leading and trailing spaces by using an update query.

> **NOTE** Using the Ltrim function removes only the leading spaces, whereas the Rtrim function removes only the trailing spaces. These functions are highlighted in Appendix A of this book.

State	SumOfDollarPotential
ca	$26,561,554.00
ny	$7,483,960.00
tx	$13,722,782.00
ca	$12,475,489.00
ny	$827,563.00
tx	$7,669,208.00

Figure 3-23 The leading spaces are preventing an accurate aggregation.

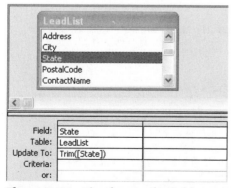

Figure 3-24 Simply pass the field name through the Trim function in an update query to remove the leading and trailing spaces.

Finding and replacing specific text

Imagine that you work in a company called BLVD, Inc. One day, the president of your company informs you that abbreviation "blvd" on all addresses is now deemed an infringement on your company's trademarked name, and must be changed to "Boulevard" as soon as possible. How would you go about meeting this new requirement? Your first thought may be to use the built-in Find and Replace functionality that exists in all Office applications. However, when your data consists of hundreds of thousands of rows, the Find and Replace function will only be able to process a few thousand records at a time. This clearly would not be very efficient.

The `Replace` function is ideal in a situation like this. As you can see in the following sidebar, the `Replace` function replaces a specified text string with a different string.

ABOUT THE REPLACE FUNCTION

`Replace(Expression, Find, Replace[, Start[, Count[, Compare]]])`

A `Replace` **function has three required arguments and three optional arguments:**

◆ `Expression` **(required): This is the full string you are evaluating. In a query environment, you can use the name of a field to specify that you are evaluating all the row values of that field.**

◆ `Find` **(required): This is the substring you need to find and replace.**

◆ `Replace` **(required): This is the substring used as the replacement.**

◆ `Start` **(optional): The position within substring to begin the search; default is 1.**

◆ `Count` **(optional): Number of occurrences to replace; default is all occurrences.**

* `Compare` **(optional): The kind of comparison to use; see Appendix A for details.**

For example:

`Replace("Pear", "P", "B")` **would return "Bear."**

`Replace("Now Here", " H", "h")` **would return "Nowhere."**

`Replace("Microsoft Access", "Microsoft", "")` **would return "Access."**

Figure 3-25 demonstrates how you would use the `Replace` **function to meet the requirements in the preceding scenario.**

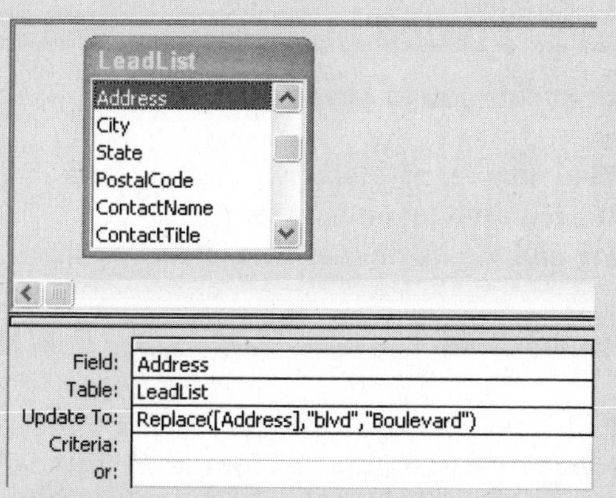

Figure 3-25 This query finds all instances of "blvd" and replaces them with "Boulevard."

Adding your own text in key positions within a string

When transforming your data, you will sometimes have to add your own text in key positions within a string. For example, in Figure 3-26, you will see two fields. The Phone field is the raw phone number received from a mainframe report, and the MyTest field is the same phone number transformed into a standard format. As you can see, the two parentheses and the dash were added in the appropriate positions within the string to achieve the correct format.

The edits demonstrated in Figure 3-26 were accomplished by using the `Right` function, the `Left` function, and the `Mid` function in conjunction with each other. See the following sidebar for more information on these functions.

Phone	MyTest
1464535550	(146) 453-5550
1464560525	(146) 456-0525
1464565066	(146) 456-5066
1464566045	(146) 456-6045
1465124411	(146) 512-4411
1462615424	(146) 261-5424
1462663146	(146) 266-3146
1463455400	(146) 345-5400
1462662666	(146) 266-2666
1462524400	(146) 252-4400

Figure 3-26 The phone number has been transformed into a standard format by adding the appropriate characters to key positions within the string.

ABOUT THE RIGHT, LEFT, AND MID FUNCTIONS

The `Right`, `Left`, **and** `Mid` **functions enable you to extract portions of a string starting from different positions.**

The `Left` **function returns a specified number of characters starting from the leftmost character of the string. The required arguments for the** `Left` **function are the text you are evaluating and the number of characters you want returned. For example:**

> `Left("70056-3504", 5)` **would return five characters starting from the leftmost character ("70056").**

The `Right` **function returns a specified number of characters starting from the rightmost character of the string. The required arguments for the** `Right` **function are the text you are evaluating and the number of characters you want returned. For example:**

> `Right("Microsoft", 4)` **would return four characters starting from the rightmost character ("soft").**

The `Mid` **function returns a specified number of characters starting from a specified character position. The required arguments for the** `Mid` **function are the text you are evaluating, the starting position, and the number of characters you want returned. For example:**

> `Mid("Lonely", 2, 3)` **would return three characters starting from the second character, or character number two in the string ("one").**

TIP In a `Mid` **function, if there are fewer characters in the text being used than the length argument, the entire text will be returned. For example,** `Mid("go",1,10000)` **will return "go". As you will see later in this chapter, this behavior comes in handy when you are working with nested functions.**

Figure 3-27 demonstrates how the MyTest field was updated to the correctly formatted phone number.

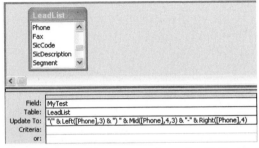

Figure 3-27 This query updates the MyTest field with a properly formatted phone number.

Take a moment to analyze the following query breakdown.

QUERY BREAKDOWN

◆ " (". **This text adds an open parenthesis to the resulting string.**

◆ &. **The ampersand is a character operator that joins strings together.**

◆ Left([Phone],3). **This function extracts the left three characters of the [Phone] field.**

◆ &. **The ampersand is a character operator that joins strings together.**

◆ ") ". **This text adds a close parenthesis and a space to the resulting string.**

◆ &. **The ampersand is a character operator that joins strings together.**

◆ Mid([Phone],4,3). **This function extracts the three characters of the [Phone] field starting from character number 4.**

◆ &. **The ampersand is a character operator that joins strings together.**

◆ " – ". **This text adds a dash to the resulting string.**

◆ &. **The ampersand is a character operator that joins strings together.**

* Right([Phone],4). **This extracts the right four characters of the [Phone] field.**

Tricks of the Trade: Padding Strings to a Specific Number of Characters

---

You may encounter a situation in which key fields are required to be a certain number of characters in order for your data to be able to interface with peripheral platforms such as ADP or SAP.

For example, imagine that the CompanyNumber field shown in Figure 3-28 must be 10 characters long. Those that are not 10 characters must be padded with enough leading zeros to create a 10-character string.

CompanyNumber
113
13792992
14280866
630
2298
3082
3128
19641288
3909
4758

Figure 3-28 You need to pad the values in the CompanyNumber field with enough leading zeros to create a 10-character string.

continues

The secret to this trick is to add 10 zeros to every company number, regardless of the current length, then pass them through a `Right` function that will extract only the right 10 characters. For example, company number 29875764 would first be converted to 000000000029875764, then would go into a `Right` function that extracted out only the right 10 characters; Right("000000000029875764",10). This would leave you with 0029875764.

Although this is essentially two steps, you can accomplish this with just one update query. Figure 3-29 demonstrates how you can do this. This query first concatenates each company number with "0000000000", and then passes that concatenated string through a `Right` function that extracts only the left 10 characters.

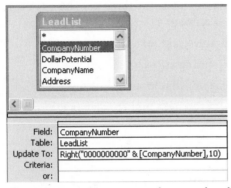

Figure 3-29   This query updates each value in the CompanyNumber field to a 10-character string with leading zeros.

Figure 3-30 shows the results of this query.

CompanyNumber
0000000113
0013792992
0014280866
0000000630
0000002298
0000003082
0000003128
0019641288
0000003909
0000004758

Figure 3-30   The CompanyNumber field now contains 10-character company numbers.

Parsing strings using character markers

Have you ever gotten a dataset where two or more distinct pieces of data were jammed into one field and separated by commas? For example, a field called Address may have a string that represents "Address, City, State, Zip." In a proper database, this string would be parsed into four fields.

In Figure 3-31, you can see that the values in the ContactName field are strings that represent "Last name, First name, Middle initial." You will need to parse this string into three separate fields.

ContactName
DINBY, IRNIST, I.
MCGEVIRN, HIGH, B.
DATTCO, KATHY, R.
TAYIH, HANABAL, T.
LIMIK, CHRASTEPHIR, O.
WALLEIGHBY, FRANK, S.
KRIMSAIK, PIRRY, D.
SANTEN, MACHEIL, S.
MSWUINIY, RACHERD, T.
PHILEN, DALE, H.
JPERTIN, HANK, G.
PITIRS, JEE, P.
KIQJA, CANDY, D.
► PERTIN, HANK, G.

Figure 3-31 You need to parse the values in the ContactName field into three separate fields.

Although this is not a straightforward undertaking, you can do it fairly easily with the help of the Instr function, which is detailed in the following sidebar.

ABOUT THE INSTR FUNCTION

`Instr(Start, String, Find, Compare)`

The `Instr` **function searches for a specified string in another string and returns its position number. An** `Instr` **function has two required arguments and two optional arguments:**

- ◆ `Start` **(optional): This is the character number to start the search; default is 1.**
- ◆ `String` **(required): This is the string to be searched.**
- ◆ `Find` **(required): This is the string to search for.**
- ◆ `Compare` **(optional): This specifies the type of string comparison.**

For example:

> `InStr("Alexander, Mike, H",",")` **would return 10 because the first comma of the string is character number 10.**

> `InStr(11,"Alexander, Mike, H",",")` **would return 16 because the first comma from character number 11 is character number 16.**

If the `Instr` **function only returns a number, how can it help you? Well, the idea is to use the** `Instr` **function with the** `Left`, `Right`, **or** `Mid` **functions in order to extract a string. For example, instead of using a hard-coded number in your** `Left` **function to pass it the required length argument, you can use a nested** `Instr` **function to return that number. For example,**
`Left("Alexander, Mike",9)` **is the same as** `Left("Alexander, Mike", Instr("Alexander, Mike", ",")-1).`

NOTE When you are nesting an `Instr` function inside of a `Left`, `Right`, or `Mid` function, you may have to add or subtract a character, depending on what you want to accomplish. For example:

`Left("Zey, Robert", Instr("Zey, Robert", ","))` **would return "Zey,".**

Why is the comma included in the returned result? The `Instr` **function returns 4 because the first comma in the string is the fourth character. The** `Left` **function then uses this 4 as a length argument, effectively extracting the left four characters "Zey,".**

If you want a clean extract without the comma, you will have to modify your function to read like this:

`Left("Zey, Robert", Instr("Zey, Robert", ",")-1)`

Subtracting 1 from the `Instr` **function would leave you with 3 instead of 4. The** `Left` **function then uses this 3 as the length argument, effectively extracting the left three characters "Zey".**

The easiest way to parse the ContactName field, shown in Figure 3-31, is to use two update queries.

WARNING This is a somewhat tricky process, so you will want to create and work in test fields. This will ensure that you give yourself a way back from any mistakes you may make.

Query 1

The first query, shown in Figure 3-32, parses out the last name in the Contact-Name field and updates the Contact_LastName field. It then updates the Contact_FirstName field with the remaining string.

If you open the LeadList table, you will be able to see the impact of your first update query. Figure 3-33 shows your progress so far.

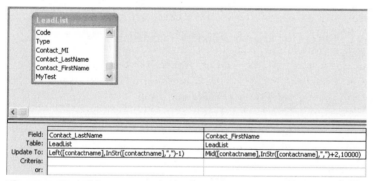

Field:	Contact_LastName	Contact_FirstName
Table:	LeadList	LeadList
Update To:	Left([contactname],InStr([contactname],",")-1)	Mid([contactname],InStr([contactname],",")+2,10000)
Criteria:		
or:		

Figure 3-32 This query updates the Contact_LastName and Contact_FirstName fields.

Contact_LastName	Contact_FirstName	Contact_MI
CILENA	THEMES, P.	
RACCI	TEM, T.	
CENE	WALLAEM, D.	
LADRIN	RACK, B.	
RACCI	TEM, T.	
KANNIY	CHERLIS, G.	
MEERE	PITIR, C.	
BIQKS	DAN, D.	
LCHERRIN	BIQTEN, M.	
FEILKIS	HILINA, P.	
DWALKIR	REBIRT, G.	
CELIY	TENAA, D.	
REPPA	DAVE, D.	
WANG	HIRBIRT, P.	
CHERIST	RACHERD, G.	
CERRELL	JEHN, P.	
BREWN	DINASE, G.	
CEPALDI	JEMIS, R.	
RIBAN	DEPHNA, D.	
KIAMAJ	JEHN, G.	

Figure 3-33 Check your progress so far.

Query 2

The second query, shown in Figure 3-34, updates the Contact_FirstName field and the Contact_MI.

After you run your second query, you can open your table and see the results, as shown in Figure 3-35.

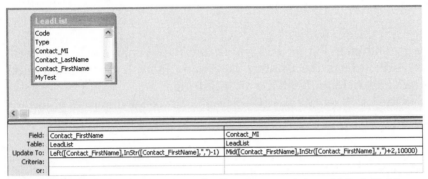

Figure 3-34 This query parses out the first name and the middle initial from the Contact_FirstName field.

ContactName	Contact_LastName	Contact_FirstName	Contact_MI
DINBY, IRNIST, I.	DINBY	IRNIST	I.
MCGEVIRN, HIGH, B.	MCGEVIRN	HIGH	B.
DATTCO, KATHY, R.	DATTCO	KATHY	R.
TAYIH, HANABAL, T.	TAYIH	HANABAL	T.
LIMIK, CHRASTEPHIR, O.	LIMIK	CHRASTEPHIR	O.
WALLEIGHBY, FRANK, S.	WALLEIGHBY	FRANK	S.
KRIMSAIK, PIRRY, D.	KRIMSAIK	PIRRY	D.
SANTEN, MACHEIL, S.	SANTEN	MACHEIL	S.
MSWUINIY, RACHERD, T.	MSWUINIY	RACHERD	T.
PHILEN, DALE, H.	PHILEN	DALE	H.
JPERTIN, HANK, G.	JPERTIN	HANK	G.
PITIRS, JEE, P.	PITIRS	JEE	P.
KIQJA, CANDY, D.	KIQJA	CANDY	D.
PERTIN, HANK, G.	PERTIN	HANK	G.
CHESIN, JENATHAN, G.	CHESIN	JENATHAN	G.
WATSEN, JECKAE, E.	WATSEN	JECKAE	E.

Figure 3-35 With two queries, you have successfully parsed the ContactName field into three separate fields.

Working with Calculations and Dates

The truth is that few organizations can analyze their raw data at face value. More often than not, some preliminary analysis with calculations and dates must be carried out before the "big-picture" analysis can be performed. Again, Excel is the preferred platform for working with calculations and dates. However, as you learn in this chapter, Access provides a wide array of tools and built-in functions that make working with calculations and dates possible.

Using Calculations in Your Analysis

If you are an Excel user trying to familiarize yourself with Access, one of the questions you undoubtedly have is "Where do the formulas go?" In Excel, you have the flexibility to enter a calculation via a formula directly into the dataset you are analyzing. You do not have this ability in Access. So the question is, where do you store calculations in Access?

As you have already learned, things work differently in Access. The natural structure of an Access database forces you to keep your data separate from your analysis. In this light, you will not be able to store a calculation (a formula) in your dataset. Now, it is true that you can store the calculated results as hard data, but using tables to store calculated results is problematic for several reasons:

- Stored calculations take up valuable storage space.
- Stored calculations require constant maintenance as the data in your table changes.
- Stored calculations generally tie your data to one analytical path.

Instead of storing the calculated results as hard data, it is a better practice to perform calculations in "real-time," at the precise moment when they are needed. This ensures the most current and accurate results, and does not tie your data to one particular analysis.

Common calculation scenarios

In Access, calculations are performed by using expressions. An *expression* is a combination of values, operators, or functions that are evaluated to return a separate value to be used in a subsequent process. For example, 2+2 is an expression that returns the integer 4, which can be used in a subsequent analysis. Expressions can be used almost anywhere in Access to accomplish various tasks: in queries, forms, reports, data access pages, and even in tables to a certain degree. In this section, you learn how to expand your analysis by building real-time calculations using expressions.

Using constants in calculations

Most calculations typically consist of hard-coded numbers, or "constants." A *constant* is a static value that does not change. For example, in the expression [Price]*1.1, 1.1 is a constant; the value of 1.1 will never change. Figure 4-1 demonstrates how a constant can be used in an expression within a query.

In this example, you are building a query that will analyze how the current price for each product compares to the same price with a 10 percent increase. The expression, entered under the alias "Increase," will multiply the price field of each record with a constant value of 1.1, calculating a price that is 10 percent over the original value in the Price field.

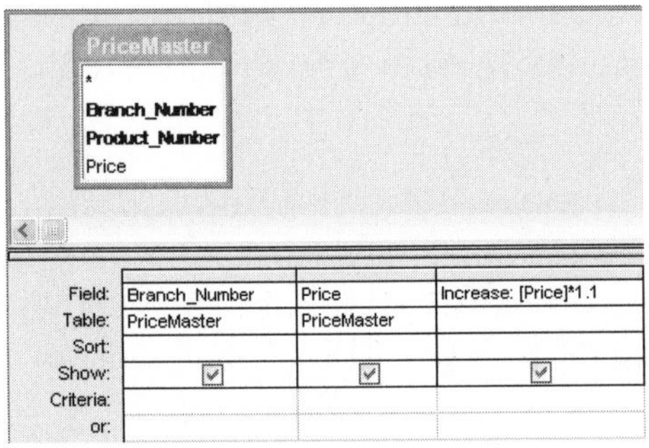

Figure 4-1 In this query, you are using a constant to calculate a 10 percent price increase.

Using fields in calculations

Not all of your calculations will require you to specify a constant. In fact, many of the mathematical operations you will carry out will be performed on data that already resides in fields within your dataset. You can perform calculations using any fields formatted as number or currency.

For instance, in the query shown in Figure 4-2, you are not using any constants. Instead, your calculation will be executed using the values in each record of the dataset. In many ways, this is similar to referencing cell values in an Excel formula.

Using the results of aggregation in calculations

Using the result of an aggregation as an expression in a calculation allows you to perform multiple analytical steps in one query. In the example in Figure 4-3, you are running an aggregate query. This query executes in the following order:

1. The query first groups your records by branch number.

2. The query calculates the count of invoices and the sum of revenue for each branch.

3. The query assigns the aliases you have defined, respectively ("Invoice Count" and "Rev").

4. The query then uses the aggregation results for each branch as expressions in your "Avg $ per Invoice" calculation.

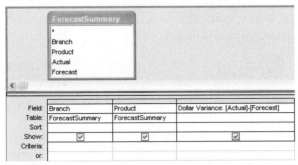

Figure 4-2 In this query, you are using two fields in a Dollar Variance calculation.

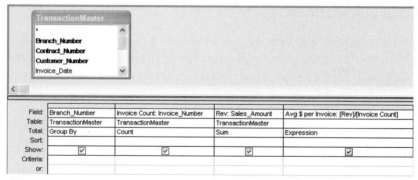

Figure 4-3 In this query, you are using the aggregation results for each branch number as expressions in your calculation.

Using the results of one calculation as an expression in another

Keep in mind that you are not limited to one calculation per query. In fact, you can use the results of one calculation as an expression in another calculation. Figure 4-4 illustrates this concept.

In this query, you are first calculating an adjusted forecast, then using the results of that calculation in another calculation that returns the variance of Actual versus Adjusted Forecast.

Using a calculation as an argument in a function

Look at the query in Figure 4-5. The calculation in this query returns a number with a fractional part. That is, it returns a number that contains a decimal point followed by many trailing digits. You would like to return a round number, however, making the resulting dataset easier to read.

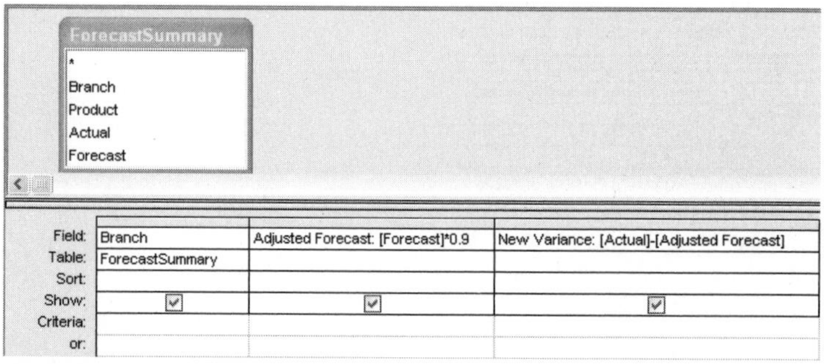

Figure 4-4 This query uses the results of one calculation as an expression in another.

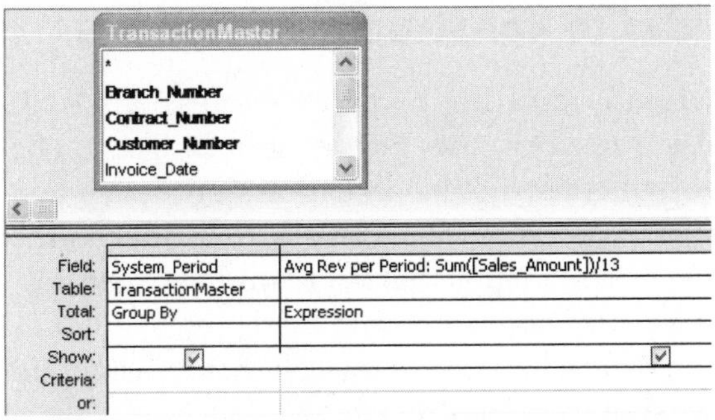

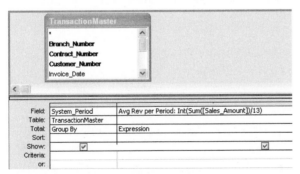

Figure 4-5 The results of this calculation will be difficult to read because they will all be fractional numbers that have many digits trailing a decimal point. Forcing the results into round numbers will make for easier reading.

To force the results of your calculation into an integer, you can use the `Int` function. The `Int` function is a mathematical function that removes the fractional part of a number and returns the resulting integer. This function takes one argument, a number. However, instead of hard coding a number into this function, you can use your calculation as the argument. Figure 4-6 demonstrates this concept.

NOTE You can use calculations that result in a number value in any function where a number value is accepted as an argument.

Figure 4-6 You can use your calculation as the argument in the `Int` function, allowing you to remove the fractional part the resulting data.

Using the Expression Builder to construct calculations

If you are not yet comfortable manually creating complex expressions with functions and calculations, Access provides the Expression Builder. The Expression Builder guides you through constructing an expression with a few clicks of the mouse. Avid Excel users may relate the Expression Builder to the Insert Function Wizard found in Excel. The idea is that you build your expression by simply selecting the necessary functions and data fields.

To activate the Expression Builder, right-click inside the cell that will contain your expression and select Build, as shown in Figure 4-7.

NOTE You can also activate the Expression Builder by selecting the Build button on the Query Design toolbar.

In fact, the Expression Builder can be activated from anywhere you would write expressions, including control properties in forms, control properties in reports, field properties in tables, as well as in the Query Design grid. Simply click the Build button on the Query Design, Form Design, Report Design, or Table Design toolbars, respectively.

As you can see in Figure 4-8, the Expression Builder has four panes to work in. The upper pane is where you enter the expression. The lower panes show the different objects available to you. In the lower-left pane you can see the five main database objects: tables, queries, forms, reports, and functions.

Figure 4-7   Activate the Expression Builder by right-clicking inside the Field row of the query grid and selecting Build.

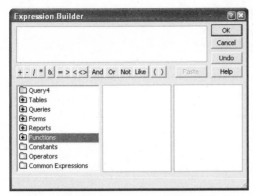

Figure 4-8 The Expression Builder displays all the database objects you can use in your expression.

Double-click any of the five main database objects to drill down to the next level of objects. By double-clicking the Functions object, for example, you will be able to drill into the built-in functions folder where you will see all the functions available to you in Access. Figure 4-9 shows the Expression Builder set to displays all the available math functions.

The idea is to double-click the function you need and Access will automatically enter the function in the upper pane of the Expression Builder. In the example shown in Figure 4-10, the selected function is the Round function. As you can see, the function is immediately placed in the upper pane of the Expression Builder and Access shows you the arguments needed to make the function work. In this case, you need a Number argument and a Precision argument.

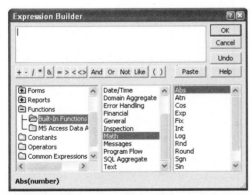

Figure 4-9 Similar to the Insert Function Wizard in Excel, the Expression Builder displays all the functions available to you.

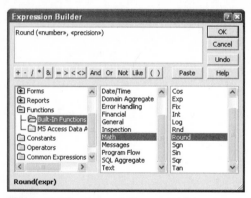

Figure 4-10 Access tells you which arguments are needed to make the function work.

If you don't know what an argument means, simply click the Help button for an explanation of the function. As shown in Figure 4-11, for example, the Round function requires a number to be rounded and an optional "Precision" argument that indicates how many places to the right of the decimal are included in the rounding.

As you can see in Figure 4-12, instead of using a hard-coded number in the Round function, an expression is used to return a dynamic value. This calculation divides the sum of [TransactionMaster]![Sales_Amount] by 13. Because the "Precision" argument is optional, that argument is left off.

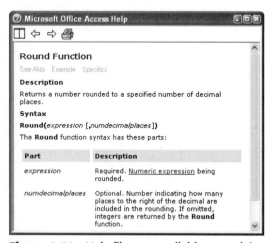

Figure 4-11 Help files are available to explain each function in detail.

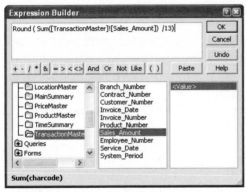

Figure 4-12 The function here rounds the results of
the calculation, ([TransactionMaster]![Sales_Amount])/13.

When you are satisfied with your newly created expression, click the OK
button to insert it into the QBE. Figure 4-13 shows that the new expression has
been added as a field. Note that the new field has a default alias of Expr1; you
can rename this to something more meaningful.

Common calculation errors

No matter what platform you are using to analyze your data, there is always
the risk of errors when working with calculations. Although Access has no
magic function that will help you prevent errors in your analysis, you can take
a few fundamental actions to avoid some of the most common calculation
errors.

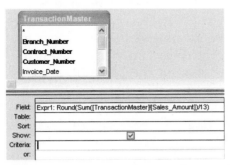

Figure 4-13 Your newly created expression has been added.

Understand the order of operator precedence

You might remember from your algebra days that when working with a complex equation, executing multiple mathematical operations, the equation does not necessarily evaluate left to right. Some operations have precedence over others and therefore must occur first. The Access environment has similar rules regarding the order of operator precedence. When you are using expressions and calculations that involve several operations, each operation is evaluated and resolved in a predetermined order. It is important to know the order of operator precedence in Access. An expression that is incorrectly built may cause errors on your analysis.

The order of operations for Access is as follows:

1. Evaluate items in parentheses.

2. Perform exponentiation (^ calculates exponents).

3. Perform negation (– converts to negative).

4. Perform multiplication (* multiplies) and division (/ divides) at equal precedence.

5. Perform addition (+ adds) and subtraction (– subtracts) at equal precedence.

6. Evaluate string concatenation (&).

7. Evaluate comparison and pattern matching operators (>, <, =, <>, >=, <=, Like, Between, Is) at equal precedence.

8. Evaluate logical operators in the following order: Not, And, Or.

NOTE Operations that are equal in precedence are performed from left to right.

How can understanding the order of operations ensure that you avoid analytical errors? Consider this basic example. The correct answer to the calculation (20+30)*4 is 200. However, if you leave off the parentheses (as in 20+30*4), Access will perform the calculation like this: 30*4 = 120 + 20 = 140. The order of operator precedence mandates that Access perform multiplication before subtraction. Therefore, entering 20+30*4 will give you the wrong answer. Because the order of operator precedence in Access mandates that all operations in parenthesis be evaluated first, placing 20+30 inside parentheses ensures the correct answer.

Watch out for Null values

A *Null value* represents the absence of any value. When you see a data item in an Access table that is empty or has no information in it, it is considered Null.

The concept of a Null value causing errors in a calculation might initially seem strange to Excel power users. In Excel, if there is a Null value within a column of numbers, the column can still be properly evaluated because Excel simply reads the Null value as zero. This is not the case in Access. If Access encounters a Null value, it does not assume that the Null value represents zero. Instead, it immediately returns a Null value as the answer. To illustrate this behavior, build the query shown in Figure 4-14.

Run the query, and you will see the results shown in Figure 4-15. Notice that the Variance calculations for the first five records do not show the expected results; instead, they show Null values. This is because the forecast values for those records are Null values.

Field:	Branch	Actual	Forecast	Variance: [Actual]-[Forecast]
Table:	ForecastSummary	ForecastSummary	ForecastSummary	
Sort:			Ascending	
Show:	☑	☑	☑	☑
Criteria:				
or:				

Figure 4-14 To demonstrate how Null values can cause calculation errors, build this query in Design view.

Branch	Actual	Forecast	Variance
701717	38,212		
101419	34,576		
101313	32,822		
806211	43,974		
806211	69,558		
806708	7,003	0	7003
305118	4,179	0	4179
601716	4,273	0	4273
806708	4,667	0	4667
202714	5,340	0	5340

Figure 4-15 As you can see, when any variable in your calculation is Null, the resulting answer is a Null value.

Looking at Figure 4-15, you can imagine how a Null calculation error can wreak havoc on your analysis, especially if you have an involved analytical process. Furthermore, Null calculation errors can be difficult to identify and fix. This is a good place to remind you that you should rarely use Null values in your tables. Instead, you should use a logical value that represents "no data" (for example, 0, "NA," or "Undefined").

That being said, you can avoid Null calculation errors by using the Nz function. The Nz function enables you to convert any Null value that is encountered to a value you specify.

Armed with this new information, you can adjust the query in Figure 4-14 to utilize the Nz function. Because the problem field is the Forecast field, you would pass the Forecast field through the Nz function. Figure 4-16 shows the adjusted query.

As you can see in Figure 4-17, the first five records now show a Variance value even though the values in the Forecast field are Null. Note that the NZ function did not physically place a zero in the Null values. The NZ function merely told access to treat the Nulls as zeros when calculating the Variance field.

Field:	Branch	Actual	Forecast	Variance: [Actual]-NZ([Forecast],0)
Table:	ForecastSummary	ForecastSummary	ForecastSummary	
Sort:			Ascending	
Show:	☑	☑	☑	☑
Criteria:				
or:				

Figure 4-16 Pass the Forecast field through the Nz function to convert Null values to zero.

Branch	Actual	Forecast	Variance
701717	38,212		38212
101419	34,576		34576
101313	32,822		32822
806211	43,974		43974
806211	69,558		69558
806708	7,003	0	7003
305118	4,179	0	4179
601716	4,273	0	4273
806708	4,667	0	4667
202714	5,340	0	5340

Figure 4-17 The first five records now show a Variance value.

ABOUT THE NZ FUNCTION

`Nz(variant, valueifnull)`
   The `Nz` **function converts any Null value to a value you specify.**

   ◆ `variant`**: The data you are working with.**

   * `valueifnull`**: The value you want returned if the** `variant` **is Null.**

   For example:

   `NZ([MyNumberField],0)` **converts any Null value in**
   `MyNumberField` **to zero.**

Watch the syntax in your expressions

Basic syntax mistakes in your calculation expressions can also lead to errors. Follow these basic guidelines to avoid slip-ups:

- If you are using fields in your calculations, enclose their names in square brackets ([ ]).

- Make sure you spell the names of the fields correctly.

- When assigning an alias to your calculated field, be sure you don't use a name that currently exists in the table(s) being calculated.

- Do not use illegal characters—period (.), exclamation mark (!), square brackets ([]), or an ampersand (&)—in your aliases.

Using Dates in Your Analysis

In Access, every possible date starting from January 1, 1900 is stored as a serial number. For example, January 1, 1900 is stored as 1; January 2, 1900 is stored as 2; and so on. This system of storing dates as serial numbers, commonly called the *1900 system,* is the default date system for all Microsoft Office applications. You can take advantage of this system to perform calculations with dates.

Simple date calculations

Figure 4-18 shows one of the simplest calculations you can perform on a date. In this query, you are adding 30 to each invoice date. This effectively returns the invoice date plus 30 days, giving you a new date.

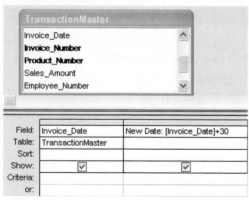

Figure 4-18 You are adding 30 to each invoice date, effectively creating a date that is equal to the invoice date plus 30 days.

WARNING To be calculated correctly dates must reside in a field that is formatted as a Date/Time field. If you enter a date into a Text field, the date will continue to look like a date, but Access will treat it like a string. The end result is that any calculation done on dates in this Text-formatted field will fail. Ensure that all dates are stored in fields that are formatted as Date/Time.

You can also calculate the number of days between two dates. The calculation in Figure 4-19, for example, essentially subtracts the serial number of one date from the serial number of another date, leaving you the number of days between the two dates.

Advanced analysis using functions

As of Access 2003, 26 built-in Date/Time functions are available. Some of these are functions you will very rarely encounter, whereas you will use others routinely in your analyses. This section discusses a few of the basic Date/Time functions that will come in handy in your day-to-day analysis.

Field:	Service_Date	Invoice_Date	Days from Service to Invoice: [Invoice_Date]-[Service_Date]
Table:	TransactionMaster	TransactionMaster	
Sort:			
Show:	☑	☑	☑
Criteria:			
or:			

Figure 4-19 In this query, you are calculating the number of days between two dates.

The Date function

The Date function is a built-in Access function that returns the current system date—in other words, today's date. With this versatile function, you never have to hard-code today's date in your calculations. That is to say, you can create dynamic calculations that use the current system date as a variable, giving you a different result every day. This section looks at some of the ways you can leverage the Date function enhance your analysis.

Finding the number of days between today and a past date

Imagine that you have to calculate aged receivables. You would need to know the current date to determine how overdue the receivables are. Of course, you could type in the current date by hand, but that can be cumbersome and prone to error.

To demonstrate how to use the Date function, create the query shown in Figure 4-20.

Using the Date function in a criteria expression

You can use the Date function to filter out records by including it in a criteria expression. For example, the query shown in Figure 4-21 returns all records with an invoice date older than 90 days.

Figure 4-21 No matter what day it is today, this query returns all invoices older than 90 days.

Calculating an age in years using the Date function

Imagine that you have been asked to provide a list of employees along with the number of years they have been employed by the company. To accomplish this task, you will have to calculate the difference between today's date and each active employee's hire date.

The first step is to build the query shown in Figure 4-22.

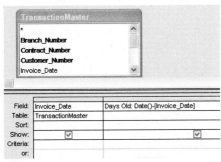

Figure 4-20 This query returns the number of days between today's date and each invoice date.

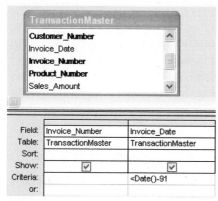

Figure 4-21 No matter what day it is today, this query returns all invoices older than 90 days.

When you look at the query results, shown in Figure 4-23, you will realize that the calculation results in the number of days between the two dates, not the number of years.

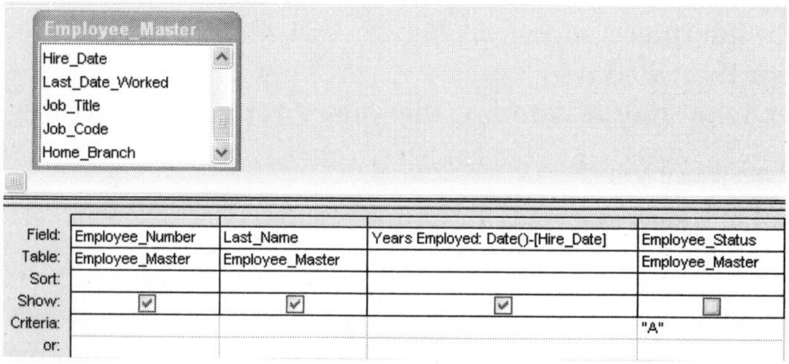

Figure 4-22   You are calculating the difference between today's date and each active employee's hire date.

Employee_Number	Last_Name	Years Employed
104	WIBB	4101
1044	BLECKMAN	4757
1054	STEMPFL	10225
106	CESTENGIAY	3366
113	TRIDIL	6096
1130	RIID	7066
1135	FERNEM	5381
1156	RACHERDS	6523
1245	HERPIR	3919
1336	RACHTIR	7041

Figure 4-23   This dataset shows the number of days, not the number of years.

To fix this, switch back to Design view and divide your calculation by 365.25. Why 365.25? That is the average number of days in a year when you account for leap years. Figure 4-24 demonstrates this change. Note that your original calculation is now wrapped in parentheses to avoid errors due to order of operator precedence.

A look at the results, shown in Figure 4-25, proves that you are now returning the number of years. All that is left to do is to strip away the fractional portion of the date using the `Int` function. Why the `Int` function? The `Int` function does not round the year up or down; it merely converts the number to a readable integer.

Wrapping your calculation in the `Int` function ensures that your answer will be a clean year without fractions (see Figure 4-26).

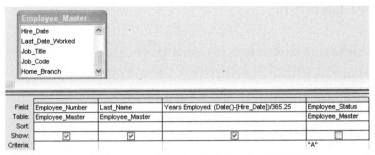

Figure 4-24   Divide your original calculation by 365.25 to convert the answer to years.

Employee_Number	Last_Name	Years Employed
104	WIBB	11.22792607803
1044	BLECKMAN	13.02395619439
1054	STEMPFL	27.99452429843
106	CESTENGIAY	9.215605749487
113	TRIDIL	16.68993839836
1130	RIID	19.34565366188
1135	FERNEM	14.73237508556
1156	RACHERDS	17.85900068446
1245	HERPIR	10.72963723477
1336	RACHTIR	19.2772073922

Figure 4-25   Your query is now returning years, but you will have to strip away the fractional portion of your answer.

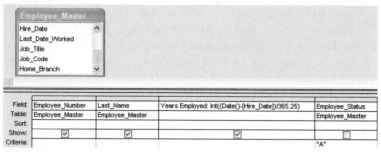

Figure 4-26 Running this query returns the number of years each employee has been with the company.

TIP You can calculate a person's age using the same method. Simply replace the hire date with the date of birth.

NOTE You will often have to wrap your date calculations inside of conversion functions such as `Int`, `Round`, and `Fix` in order to make sense of the results and/or achieve the correct analysis.

The Year, Month, Day, and Weekday functions

The `Year`, `Month`, `Day`, and `Weekday` functions are used to return an integer that represents their respective parts of a date. All of these functions require a valid date as an argument. For example:

- `Year(#12/31/1997#)` returns 1997.
- `Month(#12/31/1997#)` returns 12.
- `Day(#12/31/1997#)` returns 31.
- `Weekday(#12/31/1997#)` returns 4.

NOTE The `Weekday` function returns the day of the week from a date. In Access weekdays are numbered from 1 to 7 starting with Sunday. Therefore, if the `Weekday` function returns 4, the day of the week represented is Wednesday.

Figure 4-27 demonstrates how you would use these functions in a query environment.

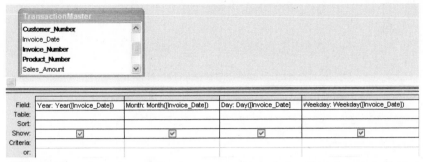

Figure 4-27 The Year, Month, Day, and Weekday functions enable you to parse out a part of a date.

Tricks of the Trade: An Easy Way to Query Only Workdays

Suppose that you have been asked to provide the total amount of revenue generated by each of your company's branches, but only on those dates that are company workdays. Workdays are defined as days that are not weekends or holidays.

The first thing you need to accomplish this task is a table that lists all the company holidays. Figure 4-28 shows that a holidays table can be nothing more than one field listing all the dates that constitute a holiday.

Holidays
1/1/2004
1/19/2004
5/31/2004
7/5/2004
9/6/2004
11/25/2004
11/26/2004
12/23/2004
12/24/2004
12/31/2004

Figure 4-28 In this database, the HolidaysMaster table contains a column called Holidays that lists all the dates that are counted as company holidays.

Once you have established a table that contains all the company holidays, it's time to build the query. Figure 4-29 demonstrates how to build a query that filters out non-workdays.

continues

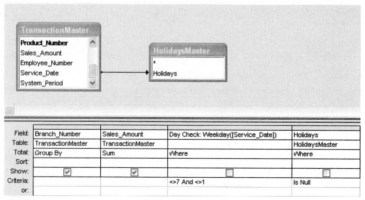

Figure 4-29   Using the HolidaysMaster table and a simple `Weekday` function, you can filter out non-workdays.

Take a moment to analyze what is going on in Figure 4-29.

1. **You create a left join from TransactionMaster to HolidaysMaster to tell Access that you want all the records from TransactionMaster.**

2. **You then use the Is Null criteria under Holidays. This limits the TransactionMaster to only those dates that do not match any of the holidays listed in the HolidaysMaster.**

3. **You then create a field called Day Check where you are returning the weekday of every service date in the TransactionMaster.**

4. **You filter the newly created Day Check field to filter out those weekdays that represent Saturdays and Sundays (1 and 7).**

The DateAdd function

A common analysis for many organizations is to determine on which date a certain benchmark will be reached. For example, most businesses want to know on what date an invoice becomes 30 days past due. Furthermore, what date should a warning letter be sent to the customer? An easy way to perform these types of analyses is to use the `DateAdd` function. The `DateAdd` function returns a date to which a specified interval has been added.

The query shown in Figure 4-30 illustrates how the `DateAdd` function can be used in determining the exact date a specific benchmark is reached. You are creating two new fields with this query: Warning and Overdue. The `DateAdd` function used in the Warning field returns the date that is three weeks from the original invoice date. The `DateAdd` function used in the Overdue field returns the date that is one month from the original invoice date.

ABOUT THE DATEADD FUNCTION

`DateAdd(interval, number, date)`

The `DateAdd` **function returns a date to which a specified interval has been added. The** `DateAdd` **function has three required arguments:**

- ◆ `interval` **(required): The interval of time you want to use. The intervals available are as follows:**

  - ■ `yyyy` **(Year)**
  - ■ `q` **(Quarter)**
  - ■ `m` **(Month)**
  - ■ `y` **(Day of year)**
  - ■ `d` **(Day)**
  - ■ `w` **(Weekday)**
  - ■ `ww` **(Week)**
  - ■ `h` **(Hour)**
  - ■ `n` **(Minute)**
  - ■ `s` **(Second)**

- ◆ `number` **(required): The number of intervals to add. A positive number returns a date in the future, whereas a negative number returns a date in the past.**

- * `date` **(required): The date value with which you are working.**

For example:

`DateAdd("ww",1,#11/30/2004#)` **returns 12/7/2004.**

`DateAdd("m",2,#11/30/2004#)` **returns 1/30/2005.**

`DateAdd("yyyy",-1,#11/30/2004#)` **returns 11/30/2003.**

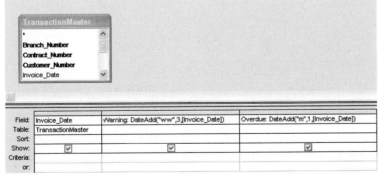

Figure 4-30   This query gives you the original invoice date, the date you should send a warning letter, and the date the invoice will be 30 days overdue.

Grouping dates into quarters

Why would you want to group your dates into quarters? Most databases store dates rather than quarter designations. Therefore, if you wanted to analyze data on a quarter-over-quarter basis, you would have to convert dates into quarters. Surprisingly, there is no Date/Time function that allows you to group dates into quarters. There is, however, the `Format` function.

The `Format` function belongs to the Text category of functions and allows you to convert a variant into a string based on formatting instructions. From the perspective of analyzing dates, you can pass several valid instructions to a `Format` function:

Format(#01/31/2004#, "yyyy") returns 2004.

Format(#01/31/2004#, "yy") returns 04.

Format(#01/31/2004#, "q") returns 1.

Format(#01/31/2004#, "mmm") returns Jan.

Format(#01/31/2004#, "mm") returns 01.

Format(#01/31/2004#, "d") returns 31.

Format(#01/31/2004#, "w") returns 7.

Format(#01/31/2004#, "ww") returns 5.

NOTE Keep in mind that the value returned when passing a date through a `Format` function is a string that cannot be used in subsequent calculations.

The query in Figure 4-31 shows how you would group all the service dates into quarters, then group the quarters to get a sum of revenue for each quarter.

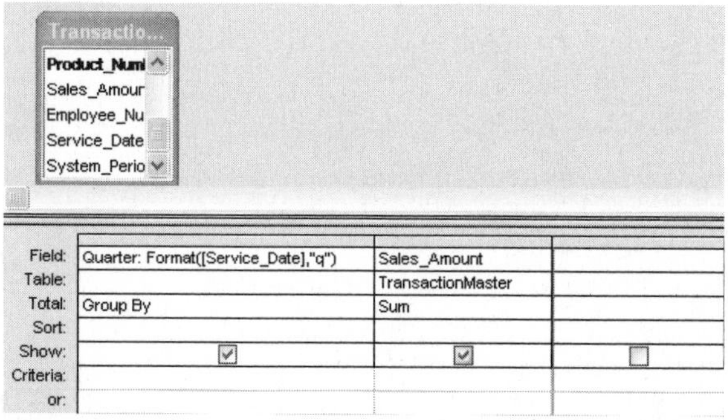

Figure 4-31 You can group dates into quarters by using the `Format` function.

If you want to get fancy, you can insert the Format function in a crosstab query, using Quarter as the column (see Figure 4-32).

As you can see in Figure 4-33, the resulting dataset is a clean look at revenue by product, by quarter.

The DateSerial function

The DateSerial function enables you to construct a date value by combining given year, month, and day components. This function is perfect for converting disparate strings that together represent a date into an actual date.

The wonderful thing about the DateSerial function is that you can pass other date expressions as arguments. For example, pretend that the system date on your PC is August 1, 2005. If you have been paying attention, this means that the Date function would return August 1, 2005. That being the case, the following expression would return August 1, 2005:

```
DateSerial ( Year(Date()) , Month(Date()) , Day(Date()) )
```

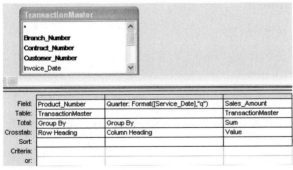

Figure 4-32   You can also use the Format function in a crosstab query.

Product_Number	1	2	3	4
16000	$575,148.34	$615,635.94	$607,250.40	$563,126.73
30300	$624,226.35	$685,701.43	$679,602.99	$638,267.25
70700	$545,062.66	$565,352.79	$551,256.32	$517,260.35
81150	$259,345.81	$295,265.31	$294,802.38	$289,182.27
87000	$294,056.23	$312,162.99	$300,570.77	$284,121.61
▶ 90830	$297,286.66	$324,844.67	$332,029.86	$322,629.36

Figure 4-33   You have successfully grouped your dates into quarters.

ABOUT THE DATESERIAL FUNCTION

`DateSerial(Year, Month, Day)`

- ◆ `Year` **(required): Any number or numeric expression from 100 to 9999.**
- ◆ `Month` **(required): Any number or numeric expression.**
- * `Day` **(required): Any number or numeric expression.**

For example:

`DateSerial(2004, 4, 3)` **returns April 3, 2004.**

NOTE `Year(Date())` **returns the current year;** `Month(Date())` **returns the current month; and** `Day(Date())` **returns the current day.**

So how is this helpful? Well, now you can put a few twists on this by performing calculations on the expressions within the `DateSerial` function. Consider some of the possibilities:

- Get the first day of last month by subtracting 1 from the current month and using 1 as the Day argument:

  `DateSerial(Year(Date), Month(Date) - 1, 1)`

- Get the first day of next month by adding 1 to the current month and using 1 as the Day argument:

  `DateSerial(Year(Date), Month(Date) + 1, 1)`

- Get the last day of this month by using 0 as the Day argument:

  `DateSerial(Year(Date), Month(Date), 0)`

- Get the last day of next month by adding 1 to the current month and using 0 as the Day argument:

  `DateSerial(Year(Date), Month(Date) +1, 0)`

TIP **Passing a 0 to the Day argument automatically gets you the last day of the month specified in the** `DateSerial` **function.**

CHAPTER 5

Performing Conditional Analysis

Until now, your analyses have been straightforward. You build a query, you add some criteria, you add a calculation, you save the query, and then you run the query whenever you need to. What happens, however, if the criteria that governs your analysis changes frequently, or if your analytical processes depend on certain conditions being met? In these situations, you would use a *conditional analysis*—the outcome of which depends on a predefined set of conditions. Barring VBA code, several tools and functions enable you to build conditional analyses, including parameter queries, the `IIf` function, and the `Switch` function. In this chapter, you learn how these tools and functions can help you save time, organize your analytical processes, and enhance your analysis.

Using Parameter Queries

You will find that when building your analytical processes, it will often be difficult to anticipate every single combination of criteria that may be needed. This is where parameter queries can help.

A *parameter query* is an interactive query that prompts you for criteria before the query is run. A parameter query is useful when you need to ask a query different questions using different criteria each time it is run. To get a firm understanding of how a parameter query can help you, build the query shown in Figure 5-1. With this query, you want to see the total revenue for each branch during the 200405 system period.

Although this query will give you what you need, the problem is that the criterion for system period is hard-coded as 200405. That means if you want to analyze revenue for a different period, you essentially have to rebuild the query. Using a parameter query allows you to create a conditional analysis; that is, an analysis based on variables you specify each time you run the query. To create a parameter query, simply replace the hard-coded criteria with text that you have enclosed in square brackets ([ ]), as shown in Figure 5-2.

Running a parameter query forces the Enter Parameter Value dialog box to open and ask for a variable. Note that the text you typed inside the brackets of your parameter appears in the dialog box. At this point, you would simply enter your parameter, as shown in Figure 5-3.

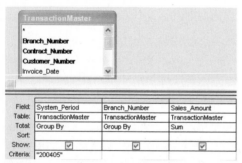

Figure 5-1 This query has a hard-coded criterion for system period.

Field:	System_Period	Branch_Number	Sales_Amount
Table:	TransactionMaster	TransactionMaster	TransactionMaster
Total:	Group By	Group By	Sum
Sort:			
Show:	☑	☑	☑
Criteria:	[Please enter the system period you would like to use]		

Figure 5-2 To create a parameter query, replace the hard-coded criteria with text enclosed in square brackets ([ ]).

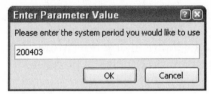

Figure 5-3   Enter your criteria in the Enter Parameter
Value dialog box and click OK.

How parameter queries work

When you run a parameter query, Access attempts to convert any text to a literal
string by wrapping the text in quotes. However, if you place square brackets ([ ])
around the text, Access thinks that it is a variable and tries to bind some value to
the variable using the following series of tests:

1. Access checks to see if the variable is a field name. If Access identifies
   the variable as a field name, that field is used in the expression.

2. If the variable is not a field name, Access checks to see if the variable is
   a calculated field. If Access determines the expression is indeed a calculated field, it simply carries out the mathematical operation.

3. If the variable is not a calculated field, Access checks to see if the variable
   is referencing an object such as a control on an open form or open report.

4. If all else fails, the only remaining option is to ask the user what the
   variable is, so Access displays the Enter Parameter Value dialog box,
   showing the text you entered in the Criteria row.

Ground rules of parameter queries

As with other functionality in Access, parameter queries come with their own
set of ground rules that you should follow in order to use them properly:

- You must place square brackets ([ ]) around your parameter. If you do
  not, Access automatically converts your text into a literal string.

- You cannot use the name of a field as a parameter. If you do, Access
  simply replaces your parameter with the current value of the field.

- You cannot use a period (.), an exclamation mark (!), square brackets
  ([]), or an ampersand (&) in your parameter's prompt text.

- You must limit the number of characters in your parameter's prompt text. Entering parameter prompt text that is too long may result in your prompt being cut off in the Enter Parameter Value dialog box. Moreover, you should make your prompts as clear and concise as possible.

TIP If you really want to use a field name in your parameter's prompt, you can follow the field name with other characters. For example, instead of using [System_Period], you could use [System_Period: ?]. As you read this, keep in mind that there is nothing magic about the colon (:) or the question mark (?). Any character will do. The idea is to allow Access to differentiate between your parameter and the field name while matching the original field name as closely as possible.

Working with parameter queries

The example shown in Figure 5-2 uses a parameter to define a single criterion. Although this is the most common way to use a parameter in a query, many ways exist to exploit this functionality. In fact, it is safe to say that the more innovative you get with your parameter queries, the more elegant and advanced your impromptu analysis will be. This section covers some of the different ways you can use parameters in your queries.

Working with multiple parameter conditions

You are not in any way limited in the number of parameters you can use in your query. Figure 5-4, on the other hand, demonstrates how you can utilize more than one parameter in a query. When you run this query, you will be prompted for both a system period and a branch number, allowing you to dynamically filter on two data points without ever having to rewrite your query.

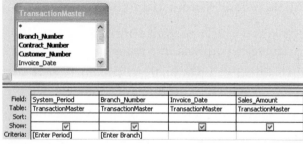

Figure 5-4 This query asks you to enter a system period and then a branch number.

Combining parameters with operators

You can combine parameter prompts with any operator you would normally use in a query. Using parameters in conjunction with standard operators allows you to dynamically expand or contract the filters in your analysis without rebuilding your query. To demonstrate how this works, build the query shown in Figure 5-5.

This query uses the BETWEEN...AND operator and the > (greater than) operator to limit the results of the query based on the user-defined parameters. Because three parameter prompts are built into this query, you will be prompted for inputs three times: once for a starting period, once for an ending period, and once for a dollar amount. The number of records returned will depend on the parameters you input. For instance, if you input 200401 as the starting period, 200403 as the ending period, and 500 as the dollar amount, you will get 175 records.

Combining parameters with wildcards

One of the problems with a parameter query is that if the parameter is ignored when the query is run, the query will return no records. One way to get around this problem is to combine your parameter with a wildcard so that if the parameter is indeed ignored, all records will be returned. To demonstrate how you can use a wildcard with a parameter, build the query shown in Figure 5-6. When you run this query, it prompts you for a branch number. Because you are using the wildcard, you have the option of filtering out a single branch by entering a branch number into the parameter, or you can ignore the parameter to return all records.

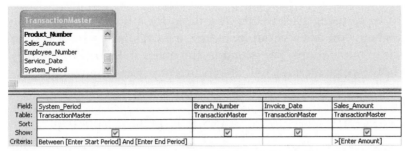

Figure 5-5 This query combines standard operators with parameters in order to limit the results.

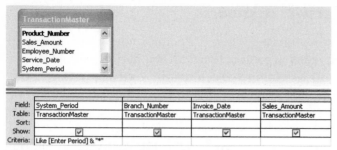

Figure 5-6 If the parameter in this query is ignored, the query will return all records thanks to the wildcard (*).

TIP Using the wildcard with a parameter also allows users to enter in a partial parameter and still get results. Suppose, for example, that the criteria in your parameter query is

```
Like [Enter Lastname] & "*"
```

Entering 'A' as the parameter would return all last names that start with the letter *A*.

Or, suppose the criteria in your parameter query is

```
Like "*" & [Enter Lastname] & "*"
```

Entering 'A' would return all last names that contain the letter *A*.

Using parameters as calculation variables

You are not limited to using parameters as criteria for a query; you can use parameters anywhere you use a variable. In fact, a particularly useful way to use parameters is in calculations. For example, the query in Figure 5-7 enables you to analyze how a price increase will affect current prices based on the percent increase you enter. When you run this query, you will be asked to enter a percentage by which you want to increase your prices. Once you pass your percentage, the parameter query uses it as a variable in the calculation.

Using parameters as function arguments

You can also use parameters as arguments within functions. Figure 5-8 demonstrates the use of the DateDiff function using parameters instead of hard-coded dates. When this query is run, you will be prompted for a start date and an end date. Those dates will then be used as arguments in the DateDiff functions. Again, this allows you to specify new dates each time you run the query without ever having to rebuild the query.

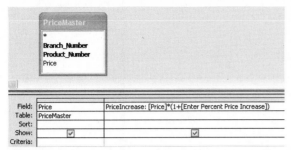

Figure 5-7   You can use parameters in calculations, enabling you to change the calculation's variables each time you run the query.

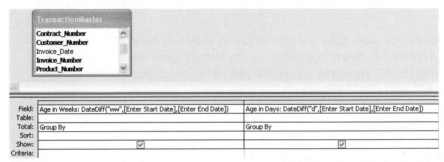

Figure 5-8   You can use parameters as arguments in functions instead of hard-coded values.

WARNING This will only work if the nature of the data you enter as your parameter fits into the function argument. For example, if you are using a parameter in a `DateDiff` function, the variable you assign to that parameter must be a Date or the function won't work.

NOTE You will notice that when you run the query in Figure 5-8, you will only have to enter the Start date and the End date one time although they are both used in two places in the query. This is because once you assign a variable to a parameter, that assignment persists to every future instance of that parameter.

Tricks of the Trade: Creating a Parameter Prompt That Accepts Multiple Entries

---

The parameter query in Figure 5-9 enables you to dynamically filter results by a variable period that you specify within the parameter. However, this query does not allow you to see results for more than one period at a time.

continues

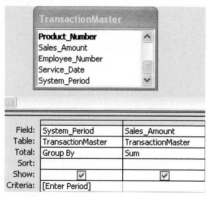

Figure 5-9 This query enables you to filter only one period at a time.

You could use more than one parameter, as shown in Figure 5-10. Unlike the query in Figure 5-9, this query allows you to include more than one period in your query results. However, you would still be limited to the number of parameters built into the query (in this case, three).

Field:	System_Period		Sales_Amount
Table:	TransactionMaster		TransactionMaster
Total:	Group By		Sum
Sort:			
Show:		☑	☑
Criteria:	[Enter 1st Period] Or [Enter 2nd Period] Or [Enter 3rd Period]		

Figure 5-10 This query enables you to filter by three periods at a time instead of one. But what if you need to filter more than three periods?

So how do you allow for any number of parameter entries? The answer is relatively easy. You create a parameter that is passed through an Instr ("in string") function to test for a position number. The query shown in Figure 5-11 demonstrates how to do this.

Notice that the parameter is not being used as criteria for the System_Period field. Instead, it is being used in an Instr function to test for the position number of the variable you enter into the parameter prompt, as follows:

```
InStr([Enter Periods separated by commas],[System_Period])
```

If the Instr function finds your variable, it returns a position number; if not, it returns 0. Therefore, you only want records that returned a position number greater than zero (hence, the criteria for the parameter).

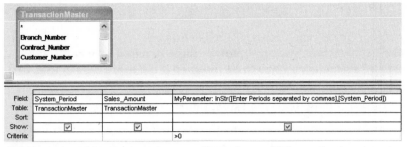

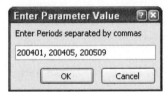

Figure 5-11   This parameter query allows for multiple entries in a parameter.

When you run this query, Access displays the standard Enter Parameter Value dialog box (see Figure 5-12). You can then type in as many variables as you want.

Enter Parameter Value
Enter Periods separated by commas
200401, 200405, 200509
OK   Cancel

Figure 5-12   Simply type in as many parameters you want.

TIP The `Instr` function searches for a specified string in another string and returns its position number. For more information about the `Instr` function, refer to Chapter 3.

NOTE This parameter query will work even without the commas separating each variable you enter. Commas are a cosmetic addition to make it easier to read the variables.

Using Conditional Functions

Parameter queries are not the only tools in Access that allow for conditional analysis. Access also has built-in functions that facilitate value comparisons, data validation, and conditional evaluation. Two of these functions are the `IIf` function and the `Switch` function. These conditional functions (also called program flow functions) are designed to test for conditions and provide different outcomes based on the results of those tests. In this section you learn how to control the flow of your analysis by utilizing the `IIf` and `Switch` functions.

ABOUT THE IIF FUNCTION

IIf(Expression, TrueAnswer, FalseAnswer)
To use the IIf **function, you must provide three required arguments: the expression to be evaluated, a value to be returned if the expression is True, and a value to be returned if the expression is False:**

- ◆ Expression **(required): The expression you want to evaluate.**

- ◆ TrueAnswer **(required): The value to return if the expression is True.**

- ◆ FalseAnswer **(required): The value to return if the expression is False.**

The IIf function

The IIf (immediate if) function replicates the functionality of an IF statement for a single operation. The IIf function evaluates a specific condition and returns a result based on a True or False determination.

TIP **Think of the commas in an** IIf **function as** THEN **and** ELSE **statements. Consider the following** IIf **function, for instance:**

```
IIf(Babies = 2 , "Twins", "Not Twins")
```

This function literally translates to: If Babies equals 2, then Twins, else Not Twins.

Using IIf to avoid mathematical errors

To demonstrate a simple problem where the IIf function comes in handy, build the query shown in Figure 5-13.

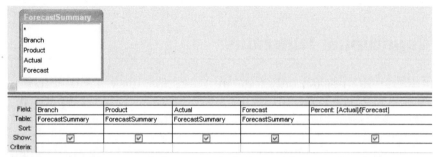

Figure 5-13 This query performs a calculation on the Actual and the Forecast fields to calculate a percent to forecast.

When you run the query, you will notice that not all the results are clean. As you can see in Figure 5-14, you are getting some errors due to division by zero. That is to say, you are dividing actual revenues by forecasts that are 0.

Although this seems like a fairly benign issue, in a more complex, multilayered analytical process, these errors could compromise the integrity of your data analysis. To avoid these errors, you can perform a conditional analysis on your dataset using the IIf function, evaluating the Forecast field for each record before performing the calculation. If the forecast is 0, you bypass the calculation and simply return a value of 0. If the forecast is not 0, you perform the calculation to get the correct value. The IIf function would look like this:

```
IIf([Forecast]=0,0,[Actual]/[Forecast])
```

Figure 5-15 demonstrates how this IIf function is put into action. As you can see in Figure 5-16, the errors have been avoided.

Branch	Product	Actual	Forecast	Percent
601310	90830	171	0	#Error
401612	90830	520	658	79.03%
940581	90830	706	727	97.11%
308118	90830	1,025	1,206	84.99%
201605	90830	1,064	1,400	76.00%
910181	90830	1,195	0	#Error
301606	90830	1,370	0	#Error
940381	90830	1,463	0	#Error
202600	90830	1,483	1,786	83.03%
102516	90830	1,522	1,951	78.01%

Figure 5-14 The errors shown in the results are due to the fact that some revenues are being divided by zero.

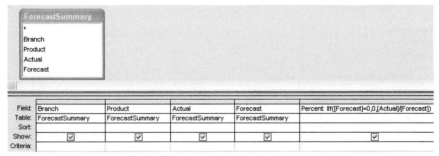

Figure 5-15 This IIf function enables you to test for forecasts with a value of 0 and bypass them when performing your calculation.

Branch	Product	Actual	Forecast	Percent
601310	90830	171	0	0.00%
401612	90830	520	658	79.03%
940581	90830	706	727	97.11%
308118	90830	1,025	1,206	84.99%
201605	90830	1,064	1,400	76.00%
910181	90830	1,195	0	0.00%
301606	90830	1,370	0	0.00%
940381	90830	1,463	0	0.00%
202600	90830	1,483	1,786	83.03%
102516	90830	1,522	1,951	78.01%

Figure 5-16   The IIf function helped you avoid the division by zero errors.

Using IIf to save time

You can also use the IIf function to save steps in your analytical processes and, ultimately, save time. For example, imagine that you need to tag customers in a lead list based on their dollar potential. You decide that you will update the MyTest field in your dataset with "LARGE" or "SMALL" based on the revenue potential of the customer.

Without the IIf function, you would have to run the two update queries shown in Figures 5-17 and 5-18 to accomplish this task.

Will the queries in Figures 5-17 and 5-18 do the job? Yes. However, you could accomplish the same task with one query using the IIf function.

The update query shown in Figure 5-19 illustrates how you can use an IIf function as the update expression.

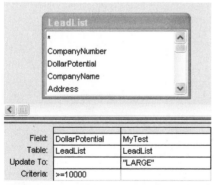

Figure 5-17   This query updates the MyTest field to tag all customers that have a revenue potential at or above 10,000 dollars with the word "LARGE".

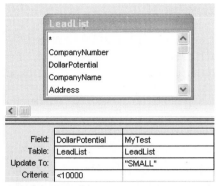

Figure 5-18 This query updates the MyTest field to tag all customers that have a revenue potential less than 10,000 dollars with the word "SMALL".

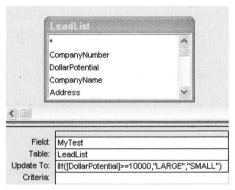

Figure 5-19 You can accomplish the same task in one query using the IIf function.

Take a moment and look at the IIf function being used as the update expression:

```
IIf([DollarPotential]>=10000,"LARGE","SMALL")
```

This function tells Access to evaluate the DollarPotential field of each record. If the DollarPotential field is greater than or equal to 10,000, use the word "LARGE" as the update value. If not, use the word "SMALL".

TIP You can use conditional operators (AND, OR, BETWEEN) within your IIf functions to add a layers to your condition expression. For example, the following function tests for a branch number and a hire date to get a True or a False value:

```
IIf([Home_Branch] = '920681' And [Hire_Date] > #1/1/1985#
,"True","False")
```

Nesting IIf functions for multiple conditions

Sometimes the condition you need to test for is too complex to be handled by a basic IF...THEN...ELSE structure. In such cases, you can use nested IIf functions—that is, IIf functions that are embedded in other IIf functions. Consider the following example:

```
IIf([VALUE]>100,"A",IIf([VALUE]<100,"C","B"))
```

This function checks to see if VALUE is greater than 100. *If* it is, *then* "A" is returned; if not (*else*), a second IIf function is triggered. The second IIf function checks to see if VALUE is less than 100. *If* yes, *then* "C" is returned; if not (*else*), "B" is returned.

The idea here is that because an IIf function results in a True or False answer, you can expand your condition by setting the "False" expression to another IIf function instead of to a hard-coded value. This triggers another evaluation. There is no limit to the number of nested IIf functions you can use.

Using IIf functions to create crosstab analyses

Many seasoned analysts use the IIf function to create custom crosstab analyses in lieu of using a crosstab query. Among the many advantages of creating crosstab analyses without a crosstab query is the ability to categorize and group otherwise unrelated data items.

In the example shown in Figure 5-20, you are returning the sum of sales amount for two groups of employees: those with a hire date before January 1, 2004 and those with a hire date after January 1, 2004. Categorizations this specific would not be possible with a crosstab query.

The result, shown in Figure 5-21, is every bit as clean and user-friendly as the results would be from a crosstab query.

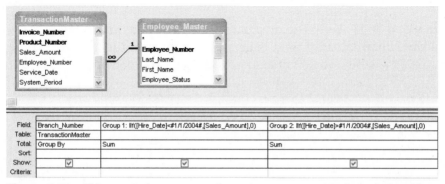

Figure 5-20   This query demonstrates how to create a crosstab analysis without using a crosstab query.

Branch_Number	Group 1	Group 2
101313	$403,589.43	$41,041.45
101419	$124,151.92	$445.23
102516	$63,227.89	$0.00
103516	$84,783.80	$16,880.48
173901	$81,848.30	$25,367.60
201605	$60,579.76	$9,237.84
201709	$87,774.28	$9,078.73
201714	$284,268.19	$4,445.38
201717	$450,524.08	$0.00
202600	$151,337.96	$0.00

Figure 5-21   The resulting dataset gives you a clean crosstab-style view of your data.

Another advantage of creating crosstab analyses without a crosstab query is the ability to include more than one calculation in your crosstab report. For example, Figure 5-22 illustrates a query where the number of transactions is being returned in addition to the sum of sales amount. Again, this would not be possible with a crosstab query.

As you can see in Figure 5-23, the resulting dataset provides a great deal of information in an easy-to-read format.

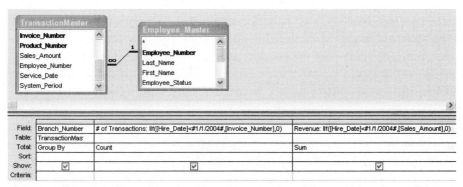

Figure 5-22   Creating crosstab-style reports using the IIf function allows you to calculate more than one value.

Branch_Number	# of Transactions	Revenue
101313	3650	$403,589.43
101419	758	$124,151.92
102516	381	$63,227.89
103516	623	$84,783.80
173901	622	$81,848.30
201605	469	$60,579.76
201709	485	$87,774.28
201714	1716	$284,268.19
201717	2709	$450,524.08
202600	1028	$151,337.96

Figure 5-23   This analysis would be impossible to create in a crosstab query, where multiple calculations are not allowed.

ABOUT THE SWITCH FUNCTION

`Switch(Expression, Value)`

◆ `Expression` **(required). The expression you want to evaluate.**

◆ `Value` **(required). The value to return if the expression is True.**

The Switch function

The `Switch` function enables you to evaluate a list of expressions and return the value associated with the expression determined to be True. To use the `Switch` function, you must provide a minimum of one expression and one value.

The power of the `Switch` function comes in evaluating multiple expressions at one time and determining which one is True. To evaluate multiple expressions, simply add another `Expression` and `Value` to the function, as follows:

```
Switch(Expression1, Value1, Expression2, Value2, Expression3, Value3)
```

When executed, this `Switch` function evaluates each expression in turn. If an expression evaluates to True, the value that follows that expression is returned. If more than one expression is True, the value for the first True expression is returned (the others are ignored). Keep in mind that there is no limit to the number of expressions you can evaluate with a `Switch` function.

WARNING **If none of the expressions in your** `Switch` **function evaluate as True, the function returns a Null value. For example, the following function evaluates** `Count` **and returns a value based on it:**

```
Switch([Count] < 10, "Low", [Count] > 15, "High")
```

The problem with this function is that if `Count` **comes in between 10 and 15, you will get a Null value because none of the expressions include those numbers. This may indirectly cause errors in other parts of your analysis.**

To avoid this scenario, you can add a "catch all" expression and provide a value to return if none of your expressions are determined to be True:

```
Switch([Count] < 10, "Low", [Count] > 15, "High", True, "Middle")
```

Adding `True` **as the last expression forces the value** `"Middle"` **to be returned instead of a Null value if none of the other expressions evaluate as True.**

Why use the Switch function?

Although the IIf function is a versatile tool that can handle most conditional analysis, the fact is that the IIf function has a fixed number of arguments that limits it to a basic IF...THEN...ELSE structure. This limitation makes it difficult to evaluate complex conditions without using nested IIf functions. Although there is nothing wrong with nesting IIf functions, there are analyses where the numbers of conditions that need to be evaluated make building a nested IIf impractical at best.

To illustrate this point, consider this scenario. It is common practice to classify customers into groups based on annual revenue, or how much they spend with your company. Imagine that your organization has a policy of classifying customers into four groups: A, B, C, and D (see Table 5-1).

You have been asked to classify the customers in the TransactionMaster table, based on each customer's sales transactions. You can actually do this using either the IIf function or the Switch function.

The problem with using the IIf function is that this situation calls for some hefty nesting. That is, you will have to use IIf expressions within other IIf expressions to handle the easy layer of possible conditions. Here is how the expression would look if you opted to use IIf:

```
IIf([REV]>=10000,"A",IIf([REV]>=5000 And [REV]<10000,"B",
IIf([REV]>1000 And [REV]<5000,"C","D")))
```

As you can see, not only is it difficult to determine what is going on here, but this is so convoluted, the chances of making a syntax or logic error are high.

In contrast to the preceding nested IIf function, the following Switch function is rather straightforward:

```
Switch([REV]<1000,"D",[REV]<5000,"C",[REV]<10000,"B",True,"A")
```

This function tells Access that if REV is less than 1000, then return a value of "D". If REV is less than 5000, then return a value of "C". If REV is less than 10000, then return "B". If all else fails, use "A". Figure 5-24 demonstrates how you would use this function in a query.

Table 5-1 Customer Classifications

ANNUAL REVENUE	CUSTOMER CLASSIFICATION
>= $10,000	A
>=5,000 but < $10,000	B
>=$1,000 but < $5,000	C
<$1,000	D

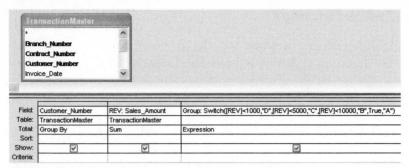

Field:	Customer_Number	REV: Sales_Amount	Group: Switch([REV]<1000,"D",[REV]<5000,"C",[REV]<10000,"B",True,"A")
Table:	TransactionMaster	TransactionMaster	
Total:	Group By	Sum	Expression
Sort:			
Show:	☑	☑	☑
Criteria:			

Figure 5-24 Using the `Switch` function is sometimes more practical than using nested `IIf` functions. This query classifies customers by how much they spend.

NOTE You may shrewdly notice that those records that are less than 1000 will also be less than 10000. So why don't all the records get tagged with a value of "B"? Remember that the `Switch` function evaluates your expressions from left to right and only returns the value of the first expression that evaluates to True.

In this light, you will want to sort the expressions in your `Switch` function accordingly, using an order that is conducive to the logic of your analysis.

When you run the query, you get the resulting dataset shown in Figure 5-25.

Customer_Number	REV	Group
2269392	$893.05	D
226945	$12,295.62	A
2270259	$8,664.52	B
2270499	$2,408.54	C
2271451	$2,583.54	C
2271878	$1,258.66	C
2272058	$554.08	D
2272123	$2,247.61	C
2272918	$983.12	D
2272929	$278.70	D

Figure 5-25 Each customer is conditionally tagged with a group designation based on annual revenue.

Advanced Analysis Techniques

Working with Subqueries and Domain Aggregate Functions

Often, you will carry out your analyses in layers, each layer of analysis using or building on the previous layer. The practice of building layers into analytical processes is actually very common. For instance, when you build a query using another query as the data source, you are layering your analysis. When you build a query based on a temporary table created by a make-table query, you are also layering your analysis.

All of these conventional methods of layering analyses have two things in common. First, they add a step to your analytical processes. Every query that has to be run in order to feed another query, or every temporary table that has to be created to advance your analysis, adds yet another task that must be completed before you get your final results. Second, they all require the creation of temporary tables or transitory queries, inundating your database with table and query objects that lead to a confusing analytical process as well as a database that bloats easily. This is where subqueries and domain aggregate functions can help.

Subqueries and domain aggregate functions allow you to build layers into your analysis within one query, eliminating the need for temporary tables or transitory queries. Sounds useful, doesn't it? So why is it that you haven't heard about these before? The primary reason is that using the conventional methods mentioned before is easy enough that most analysts don't bother looking for more options. The other reason is that both subqueries and domain aggregate functions require an understanding of SQL (Structured Query Language), and most Access users don't have the time or inclination to learn SQL.

In this chapter, you first get a solid understanding of the fundamentals of SQL. You then learn how to leverage both subqueries and domain aggregate functions to streamline your analytical processes, as well as expand and enhance your analysis.

Understanding SQL

SQL, commonly pronounced "sequel," is the language relational database management systems such as Access use to perform their various tasks. To tell Access to perform any kind of query, you must convey your instructions in SQL. You may not know that you have been speaking to Access in SQL, but you have indeed been building and using SQL statements without knowing it. A major reason your exposure to SQL is limited is that Access is more user-friendly than most people give it credit for being. The fact is that Access performs a majority of its actions in user-friendly environments that hide the real grunt work that goes on behind the scenes.

For a demonstration of this, build in Design view the query you see in Figure 6-1. In this relatively simple query, you are asking for the sum of revenue by branch and system period.

Next, select View → SQL View, and Access switches from Design view to the view you see in Figure 6-2.

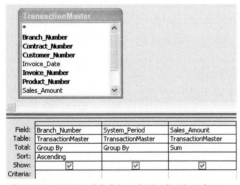

Figure 6-1 Build this relatively simple query in Design view.

SELECT TransactionMaster.Branch_Number, TransactionMaster.System_Period, Sum(TransactionMaster.Sales_Amount) AS SumOfSales_Amount
FROM TransactionMaster
GROUP BY TransactionMaster.Branch_Number, TransactionMaster.System_Period
ORDER BY TransactionMaster.Branch Number;

Figure 6-2 You can get to SQL view by selecting View → SQL View.

As you can see in Figure 6-2, while you were busy designing your query in Design view, Access was diligently creating the SQL statement that allows the query to run. This example shows that with the user-friendly interface provided by Access, you don't necessarily need to know the SQL behind each query. The question now becomes: If you can run queries just fine without knowing SQL, why bother to learn it?

Admittedly, the convenient query interface provided by Access does make it a bit tempting to go through life not really understanding SQL. However, if you want to harness the real power of data analysis with Access, it is important to understand the fundamentals of SQL. This chapter gives you a solid understanding of SQL as well as insights into some techniques that leverage it to enhance your data analysis.

The SELECT statement

The SELECT statement, the cornerstone of SQL, enables you to retrieve records from a dataset. The basic syntax of a SELECT statement is

```
SELECT column_name(s)
FROM table_name
```

Try this: Start a new query in Design view, close the Show Table dialog box (if it is open), and then select View → SQL View. In the SQL view, type in the SELECT statement shown in Figure 6-3 and run the query. Congratulations! You have just written your first query manually.

NOTE You may notice that the SQL statement automatically created by Access in Figure 6-2 has a semicolon at the end of it. This semicolon is not required for Access to run the query. The semicolon is a standard way to end a SQL statement and is required by some database programs, but it is not necessary to end your SQL statements with a semicolon in Access.

Selecting specific columns

You can retrieve specific columns from your dataset by explicitly defining the columns in your SELECT statement, as follows:

```
SELECT Employee_Number, Last_Name, First_Name
FROM Employee_Master
```

```
SELECT Employee_Number
FROM Employee_Master
```

Figure 6-3   A basic SELECT statement in SQL view.

WARNING Any column in your database that has a name which includes spaces or a non-alphanumeric character must be enclosed within brackets ([ ]) in your SQL statement. For example, the SQL statement selecting data from a column called Last Name would look like this: SELECT [Last Name] FROM EmployeeTable.

Selecting all columns

Using the wildcard (*) enables you to select all columns from a dataset without having to define every column explicitly:

```
SELECT *
FROM Employee_Master
```

Selecting unique values

The DISTINCT predicate enables you to retrieve only unique values from the selected fields in your dataset. For example, the following SQL statement selects only unique job titles from the Employee_Master table, resulting in six records:

```
SELECT DISTINCT Job_Title
FROM Employee_Master
```

Keep in mind that using SELECT DISTINCT is different from using GROUP BY or an aggregate query. There is no grouping going on here; Access is simply running through the records and retrieving the unique values.

The ORDER BY clause

The ORDER BY clause enables you to sort data by a specified field. The default sort order is ascending; therefore, sorting your fields in ascending order requires no explicit instruction. The following SQL statement sorts the resulting records in by Last_Name ascending, then First_Name ascending:

```
SELECT Employee_Number, Last_Name, First_Name
FROM Employee_Master
ORDER BY Last_Name, First_Name
```

To sort in descending order, you must use the DESC reserved word after each column you want sorted in descending order. The following SQL statement sorts the resulting records in by Last_Name descending, then First_Name ascending:

```
SELECT Employee_Number, Last_Name, First_Name
FROM Employee_Master
ORDER BY Last_Name DESC, First_Name
```

The WHERE clause

You can use the WHERE clause in a SELECT statement to filter your dataset and conditionally select specific records. The WHERE clause is always used in combination with an operator such as = (equal), <> (not equal), > (greater than), < (less than), >= (greater than or equal to), <= (less than or equal to), or BETWEEN (within general range).

The following SQL statement retrieves only those employees whose last name is Jehnsen:

```
SELECT Employee_Number, Last_Name, First_Name
FROM Employee_Master
WHERE Last_Name = "JEHNSEN"
```

And this SQL statement retrieves only those employees whose hire data is later than May 16, 2004:

```
SELECT Employee_Number, Last_Name, First_Name
FROM Employee_Master
WHERE Hire_Date > #5/16/2004#
```

NOTE Notice in the preceding two examples that the word Jehnsen is wrapped in quotes ("Jehnsen") and the date 5/16/2004 is wrapped in the number signs (#5/16/2004#). When referring to a text value in a SQL statement, you must place quotes around the value, whereas referring to a date requires that number signs be used.

The GROUP BY clause

The GROUP BY clause makes it possible to aggregate records in your dataset by column values. When you create an aggregate query in Design view, you are essentially using the GROUP BY clause.

The following SQL statement groups the Home_Branch field and gives you the count of employees in every branch:

```
SELECT Home_Branch, Count(Employee_Number)
FROM Employee_Master
GROUP BY Home_Branch
```

The HAVING clause

When you are using the GROUP BY clause, you cannot specify criteria using the WHERE clause. Instead, you need to use the HAVING clause. The following SQL statement groups the Home_Branch field and only gives you the count of employees in branch 601306:

```
SELECT Home_Branch, Count(Employee_Number)
FROM Employee_Master
GROUP BY Home_Branch
HAVING Home_Branch = "601306"
```

The AS clause

The AS clause enables you to assign aliases to your columns and tables. Generally, you would want to use aliases for two reasons: either you want to make column or table names shorter and easier to read, or you are working with multiple instances of the same table and you need a way to refer to one instance or the other.

Creating a column alias

The following SQL statement groups the Home_Branch field and gives you the count of employees in every branch. In addition, the alias MyCount has been given to the column containing the count of employee number by including the AS clause:

```
SELECT Home_Branch, Count(Employee_Number)AS MyCount
FROM Employee_Master
GROUP BY Home_Branch
```

Creating a table alias

This SQL statement gives the Employee_Master the alias "MyTable":

```
SELECT Home_Branch, Count(Employee_Number)
FROM Employee_Master AS MyTable
GROUP BY Home_Branch
```

Making sense of joins

You will often need to build queries that require two or more related tables to be joined to achieve the desired results. For example, you may want to join an employee table to a transaction table in order create a report that contains both transaction details and information on the employees who logged those transactions. The type of join used determines the records that will be output.

Inner joins

An *inner join* operation tells Access to select only those records from both tables that have matching values. Records with values in the joined field that do not appear in both tables are omitted from the query results. Figure 6-4 represents the inner join operation visually.

The following SQL statement selects only those records where the employee numbers in the Employee_Number field are in both the Employee_Master table and the TransactionMaster table:

```
SELECT Employee_Master.Last_Name, TransactionMaster.Sales_Amount
FROM Employee_Master INNER JOIN TransactionMaster
ON Employee_Master.Employee_Number = TransactionMaster.Employee_Number
```

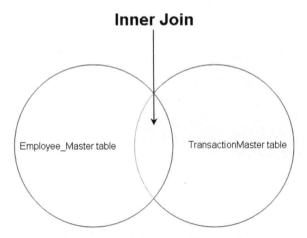

Figure 6-4 An inner join operation selects only the records that have matching values in both tables. The arrows point to the records that will be included in the results.

Outer joins

An *outer join* operation tells Access to select all the records from one table and only the records from a second table with matching values in the joined field. Two types of outer joins exist: left joins and right joins.

A *left join* operation (sometimes called an "outer left join") tells Access to select all the records from the first table regardless of matching *and* only those records from the second table that have matching values in the joined field. Figure 6-5 represents the left join operation visually.

This SQL statement selects all records from the Employee_Master table and only those records in the TransactionMaster table that have employee numbers that exist in the Employee_Master table:

```
SELECT Employee_Master.Last_Name, TransactionMaster.Sales_Amount
FROM Employee_Master LEFT JOIN TransactionMaster ON
Employee_Master.Employee_Number = TransactionMaster.Employee_Number
```

A *right join* operation (sometimes called an "outer right join") tells Access to select all the records from the second table regardless of matching *and* only those records from the first table that have matching values in the joined field (see Figure 6-6).

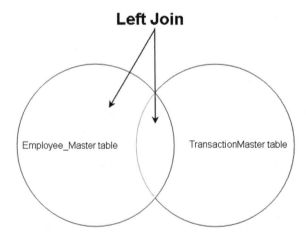

Figure 6-5 A left join operation selects all records from the first table and only those records from the second table that have matching values in both tables. The arrows point to the records that will be included in the results.

Right Join

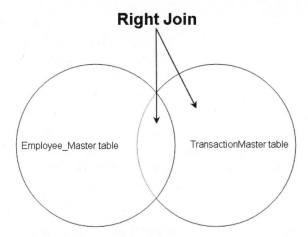

Figure 6-6   A right join operation selects all records from the second table and only those records from the first table that have matching values in both tables. The arrows point to the records that will be included in the results.

This SQL statement selects all records from the TransactionMaster table and only those records in the Employee_Master table that have employee numbers that exist in the TransactionMaster table:

```
SELECT Employee_Master.Last_Name, TransactionMaster.Sales_Amount
FROM Employee_Master RIGHT JOIN TransactionMaster ON
Employee_Master.Employee_Number = TransactionMaster.Employee_Number
```

TIP Notice that in the preceding join statements, table names are listed before each column name separated by a dot (for example, Employee_Master.Last_Name). When you are building a SQL statement for a query that utilizes multiple tables, it is generally a good practice to refer to the table names as well as field names in order to avoid confusion and errors. Access does this for all queries automatically.

Union queries in SQL

You can use union queries to merge two compatible SQL statements to produce one read-only dataset. For example, the following union query merges the results of the two SELECT statements. The first SELECT statement produces a table that shows revenue by employee for each branch. The second SELECT statement produces a table that shows total revenue by branch. When the two are merged using the union query, the result is a recordset that shows both details and totals in one table:

```
SELECT Branch_Number, Employee_Number, Revenue AS REV
FROM MainSummary
UNION
SELECT Branch_Number, "Branch Total" AS Employee, Sum(Revenue) AS REV
FROM MainSummary
GROUP BY Branch_Number
```

NOTE When you run a union query, Access matches the columns from both datasets by their position in the `SELECT` statement. That means two things: your `SELECT` statements must have the same number of columns, and the columns in both statements should, in most cases, be in the same order.

The SELECT TOP and SELECT TOP PERCENT statements

When you run a `select query`, you are retrieving all records that meet your definitions and criteria. When you run the `SELECT TOP` statement, or a top values query, you are telling Access to filter your returned dataset to show only a specific number of records.

Top values queries explained

To get a clear understanding of what the `SELECT TOP` statement does, build the aggregate query shown in Figure 6-7.

Right-click the gray area above the white query grid and select Properties. This activates the Query Properties dialog box shown in Figure 6-8. In the Query Properties dialog, change the Top Values property to 25.

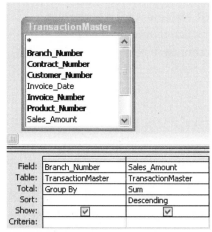

Figure 6-7   Build this aggregate query in Design view. Take note that the query is sorted descending on the Sum of Sales_Amount.

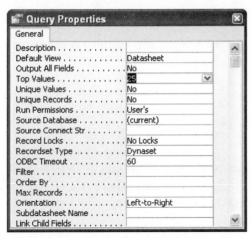

Figure 6-8   Change the Top Values property to 25.

As you can see in Figure 6-9, after you run this query, only the branches that fall into the top 25 by sum of sales amount are returned. If you want the bottom 25 branches, simply change the sort order of the sum of sales amount to ascending.

Branch_Number	SumOfSales_Amount
701715	$484,817.65
501717	$452,318.39
201717	$450,524.08
101313	$444,630.88
701309	$417,157.87
301316	$397,746.22
601306	$374,888.86
202605	$342,536.70
801211	$335,110.37
803717	$333,577.98
503405	$330,179.80
804211	$307,115.74
701407	$293,297.07
201714	$288,713.58
302301	$251,174.69
701717	$237,453.85
806211	$231,354.67
401612	$229,226.64
940381	$224,347.84
590140	$223,931.16
501619	$208,664.73
301619	$191,276.35
702309	$190,862.80
801607	$186,937.48
601716	$168,872.59

Figure 6-9   Running the query gives you the top 25 branches by sum of sales amount.

SELECT TOP

The SELECT TOP statement is easy to spot. This is the same query used to run the results in Figure 6-9:

```
SELECT TOP 25 Branch_Number, Sum(Sales_Amount) AS SumOfSales_Amount
FROM TransactionMaster
GROUP BY Branch_Number
ORDER BY Sum(Sales_Amount) DESC
```

Bear in mind that you don't have to be working with totals or currency to use a top values query. In the following SQL statement, you are returning the 25 employees that have the earliest hire date in the company, effectively producing a seniority report:

```
SELECT TOP 25 Employee_Number, Last_Name, First_Name, Hire_Date
FROM Employee_Master
ORDER BY Hire_Date ASC
```

SELECT TOP PERCENT

The SELECT TOP PERCENT statement works in exactly the same way as SELECT TOP except the records returned in a SELECT TOP PERCENT statement represent the *Nth* percent of total records rather than the *Nth* number of records. For example, the following SQL statement returns the top 25 percent of records by sum of sales amount:

```
SELECT TOP 25 PERCENT Branch_Number, Sum(Sales_Amount)
AS SumOfSales_Amount
FROM TransactionMaster
GROUP BY Branch_Number
ORDER BY Sum(Sales_Amount) DESC
```

NOTE Keep in mind that SELECT TOP PERCENT **statements only give you the top or bottom percent of the total number of records in the returned dataset, not the percent of the total value in your records. For example, the preceding SQL statement will not give you only those records that make up 25 percent of the total value of Sales_Amount. It will give you only the top 25 percent of records in the returned dataset.**

Action queries in SQL

You may not have thought about it before, but when you build an action query, you are building a SQL statement that is specific to that action. These SQL statements make it possible for you to go beyond just selecting records.

Make-table queries translated

Make-table queries use the SELECT . . . INTO statement to make a hard-coded table that contains the results of your query. The following example first selects employee number, last name, and first name, and then creates a new table called Employees:

```
SELECT Employee_Number,Last_Name,First_Name INTO Employees
FROM Employee_Master;
```

Append queries translated

Append queries use the INSERT INTO statement to insert new rows into a specified table. The following example inserts new rows into the Employee_Master table from the Employees table:

```
INSERT INTO Employee_Master (Employee_Number, Last_Name, First_Name)
SELECT Employees.Employee_Number, Employees.Last_Name,Employees.First_Name
FROM Employees
```

Update queries translated

Update queries use the UPDATE statement in conjunction with SET in order to modify the data in a dataset. This example updates the Price field in the Price-Master table to increase prices by 10 percent:

```
UPDATE PriceMaster SET Price = [Price]*1.1
```

Delete queries translated

Delete queries use the DELETE statement to delete rows in a dataset. In the example here, you are deleting all rows from the Employee_Master table that have no values in the Employee_Status field:

```
DELETE *
FROM Employee_Master
WHERE Employee_Status Is Null
```

Enhancing Your Analysis with Subqueries

Once you have a relatively firm understanding of SQL, you can start leveraging subqueries to enhance your data analysis. Subqueries (sometimes referred to as subselect queries) are select queries that are nested within other queries. The primary purpose of a subquery is to enable you to use the results of one query within the execution of another. With subqueries, you can answer a multiple-part question, specify criteria for further selection, or define new fields to be used in your analysis.

The query shown in Figure 6-10 demonstrates how a subquery is used in the design grid. As you look at this, remember that this is one example of how a subquery can be used. Subqueries are not limited to use as criteria.

If you were to build the query in Figure 6-10 and switch to SQL view, you would see the following SQL statement. Can you pick out the subquery? Look for the second SELECT statement:

```
SELECT Employee_Number, Last_Name, Home_Branch
FROM Employee_Master
WHERE Home_Branch IN
     (SELECT [Branch_Number]FROM[LocationMaster]WHERE[Market]="DALLAS")
```

NOTE Subqueries must always be enclosed in parentheses.

The idea behind a subquery is that the subquery is executed first, and the results are used in the outer query (the query in which the subquery is embedded) as a criterion, an expression, a parameter, and so on. In the example shown in Figure 6-10, the subquery first returns a list of branches that belong to the Dallas market. Then the outer query uses that list as criteria to filter out any Employee who does not belong to the Dallas market.

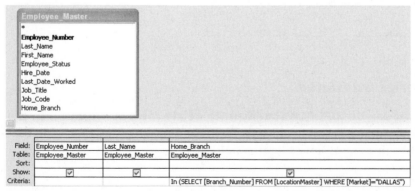

Figure 6-10   To use a subquery in the query design grid, simply enter the SQL statement.

Why use subqueries?

You should know that subqueries often run slower than a standard query using a join. This is because subqueries either are executed against an entire dataset or are evaluated multiple times—one time per each row processed by the outer query. This makes them slow to execute especially if you have a large dataset. So why use them?

Many analyses require multiple-step processes that use temporary tables or transitory queries. Although there is nothing inherently wrong with temporary tables and queries, an excess amount of them in your analytical processes could lead to a confusing analytical process as well as a database that bloats easily.

Even though using subqueries comes with a performance hit, it may be an acceptable trade for streamlined procedures and optimized analytical processes. You will even find that as you become more comfortable with writing your own SQL statements, you will use subqueries in "on-the-fly" queries to actually *save* time.

Subquery ground rules

Here are a few rules and restrictions that you must be aware of when using subqueries:

- Your subquery must have, at a minimum, a SELECT statement and a FROM clause in its SQL string.

- You must enclose your subquery in parentheses.

- Theoretically, you can nest up to 31 subqueries within a query. This number, however, is based on your system's available memory and the complexity of your subqueries.

- You can use a subquery in an expression as long as it returns a single value.

- You can use the ORDER BY clause in a subquery only if the subquery is a SELECT TOP or SELECT TOP PERCENT statement.

- You cannot use the DISTINCT keyword in a subquery that includes the GROUP BY clause.

- You must implement table aliases in queries in which a table is used in both the outer query and the subquery.

Tricks of the Trade: Creating Subqueries without Typing SQL Statements

You may have the tendency to shy away from subqueries because you may feel uncomfortable with writing your own SQL statements. Indeed, many of the SQL statements necessary to perform the smallest analysis can seem daunting.

Imagine, for example, that you have been asked to provide the number of employees that have a time in service greater than the average time in service for all employees in the company. Sounds like a relatively simple analysis, and it *is* simple when you use a subquery. But where do you start? Well, you could just write a SQL statement into the SQL view of a query and run it. But the truth is that not many Access users create SQL statements from scratch. The smart ones utilize the built-in functionalities of Access to save time and headaches. The trick is to split the analysis into manageable pieces.

In this scenario, the first step is to find the average time in service for all employees in the company. To do this, create the query shown in Figure 6-11.

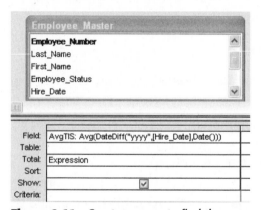

Figure 6-11   Create a query to find the average time in service for all employees.

Next, switch to SQL view, shown in Figure 6-12, and copy the SQL statement.

```
SELECT Avg(DateDiff("yyyy",[Hire_Date],Date())) AS AvgTIS
FROM Employee_Master;
```

Figure 6-12   Switch to SQL view and copy the SQL statement.

The next step is to create a query that counts the number of employees by time in service. Figure 6-13 does just that.

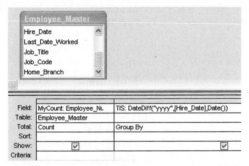

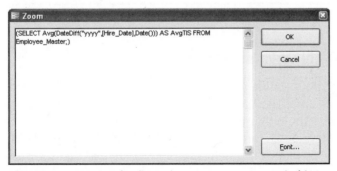

Figure 6-13 Create a query to count the number of employees by time in service.

Right-click in the Criteria row under the TIS field and select Zoom. This opens the Zoom dialog shown in Figure 6-14. The Zoom dialog does nothing more than help you more comfortably work with text that is too long to be easily seen at one time in the query grid. With the Zoom dialog box open, paste the SQL statement you copied previously into to the white input area.

NOTE Remember that subqueries must be enclosed in parentheses, so you need to enter parentheses around the SQL statement you just pasted. You also need to make sure you delete all carriage returns that were put in automatically by Access.

Figure 6-14 Paste the first SQL statement you copied into the Criteria row of the TIS field.

Finish off the query by entering a greater than (>) sign in front of your subquery and change the aggregate function of the TIS row to a WHERE clause. At this point your query should look like the one shown in Figure 6-15.

continues

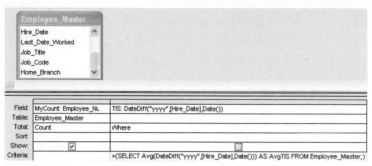

Figure 6-15 Running this query tells you that 228 employees have a time in service greater than the company average.

Now if you go to the SQL view of the query shown in Figure 6-15, you will see the following SQL statement:

```
SELECT Count(Employee_Master.Employee_Number) AS MyCount
FROM Employee_Master
WHERE (((DateDiff("yyyy",[Hire_Date],Date()))
    >(SELECT Avg(DateDiff("yyyy",[Hire_Date],Date())) AS AvgTIS
    FROM Employee_Master;))));
```

The beauty is that you didn't have to type all this syntax. You simply used your knowledge of Access to piece together the necessary actions that needed to be taken in order to get to the answer. As you become more familiar with SQL, you will find that you can create subqueries manually with no problems.

Using IN and NOT IN with subqueries

The IN and NOT IN operators enable you to run two queries in one. The idea is that the subquery will execute first, and then the resulting dataset will be used by the outer query to filter the final output.

The example SQL statement demonstrated here first runs a subquery that selects all customers that belong to branch number 101419 *and* that are based in MI (Michigan). The outer query then uses the resulting dataset as criteria to return the sum of sales amount for only those customers that match the customer numbers returned in the subquery:

```
SELECT System_Period, Sum(Sales_Amount) AS Revenue
FROM TransactionMaster
WHERE Customer_Number IN
(SELECT [Customer_Number] FROM [CustomerMaster] WHERE [Branch_Num] = "101419"
AND [State] = "MI")
GROUP BY System_Period
```

You would use NOT IN to go the opposite way and return the sum of sales amount for those customers that do not match the customer numbers returned in the subquery.

> **TIP** You can find the examples in this section in the sample database for this book, located at www.wiley.com/go/accessdataanalysis.

Using subqueries with comparison operators

As its name implies, a comparison operator (=, <, >, <=, >=, <>, and so on) compares two items and returns True or False. When you use a subquery with a comparison operator, you are asking Access to compare the resulting dataset of your outer query to that of the subquery.

For example, to analyze the employees that have an annual revenue less than the average annual revenue of all employees in the company, you can use the following SQL statement:

```
SELECT Branch_Number, Employee_Number, Revenue
FROM MainSummary
WHERE Revenue
      <(SELECT Avg(Revenue)FROM MainSummary)
```

The subquery runs first, giving you the average revenue of all employees. This is a single value that Access then uses to compare the outer query's resulting dataset. In other words, the annual revenue for each employee is compared to the company average. If an employee's annual revenue is less than the company average, it is included in the final output; otherwise, it is excluded.

> **NOTE** A subquery that is used with a comparison operator must return a single value.

Using subqueries as expressions

In every example so far you have used subqueries in conjunction with the WHERE clause, effectively using the results of a subquery as criteria for your outer query. However, you can also use a subquery as an expression, as long as the subquery returns a single value. The query shown in Figure 6-16 demonstrates how you can use a subquery as an expression in a calculation.

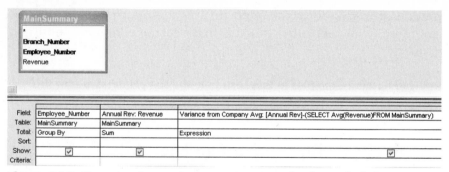

Figure 6-16   You are using a subquery as an expression in a calculation.

This example uses a subquery to get the average revenue per employee for the entire company; that subquery returns a single value. You are then using that value in a calculation to determine the variance between each employee's annual revenue and the average revenue for the company. The output of this query is shown in Figure 6-17.

Using correlated subqueries

A *correlated query* is essentially a subquery that refers back to a column that is in the outer query. What makes correlated subqueries unique is that whereas standard subqueries are evaluated one time to get a result, a correlated subquery has to be evaluated multiple times—once for each row processed by the outer query. To illustrate this point, consider the following two SQL statements.

Uncorrelated subqueries

This first SQL statement is using an uncorrelated subquery. How can you tell? The subquery is not referencing any column in the outer query. This subquery is evaluated one time to give you the average revenue for the entire dataset:

```
SELECT MainSummary.Branch_Number,
    (SELECT Avg(Revenue)FROM MainSummary)
    FROM MainSummary
```

Employee_Number	Annual Rev	Variance from Company Avg
104	$9,023.50	($6,985.6998)
1044	$447.33	($15,561.86)
1050	$179.74	($15,829.46)
1054	$54,147.73	$38,138.53
106	$38,013.36	$22,004.17
113	$963.06	($15,046.14)
1130	$67,961.15	$51,951.95
1135	$1,477.21	($14,531.98)
1156	$192.07	($15,817.13)
1245	$38,189.81	$22,180.61

Figure 6-17   Your query result.

Correlated subqueries

This second SQL statement is using a correlated subquery. The subquery is reaching back into the outer query and referencing the Branch_Number column, effectively forcing the subquery to be evaluated for every row that is processed by the outer query. The end result of this query is a dataset that shows the average revenue for every branch in the company.

```
SELECT MainSummary.Branch_Number,
     (SELECT Avg(Revenue)FROM MainSummary AS M2
     WHERE M2.Branch_Number = MainSummary.Branch_Number) AS AvgByBranch
FROM MainSummary
```

TIP Try to give your tables alias names that make sense. For example, if both your outer query and subquery are using the MainSummary table, you could give the table an alias of M1 in your outer query, and name the same table M2 in your subquery. This would give you an easy visual indication of which table you are referring to.

Using a correlated subquery as an expression

You can use a correlated subquery to peel back different layers from your data. The example shown in Figure 6-17 used an uncorrelated subquery to determine the variance between each employee's annual revenue and the average revenue for the company.

Adding a correlation for each branch number allows you to determine the variance between each employee's annual revenue and the average revenue for that employee's branch:

```
SELECT M1.Employee_Number, Sum(M1.Revenue) AS YrRevenue, [YrRevenue]-
     (SELECT Avg(Revenue) FROM MainSummary AS M2
     WHERE M2.Branch_Number = M1.Branch_Number)
AS Variance
FROM MainSummary AS M1
GROUP BY M1.Branch_Number, M1.Employee_Number
```

Using subqueries within action queries

Action queries can be fitted with subqueries just as easily as select queries can. Here are a few examples of how you would use a subquery in an action query.

USING ALIASES WITH CORRELATED SUBQUERIES

Notice that in the correlated subquery, you are using the AS clause to establish a table alias of "M2". The reason for this is that the subquery and the outer query are both utilizing the same table. By giving one of the tables an alias, you allow Access to distinguish exactly which table you are referring to in your SQL statement. Although the alias in this SQL statement is assigned to the subquery, you can just as easily assign an alias to the table in the outer query.

Note that the character "M2" holds no significance. In fact, you can use any text string you like, as long as the alias and the table name combined do not exceed 255 characters.

To assign an alias to a table in Design view, simply right-click the field list and select Properties, as shown in Figure 6-18.

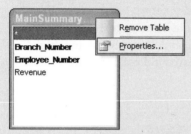

Figure 6-18   Right-click the field list and select Properties.

Next, edit the Alias property to the one you would like to use (see Figure 6-19). You will know that it took effect when the name on the field list changes to your new alias.

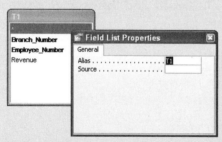

Figure 6-19   Enter the table alias into the Alias property.

TIP   Try to give your tables alias names that make sense. For example, if both your outer query and subquery are using the MainSummary table, you could give the table an alias of M1 in your outer query, and name the same table M2 in your subquery. This would give you an easy visual indication of which table you are referring to.

A subquery in a make-table query

This example illustrates how to use a subquery within a make-table query:

```
SELECT E1.Employee_Number, E1.Last_Name, E1.First_Name
INTO OldSchoolEmployees
FROM Employee_Master as E1
WHERE E1.Employee_Number IN
    (SELECT E2.Employee_Number
    FROM Employee_Master AS E2
    WHERE E2.Hire_Date <#1/1/1995#)
```

A subquery in an append query

This example uses a subquery within an append query:

```
INSERT INTO CustomerMaster ( Customer_Number, Customer_Name, State )
SELECT CompanyNumber,CompanyName,State
FROM LeadList
WHERE CompanyNumber Not In
    (SELECT Customer_Number from CustomerMaster)
```

A subquery in an update query

This example uses a subquery in an update query:

```
UPDATE PriceMaster SET Price = [Price]*1.1

WHERE Branch_Number In

    (SELECT Branch_Number from LocationMaster WHERE Region =  "South")
```

A subquery in a delete query

This example uses a subquery in a delete query:

```
DELETE CompanyNumber
FROM LeadList
WHERE CompanyNumber In
    (SELECT Customer_Number from CustomerMaster)
```

Tricks of the Trade: Getting the Second Quartile of a Dataset with One Query

You can easily pull out the second quartile of a dataset by using a top values subquery. The first step is to create a top values query that returns the top 25 percent of your dataset. In the example shown in Figure 6-20, you are returning the top 25 percent of branches by revenue.

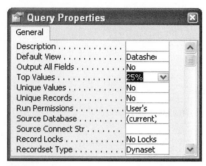

Figure 6-20   Create a query that returns the top 25 percent of your dataset.

NOTE   Again, to get to the Query Properties dialog box shown in 6-20, simply right-click the gray area above the white query grid and select Properties.

Next, switch to SQL view, shown in 6-21, and copy the SQL string.

```
SELECT TOP 25 PERCENT MainSummary.Branch_Number, Sum(MainSummary.Revenue) AS SumOfRevenue
FROM MainSummary
GROUP BY MainSummary.Branch_Number
ORDER BY Sum(MainSummary.Revenue) DESC;
```

Figure 6-21   Copy the SQL statement that makes up the query.

Switch back to Design view. The idea is to paste the SQL statement you just copied into the Criteria row of the Branch_Number field. To do this, right-click inside the Criteria row of the Branch_Number field and select Zoom. Then paste the SQL statement inside the Zoom dialog box, as shown in Figure 6-22.

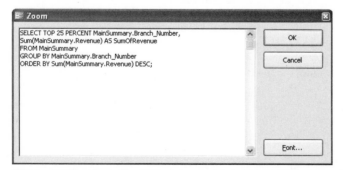

Figure 6-22   Paste the SQL statement into the Criteria row of Branch_Number.

This next part is a little tricky. You will need to perform the following edits on the SQL statement in order to make it work for this situation:

1. Because this subquery is a criterion for the Branch_Number field, you only need to select Branch_Number in the SQL statement; therefore, you can remove the line `Sum(MainSummary.Revenue) AS SumOfRevenue`.

2. Remove the comma at the end of the first line.

3. Delete all carriage returns.

4. Place parentheses around the subquery and put the `NOT IN` operator in front of it all.

At this point, your Zoom dialog box should look like the one shown in Figure 6-23.

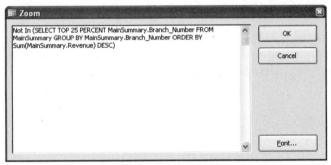

Figure 6-23   After some cleanup, your query is ready to run.

There you have it. Running this query returns the second quartile in the dataset. To get the third quartile, simply replace `TOP 25 PERCENT` in the subquery with `TOP 50 PERCENT`; to get the fourth quartile, use `TOP 75 PERCENT`.

NOTE Be sure to check this book's sample file to get a few more examples that highlight how subqueries can help you find solutions to common analytical needs.

Domain Aggregate Functions

Domain aggregate functions enable you to extract and aggregate statistical information from an entire dataset (a domain). These functions differ from aggregate queries in that an aggregate query groups data before evaluating the values, whereas a domain aggregate function evaluates the values for the entire dataset; thus, a domain aggregate function will never return more than one value. To get a clear understanding of the difference between an aggregate query and a domain aggregate function, build the query shown in Figure 6-24.

Run the query to get the results you see in Figure 6-25. You will notice that the SumOfSales_Amount column contains a different total for each branch number, whereas the Domain column (the domain aggregate function) contains only one total (for the entire dataset).

NOTE Although the examples in this chapter show domain aggregate functions being used in query expressions, keep in mind that you can use these functions in macros, modules, or the calculated controls of forms and reports.

Figure 6-24 This query shows you the difference between an aggregate query and a domain aggregate function.

Branch_Number	SumOfSales_Amount	Domain
101313	$444,630.88	10774189.4594
101419	$124,597.15	10774189.4594
102516	$63,227.89	10774189.4594
103516	$101,664.28	10774189.4594
173901	$107,215.90	10774189.4594
201605	$69,817.60	10774189.4594
201709	$96,853.01	10774189.4594
201714	$288,713.58	10774189.4594
201717	$450,524.08	10774189.4594
202600	$151,337.96	10774189.4594

Figure 6-25 You can clearly see the difference between an aggregate query and a domain aggregate function.

The anatomy of domain aggregate functions

Twelve different domain aggregate functions exist, but they all have the same anatomy.

Understanding the different domain aggregate functions

DSum

The DSum function returns the total sum value of a specified field in the domain. For example, DSum("[Sales_Amount]", "[TransactionMaster]") returns the total sum of sales amount in the TransactionMaster table.

DAvg

The DAvg function returns the average value of a specified field in the domain. For example, DAvg("[Sales_Amount]", "[TransactionMaster]") returns the average sales amount in the TransactionMaster table.

DCount

The DCount function returns the total number of records in the domain. DCount("*", "[TransactionMaster]"), for example, returns the total number of records in the TransactionMaster table.

DLookup

The DLookup function returns the first value of a specified field that matches the criteria you define within the DLookup function. If you don't supply a criterion, the DLookup function returns a random value in the domain. For example, DLookUp("[Last_Name]","[Employee_Master]","[Employee_Number]='42620' ") returns the value in the Last_Name field of the record where the Employee_Number is '42620'.

> **NOTE** DLookup **functions are particularly useful when you need to retrieve a value from an outside dataset.**

DMin and DMax

The DMin and DMax functions return the minimum and maximum values in the domain, respectively. For example, DMin("[Sales_Amount]", "[TransactionMaster]") returns the lowest sales amount in the TransactionMaster table, whereas DMax ("[Sales_Amount]", "[TransactionMaster]") returns the highest sales amount.

USING DOMAIN AGGREGATE FUNCTIONS

```
FunctionName("[Field Name]","[Dataset Name]",
"[Criteria]")
```

 ◆ FunctionName. **This is the name of the domain aggregate function you are using.**

 ◆ Field Name **(required). This expression identifies the field containing the data with which you are working.**

 ◆ Dataset Name **(required). This expression identifies the table or query you are working with; also known as the domain.**

 ◆ Criteria **(optional). This expression is used to restrict the range of data on which the domain aggregate function is performed. If no criteria are specified, the domain aggregate function is performed against the entire dataset.**

NOTE You cannot use a parameter query with a domain aggregate function.

DFirst and DLast

The DFirst and DLast functions return the first and last values in the domain, respectively. For example, DFirst("[Sales_Amount]", "[TransactionMaster]") returns the first sales amount in the Transaction Master table, whereas DLast("[Sales_Amount]", "[Transaction Master]") returns the last.

DStDev, DStDevP, DVar, and DvarP

You can use the DStDev and DStDevP functions to return the standard deviation across a population sample and a population, respectively. Similarly, the DVar and the DVarP functions return the variance across a population sample and a population, respectively. For example, DStDev("[Sales_Amount]", "[TransactionMaster]") returns the standard deviation of all sales amounts in the TransactionMaster table. DVar ("[Sales_Amount]", "[TransactionMaster]") returns the variance of all sales amounts in the TransactionMaster.

Examining the syntax of domain aggregate functions

Domain aggregate functions are unique in that the syntax required to make them work actually varies depending on the scenario. This has led to some very frustrated users who have given up on domain aggregate functions altogether. This section describes some general guidelines that will help you in building your domain aggregate functions.

Using no criteria

In this example, you are summing the values in the Sales_Amount field from the TransactionMaster table (domain). Your field names and dataset names must always be wrapped in quotes:

```
DSum("[Sales_Amount]","[TransactionMaster]")
```

Also, note the use of brackets. Although not always required, it is generally a good practice to use brackets when identifying a field, a table, or a query.

Using text criteria

In this example, you are summing the values in the Sales_Amount field from the TransactionMaster table (domain) where the value in the System_Period field is 200405. Note that the System_Period field is formatted as text. When specifying criteria that is textual or a string, your criterion must be wrapped in single quotes. In addition, your entire criteria expression must be wrapped in double quotes:

```
DSum("[Sales_Amount]", "[TransactionMaster]", "[System_Period] = '200405' ")
```

TIP You can use any valid WHERE clause in the criteria expression of your domain aggregate functions. This adds a level of functionality to domain aggregate functions, because they can support the use of multiple columns and logical operators such as AND, OR, NOT, and so on. An example would be

```
DSum("[Field1]", "[Table]", "[Field2] = 'A' OR [Field2] = 'B' AND [Field3] = 2")
```

If you are referencing a control inside of a form or report, the syntax will change a bit:

```
DSum("[Sales_Amount]", "[TransactionMaster]", "[System_Period] =
' " & [MyTextControl] & " ' " )
```

Notice that you are using single quotes to convert the control's value to a string. In other words, if the value of the form control is 200405, then " [System_ Period] = ' " & [MyTextControl] & " ' " is essentially translated to read " [System_Period] = '200405' ".

Using number criteria

In this example, you are summing the values in the Sales_Amount field from the TransactionMaster table (domain) where the value in the Sales_Amount field is greater than 500. Notice that you are not using the single quotes because the Sales_Amount field is an actual number field:

```
DSum("[Sales_Amount]", "[TransactionMaster]", "[Sales_Amount] > 500 ")
```

If you are referencing a control inside of a form or report, the syntax will change a bit:

```
DSum("[Sales_Amount]", "[TransactionMaster]", "[Sales_Amount] >"
[MyNumericControl])
```

Using date criteria

In this example, you are summing the values in the Sales_Amount field from the TransactionMaster table (domain) where the value in the Service_Date field is 01/05/2004:

```
DSum("[Sales_Amount]", "[TransactionMaster]", "[Service_Date] = #01/05/04# ")
```

If you are referencing a control inside of a form or report, the syntax will change a bit:

```
DSum("[Sales_Amount]", "[TransactionMaster]", "[Service_Date] =
#" & [MydateControl] & "#")
```

Notice that you are using number signs to convert the control's value to a date. In other words, if the value of the form control is 01/05/2004, then `"[Service_Date] = #" & [MydateControl] & "#"` is essentially translated to read `"[Service_Date] = #01/05/2004# "`.

Using domain aggregate functions

Like subqueries, domain aggregate functions are not very efficient when it comes to performing large-scale analyses and crunching very large datasets. These functions are better suited for use in specialty analyses with smaller subsets of data. Indeed, you will most often find domain aggregate functions in environments where the dataset being evaluated is predictable and controlled (form example, functions, forms, and reports). This is not to say, however, that domain aggregate functions don't have their place in your day-to-day data analysis. This section walks through some examples of how you can use domain aggregate functions to accomplish some common tasks.

Calculating the percent of total

The query shown in Figure 6-26 returns products by group and the sum of sales amount for each product. This is a worthwhile analysis, but you could easily enhance it by adding a column that would give you the percent of total revenue for each product.

To get the percent of the total dollar value that each product makes up, you naturally would have to know the total dollar value of the entire dataset. This is where a DSum function can come in handy. The following DSum function returns the total value of the dataset:

```
DSum("[Sales_Amount]","[TransactionMaster]")
```

Now you can use this function as an expression in the calculation that returns the "percent of total" for each product group. Figure 6-27 demonstrates how.

The result, shown in Figure 6-28, proves that this is a quick and easy way to get both total by group and percent of total with one query.

Product_Description	SumOfSales_Amount
Cleaning & Housekeeping Services	$1,138,595.78
Facility Maintenance and Repair	$2,361,161.41
Fleet Maintenance	$2,627,798.02
Green Plants and Foliage Care	$1,276,790.55
Landscaping/Grounds Care	$1,190,911.60
Predictive Maintenance/Preventative Maintenance	$2,178,932.11

Figure 6-26   You want to add a column that shows the percent of total revenue for each product.

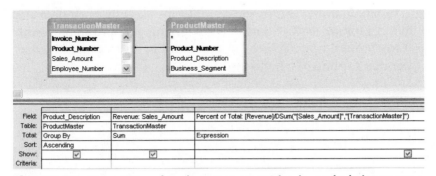

Figure 6-27   Use a DSum function as an expression in a calculation to get "Percent of Total."

Product_Description	Revenue	Percent of Total
Cleaning & Housekeeping Services	$1,138,595.78	10.57%
Facility Maintenance and Repair	$2,361,161.41	21.91%
Fleet Maintenance	$2,627,798.02	24.39%
Green Plants and Foliage Care	$1,276,790.55	11.85%
Landscaping/Grounds Care	$1,190,911.60	11.05%
Predictive Maintenance/Preventative Maintenance	$2,178,932.11	20.22%

Figure 6-28   You retrieved both total by group and percent of total with one query.

Creating a running count

The query in Figure 6-29 uses a DCount function as an expression to return the number of invoices processed on the each specific invoice day.

Take a moment to analyze what this DCount function is doing:

```
DCount("[Invoice_Number]","[TransactionMaster]","[Invoice_Date] = #" &
[Invoice_Date] & "#")
```

This DCount function gets the count of invoices where the invoice date equals (=) each invoice date returned by the query. So, in context of the query shown in Figure 6-29, the resulting dataset shows each invoice date and its own count of invoices.

What would happen if you were to alter the DCount function to tell it to return the count of invoices where the invoice date equals or is earlier than (<=) each invoice date returned by the query, as follows?

```
DCount("[Invoice_Number]","[TransactionMaster]","[Invoice_Date] <= #" &
[Invoice_Date] & "#")
```

The DCount function would return the count of invoices for each date *and* the count of invoices for any earlier date, thereby giving you a running count.

To put this into action, simply replace the = operator in the DCount function with the <= operator, as shown in Figure 6-30.

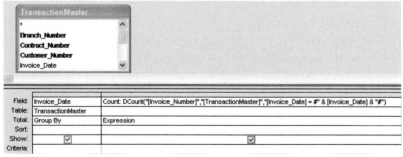

Figure 6-29   This query returns all invoice dates and the number of invoices processed on each date.

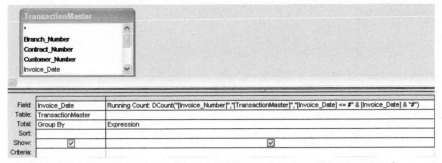

Figure 6-30   Use the <= operator in your DCount function to return the count of invoice dates that equals or is less than the date returned by the query.

Figure 6-31 shows the resulting running sum.

TIP You can achieve a running sum instead of a running count by using the DSum **function.**

Using a value from the previous record

The query in Figure 6-32 uses a DLookup function to return the revenue value from the previous record. This value is placed into a new column called "Yesterday."

Invoice_Date	Running Count
1/5/2004	8
1/6/2004	195
1/7/2004	406
1/8/2004	623
1/9/2004	884
1/12/2004	1120
1/13/2004	1344
1/14/2004	1540
1/15/2004	1802
1/16/2004	1996
1/19/2004	2237
1/20/2004	2356
1/21/2004	2521
1/22/2004	2694
1/23/2004	2912

Figure 6-31   You now have a running count in your analysis.

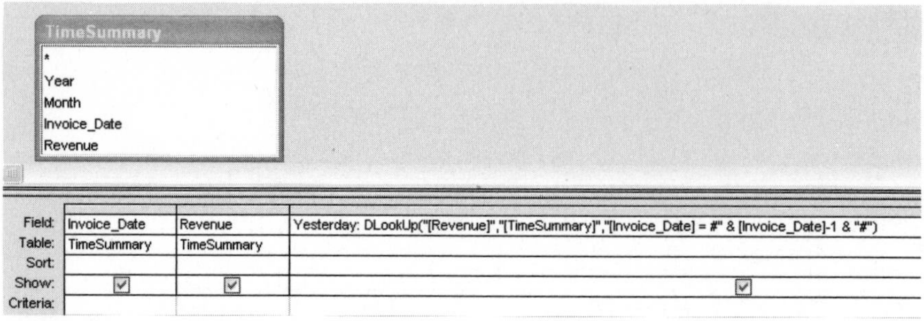

Figure 6-32   This query uses a DLookup to refer to the previous revenue value.

This method is similar to the one used when creating a running sum in that it revolves around manipulating a comparison operator in order to change the meaning of the domain aggregate function. In this case, the DLookup searches for the revenue value where the invoice date is equal to each invoice date returned by the query minus one (-1). If you subtract one from a date, you get yesterday's date!

```
DLookUp("[Revenue]","[TimeSummary]","[Invoice_Date] =          #" &
[Invoice_Date]-1 & "#")
```

TIP   If you add 1 you will get the next record in the sequence. However, this trick will not work with textual fields. This only works with date and numeric fields. If you are working with a table that does not contain any numeric or date fields, create an autonumber field. This will give you a unique numeric identifier that you can use.

Running the query in Figure 6-32 yields the results shown in Figure 6-33.

You can enhance this analysis by adding a calculated field that gives you the dollar variance between today and yesterday. Create a new column and enter **[Revenue]-NZ([Yesterday],0)**, as shown in Figure 6-34. Note that the Yesterday field is wrapped in an NZ function in order to avoid errors caused by Null fields.

Invoice_Date	Revenue	Yesterday
1/5/2004	$1,218.87	
1/6/2004	$29,280.65	1218.8734
1/7/2004	$34,418.48	29280.6534
1/8/2004	$34,437.67	34418.4828
1/9/2004	$41,319.75	34437.6745
1/12/2004	$37,923.82	
1/13/2004	$37,900.75	37923.8214
1/14/2004	$33,318.55	37900.7498
1/15/2004	$44,478.61	33318.5515
1/16/2004	$31,350.05	44478.6144
1/19/2004	$39,003.20	
1/20/2004	$19,304.81	39003.2
1/21/2004	$27,029.77	19304.8096
1/22/2004	$30,825.20	27029.7725
1/23/2004	$35,443.71	30825.1963
1/26/2004	$31,398.60	
1/27/2004	$29,787.17	31398.5956
1/28/2004	$38,793.62	29787.165
1/29/2004	$29,912.85	38793.6207
1/30/2004	$74,719.80	29912.8486

Figure 6-33   You can take this functionality a step further and perform a calculation on the Yesterday field.

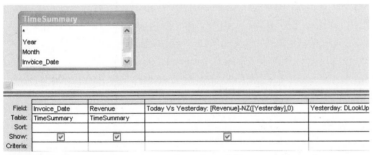

Figure 6-34   Enhance your analysis by adding a variance between today and yesterday.

Figure 6-35 shows the result.

Invoice_Date	Revenue	Yesterday	Today Vs Yesterday
1/5/2004	$1,218.87		$1,218.87
1/6/2004	$29,280.65	1218.8734	$28,061.78
1/7/2004	$34,418.48	29280.6534	$5,137.83
1/8/2004	$34,437.67	34418.4828	$19.19
1/9/2004	$41,319.75	34437.6745	$6,882.07
1/12/2004	$37,923.82		$37,923.82
1/13/2004	$37,900.75	37923.8214	($23.07)
1/14/2004	$33,318.55	37900.7498	($4,582.20)
1/15/2004	$44,478.61	33318.5515	$11,160.06
1/16/2004	$31,350.05	44478.6144	($13,128.57)
1/19/2004	$39,003.20		$39,003.20
1/20/2004	$19,304.81	39003.2	($19,698.39)
1/21/2004	$27,029.77	19304.8096	$7,724.96
1/22/2004	$30,825.20	27029.7725	$3,795.42
1/23/2004	$35,443.71	30825.1963	$4,618.51
1/26/2004	$31,398.60		$31,398.60
1/27/2004	$29,787.17	31398.5956	($1,611.43)
1/28/2004	$38,793.62	29787.165	$9,006.46
1/29/2004	$29,912.85	38793.6207	($8,880.77)
1/30/2004	$74,719.80	29912.8486	$44,806.95

Figure 6-35   Another task made possible by domain aggregate functions.

CHAPTER 7

Running Descriptive Statistics in Access

Descriptive statistics enable you to present large amounts of data in quantitative summaries that are simple to understand. When you sum data, count data, and average data, you are producing descriptive statistics. It is important to note that descriptive statistics are used only to profile a dataset and enable comparisons that can be used in other analyses. This is different from *inferential statistics*, where you infer conclusions that extend beyond the scope of the data. To help solidify the difference between descriptive and inferential statistics, consider a customer survey. Descriptive statistics summarize the survey results for all customers and describe the data in understandable metrics, whereas inferential statistics infer conclusions, such as customer loyalty, based on the observed differences between groups of customers.

When it comes to inferential statistics, Excel is better suited to handle these types of analyses than Access. Why? First, Excel comes with a plethora of built-in functions and tools that make it easy to perform inferential statistics, tools that Access simply does not have. Second, inferential statistics is usually performed on small subsets of data that can be analyzed flexibly and presented by Excel. Running descriptive statistics, on the other hand, is quite practical in Access. In fact, running descriptive statistics in Access rather than in Excel is often the smartest option due to the structure and volume of the dataset.

TIP All the examples in this chapter are located in the sample database for this book, which you can find at www.wiley.com.

Basic Descriptive Statistics

This section discusses some of the basic tasks you can perform by using descriptive statistics, including

- Running descriptive statistics with aggregate queries
- Ranking records in a dataset
- Determining the mode and median of a dataset
- Creating random samplings from a dataset

Running descriptive statistics with aggregate queries

At this point in the book, you have run many Access queries, some of which have been aggregate queries. Little did you know that when you ran those aggregate queries, you were actually creating descriptive statistics. It's true. The simplest descriptive statistics can be generated using an aggregate query. To demonstrate this point, build the query shown in Figure 7-1.

Similar to the descriptive statistics functionality found in Excel, the result of this query, shown in Figure 7-2, provides key statistical metrics for the entire dataset.

You can easily add layers to your descriptive statistics. In Figure 7-3, you are adding the Branch_Number field to your query. This will give you key statistical metrics for each branch.

As you can see in Figure 7-4, you can now compare the descriptive statistics across branches to measure how they perform against each other.

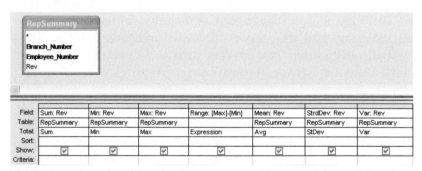

Field:	Sum: Rev	Min: Rev	Max: Rev	Range: [Max]-[Min]	Mean: Rev	StrdDev: Rev	Var: Rev
Table:	RepSummary	RepSummary	RepSummary		RepSummary	RepSummary	RepSummary
Total:	Sum	Min	Max	Expression	Avg	StDev	Var
Sort:							
Show:	✓	✓	✓	✓	✓	✓	✓
Criteria:							

Figure 7-1 Running this aggregate query provides a useful set of descriptive statistics.

Sum	Min	Max	Range	Mean	StrdDev	Var
$10,774,189.4	$86	$137,707	$137,621	$16,009	$21,059	$443,482,958

Figure 7-2 Key statistical metrics for the entire dataset.

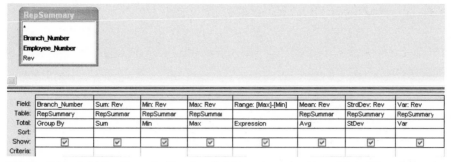

Field:	Branch_Number	Sum: Rev	Min: Rev	Max: Rev	Range: [Max]-[Min]	Mean: Rev	StrdDev: Rev	Var: Rev
Table:	RepSummary	RepSummar	RepSummar	RepSummar		RepSummar	RepSummary	RepSummary
Total:	Group By	Sum	Min	Max	Expression	Avg	StDev	Var
Sort:								
Show:	☑	☑	☑	☑	☑	☑	☑	☑
Criteria:								

Figure 7-3   Add the Branch_Number field to your query to add another dimension to your analysis.

Branch_Number	Sum	Min	Max	Range	Mean	StrdDev	Var
101313	$444,631	$124	$78,824	$78,700	$22,232	$29,111	$847,454,523
101419	$124,597	$99	$46,645	$46,546	$20,766	$19,027	$362,039,701
102516	$63,228	$678	$36,387	$35,709	$21,076	$18,390	$338,192,979
103516	$101,664	$151	$31,428	$31,277	$6,778	$9,338	$87,200,338
173901	$107,216	$402	$33,136	$32,734	$13,402	$13,371	$178,773,758
201605	$69,818	$624	$27,657	$27,033	$8,727	$9,496	$90,165,337
201709	$96,853	$184	$42,778	$42,593	$6,918	$12,375	$153,131,218
201714	$288,714	$145	$57,803	$57,658	$12,553	$15,901	$252,833,070
201717	$450,524	$169	$61,521	$61,352	$34,656	$25,160	$633,007,891
202600	$151,338	$277	$58,473	$58,196	$18,917	$25,557	$653,147,704

Figure 7-4   You have a one-shot view of the descriptive statistics for each branch.

Determining rank, mode, and median

Ranking the records in your dataset, getting the mode of a dataset, and getting the median of a dataset are all tasks that a data analyst will need to perform from time to time. Unfortunately, Access does not provide built-in functionality to perform these tasks easily. This means you will have to come up with a way to carry out these descriptive statistics. In this section, you learn some of the techniques you can use to determine rank, mode, and median.

Ranking the records in your dataset

You will undoubtedly encounter scenarios where you will have to rank the records in your dataset based on a specific metric such as revenue. A record's rank is not only useful in presenting data, it is also a key variable when calculating advanced descriptive statistics such as median, percentile, and quartile.

The easiest way to determine a record's ranking within a dataset is by using a correlated subquery. The query shown in Figure 7-5 demonstrates how a rank is created using a subquery.

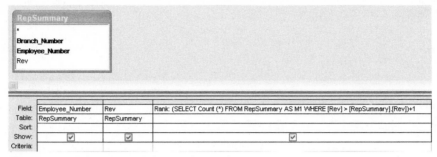

Figure 7-5 This query ranks employees by revenue.

Take a moment to examine the subquery that generates the rank:

```
(SELECT Count(*)FROM RepSummary AS M1 WHERE [Rev]>[RepSummary].[Rev])+1
```

This correlated subquery returns the total count of records from the M1 table (this is the RepSummary table with an alias of M1), where the Rev field in the M1 table is greater than the Rev field in the RepSummary table. The value returned by the subquery is then increased by one. Why increase the value by one? If you don't, the record with the highest value will return 0 because zero records are greater than the record with the highest value. The result would be that your ranking starts with 0 instead of 1. Adding one effectively ensures that your ranking starts with 1.

NOTE Because this is a correlated subquery, this subquery is evaluated for every record in your dataset, thereby giving you a different rank value for each record. Correlated subqueries are covered in detail in Chapter 6.

Figure 7-6 shows the result.

TIP This technique is also useful when you want to create an autonumber field within a query.

Employee_Number	Rank	Rev
64621	1	$137,707.14
4136	2	$111,681.81
5060	3	$106,299.32
56422	4	$102,239.87
56405	5	$83,525.72
160034	6	$78,823.82
60425	7	$77,452.50
3466	8	$76,789.52
52635	9	$76,684.54
52404	10	$76,532.26

Figure 7-6 You have created a Rank column for your dataset.

Getting the mode of a dataset

The *mode* of a dataset is the number that appears the most often in a set of numbers. For instance, the mode for 4, 5, 5, 6, 7, 5, 3, 4 is 5.

Unlike Excel, Access does not have a built-in Mode function, so you will have to create your own method of determining the mode of a dataset. Although there are various ways to get the mode of a dataset, one of the easiest is to use a query to count the occurrences of a certain data item, and then filter for the highest count. To demonstrate this method, build the query shown in Figure 7-7.

The results, shown in Figure 7-8, do not seem very helpful, but if you turn this into a top values query, returning only the top 1 record, you would effectively get the mode.

Figure 7-7 This query groups by the Rev field and then counts the occurrences of each number in Rev field. The query is sorted in descending order by Rev.

Rev	CountOfRev
$154.55	4
$158.60	4
$145.02	3
$185.27	3
$122.89	3
$245.78	3
$309.11	3
$151.03	3
$179.99	2
$654.26	2
$650.24	2
$168.82	2
$431.98	2
$254.34	2
$401.57	2

Figure 7-8 Almost there. Turn this into a top values query and you'll have your Mode.

Change the Top Values property to 1, as shown in Figure 7-9, and you will get one record with the highest count.

As you can see in Figure 7-10 you now have only one Rev figure—the one that occurs the most often. This is your mode.

> **NOTE** Keep in mind that in the event of a tie, a top values query will show all records. This will effectively give you more than one mode. You will have to make a manual determination which mode to use.

Getting the median of a dataset

The *median* of a dataset is the number that is the middle number in the dataset. In other words, half of the numbers have values that are greater than the median, and half have values that are less than the median. For instance, the median number in 3, 4, 5, 6, 7, 8, 9 is 6 because 6 is the middle number of the dataset.

> **TIP** Why can't you just calculate an average and be done with it? Sometimes, calculating an average on a dataset that contains outliers can dramatically skew your analysis. For example, if you were to calculate an average on the numbers 32, 34, 35, 37, and 89, you would get an answer of 45.4. The problem is that 45.4 does not accurately represent the central tendency of this sampling of numbers. Using the median on this sample makes more sense. The median in this case would be 35, which is more representative of what's going on in this data.

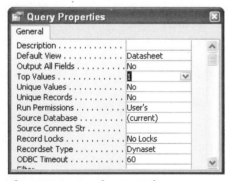

Figure 7-9   Set the Top Values property to 1.

Rev	CountOfRev
$158.60	4

Figure 7-10   This is your mode.

Access does not have a built-in Median function, so you will have to create your own method of determining the median of a dataset. An easy way to get the median is to build a query in two steps. The first step is to create a query that sorts and ranks your records. The query shown in Figure 7-11 sorts and ranks the records in the RepSummary table.

The next step is to identify the middle-most record in your dataset by counting the total number of records in the dataset and then dividing that number by two. This will give you a middle value. The idea is that because the records are now sorted and ranked, the record that has the same rank as the middle value will be the median. Figure 7-12 shows the subquery that returns a middle value for the dataset. Note that the value is wrapped in an `Int` function to strip out the fractional portion of the number.

As you can see in Figure 7-13, the middle value is 336. You can go down to record 336 to see the median.

If you want to return only the median value, simply use the subquery as a criterion for the Rank field, as shown in Figure 7-14.

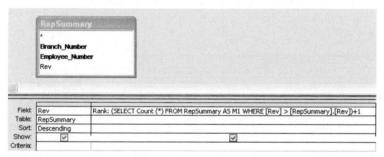

Field:	Rev	Rank: (SELECT Count (*) FROM RepSummary AS M1 WHERE [Rev] > [RepSummary].[Rev])+1
Table:	RepSummary	
Sort:	Descending	
Show:	☑	☑
Criteria:		

Figure 7-11 The first step in finding the median of a dataset is to assign a rank to each record.

Field:	Rev	Rank: (SELECT	Middle Value: Int((SELECT Count(*) FROM RepSummary)/2)
Table:	RepSummary		
Sort:	Descending		
Show:	☑	☑	☑
Criteria:			

Figure 7-12 The Middle Value subquery counts all the records in the dataset and then divides that number by 2.

Rev	Rank	Middle Value
$137,707.14	1	336
$111,681.81	2	336
$106,299.32	3	336
$102,239.87	4	336
$83,525.72	5	336
$78,823.82	6	336
$77,452.50	7	336
$76,789.52	8	336
$76,684.54	9	336
$76,532.26	10	336
$75,690.33	11	336
$75,489.77	12	336
$75,358.76	13	336
$74,653.99	14	336
$71,427.33	15	336

Figure 7-13   Go down to record 336 to get the median value of the dataset.

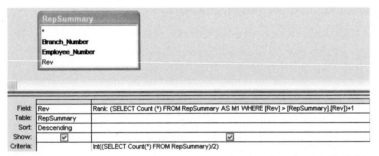

Figure 7-14   Using the subquery as a criterion for the Rank field ensures that only the median value is returned.

Pulling a random sampling from your dataset

Although the creation of a random sample of data does not necessarily fall into the category of descriptive statistics, a random sampling is often the basis for statistical analysis.

Many ways exist to create a random sampling of data in Access, but one of the easiest is to use the Rnd function within a top values query. The Rnd function returns a random number based on an initial value. The idea is to build an expression that applies the Rnd function to a field that contains numbers, and then limit the records returned by setting the Top Values property of the query.

To demonstrate this method, start a query in Design view on the TransactionMaster table. Create a Random ID field, as shown in Figure 7-15, and then sort the field (either ascending or descending will work).

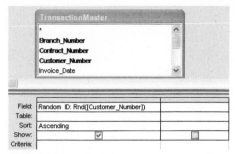

Figure 7-15   Start by creating a Random ID field using the Rnd function with the Customer_Number field.

NOTE The Rnd **function will not work with fields that contain text or Null values. Strangely enough, though, the** Rnd **function will work with fields that contain all numerical values even if the field is formatted as a Text type field.**

If your table is made up of fields that only contain text, you can add an Autonumber field to use with the Rnd **function. Another option is to pass the field containing text through the** Len **function, and then use that expression in your** Rnd **function. For example:** Rnd(Len([Mytext])).

Next, change the Top Values property of the query to the number of random records you want returned. The scenario shown in Figure 7-16 limits this dataset to 1,000 records.

The last step is to set the Show row for the Random ID field to False and add the field you will want to see in your dataset. Run the query and you will have a completely random sampling of data.

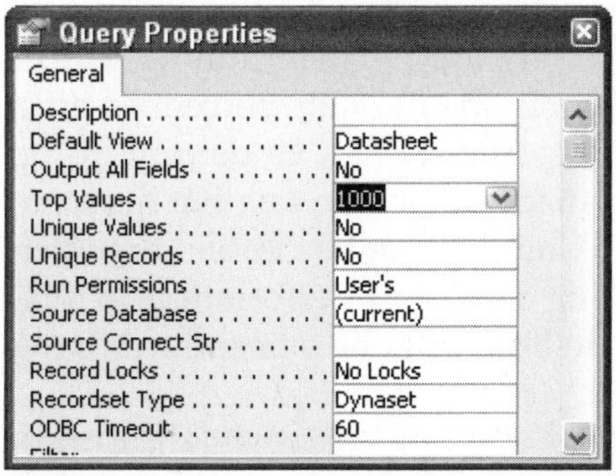

Figure 7-16   Limit the number of records returned by setting the Top Values property of the query.

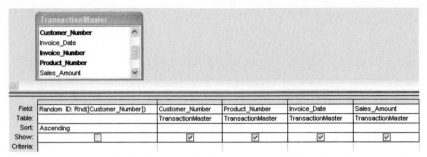

Figure 7-17 Running this query produces a sample 1,000 random records.

WARNING Re-running the query, switching the view state, or sorting the dataset will result in a different set of random records. If you want to perform extensive analysis on an established set of random records that will not change, you will need to run this query as a make-table query in order to create a hard table.

Advanced Descriptive Statistics

You will find that when working with descriptive statistics, a little knowledge goes a long way. Indeed, basic statistical analyses often lead to more advanced statistical analyses. In this section you build on the fundamentals you have just learned to create advanced descriptive statistics.

Calculating percentile ranking

A *percentile rank* indicates the standing of a particular score relative to the normal group standard. Percentiles are most notably used in determining performance on standardized tests. If a child scores in the 90th percentile on a standardized test, this means that his score is higher than 90 percent of the other children taking the test. Another way to look at it is to say that his score is in the top 10 percent of all the children taking the test. Percentiles are often used in data analysis as a method of measuring a subject's performance in relation to the group as a whole—for instance, determining the percentile ranking for each employee based on annual revenue.

Calculating a percentile ranking for a dataset is simply a mathematical operation. The formula for a percentile rank is `(Record Count−Rank)/Record Count`. The trick is getting all the variables needed for this mathematical operation.

To start, build the query you see in Figure 7-18. This query starts by ranking each employee by annual revenue. Be sure to give your new field an alias of "Rank."

Next, add a field that counts all the records in your dataset. As you can see in Figure 7-19, you are using a subquery to do this. Be sure to give your new field an alias of "RCount."

Finally, create a calculated field with the expression (RCount-Rank)/ RCount. At this point, your query should look like the one shown in Figure 7-20.

Running the query gives you the results shown in Figure 7-21.

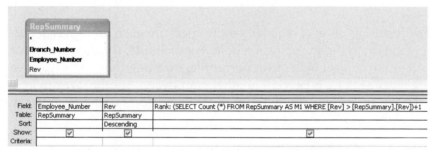

Figure 7-18 Start with a query that ranks employees by revenue.

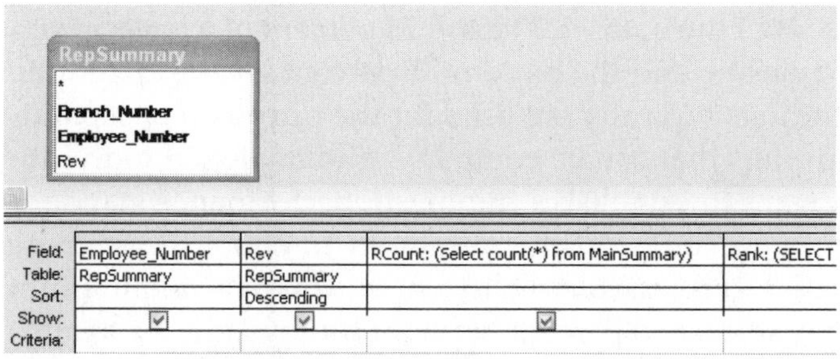

Figure 7-19 Add a field that returns a total dataset count.

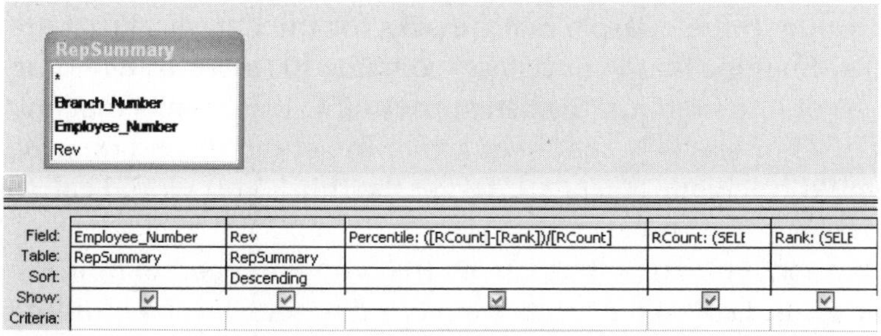

Figure 7-20 The final step is to create a calculated field that gives you the percentile rank for each record.

Employee_Number	Rank	Percentile	Rev	RCount
64621	1	99.85%	$137,707.14	673
4136	2	99.70%	$111,681.81	673
5060	3	99.55%	$106,299.32	673
56422	4	99.41%	$102,239.87	673
56405	5	99.26%	$83,525.72	673
160034	6	99.11%	$78,823.82	673
60425	7	98.96%	$77,452.50	673
3466	8	98.81%	$76,789.52	673
52635	9	98.66%	$76,684.54	673
52404	10	98.51%	$76,532.26	673
3660	11	98.37%	$75,690.33	673
1336	12	98.22%	$75,489.77	673
56416	13	98.07%	$75,358.76	673
55144	14	97.92%	$74,653.99	673
60224	15	97.77%	$71,427.33	673

Figure 7-21 You've successfully calculated the percentile rank for each employee.

Again, the resulting dataset enables you to measure each employee's performance in relation to the group as a whole. For example, the employee that is ranked 6th in the dataset is the 99th percentile, meaning that this employee earned more revenue than 99 percent of other employees. Another way to look at it is that the top six employees make up roughly 1 percent of the revenues in this group of employees.

Determining the quartile standing of a record

A *quartile* is a statistical division of a dataset into four equal groups, with each group making up 25 percent of the dataset. The top 25 percent of a collection is considered to be the 1st quartile, and the bottom 25 percent is considered the 4th quartile. Quartile standings typically are used for the purposes of separating data into logical groupings that can be compared and analyzed individually. For example, if you want to establish a minimum performance standard around monthly revenue, you could set the minimum to equal the average revenue for employees in the 2nd quartile. This ensures you have a minimum performance standard that at least 50 percent of your employees have historically achieved or exceeded.

Establishing the quartile for each record in a dataset does not involve a mathematical operation; rather, it is a question of comparison. The idea is to compare each record's rank value to the quartile benchmarks for the dataset. What are quartile benchmarks? Imagine that your dataset contains 100 records. Dividing 100 by 4 would give you the first quartile benchmark (25). This means that any record with a rank of 25 or less is in the 1st quartile. To get the second quartile benchmark, you would calculate 100/4*2. To get the third, you would calculate 100/4*3 and so on.

Given that information, you know right away that you will need to rank the records in your dataset and count the records in your dataset. Start by building the query shown in Figure 7-22. Build the Rank field the same way you did in Figure 7-18. Build the RCount field the same way you did in Figure 7-19.

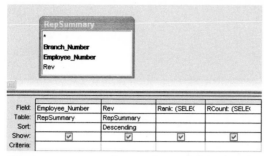

Figure 7-22   Start by creating a field named Rank that ranks each employee by revenue and a field named RCount that counts the total records in the dataset.

Once you have created the Rank and RCount fields in your query, you can use these fields in a `Switch` function that will tag each record with the appropriate quartile standing. Take a moment and look at the `Switch` function you will be using:

```
Switch([Rank]<=[RCount]/4*1,"1st",[Rank]<=[RCount]/4*2,"2nd",
[Rank]<= [RCount]/4*3,"3rd",True,"4th")
```

This `Switch` function is going through four conditions, comparing each record's rank value to the quartile benchmarks for the dataset.

NOTE For more information on the `Switch` function, see Chapter 5.

Figure 7-23 demonstrates how this `Switch` function fits into the query. Note that you are using an alias of quartile here.

As you can see in Figure 7-24, you can sort the resulting dataset on any field without compromising your quartile standing tags.

Field:	Empl	Rev	Quartile: Switch([Rank]<=[RCount]/4*1,"1st",[Rank]<=[RCount]/4*2,"2nd",[Rank]<=[RCount]/4*3,"3rd",True,"4th")
Table:	RepS	RepS	
Sort:		Desc	
Show:	☑	☑	☑
Criteria:			

Figure 7-23   Create the quartile tags using the `Switch` function.

Employee_Number	Rev	Rank	Quartile	RCount
104	$9,023.50	294	2nd	673
1044	$447.33	520	4th	673
1050	$179.74	614	4th	673
1054	$54,147.73	55	1st	673
106	$38,013.36	105	1st	673
113	$963.06	458	3rd	673
1130	$67,961.15	18	1st	673
1135	$1,477.21	429	3rd	673
1156	$192.07	602	4th	673
1245	$38,189.81	103	1st	673
1336	$75,489.77	12	1st	673
1344	$12,242.75	268	2nd	673
1416	$1,120.57	445	3rd	673
142	$1,622.30	421	3rd	673
1435	$43,118.02	89	1st	673

Figure 7-24   Your final dataset can be sorted in any way without the danger of losing your quartile tags.

Creating a frequency distribution

A *frequency distribution* is a special kind of analysis that categorizes data based on the count of occurrences where a variable assumes a specified value attribute. Figure 7-25 illustrates a frequency distribution created by using the `Partition` function.

CountOfEmployee_Number	Dollars
158	: 499
183	500: 5499
49	5500: 10499
43	10500: 15499
31	15500: 20499
34	20500: 25499
36	25500: 30499
22	30500: 35499
23	35500: 40499
13	40500: 45499
19	45500: 50499
15	50500: 55499
17	55500: 60499
10	60500: 65499
5	65500: 70499
4	70500: 75499
6	75500: 80499
1	80500: 85499
4	100001:

Figure 7-25   This frequency distribution was created by using the `Partition` function.

ABOUT THE PARTITION FUNCTION

Partition(Number, Range Start, Range Stop, Interval)
   The Partition **function identifies the range that a specific number falls into, indicating where the number occurs in a calculated series of ranges. The** Partition **function requires the following four arguments:**

- Number **(required). This is the number you are evaluating. In a query environment, you typically use the name of a field to specify that you are evaluating all the row values of that field.**

- Range Start **(required). This is a whole number that is to be the start of the overall range of numbers. Note that this number cannot be less than zero.**

- Range Stop **(required). This is a whole number that is to be the end of the overall range of numbers. Note that this number cannot be equal to or less than the** Range Start.

- Interval **(required). This is a whole number that is to be the span of each range in the series from** Range Start **to** Range Stop. **Note that this number cannot be less than one.**

With this frequency distribution, you are clustering employees by the range of revenue dollars they fall in. For instance, 183 employees fall into the 500:5999 grouping, meaning that 183 employees earn between 500 and 5,999 revenue dollars per employee. Although several ways exist to get the results you see here, the easiest way to build a frequency distribution is to use the Partition function.

To create the frequency distribution you saw in Figure 7-25, build the query shown in Figure 7-26. As you can see in this query, you are using a Partition function to specify that you want to evaluate the Revenue field, start the series range at 500, end the series range at 100,000, and set the range intervals to 5,000.

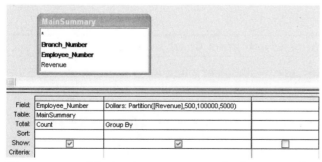

Figure 7-26   This simple query creates the frequency distribution you see in Figure 7-25.

You can also create a frequency distribution by group by adding a Group By field to your query. Figure 7-27 demonstrates this by adding the Branch_Number field.

Figure 7-28 shows the resulting dataset that contains a separate frequency distribution for each branch, detailing the count of employees in each revenue distribution range.

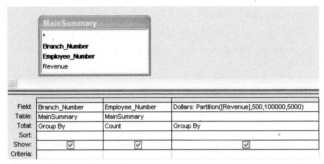

Figure 7-27 This query creates a separate frequency distribution for each branch number in your dataset.

Branch_Number	CountOfEmployee_Number	Dollars
490260	6	: 499
490260	5	500: 5499
490260	3	5500: 10499
490260	2	10500: 15499
490260	3	15500: 20499
490260	1	20500: 25499
490360	1	: 499
490360	1	25500: 30499
490360	1	30500: 35499
490360	1	35500: 40499
490460	5	: 499
490460	5	500: 5499
490460	1	25500: 30499
490460	1	35500: 40499

Figure 7-28 You have successfully created multiple frequency distributions with one query.

Tricks of the Trade: Creating a Histogram Chart in Access

A *histogram chart* is a graphic representation of a frequency distribution. You can use these types of charts to easily pick out anomalies in a data collection.

TIP This trick involves using a PivotChart view to create a histogram chart. Chapter 8 discusses PivotTable and PivotChart views in detail.

Start your histogram chart by building the query shown in Figure 7-29.

Next, from the application menu, select View → PivotChart View. At this point, your screen should look like Figure 7-30.

Go up to the application menu again and select View → Field List. This activates the Chart Field List dialog box shown in Figure 7-31.

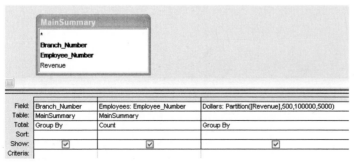

Field:	Branch_Number	Employees: Employee_Number	Dollars: Partition([Revenue],500,100000,5000)
Table:	MainSummary	MainSummary	
Total:	Group By	Count	Group By
Sort:			
Show:	☑	☑	☑
Criteria:			

Figure 7-29 Build a query using the `Partition` function to create a frequency distribution.

Figure 7-30 Switch to PivotChart view.

continues

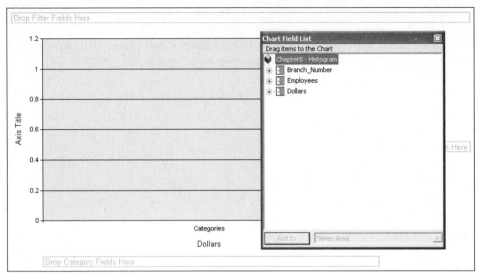

Figure 7-31   Activate the Chart Field List dialog box.

The idea is to drag your data fields into the appropriate areas of the PivotChart.

◆ **Employees.** The Employees field holds the data values in this dataset (the number of employees in each branch). Drag this field into the gray data area.

◆ **Dollars.** The Dollars field holds the ranges in your frequency distribution. This field needs to be on the X axis of the chart. Therefore, you need to drag this field to the "Drop Category Fields Here" area.

◆ **Branch_Number.** You will use the Branch_Number field as a filter to be able to parse out a specific branch. So, you need to drag the Branch_Number field to the "Drop Filter Fields" area.

Once you drag these three fields to the appropriate areas, your PivotChart should look similar to the one shown in Figure 7-32. You have successfully created a histogram chart.

As if that isn't impressive enough, remember you have given yourself the ability to filter by branch number. To filter out one branch, click the drop-down arrow next to the Branch_Number field, shown in Figure 7-33, and remove the check from the "All" checkbox.

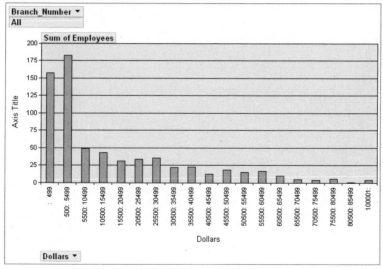

Figure 7-32   Your histogram chart is complete.

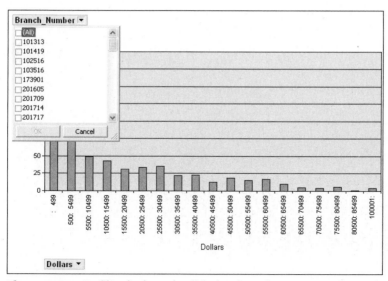

Figure 7-33   To filter by branch, click the drop-down arrow next to the Branch_Number field.

   Place a check in the checkbox for the branch you want to show and click OK. The PivotChart in Figure 7-34 presents the histogram chart for branch 301316.

continues

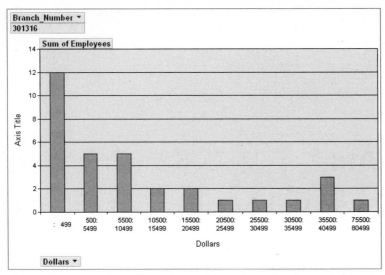

Figure 7-34 You have filtered out all branches, showing only branch 301316.

CHAPTER 8

Analyzing Data with Pivot Tables and Pivot Charts

A *pivot table* is a robust tool that helps you group data, summarize information, and perform a wide variety of calculations in a fraction of the time it takes by hand. The most impressive functionality of a pivot table is the ability to interactively change its content, shape data, and alter its overall utility. With pivot tables, you can drag and drop fields, dynamically change your perspective, recalculate totals to fit the current view, and interactively drill down to the detail records. In short, pivot tables enable you to customize your analysis on-the-fly without rewriting your query or turning to code. In this chapter, you learn how to leverage pivot tables and pivot charts in Access to enhance your analysis.

Working with Pivot Tables in Access

For years, pivot tables could only be found in Excel. The closest equivalent to this functionality in pre-2000 versions of Access was the traditional crosstab query, which didn't come close to the analytical power of pivot tables. The first attempts at an "Access pivot table" came with Access 2000, where users had the ability to embed an Excel pivot table report inside of a form. Unfortunately, this feature was a bit clunky and left users with an interface that felt clumsy at best. However, Office 2000 also introduced a promising new technology in the form of Office Web Components. Office Web Components enabled users to create interactive Web pages with functionality normally found only in Excel.

One of these components was the PivotTable component. Although this component did expose pivot table functionality to Access, the fact that it was limited for use only on Data Access Pages made it an impractical tool for day-to-day data analysis. With the release of Office XP, Microsoft gave Access users the ability to use the PivotTable component in both the Query and Form environments. This finally allowed for practical data analysis using pivot tables in Access.

Although this functionality remains one of the most significant new features of Access, it has received surprisingly little fanfare. So why should you get excited about pivot tables? From a data analysis point of view, this is one of the most powerful data-crunching tools found in Access today. Consider these capabilities:

- You can create multidimensional analyses that far surpass the limitations of traditional crosstab queries.

- You can interactively change your analysis without rewriting your query.

- You can dynamically sort, filter, group, and add custom calculations with a few clicks of the mouse.

- You have drill-down capabilities that allow you to collapse and expand analytical details without writing code.

- You can perform more of your analysis in Access instead of spending time exporting raw data back and forth to Excel.

In this chapter, you will come to know pivot tables and pivot charts, and you learn how leveraging these powerful tools can change the way you analyze your Access data.

The anatomy of a pivot table

Figure 8-1 shows an empty pivot table. As you can see, a pivot table is comprised of four areas. Because how you choose to utilize these areas defines both the utility and the appearance of your pivot table, it's important to understand the functionality of each area.

Figure 8-1   An empty pivot table in Access.

Totals and detail area

The *totals and detail area*, highlighted in Figure 8-2, is the area that calculates and supplies the details for your report. You can recognize this area by the words "Drop Totals or Detail Fields Here." This area tends to be confusing for first-time users because it has a dual role. First, it displays aggregate totals such as revenue sums, unit counts, and average prices. Second, it stores detailed row data that is exposed when the Row and Column fields are expanded.

Row area

The *row area*, highlighted in Figure 8-3, is the area that creates the headings down the left side of the pivot table. You can recognize this area by the words "Drop Row Fields Here." Dropping a field into the row area displays each unique value in that field down the left side of the pivot table. The types of data fields that you would drop here would be things you would want to group and categorize—for example, locations, customer names, and products.

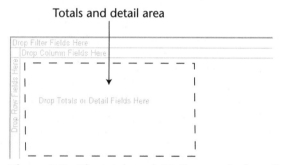

Figure 8-2   The totals and detail area calculates fields and stores record details.

Figure 8-3   The row area displays values down the left side of the pivot table.

Column area

The *column area*, highlighted in Figure 8-4, makes up the headings that span across the top of the pivot table. You can recognize this area by the words "Drop Column Fields Here." Dropping a field into the column area displays each unique value in the field in a column-oriented perspective. The column area is ideal for showing trends over time. Some examples of fields you would drop here would be Months, Periods, and Years.

Filter area

The *filter area*, highlighted in Figure 8-5, allows for dynamic filtering of your pivot table based on a value in a field. You can recognize this area by the words "Drop Filter Fields Here." The fields dropped here would be things you would want to isolate and focus on, such as locations, employee names, and products.

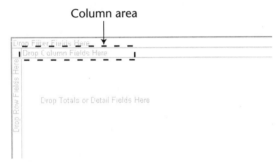

Column area

Figure 8-4   The column area displays values across the top of the pivot table.

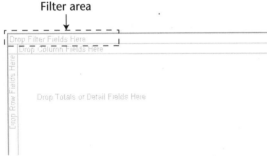

Filter area

Figure 8-5   The filter area enables you to filter the data in your pivot table.

Creating a basic pivot table

To create a basic pivot table, first build the query you see in Figure 8-6, and then select View → PivotTable View.

At this point, you will see an empty pivot table, shown in Figure 8-7, and a list of fields that are in your dataset.

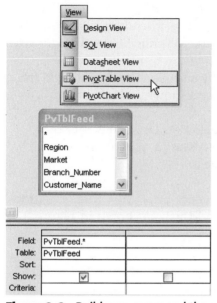

Figure 8-6   Build your query and then switch to PivotTable view.

Figure 8-7   Use the field list to build your pivot table.

The idea is to drag the fields you need into the pivot table's drop areas. How do you know which field goes where? To answer this question, consider two things: what are you measuring, and how do you want it presented? The answer to the first question will tell you which fields in your data source you will need to work with, and the answer to the second question will tell you where to place the fields. For example, if you want to measure the amount of revenue by region, you automatically know that you will need to work with the Revenue field and the Region field. In addition, you want regions to go down the left side of the report and revenues to be calculated for each region. Therefore, you know that the Region field will go into the row area and the Revenue field will go into the detail area.

Now that you know what you need, start by selecting the Region field from your field list and dragging it to the row area, as shown in Figure 8-8.

TIP If you accidentally close out your PivotTable Field List, simply right-click inside the pivot table and select Field List to reactivate it. You can also select Field List on the PivotTable toolbar to reactivate it.

Next, select the Revenue field, and then select Data Area from the drop-down box at the bottom of the PivotTable field list, as shown in Figure 8-9. Click the Add to button.

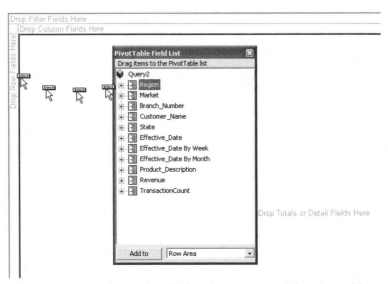

Figure 8-8   Drag the Region field to the row area of the pivot table.

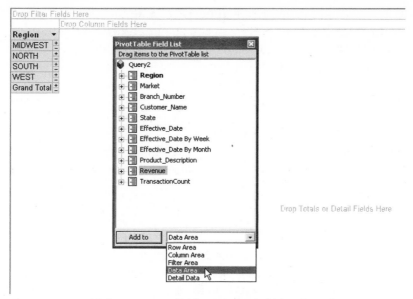

Figure 8-9   Add the Revenue field using the field list drop-down.

NOTE   Why not just drag the Revenue field to the detail area? The reason is that the Pivot Table Web Component requires that you view detail data before you add totals. So, if you simply drag the Revenue field to the data area, the pivot table will not display the sum of revenue; instead, it would display the detailed revenue for each record in your dataset.

Keep in mind that in order to use the method shown in Figure 8-9, the field you are adding must be a numeric or currency field.

At this point, your pivot table should look like the one shown in Figure 8-10.

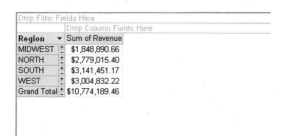

Figure 8-10   You have created your first pivot table report!

You can add some dimension to this report by dragging the Product_ Description field to the column area. As you can see in Figure 8-11, you now have a cross tabular view of revenue by region and product.

Drop Filter Fields Here				
Product_Description ▼				
	Cleaning & Housekeeping Services	Facility Maintenance and Repair	Fleet Maintenance	Green Plants and Foliage Care
	+ –	+ –	+ –	+ –
Region ▼	Sum of Revenue	Sum of Revenue	Sum of Revenue	Sum of Revenue
MIDWEST ±	$174,518.08	$463,078.85	$448,800.61	$93,560.99
NORTH ±	$534,284.19	$606,748.65	$610,791.49	$155,020.39
SOUTH ±	$283,170.17	$846,508.06	$1,046,229.86	$157,820.88
WEST ±	$146,623.34	$444,825.85	$521,976.06	$870,388.29
Grand Total ±	$1,138,595.78	$2,361,161.41	$2,627,798.02	$1,276,790.55

Figure 8-11   Drag the Product_Description field to the column area of the pivot table.

Now add the Market field to the row area and drag the Region field to the filter area (the area that reads "Drop Filter Fields Here"). Your pivot table should look like the one shown in Figure 8-12. With just a few mouse clicks, you not only have a totally new perspective on the same data, but you can now filter by region.

TIP   If you need to remove a field from your pivot table, an alternative to dragging it off is to right-click the field name and select Remove.

Region ▼				
All				
	Product_Description ▼			
	Cleaning & Housekeeping Services	Facility Maintenance and Repair	Fleet Maintenance	Green Plants and Foliage Care
	+ –	+ –	+ –	+ –
Market ▼	Sum of Revenue	Sum of Revenue	Sum of Revenue	Sum of Revenue
BUFFALO ±	$66,844.23	$69,568.80	$86,461.34	$34,830.18
CALIFORNIA ±	$37,401.55	$281,203.86	$337,224.62	$830,422.28
CANADA ±		$294,258.33	$273,175.05	$15,965.46
CHARLOTTE ±	$170,341.83	$223,346.86	$245,119.74	$46,483.15
DALLAS ±	$18,807.34	$136,844.19	$156,152.05	$16,082.87
DENVER ±	$12,563.96	$160,325.12	$170,188.42	$42,407.50
FLORIDA ±	$20,448.86	$410,039.45	$556,003.84	$85,133.63
KANSASCITY ±	$65,439.45	$132,119.42	$133,170.10	$35,315.29
MICHIGAN ±	$243,451.28	$65,079.56	$66,408.19	$80,175.55
NEWORLEANS ±	$73,572.13	$76,277.55	$88,954.24	$10,121.23
NEWYORK ±	$223,988.68	$177,841.95	$184,746.91	$24,049.20
PHOENIX ±	$96,685.78	$125,522.50	$150,788.58	$28,986.31
SEATTLE ±	$12,536.02	$38,099.49	$33,962.86	$10,979.70
TULSA ±	$96,514.67	$170,634.31	$145,442.10	$15,838.20
Grand Total ±	$1,138,595.78	$2,361,161.41	$2,627,798.02	$1,276,790.55

Figure 8-12   Adding the Market field and dragging the Region field to the filter area enables you to analyze market revenue for a specific region.

A WORD ABOUT DRAGGING FIELDS FROM ONE AREA TO ANOTHER

When you are dragging your fields from one area of a pivot table to another, it's sometimes difficult to discern which area your cursor is in. A few trips in the wrong direction can place your field in the wrong area.

The key to telling which area you are hovering over is to watch the blue area of the cursor.

Creating an advanced pivot table with details

This section demonstrates how you can incorporate record details into your pivot table, effectively building an analysis that can drill down to the record level.

To begin, create the pivot table shown in Figure 8-13 by performing the following steps:

1. Build the query you see in Figure 8-6, and then select View → Pivot-Table View.

2. Drag the Market and Product_Description fields to the row area of the pivot table.

3. Select the Revenue field, then select Data Area from the drop-down box at the bottom of the PivotTable field and click the Add to button.

Market	Product_Description	Sum of Revenue
⊟ BUFFALO	Cleaning & Housekeeping Services	$66,844.23
	Facility Maintenance and Repair	$69,568.80
	Fleet Maintenance	$86,461.34
	Green Plants and Foliage Care	$34,830.18
	Landscaping/Grounds Care	$65,464.84
	Predictive Maintenance/Preventative Maintenance	$127,309.32
	Total	$450,478.72
⊟ CALIFORNIA	Cleaning & Housekeeping Services	$37,401.55
	Facility Maintenance and Repair	$281,203.86
	Fleet Maintenance	$337,224.62
	Green Plants and Foliage Care	$830,422.28
	Landscaping/Grounds Care	$248,343.46
	Predictive Maintenance/Preventative Maintenance	$520,155.87
	Total	$2,254,751.64
⊟ CANADA	Facility Maintenance and Repair	$294,258.33
	Fleet Maintenance	$273,175.05
	Green Plants and Foliage Care	$15,965.46
	Landscaping/Grounds Care	$76,751.57
	Predictive Maintenance/Preventative Maintenance	$116,097.37
	Total	$776,247.78
⊟ CHARLOTTE	Cleaning & Housekeeping Services	$170,341.83
	Facility Maintenance and Repair	$223,346.86
	Fleet Maintenance	$245,119.74
	Green Plants and Foliage Care	$46,483.15
	Landscaping/Grounds Care	$80,239.54

Figure 8-13 Build the pivot table shown here.

Take a moment and look at what you have so far. You've created a basic analysis that reveals the amount of revenue by product for each market. Now you can enhance this analysis by adding customer details to the pivot table. This allows you to drill into a product segment and view all the customers that make up that product's revenue.

4. Select the Customer_Name field, then select Detail Area from the drop-down box at the bottom of the PivotTable field and click the Add to button.

5. Select the Effective_Date field, then select Detail Area from the drop-down box at the bottom of the PivotTable field and click the Add to button.

6. Select the Revenue field, then select Detail Area from the drop-down box at the bottom of the PivotTable field and click the Add to button.

At this point, it looks as though your pivot table hasn't changed. However, if you click the plus sign next to any one of the product segments, you will see the customer details for every customer that contributed to that segment's total revenue (see Figure 8-14).

TIP You can drill into all details at one time by right-clicking the field names and selecting Show Details. Conversely, you can hide the details by selecting Hide Details. You also have the option of selecting Show Details and Hide Details on the PivotTable toolbar.

Market	Product_Description	Customer_Name	Effective_Date	Revenue
⊟ BUFFALO	Cleaning & Housekeeping Services	▶ BAUDUS Corp.	1/13/2004	$5,417.95
		CUNUME Corp.	1/19/2004	$3,750.89
		FSULLA Corp.	6/9/2004	$1,250.30
		GOSBOR Corp.	1/7/2004	$3,750.89
		KUYSTU Corp.	1/20/2004	$3,750.89
		LATREB Corp.	1/5/2004	$6,668.24
		LATRUN Corp.	2/2/2004	$2,083.83
		PPGAND Corp.	1/29/2004	$3,750.89
		SPUCAA Corp.	1/8/2004	$10,835.90
		VARGAN Corp.	1/8/2004	$3,750.89
		VUUDUS Corp.	1/12/2004	$5,417.95
		LUXANG Corp.	1/19/2004	$6,668.85
		PRUUUC Corp.	9/27/2004	$1,025.98
		SUNUCA Corp.	1/14/2004	$2,564.94
		THEHAL Corp.	1/21/2004	$3,077.93
		Sum of Revenue		$66,844.23
	Facility Maintenance and Repair	Sum of Revenue		$69,568.80
	Fleet Maintenance	Sum of Revenue		$86,461.34
	Green Plants and Foliage Care	Sum of Revenue		$34,830.18
	Landscaping/Grounds Care	Sum of Revenue		$65,464.84
	Predictive Maintenance/Preventative Maintenance	Sum of Revenue		$127,309.32
	Total	Sum of Revenue		$450,478.72

Figure 8-14 You now have the ability to drill down into the details that make up your revenue totals.

WARNING Incorporating record details into your pivot tables is a technique that should be limited to smaller datasets. Because the PivotTable component opens a separate ADO recordset for each cell it contains, accessing a large amount of details through your pivot table can lead to performance issues. If you absolutely need to view all row and column details for a large dataset, you should consider using a query or form.

Setting the PivotTable view as the default view

It's important to remember that when you are building your analysis with a pivot table, you are actually working with a query in a "PivotTable view." Therefore, when you save your analysis, it will save as a query. You will notice that the next time you open the query it will open in Datasheet view. This doesn't mean your pivot table is lost. Just switch back to PivotTable view to see your pivot table.

If you want your query to run in PivotTable view by default, just change the Default View property of the query. To do this, open your query in Design view and select View → Properties. This activates the Query Properties dialog box shown in Figure 8-15. Change the Default View property to PivotTable View. The next time you open your query, it will open in PivotTable view.

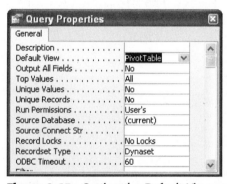

Figure 8-15 Setting the Default View property of your query to PivotTable view ensures that each time you open your query it will open in a PivotTable view.

Tricks of the Trade: Sending Your Pivot Table Analysis to Excel

Want to export your pivot table to Excel? You can easily send your analysis to Excel by hitting Ctrl+E on your keyboard when you are in PivotTable view. This will send your pivot table and the raw data to an Excel HTM document. You can save the document as an Excel XLS document if you like. In addition to the data, any formatting you applied to the pivot table in Access persists in Excel.

continues

You can also send your analysis to Excel by selecting PivotTable → Export to Microsoft Excel.

WARNING If the dataset used to create the pivot table contains more than 65,536 rows of data, the export will fail. That being said, a general rule of thumb is that PivotTable views ideally are used with datasets that have already been massaged down to a manageable size.

Pivot table options

You will often find that you need to tweak your pivot tables to get the result you're looking for. This section covers some of the pivot table options you can adjust to enhance your analysis. To prepare for the examples in this section, create the pivot table shown in Figure 8-16 by performing the following steps:

1. Build the query from Figure 8-6, and then select View → PivotTable View.

2. Drag the Region, Market, and Customer Name fields to the row area of the pivot table.

3. Select the Revenue field, then select Data Area from the drop-down box at the bottom of the PivotTable field and click the Add to button.

4. Select the TransactionCount field, then select Data Area from the drop-down box at the bottom of the PivotTable field and click the Add to button.

Region ▾	Market ▾	Customer_Name ▾	Sum of Revenue	Sum of TransactionCount
⊟ MIDWEST	⊟ DENVER	ADOMSC Corp.	$1,190.30	6
		ADVANC Corp.	$1,709.64	12
		ALLAAN Corp.	$625.25	4
		ALLFAN Corp.	$448.02	4
		ALPANE Corp.	$4,578.26	25
		ALUXAN Corp.	$1,139.76	8
		AMPRUT Corp.	$448.02	4
		AMPUST Corp.	$5,592.04	30
		AMUSYS Corp.	$937.88	6
		ANAQAE Corp.	$1,172.20	8
		ANATUD Corp.	$4,644.84	24
		ANCLEM Corp.	$716.28	6
		ANDALU Corp.	$997.29	7
		ANDART Corp.	$2,421.99	17
		ANDUQU Corp.	$1,318.73	9
		ANDUSS Corp.	$448.02	4
		ANFANA Corp.	$434.06	4
		ANGUSS Corp.	$1,318.73	9
		ANITU Corp.	$434.06	4

Figure 8-16 Build the pivot table shown here.

Expanding and collapsing fields

It's always difficult to perform an effective analysis on a large volume of data. So when you are analyzing a large amount of data in a pivot table such as the one shown in Figure 8-16, it's helpful to see small chunks of data at a time.

Access enables you to expand or collapse details easily by clicking the plus and minus signs shown in the pivot tables. You can also expand or collapse all values in a field at once. For example, right-click the Market field and select Collapse. As you can see in Figure 8-17, all the customer details for each market are now hidden, which makes this pivot table easier to read. Now you can analyze the customer detail for one market at a time by clicking the plus sign for that market.

Changing field captions

Access often attempts to name aggregated fields with its own name such as "Sum of TransactionCount." You can imagine how titles like this can be confusing to the consumer. You can customize your field captions by changing the Caption property of the field.

To demonstrate this, right-click the Sum of TransactionCount field heading and select Properties. This activates the Properties dialog box shown in Figure 8-18. Click the Captions tab and enter **Count of Transactions** in the Caption input box. Close the dialog box and your changes will immediately take effect.

Region	Market	Customer_Name	Sum of Revenue	Sum of TransactionCount
⊟ MIDWEST	⊞ DENVER		$645,584.10	4231
	⊞ KANSASCITY		$574,899.15	3784
	⊞ TULSA		$628,407.41	4417
	Total		$1,848,890.66	12432
⊟ NORTH	⊞ BUFFALO		$450,478.72	2625
	⊞ CANADA		$776,247.78	4981
	⊞ MICHIGAN		$678,708.11	3689
	⊞ NEWYORK		$873,580.79	4808
	Total		$2,779,015.40	16103
⊟ SOUTH	⊞ CHARLOTTE		$890,514.49	5389
	⊞ DALLAS		$467,086.11	3392
	⊞ FLORIDA		$1,450,397.76	11486
	⊞ NEWORLEANS		$333,452.80	1920
	Total		$3,141,451.17	22187
⊟ WEST	⊞ CALIFORNIA		$2,254,751.64	13617
	⊞ PHOENIX		$570,254.17	3222
	⊞ SEATTLE		$179,826.42	1053
	Total		$3,004,832.22	17892
Grand Total			$10,774,189.46	68614

Figure 8-17   Collapsing fields makes your pivot tables easier to read.

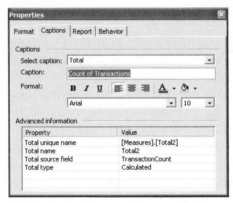

Figure 8-18   You can change a field's name by setting the Caption property of the field.

Sorting data

By default, pivot tables are initially sorted in ascending order. However, you may prefer to present your data in an order that makes more sense in your situation. To change the sort order of a particular field or aggregation, simply right-click the chosen field or aggregation and select Sort Ascending or Sort Descending.

Grouping data

A particularly useful feature in pivot tables is the ability to create a new layer of analysis by grouping and summarizing unrelated data items. Imagine that you need to group the products shown in Figure 8-19 into two segments: outside services and inside services. "Green Plants and Foliage Care" and "Landscaping/ Grounds Care" need to be classified as "Outside Services" whereas the rest would be considered "Inside Services."

To accomplish this task, hold down the Ctrl key and select both "Green Plants and Foliage Care" and "Landscaping/Grounds Care." Then right-click and select Group Items, as shown in Figure 8-20.

Drop Filter Fields Here	
	Drop Column Fields Here
Product_Description ▾	Sum of Revenue
Cleaning & Housekeeping Services	$1,138,595.78
Facility Maintenance and Repair	$2,361,161.41
Fleet Maintenance	$2,627,798.02
Green Plants and Foliage Care	$1,276,790.55
Landscaping/Grounds Care	$1,190,911.60
Predictive Maintenance/Preventative Maintenance	$2,178,932.11
Grand Total	$10,774,189.46

Figure 8-19   You need to group these products into two groups.

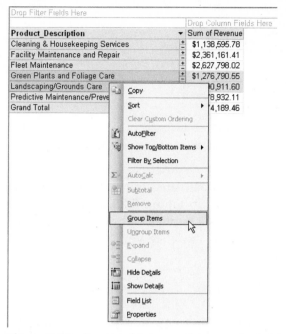

Figure 8-20   You need to group these products into two groups.

At this point, your pivot table should look similar to the one shown in Figure 8-21. As you can see, you have essentially created a new field with two data items: Group1 and Other. All that is left to do now is to change the captions on these newly created objects to reflect their true meaning.

Figure 8-22 illustrates what the final report with a new Product Segment field should look like.

Product_Description1 ▾	Product_Description		Sum of Revenue
⊟ Group1	Green Plants and Foliage Care	±	$1,276,790.55
	Landscaping/Grounds Care	±	$1,190,911.60
	Total	±	$2,467,702.15
⊟ Other	Cleaning & Housekeeping Services	±	$1,138,595.78
	Facility Maintenance and Repair	±	$2,361,161.41
	Fleet Maintenance	±	$2,627,798.02
	Predictive Maintenance/Preventative Maintenance	±	$2,178,932.11
	Total	±	$8,306,487.31
Grand Total		±	$10,774,189.46

Figure 8-21   You've successfully grouped two of your product descriptions into their own segment.

Drop Filter Fields Here		
		Drop Column Fields Here
Product Segment ▾	**Product_Description**	**Sum of Revenue**
⊟ Outside Services	Green Plants and Foliage Care	$1,276,790.55
	Landscaping/Grounds Care	$1,190,911.60
	Total	$2,467,702.15
⊟ Inside Services	Cleaning & Housekeeping Services	$1,138,595.78
	Facility Maintenance and Repair	$2,361,161.41
	Fleet Maintenance	$2,627,798.02
	Predictive Maintenance/Preventative Maintenance	$2,178,932.11
	Total	$8,306,487.31
Grand Total		$10,774,189.46

Figure 8-22   In just a few clicks, you have added another layer to your analysis.

One last note about grouping data. If you activate your field list and drill into the Product_Description field, as shown in Figure 8-23, you will notice that your newly created grouping is listed as a subfield. This means you can treat this field as any other in your field list. To delete your grouping, right-click its entry in the field list and select Delete.

Using date groupings

Notice that in Figure 8-24 you see a field called Effective_Date and directly underneath that field you see "Effective_Date by Week" and "Effective_Date by Month." Unlike Excel where you would have to explicitly create date groupings, Access automatically creates these groupings for any field that is formatted as a date field.

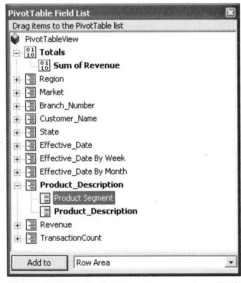

Figure 8-23   To delete your grouping, find it in the PivotTable Field List, right-click it, and then click Delete.

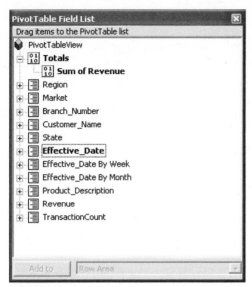

Figure 8-24 Access automatically creates date groupings for any field that is formatted as a date field.

Figure 8-25 illustrates how these date groupings are readily available to be dragged onto your pivot table just as you would any other field.

NOTE One drawback to using the Access-provided date groupings is that you can't separate them. For instance, you cannot drag the Year grouping into the column area and then drag the Month grouping into the row area.

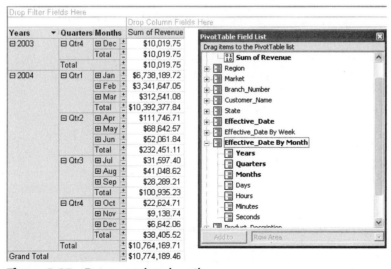

Figure 8-25 Date groupings in action.

Filtering for top and bottom records

You can filter your pivot table to show the top or bottom Nth records with just a few clicks of the mouse. In the example illustrated in Figure 8-26, you have a list of customers and want to limit the list to the top 10 customers by sum of revenue. Right-clicking the Customer_Name field heading exposes a shortcut menu where you would select Show Top/Bottom Items → Show Only the Top → 10.

As you can see in Figure 8-26, the filtering options also include the ability to filter by percent of records. You can remove the applied filter by right-clicking the field heading and selecting AutoFilter.

TIP You can actually use two methods to remove an applied filter from a field:

Method 1: Right-click the field heading and select AutoFilter.

Method 2: Right-click the field heading and select Show Top/Bottom Items, and then select Show All.

Method 1 has an added advantage in that it allows you to reapply the last known filter to the field at any time by right-clicking the field heading and selecting AutoFilter. Method 2, on the other hand, clears the filter settings altogether.

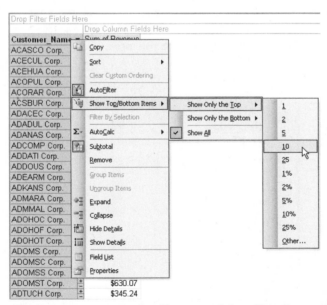

Figure 8-26 An example of how easy it is to filter the top 10 customers.

Adding a calculated total

Once you create a pivot table, you may find it useful to expand your analysis by performing calculations on summary totals. To demonstrate this, create the pivot table shown in Figure 8-27. This analysis calculates total revenue and total count of transactions. Upon reviewing these results, you determine that you need to get an average dollar per transaction.

Select PivotTable → Calculated Totals and Fields → Create Calculated Total. This sets off two events. First, a new field called New Total appears in your pivot table, as shown in Figure 8-28. Second, the Properties dialog box for this field activates.

Market	Sum of Revenue	Sum of TransactionCount
BUFFALO	$450,478.72	2625
CALIFORNIA	$2,254,751.64	13617
CANADA	$776,247.78	4981
CHARLOTTE	$890,514.49	5389
DALLAS	$467,086.11	3392
DENVER	$645,584.10	4231
FLORIDA	$1,450,397.76	11486
KANSASCITY	$574,899.15	3784
MICHIGAN	$678,708.11	3689
NEWORLEANS	$333,452.80	1920
NEWYORK	$873,580.79	4808
PHOENIX	$570,254.17	3222
SEATTLE	$179,826.42	1053
TULSA	$628,407.41	4417
Grand Total	$10,774,189.46	68614

Figure 8-27 You need to calculate the average dollar per transaction for each market.

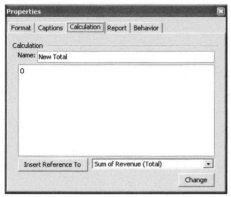

Figure 8-28 Adding a new calculated total creates a new field in your pivot table.

The idea here is to enter the calculation you need into the dialog box, as follows:

1. Enter **Dollars per Transaction** into the Name input box.

2. Delete the 0 from the large input box below Name.

3. Select Sum of Revenue (Total) from the drop-down and click the Insert Reference To button.

4. Type a forward slash (/) to indicate division.

5. Select Sum of TransactionCount (Total) from the drop-down and click the Insert Reference To button.

At this point, your dialog box should look similar to Figure 8-29.

6. Click the Change button.

7. Go to the Format Tab and select Currency from the Number input box.

As you can see in Figure 8-30, your new calculation looks and acts like any other Totals field in your pivot table.

To adjust the calculation behind your calculated total, right-click the field heading and select Properties. This opens the Properties dialog box where you can change the calculation in the Calculation tab.

To delete your calculated total, right-click its entry in the field list, shown in Figure 8-31, and select Delete.

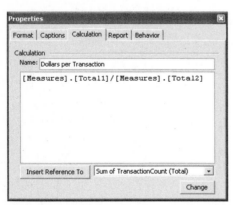

Figure 8-29   Your dialog box should look like this.

Market ▼	Dollars per Transaction	Sum of Revenue	Sum of TransactionCount
BUFFALO	$171.61	$450,478.72	2625
CALIFORNIA	$165.58	$2,254,751.64	13617
CANADA	$155.84	$776,247.78	4981
CHARLOTTE	$165.25	$890,514.49	5389
DALLAS	$137.70	$467,086.11	3392
DENVER	$152.58	$645,584.10	4231
FLORIDA	$126.28	$1,450,397.76	11486
KANSASCITY	$151.93	$574,899.15	3784
MICHIGAN	$183.98	$678,708.11	3689
NEWORLEANS	$173.67	$333,452.80	1920
NEWYORK	$181.69	$873,580.79	4808
PHOENIX	$176.99	$570,254.17	3222
SEATTLE	$170.78	$179,826.42	1053
TULSA	$142.27	$628,407.41	4417
Grand Total	$157.03	$10,774,189.46	68614

Drop Filter Fields Here
Drop Column Fields Here

Figure 8-30 You have enhanced your analysis with a calculated total.

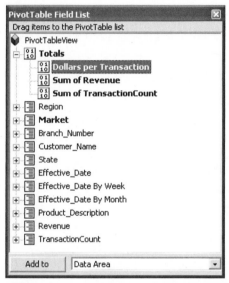

Figure 8-31 To delete your calculated total, find it in the PivotTable Field List, right-click it, and then click Delete.

NOTE You can also create a calculated detail field using the same steps just illustrated. However, it's generally a better idea to perform calculations on details in a query as opposed to a pivot table. This way, the Microsoft Jet database performs the calculation instead of the PivotTable component, making your PivotTable view perform better.

Working with Pivot Charts in Access

A *pivot chart* is essentially a pivot table in chart form. Once you learn the basics of using a pivot table, a pivot chart will feel quite intuitive. There are, however, slight differences in the anatomy of a pivot chart.

The anatomy of a pivot chart

Figure 8-32 shows an empty pivot chart where you can see four distinct areas. Just as in pivot tables, how you choose to utilize these areas defines both the utility and the appearance of your pivot chart.

Data area

The *data area*, highlighted in Figure 8-33, is the area that calculates and supplies the data points for your chart. You can recognize this area by the words "Drop Data Fields Here."

Series area

The *series area*, highlighted in Figure 8-34, is the area that makes up the Y axis of your chart. You can recognize this area by the words "Drop Series Fields Here." This area corresponds to the column area of a pivot table. In other words, if you create a pivot table and switch to PivotChart view, the fields in the column area of the pivot table will become the Y axis series.

Figure 8-32   An empty pivot chart in Access.

Data area

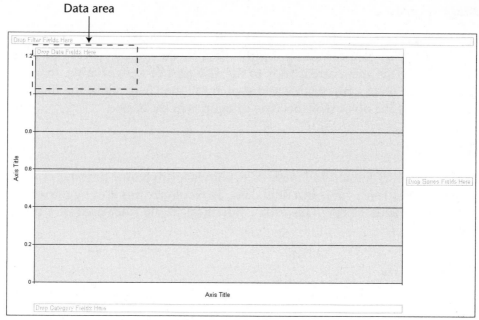

Figure 8-33   The data area supplies the data points for your chart.

Series area

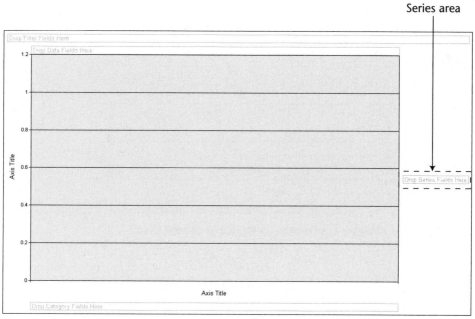

Figure 8-34   The series area makes up the Y axis of your chart.

Category area

The *category area*, highlighted in Figure 8-35, is the area that makes up the X axis of your chart. You can recognize this area by the words "Drop Category Fields Here." This area corresponds to the row area of a pivot table. In other words, if you create a pivot table and switch to PivotChart view, the fields in the row area of the pivot table become categories in the X axis.

Filter area

The *filter area*, highlighted in Figure 8-36, allows for dynamic filtering of your pivot chart based on a value in a field. You can recognize this area by the words "Drop Filter Fields Here." This area is identical to the filter area of a pivot table.

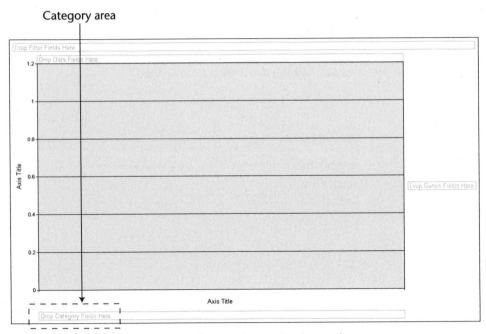

Figure 8-35 The category area makes up the X axis of your chart.

Filter area

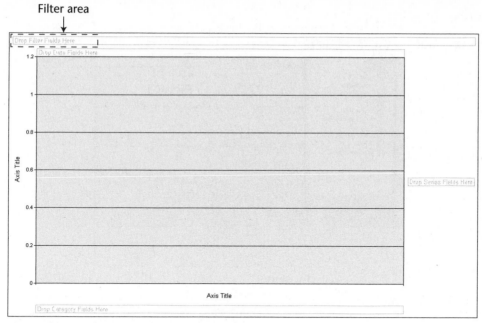

Figure 8-36   The filter area enables you to filter your pivot chart.

Creating a basic pivot chart

To create a pivot chart, first build the query you see in Figure 8-37, and then select View → PivotChart View.

At this point, you will see an empty pivot chart, as shown in Figure 8-38, and a list of fields that are in your dataset.

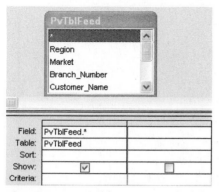

Figure 8-37   Build your query and then switch to PivotChart view.

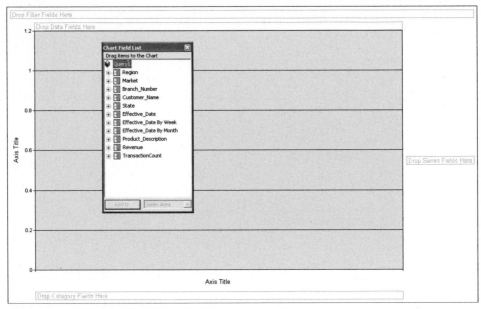

Figure 8-38 Use the field list to build your pivot table.

Just as in a pivot table, the idea is to drag the fields you need into the pivot chart's drop areas. Build a basic chart by dragging the Revenue field to the data area, then the Market field to the category area. Finally drag the Region field to the filter area. Your completed chart should look like the one illustrated in Figure 8-39.

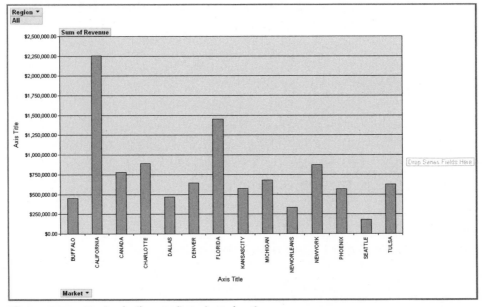

Figure 8-39 You've built your first pivot chart!

Formatting your pivot chart

The key to formatting a pivot chart in Access is to remember that everything revolves around property settings. Each object on the chart has its own properties that can be adjusted. To demonstrate this, right-click your pivot chart, select Properties, which activates the Properties dialog box shown in Figure 8-40, and then select the General tab.

The idea is here is to select the object with which you want to work in order to expose the adjustable properties. For example, if you want to add labels to your series, select Series from the Select drop-down list, as demonstrated in Figure 8-41.

Figure 8-40   Select the General tab of the pivot chart's Properties dialog box.

Figure 8-41   Selecting the Series object exposes its modifiable properties.

With the Series properties exposed, you can tailor its properties to suit your needs. In Figure 8-42, you are adding data labels to your pivot chart.

Of course, data labels have properties that can be modified as well. Go back to the General tab of the Properties dialog box and select the series data labels you just added. As you can see in Figure 8-43, the Select drop-down list has been updated to include Series Data Labels 1.

Twenty minutes of experimenting with each object's properties will give you a solid level of proficiency at formatting pivot charts in Access.

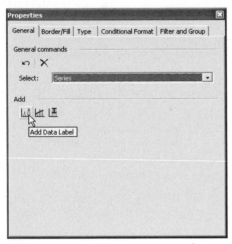

Figure 8-42   Adding data labels to your pivot chart.

Figure 8-43   The Select drop-down list is updated every time you add a new object to your chart.

Automating
Data Analysis

Scheduling and Running Batch Analysis

In the realm of Microsoft Access, the term "automation" actually has two meanings. First, it's used to describe the computerization of a process where Access self-regulates a procedure based on predetermined requirements you supply. It is also used to define the means of manipulating another application's objects with the use of Access Visual Basic for Applications (VBA). In the context of this book, the term automation involves the former.

Access provides you with two key methods of automating your analytical processes: macros and VBA. This chapter focuses on using macros to automate your processes and run batch analysis on your data. Why should you care? Well, leveraging macro functionality is not just a cool way to use Access, it offers the following advantages:

- **Higher productivity.** Just because you have the skills to analyze data in Access doesn't mean you have the time. With automation, you can have Access carry out redundant analyses and recurring analytical processes, leaving you free to work on other tasks.

- **Quality control.** Human beings make mistakes. The more you touch a set of analyses, the greater the chance there is for errors. Automation takes humans (you) out of the equation.

- **Reproducibility.** There's an old quip among data analysts: "It's okay to produce the wrong answer, as long as you produce the same wrong answer consistently." Although you obviously don't want to produce a wrong answer, the point is you want to be able to reproduce the analysis you have established. If your answer changes from one analysis to the next, you'll find yourself wondering whether you've done something differently. Automating your analytical processes will ensure that Access executes your analyses in the same way every time.

Introduction to Access Macros

Access macros are very different from Excel macros. In Excel, macros are used as a way to record actions that can be played back when needed. Excel macros are analogous to programming a phone to dial a specific telephone number when you hit a special key. In Access, however, macros are used to execute a set of pre-programmed functions, much like a list of menu options on your TV that can be fired when selected. These pre-programmed functions are called *actions*. The idea behind building a macro in Access is to choose a set of actions you want the macro to carry out when it is executed. Figure 9-1 illustrates an Access macro that carries out three actions when run.

Again, none of the actions shown in Figure 9-1 were recorded by the user. They are all actions that came pre-packaged for use in a macro.

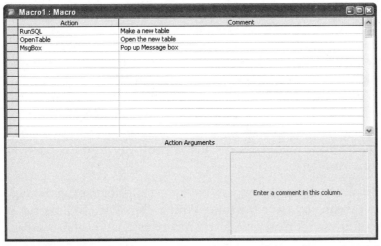

Figure 9-1   This macro runs a SQL statement that makes a new table, opens the new table, and throws up a message box.

Creating your first macro

To get a solid understanding of how an Access macro works, try creating the macro in Figure 9-1.

Start by initializing a new macro. To do this, click Macro in the Database window, and then click New (see Figure 9-2).

This activates the Macro window shown in Figure 9-3. As you can see, this is essentially a grid with two columns (Action and Comment) and many rows. The idea is to fill each row with an action selected from the drop-down box in the Action column.

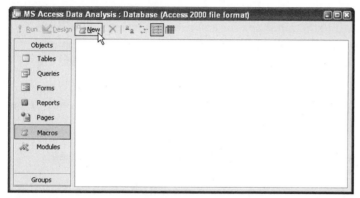

Figure 9-2   Start a new macro.

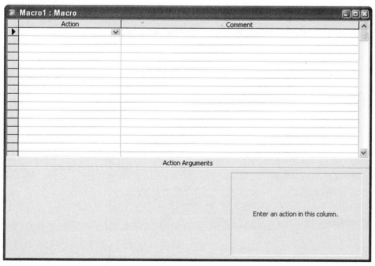

Figure 9-3   The Macro window is essentially a grid where each row defines a specified action to carry out.

The first action you want to run is a RunSQL action, so select RunSQL from the Action drop-down box. Once you select your action, you will see some new input boxes in the gray area underneath the grid. These new input boxes are called *action arguments*. Every action comes with a unique set of arguments that you can tailor to fit your needs. As you can see in Figure 9-4, the RunSQL action requires two arguments: SQL Statement and Use Transaction.

Click inside the SQL Statement input and enter **SELECT Customer_Number INTO MyTable FROM CustomerMaster**. This action runs a make-table query in order to make a new table called MyTable. In addition, enter a comment about this action in the Comment column. Although this is optional, it is generally a good practice to add comments for documentation.

TIP When you click inside the input box for an action argument, you will see some quick tips for that argument in blue lettering in the lower-right corner of the Macro window. In addition, pressing F1 on your keyboard while inside the input box brings up a help file pertaining to that argument.

Add the OpenTable action and enter **MyTable** in the Table Name input, as shown in Figure 9-5. This action opens the MyTable table.

NOTE Although there is no table called MyTable currently in the database, there will be once the RunSQL action runs. In the meantime, the macro doesn't care that there is no table called MyTable and will save with no problem. This illustrates the fact that, unlike VBA modules, macros don't compile to identify unrecognized objects or other errors.

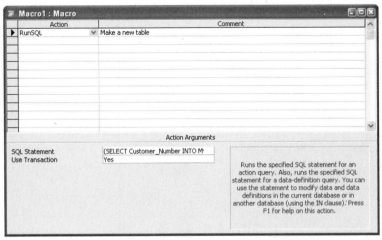

Figure 9-4   Add the RunSQL action and specify its arguments.

Add the `MsgBox` action and enter **Table has been created** in the Message input, as shown in Figure 9-6. This action activates a message box.

At this point, you are ready to save your macro by selecting File → Save. Access will prompt you to give your new macro a name. Once you name your macro, it will be saved in the Macros collection in your Database window. To run it, simply double-click it. If you built your macro correctly, it should paste 9253 records into a new table called MyTable, and then open the table and throw up a message box that reads "Table has been created."

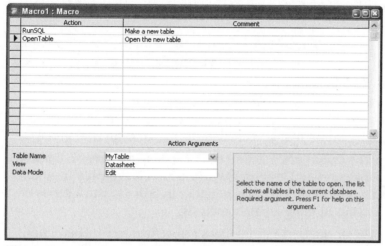

Figure 9-5   Add the `OpenTable` action and specify its arguments.

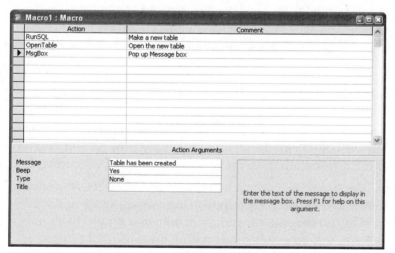

Figure 9-6   Add the `MsgBox` action and specify its arguments.

Essential macro actions

Access has more than 50 macro actions, covering a wide range of functionalities. Trying to determine which macro actions benefit the automation of your data analysis can be overwhelming. A set of 18 macro actions, however, is ideal for automating your analytical processes. When trying to familiarize yourself with the macro actions that are available to you, the actions in this section should be first on your list.

Actions that manipulate forms, queries, reports, and tables

- **Close.** The Close action closes a specified form, query, report, or table. This is useful when you want to ensure that a particular object is closed before running a process.

- **DeleteObject.** The DeleteObject action deletes a specified form, query, report, or table. This action comes in handy when you need to delete temporary tables that you created during an analytical process.

- **OpenQuery.** The OpenQuery action runs a specified query or, if indicated, opens the query in Design view. The action is typically used to string multiple OpenQuery actions together in order to run a series of queries, effectively running a batch analysis.

- **OpenForm.** The OpenForm action opens a specified form. This action can be used to open a form that supplies the values needed for your analytical process.

- **OpenReport** and **OpenTable.** The OpenReport and OpenTable actions allow you to open a specified report and table, respectively. These are useful for presenting a final result after your batch analysis.

Actions that affect the Access environment

- **Quit.** The Quit action closes the entire Access application. This action comes in handy when you are running a scheduled process and you want to close the application once the macro has finished executing.

- **SetWarnings.** The SetWarnings action forces an OK or Yes response to all system messages, effectively suppressing message pop-ups while a macro runs. Without the SetWarnings action, you would have to be there to click Yes or OK on every confirmation message that popped up while your macro was running.

Actions that control the execution of processes

- **RunCode.** The `RunCode` action executes an existing VBA function. This action is ideal when you need to initialize a procedure that can only be accomplished with VBA, such as automating Excel.

- **RunMacro.** The `RunMacro` action executes another macro. This action can be used in a conditional macro where the resulting decision requires that another macro be executed.

- **RunSQL.** The `RunSQL` action executes a valid SQL string. Bear in mind that only `Insert`, `Delete`, `Select...Into`, or `Update` statements are valid in the macro environment. This action comes in handy when you need to run action queries, but you don't want to inundate your database with superfluous query objects.

- **StopMacro.** The `StopMacro` stops the current macro. You can use this action in a conditional macro where the resulting decision indicates no further processing is needed.

Actions that export or output data

- **PrintOut.** The `PrintOut` action prints the active datasheet, form, or report. This action is ideal for ensuring that a hardcopy of analytical results is produced.

- **OutputTo.** The `OutputTo` action outputs a table, query, form, or report to an external document. Output options include outputting to Excel, Word, HTML, or text. Note that this action is memory intensive and does not work well with very large datasets.

- **TransferDatabase.** The `TransferDatabase` action exports and imports data to and from an external database. This action is ideal for backing up your database to an external location. You can even schedule nightly backups of your data using this macro action.

- **TransferSpreadsheet** and **TransferText.** The `TransferSpreadsheet` and `TransferText` actions export and import data to and from external spreadsheets and text files, respectively. These actions are equivalent to the Export menu option in Access, saving the data into a file.

- **SendObject.** The `SendObject` action outputs an object to an Excel, text, or HTML file, then attaches that file to an email message that can be sent to specified address with additional text. This action works with any 32-bit email program that conforms to Mail Application Programming Interface (MAPI) standards.

Setting Up and Managing Batch Analysis

An analytical process involves a series of queries that run in a logical order, giving you the needed set of analyses. A batch analysis is nothing more than automating the execution of one or more of your analytical processes. In this section, you learn how to set up and manage your own automated batch analysis.

Getting organized

Creating a batch analysis is as simple as defining which queries and actions you need to run. This involves pointing your macro to specific objects. However, if your database is inundated with temporary queries and tables, or queries that have no logical name or order, it becomes difficult to determine which object does what, let alone point a macro to the right set of objects. That being said, there are a few things you can do to ensure that you keep your database organized.

Using a logical naming convention

The long-standing guideline on using naming conventions in Access is that you preface each type of object in your database with a prefix describing that object. For example, an appropriate name for a query would be *qryMonthlyRevenue*, a table could be called *tblCustomers*, and a form could be named *frmMain*.

What you are about to read will be considered blasphemy in many Access circles, but the fact is that this is not always the best naming convention you can use.

The database in Figure 9-7 is a good example. This database contains 15 queries that make up two separate analytical processes. As you can see, it's difficult to determine which query belongs to which process.

Adding "qry" to each query, as shown in Figure 9-8, doesn't help much in this situation.

So, what do you do? In a database that is used primarily for data analysis, the best way to organize your queries is to take advantage of the fact that the default sort order is alphabetical. Preface your query names with text describing the analysis followed by a logical numbering system. For example, instead of AppendCredits, you could use PSmry_2A_AppendCredits. Figure 9-9 demonstrates this naming convention. Keep in mind that there is nothing special about the prefix "PSmry"; it is simply a description that allows for easy recognition of the analyses that have to do with creating the period summary.

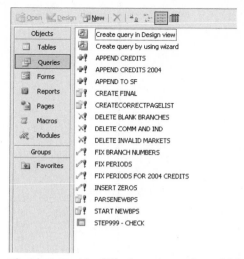

Figure 9-7   It's difficult to determine which query belongs to which analytical process.

Figure 9-8   Prefixing each query with "qry" does not clear things up at all.

NOTE Note the use of the underscore in place of spaces. It's generally a good practice not to use spaces in your object names in order to avoid complications when writing SQL strings or using VBA code.

You should also make your object names "camel case," meaning that the first letter of each word is capitalized. This makes your object names easier to read. Figure 9-10 demonstrates this naming convention.

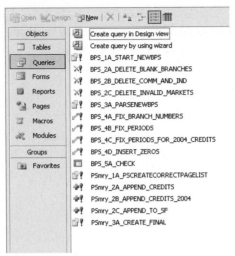

Figure 9-9 With this naming convention, you can not only distinguish between the two analyses, but you can see the correct order in which each query should be run.

Figure 9-10 Using "camel case" makes your object names easier to read.

Using the Description property

Each object has a Description property that you use to describe the object in detail. To adjust an object's Description property, right-click the object and select Properties. This activates a properties dialog box for that object, as shown in Figure 9-11. You can use up to 250 characters to describe the object.

Change your database view to Details view by going up to the application menu and selecting View → Details. This shows you a series of details to include the description you entered. Figure 9-12 shows a database in Details view.

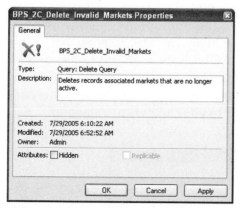

Figure 9-11 Use the Description property to describe the object in detail.

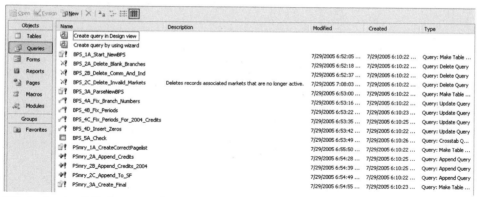

Figure 9-12 Switch to Details view to see the description you added.

Grouping database objects

Access has a built-in grouping functionality that allows you to create a group of shortcuts to related database objects. As you can see in Figure 9-13, the Groups section comes with a default Favorites group.

The idea is create a new group and assign objects to it. To demonstrate this, go up to the application toolbar and select Edit → Groups → New Group. This opens the New Group dialog box, as shown in Figure 9-14, where you can specify a name for your new group.

Now you can simply drag all the queries that are related to Chapter 8 into the new Chapter8 group. After you drag the appropriate queries into the group, open it by clicking it. As you can see in Figure 9-15, you now have a set of shortcuts inside the group. You can work with these shortcuts just as you would with the objects themselves, opening them, designing them, and so on.

Figure 9-16 illustrates that you can create several groups that are analysis-specific, giving you an organized structure to your analytical databases.

Click Groups to see the grouped database objects

Figure 9-13 Use Groups to help organize related database objects.

Figure 9-14 Start a new group called Chapter8.

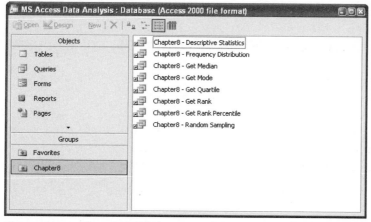

Figure 9-15   The grouped shortcuts allow you to work with them just as you would with the objects themselves.

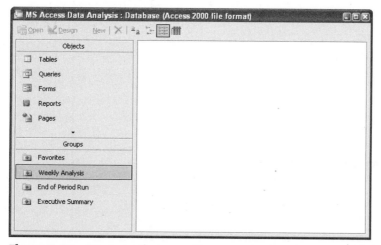

Figure 9-16   Create analysis-specific groups to organize your analytics.

Setting up a basic batch analysis

Setting up a basic batch analysis involves little more than creating a macro that executes a set of analytical processes in a logical order conducive to your analysis. For example, the database in Figure 9-17 is used to run three queries that work together to accomplish a set of analytics.

The macro being built in Figure 9-18 starts with a SetWarnings action to ensure that no system messages interrupt the process. From, here, it's simply a question of adding the queries that need to be executed in order.

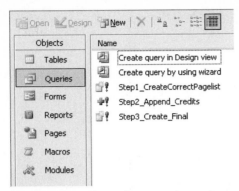

Figure 9-17 These three queries make up a simple analytical process.

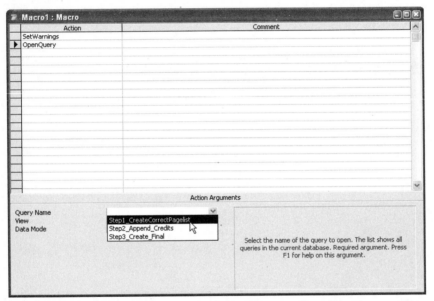

Figure 9-18 Building a macro to automate the execution of the three queries.

TIP Instead of selecting queries from the argument dropdown as shown in Figure 9-18, you can drag your queries and into the Macro window. This automatically enters an OpenQuery action for that query.

After all queries are added, a second SetWarnings action is called to reinstate system messages, and then a Msgbox is thrown up to indicate completion of the macro. The completed macro, shown in Figure 9-19, is then saved and run as a batch analysis.

You can even create a macro that runs multiple batch analyses at once. The "Big 5 Analysis" macro, shown in Figure 9-20, runs five macros, each of which executes its own batch analysis.

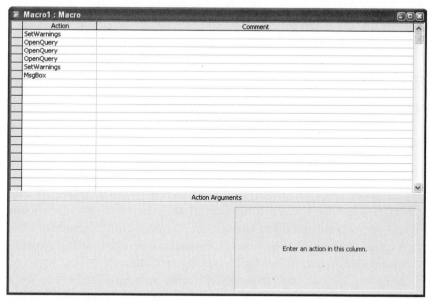

Figure 9-19   When completed and saved, the macro can be run anytime as a batch analysis.

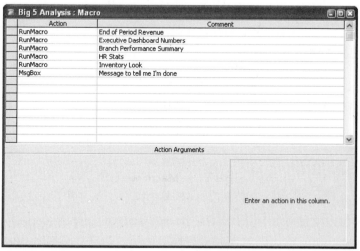

Figure 9-20   You can create a master macro to run all your batch analyses at once.

Building smarter macros

Did you know that you can use `If...Then...Else` statements through a macro? Well, not exactly, but you can simulate that decision-making functionality by building conditions into your macros. A *condition* is a logical expression that is evaluated in order to return a True or False answer. With conditions, you simulate an `If...Then` scenario or even an `If...Then...Else` scenario.

Simulating If...Then

To demonstrate how to build a basic `If...Then` scenario, write a simple macro that analyzes a number entered into an input box and then makes a decision based on that number. Start by building the macro shown in Figure 9-21. Note that the Message argument for the `MsgBox` action is "That number is over 10."

Now go up to the application menu and select View → Conditions. At this point, your Macro window should look similar to the one shown in Figure 9-22. As you can see, a column called Condition has been unhidden. The idea is to enter an expression here that will evaluate as True or False. If the expression evaluates as True, the action next to it will be executed.

Enter the following expression: **InputBox("Enter any number")>10**. Your Macro window should look similar to the one shown in Figure 9-23. This expression activates an input box and asks you to enter a number. The number you enter is then evaluated to determine if it is greater than 10. If the number you enter is greater than 10, the expression returns a True answer, otherwise, it returns a False answer.

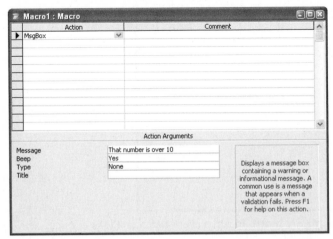

Figure 9-21 Start a new macro with one `MsgBox` action.

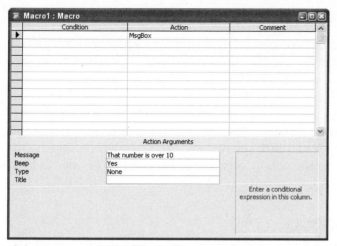

Figure 9-22   The Condition column is hidden by default until you explicitly unhide it.

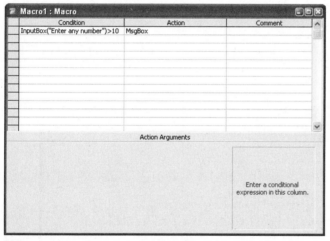

Figure 9-23   This expression evaluates the number you enter to determine if it is greater than 10.

NOTE The `InputBox` function enables you to get information from a user. You can think of it as a `MsgBox` in reverse. A `MsgBox` function outputs information, whereas an `InputBox` inputs information.

Close the macro and save it as **Macro1**. When you run the macro, you see the input box shown in Figure 9-24. If you enter a number less than or equal to 10, nothing happens. If you enter a number greater than 10, a message pops up telling you your number is greater than 10.

Simulating If...Then...Else

You can expand the scope of your conditions by adding If...Then...Else
functionality. To demonstrate this, create a new macro and unhide the Condition
column. Then, enter the following condition in the first row: **InputBox("Guess
How Many Locations There are")=DCount("[Branch_Number]","[Location
Master]")**.

With this condition, you are comparing the user's input to the number of
records in the LocationMaster table. If the two are equal, the expression evaluates as True. Select Beep as the action, and your Macro window should look
similar to Figure 9-25.

Figure 9-24   Running the macro activates an input box where you enter your chosen
number.

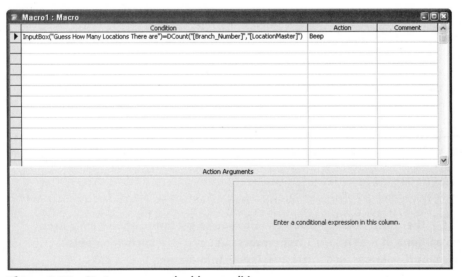

Figure 9-25   Start a macro and add a condition.

On the next two lines, enter three periods (also called an "ellipsis") as the condition. Any macro action that has an ellipsis as the condition will be run only if the preceding condition evaluated as True; otherwise, those actions will be skipped.

Select the MsgBox action and then select the StopMacro action. Note that the Message argument for MsgBox is "That's Right". At this point, your Macro window should look similar to the one shown in Figure 9-26.

On the next line, select the MsgBox action and enter **"The Answer is 59"** in the Message argument. On the line below that, select the RunMacro action and enter **"ConditionalMacro"** as the Macro Name argument. At this point, your Macro window should look similar to the one shown in Figure 9-27. Notice that there is no ellipsis in the condition inputs of the newly added actions. This is because you don't want these actions to run if the correct answer was selected.

Go up to the application menu and select File → Save. When asked to name your macro, be sure to name it **ConditionalMacro**.

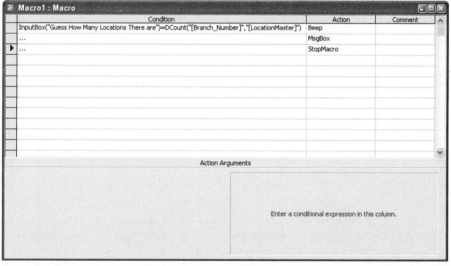

Figure 9-26 Using an ellipsis in the Condition inputs tells the macros to execute the action on that line only if the condition in the preceding line is True.

Now look at the macro in Figure 9-27 and take a moment to consider what happens when you run it:

1. It gives you an input box where you guess how many locations there are. It then compares your answer to the real record count from the LocationMaster table. As you can see, this essentially gives you the `If...Then...Else` effect. *If* your answer matches the actual record count, *then* the macro performs steps 2 and 3; *Else*, the macro skips to step 4.

2. If your macro goes to step 2, it means you got the answer right. A message box is thrown up to tell you so.

3. The macro stops.

4. If your macro goes directly to step 4, it means you got the answer wrong. A message box is thrown up to tell you the correct answer.

5. The macro is run again to give you another chance.

You have successfully built a macro that executes actions based on a condition. Beyond that, however, this example also demonstrates a functionality that adds even more value to macros: looping.

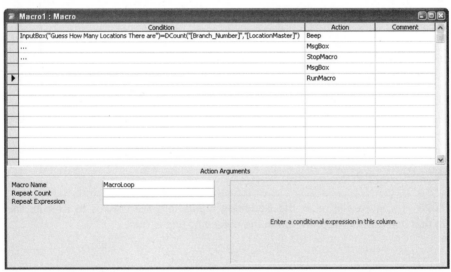

Figure 9-27 Notice that you are not using the ellipsis in the Condition inputs for your newly added actions. This means that these actions will only be run if you did not enter the correct answer in the input box.

Looping with macros

First, your trustworthy author has to confess that the phrase "looping with macros" is admittedly a tad misleading. *Looping* implies that the macro's actions are continuously being run in the same instance of execution. What is really happening is that the macro is being started repeatedly until a condition is met. However, the fact that you can simulate looping behavior through macros does open up some interesting possibilities if you are not yet comfortable with VBA.

To demonstrate the concept of a looping macro, imagine that you have been asked to provide a list of the top 10 customers by market at the end of every month. Instead of running a top values query for each market by hand every month, you decide to use macros to automate the process. For this particular scenario, you will need four queries and two macros.

> **TIP** You can find a working version of the example illustrated here in the sample database for this book (www.wiley.com/go/AccessData Analysis). Refer to the sample database if you run into problems.

1. Create the make-table query shown in Figure 9-28. Name the table being created **TopTenList**. Running this query creates an empty table that will eventually contain the final results. Be sure to save this query as **TopTen_Step1**.

> **NOTE** Run the query you created in step 1 at least one time. You will need the table it creates for step 3.

2. Create the make-table query shown in Figure 9-29. Name the table being created **LoopList**. Running this query creates a list of unique market names that will be used to loop through. Be sure to save this query as **TopTen_Step2**.

Field:	Region	Market: " "	CustomerName: " "	Revenue: 0
Table:	LocationMaster			
Sort:				
Show:	☐	☑	☑	☑
Criteria:	"0"			
or:				

Figure 9-28 Save this make-table query as TopTen_Step1.

NOTE Run the query you created in step 2 at least one time. You will need the table it creates for step 4.

3. Create the append query shown in Figure 9-30. You will append to the TopTenList table you created in step 1. Note that the Top Values property has been set to 10 in order to return only the top 10 values. Also note the criteria under Market. This criteria ensures that only one market is included in the query: the one whose first letter is closest to the letter A. Be sure to save this query as **TopTen_Step3**.

Figure 9-29   Save this make-table query as TopTen_Step2.

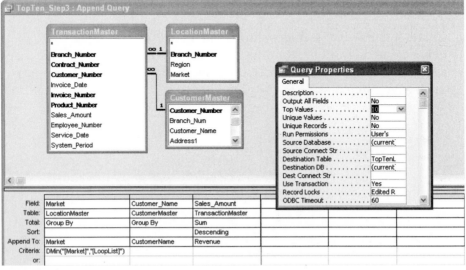

Figure 9-30   Save this append query as TopTen_Step3.

4. Create the delete query shown in Figure 9-31. Running this query deletes the market whose first letter is closest to the letter A from the LoopList. This ensures that the market can never again be used in the TopTen_Step3 query. If you ran this query 14 times, you would eventually run out of markets. Be sure to save this query as **TopTen_Step4**.

5. Start a new macro and add the following actions:

   - **SetWarnings.** Set the Warnings No argument to No.
   - **OpenQuery.** Set the Query Name argument to TopTen_Step1.
   - **OpenQuery.** Set the Query Name argument to TopTen_Step2.
   - **RunMacro.** Set the Macro Name argument to TopTenB_Child.
   - **SetWarnings.** Set the Warnings No argument to Yes.

   At this point, your Macro window should look similar to the one shown in Figure 9-32. This macro does the setup work, creating the tables necessary for the looping action. Once the tables are created, it calls the child macro, TopTenB_Child. Be sure to save this query as **TopTenA_Parent**.

Figure 9-31   Save this delete query as TopTen_Step4.

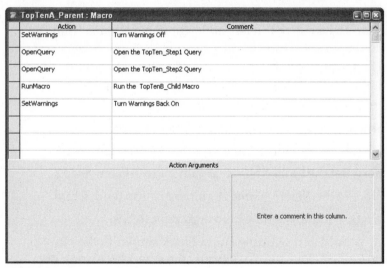

Figure 9-32 Save this macro as TopTenA_Parent.

6. Start a new macro and add the following actions:

- **Beep.** Set the Condition to DCount("[Market]","[LoopList]")>0. This condition specifies that the record count of the LoopList table must be greater than zero in order to continue with the actions that have the ellipsis condition.

- **SetWarnings.** Give this action an ellipsis condition. Set the Warnings No argument to No.

- **OpenQuery.** Give this action an ellipsis condition. Set the Query Name argument to TopTen_Step3.

- **OpenQuery.** Give this action an ellipsis condition. Set the Query Name argument to TopTen_Step4.

- **RunMacro.** Give this action an ellipsis condition. Set the Macro Name argument to TopTenB_Child. This action starts the macro over. The idea is that this macro will repeatedly start over until the condition in the first line of the macro is false.

- **DeleteObject.** This is the first action that runs when the condition in the first line of the macro is false. Set the ObjectType argument to Table and the Object Name argument to LoopList. This action deletes the LoopList table because it is no longer needed.

- **SetWarnings.** Set the Warnings No argument to Yes.

- **MsgBox.** Set the Message argument to "Top Ten Customers by Market can now be found in the TopTenList table."

- **StopAllMacros.** This action is used as a clean sweep to ensure no rogue macro actions are still executing and that all system warnings are turned back on.

When you are done, your Macro window should look similar to the one shown in Figure 9-33. Be sure to save this query as **TopTenB_Child**.

7. There is nothing left to do but run the macro. Double-click the TopTenA_Parent macro to start the loop. After the macro is done, you will get a message telling you that you can find your results in the TopTenList table. Open the table to see the results.

You may be thinking that this is a lot of work. However, remember that you are not only performing some hefty analytics on 14 markets with a click of the mouse, but now that this process is built, you can run it whenever you need to.

TIP Instead of using the OpenQuery action in your macro, which requires that you create a query object, you can use a SQL statement in a RunSQL action. This can help you cut back on the number of superfluous queries in your database.

Keep in mind that the SQL statements used in RunSQL actions cannot be more than 256 characters in length.

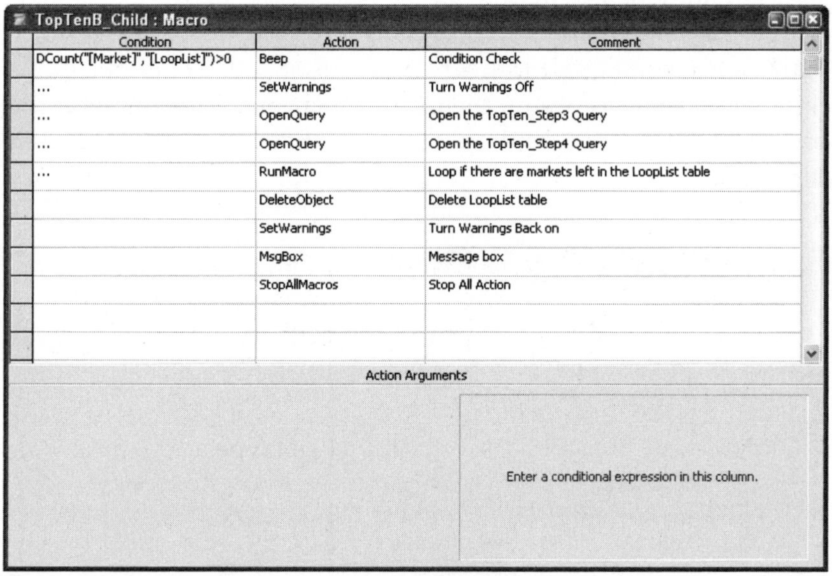

Condition	Action	Comment
DCount("[Market]","[LoopList]")>0	Beep	Condition Check
...	SetWarnings	Turn Warnings Off
...	OpenQuery	Open the TopTen_Step3 Query
...	OpenQuery	Open the TopTen_Step4 Query
...	RunMacro	Loop if there are markets left in the LoopList table
	DeleteObject	Delete LoopList table
	SetWarnings	Turn Warnings Back on
	MsgBox	Message box
	StopAllMacros	Stop All Action

TopTenB_Child : Macro

Action Arguments

Enter a conditional expression in this column.

Figure 9-33 Save this macro as TopTenB_Child.

Scheduling Macros to Run Nightly

Although automating a process to run with a click of the mouse is impressive, the ultimate in automation is not even being there. How many times have you heard someone say, "Yeah, I just run a nightly routine" while you nod your head and pretend to know what that means. Meanwhile, you're trudging into work at 5 A.M. to make sure you have the reports ready by 8 A.M. The good news is that there is an easy way to schedule your macros to run every night, every Monday, on the fifteenth of every month, or whenever you like.

Unfortunately, as of Office 2003, Access does not yet have an internal macro scheduler. Until the time it does, you can use the Windows Task Scheduler to schedule a macro to run at specific times. The question is, how do you tell Access which macro to run through a completely unrelated program (Windows Task Scheduler)? You have two options: use an AutoExec macro or use a command-line switch.

Using an AutoExec macro to schedule tasks

If you name a macro AutoExec, that macro will be run automatically when your database is opened. How does that help you? The idea is to create a macro that contains your batch analysis and save it as AutoExec. When the Windows Task Scheduler opens your database at 3:00 a.m., the AutoExec automatically executes your batch analysis.

To demonstrate this, create the macro shown in Figure 9-34. The `MsgBox` action with Message argument set to read "A bunch of actions are executed" will represent a batch analysis. Using the `Quit` action makes certain that the database closes once the macro completes execution. Save your newly created macro as **AutoExec**.

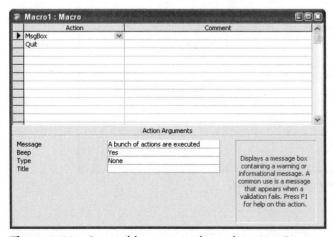

Figure 9-34   Create this macro and save it as AutoExec.

TIP If you need to run multiple batch analyses, you can create a "master" macro that runs other macros, and then save it as AutoExec.

Once you save your macro as AutoExec, close the database to test it. When you open your database again, you should see the message box you entered into the AutoExec; then the database closes. Now you are ready to schedule your newly created macro with the Windows Task Scheduler.

TIP How do you get back into your database? Simply hold down the Shift key while you open the database. This prevents the AutoExec macro from running.

You may be tempted to remove the Quit action from your macro, but keep in mind that during a nightly routine, you want the database to close automatically. Removing the Quit action causes the database to stay open.

Using the Windows Task Scheduler

Open the Windows Control Panel by clicking the Start button, selecting Setting, and then Control Panel. Once you are in Control Panel, double-click the Scheduled Tasks icon, shown in Figure 9-35.

Once you are in the Scheduled Tasks folder, double-click the Add Scheduled Task icon to activate the Scheduled Task Wizard shown in Figure 9-36, and then click Next.

The next window, shown in Figure 9-37, asks you to select the program you would like to run. Select Microsoft Access from the program list and click the Next button.

At this point, you will see the window shown in Figure 9-38, where you will name your scheduled task and specify when you want the task to be performed. In this example, the task will be performed daily.

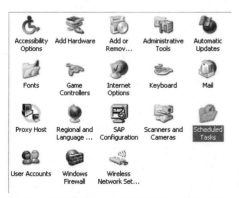

Figure 9-35 Double-click Scheduled Tasks.

Figure 9-36   Activate the Scheduled Task Wizard and click the Next button.

Figure 9-37   Select Microsoft Access from the program list and click Next.

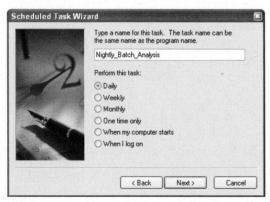

Figure 9-38   Specify when you want the task to be performed and click Next.

In the next window, you will set up the time and interval for the task. In the example illustrated in Figure 9-39, the task will be performed at 3:00 a.m. every day, starting on July 31, 2005.

TIP Spend some time playing with the controls here. You will quickly realize that you have a wide array of options when scheduling a task.

In the next window, shown in Figure 9-40, you will have to enter the user ID and password you use to log in. This is important, because the scheduled task will not run without it.

WARNING The Windows Task Scheduler does not keep track of expired or changed passwords. You will have to reconfigure your task if you change your password.

Figure 9-39   Indicate the time and interval you want the task to be performed and click Next.

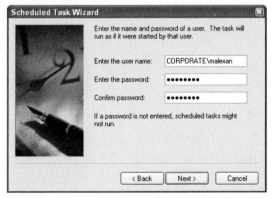

Figure 9-40   Enter your security information and click Next.

Once you get to Figure 9-41, you're almost done. Place a check in the checkbox next to "Open advanced properties for this task when I click Finish."

TIP **If you accidentally click Finish before placing a check in the advanced properties checkbox, you can get back to the advanced properties by simply right-clicking your task and selecting Properties.**

The last step is to click the Browse button, shown in Figure 9-42, and point the Scheduler to the database that contains the AutoExec macro.

NOTE **Be sure to change the Files of Type setting to "All Files (*.*)" in the Browse dialog box.**

Figure 9-41 Place a check in the advanced properties checkbox and click Finish.

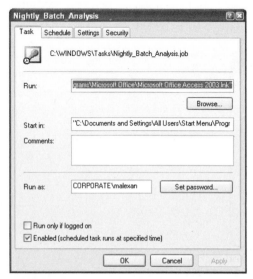

Figure 9-42 Click the Browse button and point the Scheduler to your database.

Now you can test the task to make sure it runs properly by right-clicking its name and selecting Run, as demonstrated in Figure 9-43.

Your task is now scheduled! One thing to keep in mind is that the PC on which the task is scheduled obviously must stay on. Also, based on your PC's configuration, you must be logged in for the task to run. That is to say that if you log out, the task may not run. A workaround to this problem is to lock the workstation, which effectively keeps your user ID logged in without compromising security.

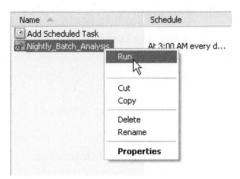

Figure 9-43 Be sure to test your task to make sure it runs properly.

Using command lines to schedule tasks

Command lines are nothing more than commands you can pass to your Access database to modify its startup process. In other words, you can tell Access to do something on startup. For example, the following command line tells the DB1 database to open exclusively and fire the STATS macro:

```
"C:\Program Files\Microsoft Office\Office\msaccess.exe"
"C:\Data\DB1.mdb"/Excl/X STATS
```

A command line is made up of three basic parts:

- The path to the msaccess.exe

  ```
  "C:\Program Files\Microsoft Office\Office\msaccess.exe"
  "C:\Data\DB1.mdb"/Excl/X STATS
  ```

- The path of the affected database

  ```
  "C:\Program Files\Microsoft Office\Office\msaccess.exe"
  "C:\Data\DB1.mdb"/Excl/X STATS
  ```

- The command-line switch(es) being used

  ```
  "C:\Program Files\Microsoft Office\Office\msaccess.exe"
  "C:\Data\DB1.mdb"/Excl/X STATS
  ```

In this example, the /Excl switch tells the database to open exclusively. The /X STATS switch tells the database to run the STATS macro upon opening.

> **NOTE** Here's a quick list of the more useful command-line switches:
>
> - /excl **opens the specified database exclusively.**
> - /ro **opens the specified database as read-only.**
> - /user **starts Access by using the specified user name.**
> - /pwd **starts Access by using the specified password.**
> - /profile **starts Access by using the options in the specified user profile.**
> - /compact **compacts and repairs the specified database.**
> - /X MacroName **starts the specified database and runs the specified macro.**
> - /wrkgrp **starts Access by using the specified workgroup information.**

When to use command lines to schedule tasks instead of AutoExec

Microsoft recommends that you use an AutoExec macro in lieu of command-line switches. However, in some situations a command line makes more sense. Consider the following when deciding which method to use to schedule your batch analysis:

- **AutoExec affects the startup of your database every time you open it.** You already know that holding the Shift key while you open the database bypasses the AutoExec macro. However, working with a database where you constantly have to remember to hold down the Shift key can be quite annoying. In contrast, a command-line switch does not become part of the database. This means you can fire it whenever you like. If you regularly work in the same database used to run scheduled tasks, consider using command lines.

- **Each macro can have its own schedule.** The problem with combining all your analytical processes into one AutoExec macro is that you run them *all* when you run AutoExec. If you want to schedule some of your analyses to run on Monday while others run on Wednesday, you'll have to create another database with a separate AutoExec macro. Command lines, on the other hand, allow you to have multiple macros run on different schedules without creating new databases. If you have multiple tasks that need to be scheduled at different time, consider using command lines.

Scheduling a macro to run using a command line

To schedule a task using a command line, follow the steps you performed in the section "Using the Windows Task Scheduler" (shown in Figures 9-35 to 9-42). In the advanced properties dialog box shown in Figure 9-42, enter the following in the Run input box:

- The path to msaccess.exe in quotes. In most cases it will be "C:\Program Files\Microsoft Office\OFFICExx\msaccess.exe," where xx is the version of Office.

- A space.

- The path to the database that contains the macro you want to run in quotes.

- The command-line switch for running a macro (/X MacroName).

The following is an example of a valid command-line switch:

```
"C:\Program Files\Microsoft Office\OFFICE11\msaccess.exe"
"C:\Data\MyDatabase.mdb"/X MyMacro
```

As you can see in Figure 9-44, to use this command line, you would simply enter it into the Run input box.

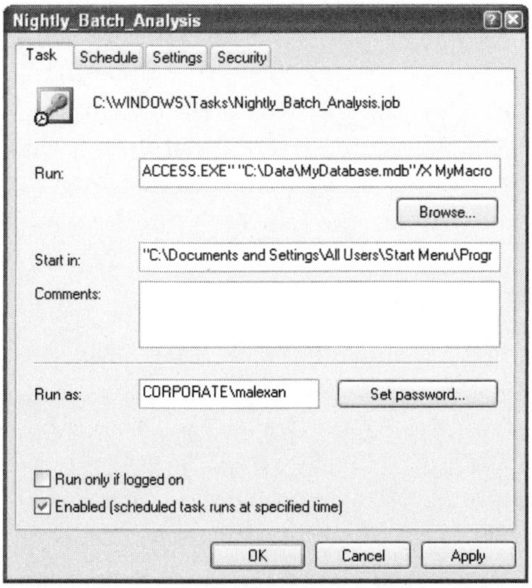

Figure 9-44 Simply enter the command line into the Run input box.

Your task is now scheduled!

TIP You can create a new shortcut on your desktop and use a command line as the target. This will enable you to run a macro from a shortcut, compact and repair your database from a shortcut, and so forth.

CHAPTER 10

Leveraging VBA to Enhance Data Analysis

Many Access users are not programmers, and it would be fair to say that most do not aspire to be programmers. In fact, you are probably just trying to survive the projects you are juggling now; who has the time to learn VBA?

If you are tempted to take a polite look at this chapter and then move on, you should definitely fight that urge. Why? Because leveraging VBA (Visual Basic for Applications) in your analytical processes can make your life easier in the long run. VBA can help you do things faster and more efficiently. In fact, just a few lines of code can save you hours of work, freeing you up to do other things, and increasing your productivity. Consider some of the advantages that VBA offers:

- VBA can help you automate redundant analyses and recurring analytical processes, leaving you free to work on other tasks.

- VBA allows you to process data without the need to create and maintain queries and macros.

- With VBA, you can automate external programs such as Excel to expand the reporting capabilities.

- With VBA, you can perform complex, multi-layered procedures that involve looping, record level testing, and `If...Then...ElseIf` statements.

- You can tailor your own error-handling procedures using VBA, allowing you to anticipate and plan for process flow changes in the event of an error.

This chapter covers some fundamental concepts and techniques that will lay the groundwork for your own ideas about how to enhance your analytical processes with VBA.

> **TIP** True to its purpose, all the techniques in this chapter involve writing some basic code. In order to keep this chapter focused on the data analysis aspect of these techniques, this chapter does not spend much time explaining the VBA behind them. If you are new to VBA, you may want to refer to Appendix B, "VBA Fundamentals," which gives you a firm understanding of the basic concepts used in this chapter.

Creating and Using Custom Functions

The developers at Microsoft have put in thousands of man-hours developing functions that are expansive enough to fit the needs of most users. In most cases, the functions available in Access more than satisfy user requirements. In fact, many users will never use a majority of the functions available, typically gravitating toward only those that fit their needs.

On the other end of the spectrum, there are those users whose daily operations involve tasks not covered by the functions in Access. These tasks can involve a business-specific calculation or a complex expression that achieves a particular result. In most cases, these tasks would be accomplished by building expressions. For example, suppose that your analysis routinely calls for the last day of the current week. Because no built-in function exists to help you determine the last day of the current week, you would use the following expression wherever you need this data:

```
Date() - WeekDay(Date()) + 7
```

The alternative to using such an expression is to build a custom function (sometimes referred to as a user-defined function). *Custom functions* are VBA procedures that expose your expressions to other objects in your database as a function, much like Access's built-in functions. This essentially means that instead of creating and using expressions in a query or form, you build your expressions into a VBA procedure, and then call it whenever you need it. Why bother with custom functions? Well, consider the following inherent advantages to converting your expressions into custom functions:

- Expressions, in and of themselves, generally perform operations that are simple and linear in nature. They don't allow for complex operations that involve looping or `If...Then...ElseIf` logic. Building a custom function gives you the flexibility to perform complex, multi-layered procedures that involve looping, record-level testing, and `If...Then...ElseIf` logic.

■ Expressions don't allow you to define explicitly what happens in the event of an error. Building a custom function in a VBA environment allows you to include error-handling procedures with your expressions, empowering you to anticipate and plan for process flow changes in the event of an error.

■ When you change the definition of an expression, you have to find and modify that expression in every place it is used. A custom function resides in one module; therefore, when there is a change in your expression or procedure, you have to update it in only one location.

■ There is an increased risk of error when you are forced to manually type expressions repeatedly. For example, the expression, `Date() - WeekDay(Date()) + 7` contains syntax that could easily be keyed incorrectly or omitted. By using a custom function, you ensure that your expression is performed the same way every time, without the risk of a typing mistake.

Creating your first custom function

For your first custom function, you will build a function that returns the last day of the current week.

1. Start a new module by selecting Insert → Module. At this point, your screen should look similar to Figure 10-1.

2. Create a new function by entering the following code:

```
Function LastDayThisWeek()
```

NOTE There is nothing special about the name "LastDayThisWeek." It's simply a descriptive name that coincides with the purpose of the function. When creating your own custom functions, it is a good practice to give them simple names that are descriptive and easy to remember.

3. On the next line, assign the needed expression to the function, giving your custom function its utility.

```
LastDayThisWeek = Date - Weekday(Date) + 7
```

At this point, your module should look similar to the one shown in Figure 10-2.

4. Save the module and close it.

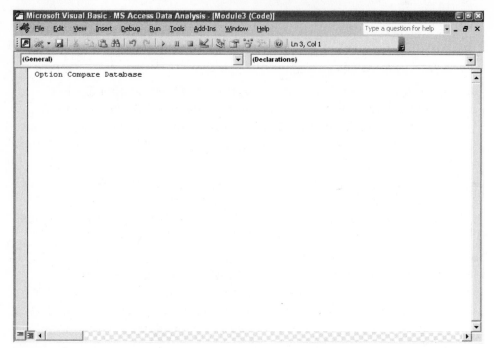

Figure 10-1   Start a new module.

Figure 10-2   You have created your first custom function.

To test your newly created custom function, create the query you see in Figure 10-3 and run it. In this query, you first determine the last day of the current week by using your newly created function, and then you use that value to calculate how many days are left in the current week.

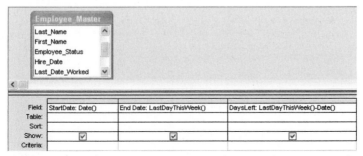

Field:	StartDate: Date()	End Date: LastDayThisWeek()	DaysLeft: LastDayThisWeek()-Date()
Table:			
Sort:			
Show:	☑	☑	☑
Criteria:			

Figure 10-3   This query uses your newly created function to determine how many days are left in the current week.

Tricks of the Trade: Creating a Central Repository of Custom Functions
---

You don't have to create a separate module for each custom function in your database; you can create one module to hold them all. In the sample database that comes with this book, you will see a module called "My_Custom_Functions." If you open it, you will see the seven separate custom functions shown in Figure 10-4. These functions can be used separately in various analyses.

This method of storing your custom functions makes finding and editing your functions easy. Figure 10-5 illustrates another advantage of this method. When you activate the Expression Builder, you can drill into all the modules you have created in your database. Having one module that contains all your custom functions provides you with a complete list of your functions.

continues

```
Function FirstDayThisWeek()
FirstDayThisWeek = Date - Weekday(Date) + 1
End Function

Function LastDayThisWeek()
LastDayThisWeek = Date - Weekday(Date) + 7
End Function

Function FirstDayThisQtr()
FirstDayThisQtr = DateSerial(Year(Date), Int((Month(Date) - 1) / 3) * 3 + 1, 1)
End Function

Function LastDayThisQtr()
LastDayThisQtr = DateSerial(Year(Date), Int((Month(Date) - 1) / 3) * 3 + 4, 0)
End Function

Function LastDayThisMonth()
LastDayThisMonth = DateSerial(Year(Date), Month(Date) + 1, 0)
End Function

Function LastDayNextMonth()
LastDayNextMonth = DateSerial(Year(Date), Month(Date) + 2, 0)
End Function

Function FirstDayLastMonth()
FirstDayLastMonth = DateSerial(Year(Date), Month(Date) - 1, 1)
End Function
```

Figure 10-4   Creating one module that holds all your custom functions allows you to quickly find and edit any of your user-defined functions.

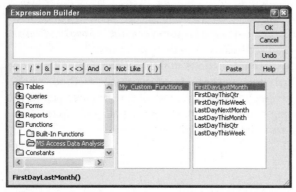

Figure 10-5   Creating one module that holds all your custom functions allows you to quickly find and edit any of your user-defined functions.

Creating a custom function that accepts arguments

Sometimes the operation that is performed by your custom function requires arguments that cannot be supplied internally by Access. In these situations, you will need to create a custom function that accepts arguments. To illustrate this concept, look at the query in Figure 10-6.

In this query, the Revenue field is being annualized—that is, the revenue value of each row is being translated to an annual rate for comparative purposes. The nature of this operation requires three arguments: the value being annualized, the number of periods already completed, and the number of periods that make up an entire year. As you can see in this query, the value being annualized is revenue, the number of periods completed is 8, and the number of periods that make up a year is 12.

In order to convert this expression to a custom function, you will have to allow the user to pass the required arguments. Walk through the following steps:

1. Start a new module by selecting Insert → Module.

2. Create and name your new function by entering the following code:

   ```
   Function Annualized()
   ```

3. Inside the parentheses, declare a variable and type for each argument that will be passed to the function:

   ```
   Function Annualized(MyValue as Long, PeriodsCompleted as Integer,
   PeriodsinYear as Integer )
   ```

4. On the next line, assign the needed expression to the function, giving your custom function its utility. Instead of using hard-coded values, you will use the values passed to the declared variables.

   ```
   Annualized = MyValue / PeriodsCompleted * PeriodsinYear
   ```

At this point, your module should look similar to the one shown in Figure 10-7.

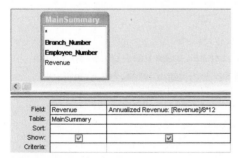

Figure 10-6 This query is using an expression that annualizes a revenue value.

Figure 10-7   This custom function accepts three variables and uses them in an expression.

To test your newly created Annualized function, create the query you see in Figure 10-8 and run it. Note that you are using your newly created function in an alias called "AnlzdRev."

TIP   You can hard-code selected arguments in your custom function to limit the number of arguments that need to be passed. For instance, the following code demonstrates how you can change the procedure for the Annualized function to hard-code the number of periods in a year:

```
Function Annualized(MyValue As Long, PeriodsCompleted As Integer)
Annualized = MyValue / PeriodsCompleted * 12
End Function
```

As you can see, the number of periods in a year has been hard-coded to 12, so when using this function you only have to pass two arguments. For example:

```
Annualized([Revenue], 8).
```

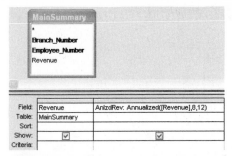

Figure 10-8   This query uses your newly created function to get the annualized revenue for each record.

A WORD ABOUT USING CUSTOM FUNCTIONS

Up to this point, you have tested your custom functions using queries. Although you will most commonly use your custom functions in queries, it is important to note that you can use them anywhere you would use any one of Access's built-in functions. Here are a few examples of how you can utilize your custom functions.

In a query environment, you can use your custom functions in the same ways you would use built-in Access functions. Figure 10-9 demonstrates some of the ways you can use a custom function in a query.

Field:	Hire_Date	LastMonth: FirstDayLastMonth()	Days: [Hire_Date]-FirstDayLastMonth()
Table:	Employee_Master		
Sort:			
Show:	☑	☑	☑
Criteria:	>FirstDayLastMonth()		

Figure 10-9   Using custom functions in a query.

Figure 10-10 illustrates how in a form, you can tie the Control Source for a text box to one of your custom functions. This same method works in Access reports. In this example, this form automatically executes the `FirstDay LastMonth` function each time it is opened to provide a value to the assigned text box.

(continued)

A WORD ABOUT USING CUSTOM FUNCTIONS *(continued)*

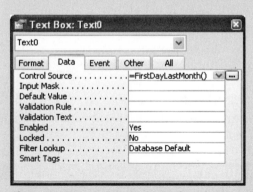

Figure 10-10 Using a custom function in a form.

Figure 10-11 illustrates how your custom functions can be used in other VBA procedures. This procedure uses the `FirstDayLastMonth` function to find the first day of last month, and then puts that date into a message box.

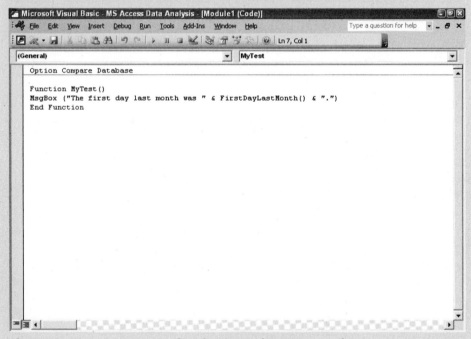

Figure 10-11 Using a custom function in another VBA procedure.

Controlling Analytical Processes with Forms

An Access form is nothing more than a database object that can accept user input and display data using a collection of controls. Access forms are often thought of as part of the presentation layer of a database, primarily being used as the front-end of an application. Though it is true that the primary purpose of forms is to act as an interface between Access and a user, this does not mean the user cannot be you (the designer of the database). In this section, you learn how Access forms can be leveraged on the back end of a database as a data analysis tool that interacts with your analyses and further automates your analytical processes.

The basics of passing data from a form to a query

The idea behind passing data from a form to a query is that instead of using parameters in a query to collect the data for your analysis, you collect the data through a form. To get a firm understanding of the basics of passing parameters from a form to a query, perform the following steps:

1. Start by creating a new form. Click Forms in the Database window, shown in Figure 10-12, and select Create form in Design View.

2. Select View → ToolBox. This activates the Toolbox shown in Figure 10-13. Select the Text Box control, then click anywhere on your form. At this point, you should have a form with one text box control.

3. Right-click the text box and select Properties. Click the All tab, and then give the newly created text box a distinctive name by entering **txtParam** as the Name property, as shown in Figure 10-14.

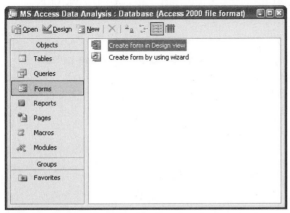

Figure 10-12   Start a new form in Design view.

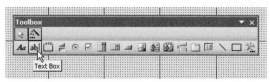

Figure 10-13 Activate the Toolbox toolbar and add a text box control to your form.

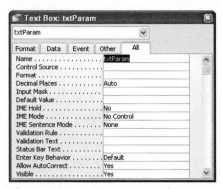

Figure 10-14 Give your text box control a distinctive name.

NOTE Each control on your form must have a valid name in the Name property. The Name property is a unique identifier that allows Access to reference a control in other parts of your database. Access automatically assigns generic names to newly created controls. However, you should always make it a point to give each of your controls your own descriptive name. This makes referencing and recognizing your controls much easier.

4. Go back to the Toolbox toolbar, select the Command Button control, as shown in Figure 10-15, and then click anywhere on your form. This places a command button on your form.

NOTE If the Command Button Wizard activates, click Cancel to close it. You will not need that wizard for this exercise.

5. Right-click the newly created command button and select Properties. Click the All tab, and adjust the Name property of your command button to read **btnRunQuery**. Then adjust the Caption property to read **Run Query**.

6. Next, while still in the command button's properties, click the Event tab and select [Event Procedure] from the On Click event, as shown in Figure 10-16. Next, click the ellipsis button (the button next to the dropdown).

7. At this point, you should be inside the VBA editor where you will enter a DoCmd action that will run the query called "Chapter10_Example_A." Enter the following code, just as you see in Figure 10-17:

```
DoCmd.OpenQuery "Chapter10_Example_A", acViewNormal
```

Figure 10-15   Add a command button control to your form.

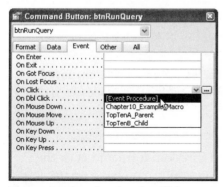

Figure 10-16   Set the On Click event to run an [Event Procedure] and click the ellipsis button.

Figure 10-17 Use the Docmd.OpenQuery method to execute the "Chapter10_Example_A" query.

NOTE The DoCmd.OpenQuery **method enables you to execute any saved query from code. This method is perfect for simple automation processes such as this.**

8. Once you are done, save your form as "frmMain" and close it.

9. It's time to test. Open the newly created frmMain form and click the Run Query button. If the query runs successfully, you have set up your form correctly. Now you can prepare your query to accept parameters from this form!

10. Open the "Chapter10_Example_A" query in Design view. Enter **[Forms]![frmMain].[txtParam]** as the criteria for the System_Period field, as shown in Figure 10-18.

11. Save and close the query.

Now you can open the frmMain form and enter a parameter for your query through a form! Enter **200401** in the text box, as shown in Figure 10-19, and then run the query. This returns all revenues earned in the 200401system period.

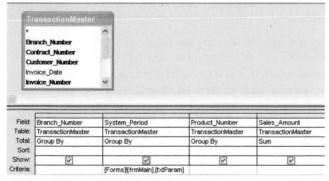

The query grid shows the following fields:

Field:	Branch_Number	System_Period	Product_Number	Sales_Amount
Table:	TransactionMaster	TransactionMaster	TransactionMaster	TransactionMaster
Total:	Group By	Group By	Group By	Sum
Sort:				
Show:	✓	✓	✓	✓
Criteria:		[Forms]![frmMain].[txtParam]		

Figure 10-18 This query filters on the System_Period field based on the value of the txtParam text box in the frmMain form.

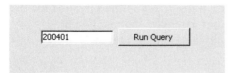

Figure 10-19 Now you can pass your parameters to your query through a form.

NOTE You will notice that if you leave the text box blank, your query will not return any results. This is the same issue you encounter using parameter queries. One way to get around this problem is to combine your expression with a wildcard so that if the text box is blank, all records will be returned. In this scenario, for instance, you would change your expression to read:

```
Like [Forms]![frmMain].[txtParam] & "*"
```

TIP You can reference any form control that has a value property, including combo boxes, list boxes, text boxes, and option groups.

Enhancing automation with forms

Access forms can help you enhance your automated processes using little more than a few controls and some light VBA coding. The idea is to turn your forms into something more than just a tool to pass parameters; you can create a robust central control point for your analysis.

UNDERSTANDING THE SYNTAX FOR REFERENCING A FORM

◆ *Brackets ([ ])*: Brackets are used to identify the name of an object. For instance, if you were referring to the CustomerMaster table, you would refer to it as [CustomerMaster]. If you were referring to a query called TopTen_Step1, you would refer to it as [TopTen_Step1]. This not only helps Access identify objects, but it also makes your code easier to read.

◆ *The collection operator (!)*: The collection operator (sometimes referred to as the bang operator) is used to tell Access that the object with which you are working belongs to a particular collection of objects. For example, if you are working with a form called "Main," you would refer to it as [Forms]![Main] because the form [Main] belongs to the Forms collection.

◆ *The dot operator (.)*: The dot operator is used to point to a property belonging to an object. For example, while [CustomerMaster] refers to the CustomerMaster table, [CustomerMaster].[City] refers to the City field in the CustomerMaster table. Here is another example: [Forms]![Main] refers to the form "Main", while [Forms]![Main].[Fname] refers to a control called Fname located in "Main."

To help illustrate the power of incorporating Access forms into your analysis, open the frmMktRpts form in the sample database, shown in Figure 10-20. The purpose of this form is to control the execution of an analysis that involves creating market reports. The idea is to select a market, run the process that executes a query, and then send the results to an Excel file in the C:\Access DataAnalysis directory.

Figure 10-20   This form enables you to control the execution of an analytical process.

Open the form in Design view to see how this works. As you can see, there are three controls on this form.

- **The txtPath text box.** The txtPath text box uses the market value from the combo box to construct a file path. This allows you to dynamically create a separate path for each market. This path is constructed by concatenating two strings and a control reference.

  - **C:\AccessDataAnalysis\.** This is the first part of the file path, pointing to the AccessDataAnalysis directory in the C drive.

  - **[cboLocations].** This is the name of the combo box where you select your market. This becomes the file name.

  - **.xls.** This string finishes the path by assigning the file extension that identifies the file as an Excel file.

  If you open the MktExports macro, shown in Figure 10-21, you will notice that the Output File path is referencing this text box. This allows the macro to avoid using a hard-coded file path.

- **The cboLocations combo box.** This combo box helps do two things. First, this combo box feeds the txtPath text box a market to use in the construction of a file path. Second, it feeds the MarketExports query its parameter. If you open the MarketExports query, shown in Figure 10-22, you will notice that filter criteria for the Market field is referencing this combo box. This allows the query to avoid using a hard-coded market.

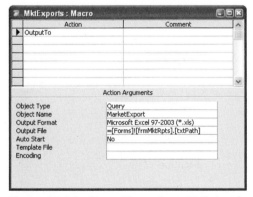

Figure 10-21 You will use the txtPath text box to dynamically feed your macro the Output File path for each market.

- **The btnRunMarket command button.** Right-click this command button and click Build Event. This takes you to the VBA editor shown in Figure 10-23. As you can see, this button simply runs the MktExports macro, and then throws up a message box announcing the location of your new file.

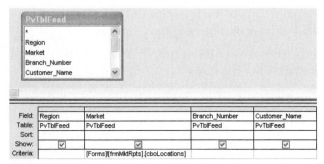

Figure 10-22 You are using the cboLocations combo box as the filter criteria for the Market field.

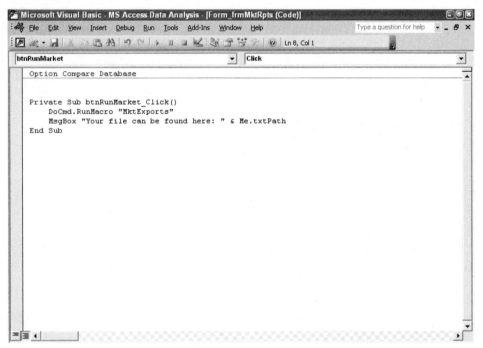

Figure 10-23 When you click the command button, a DoCmd action runs the macro and then calls a message box.

Now that you have a firm grasp of how this form works, you can enhance it even further. Instead of running one market at a time, wouldn't it be useful to run all markets at once? You can do this by using VBA to enumerate through all the markets in the combo box, running the MktExports as you go.

Enumerating through a combo box

Open the frmMktRpts form and take a look at the combo box on the form. The entries, or rows, you see within the combo box are indexed—that is, each row has an index number starting from 0 and continuing to however many rows there are. For example, the first row is index number 0, the second row is index number 1, the third row is index number 2, and so on. The idea behind enumerating through a combo box is to capture one index at a time, and then change the value of the combo box to match the row value assigned to that index number.

1. Start by opening the frmMktRpts form in Design view and adding a second command button.

2. Adjust the Name property of your newly created command button to read **btnRunAll**, and then adjust the Caption property to read **Run All**.

   At this point, your form should look similar to Figure 10-24.

3. Right-click the button and select Build Event. Select Code Builder from the Choose Builder dialog box and click OK. This opens the VBA Editor. As you can see in Figure 10-25, this creates a separate subprocedure.

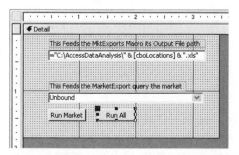

Figure 10-24   Add a second command button called "Run All" to the form.

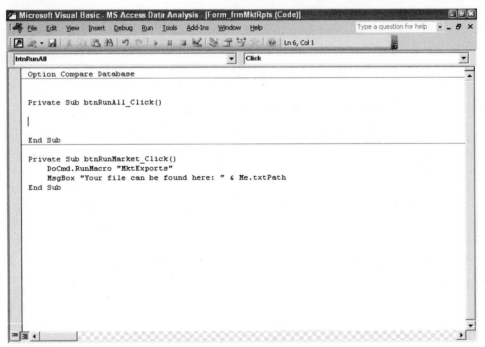

Figure 10-25 Build an "On Click" event for the newly created btnRunAll command button.

4. Start the code by declaring an integer variable called IndexNumber. This will be used to trap the index number of each entry of the combo box.

```
Dim IndexNum As Integer
```

5. Initiate a `For...Next` loop with the IndexNum variable. This line of code ensures that the procedure will run for each index number in the combo box.

```
For IndexNum = 0 To Me.cboLocations.ListCount - 1
```

NOTE Why subtract 1 from the combo box's list count? You must do this to adjust for the fact that index numbers of a combo box start at 0. If there are 10 rows in a combo box, the ListCount property starts counting at 1, returning a count of 10 rows. However, the index numbers in the same combo box range from 0 to 9. Subtracting 1 from the list count removes the extra number and corrects the discrepancy.

6. Set the value of the combo box equal to the value of the row assigned to the current index number. After the new value has been set, run the pre-defined macro.

```
Me.cboLocations.Value = Me.cboLocations.ItemData(IndexNum)
DoCmd.RunMacro "MktExports"
```

7. Repeat the process for the next index number. The message will alert you when the procedure has completed its execution.

```
Next IndexNum
MsgBox "Your files can be found in the C:\AccessDataAnalysis
directory."
```

If you have done everything correctly, your procedure should look similar to Figure 10-26.

8. Save your form and test the newly created functionality by clicking the Run All button.

Once the procedure has completed running, look under the C:\AccessData Analysis directory to see all the Excel files that where created (see Figure 10-27).

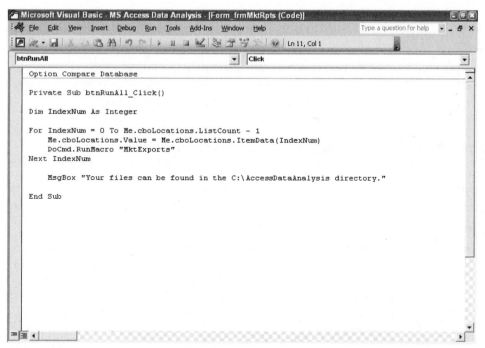

Figure 10-26 This procedure will enumerate through a combo box, running a macro for each entry.

Figure 10-27   All of these Excel files were created with automation.

Needless to say, this example is just one of the hundreds of ways you can enhance your analytical processes using forms. The flexibility and functionality you gain by using a few controls and a handful of code is simply incredible. Even simple techniques such as passing parameters from a form to a query can open the doors to a completely new set of analytical functionality.

Processing Data Behind the Scenes

One of the benefits of using VBA is that you can perform much of your data processing in the background without the use of queries and macros. This can be beneficial in several ways:

- **Reduce the number of query objects in your database.** Every analytical process will have intermediate steps that serve as a means to an end. These steps typically involve action queries that massage and transform the data for the bigger analysis. Too many of these peripheral queries can inundate your database with query objects, making your analytical processes difficult to manage and change. Processing your data in the background using VBA can help you streamline your processes by reducing the number query objects in your database, making both the management and the maintenance of your analyses more practical.

- **Better organize your analytical processes.** Have you ever seen a process that involves queries that link to forms that, in turn, link to macros that reference tables created by other queries, and so on? You will undoubtedly run into analyses that involve complicated processes, and there is nothing wrong with utilizing the tools Access provides. However, engineering overly elaborate systems that involve macros, queries, and forms can make your processes difficult to manage and maintain. Processing your data in the background using VBA can help you centralize your analysis into one procedure, organizing your tasks in a clearly defined set of instructions that are easy to locate, update, and manage.

- **Protect your processes in shared environments.** Processing your data in the background using VBA can help you protect your analytical processes working in a shared database. Building your processes in VBA can reduce the risk of someone changing your queries or accidentally deleting objects.

- **Enhance your processes with VBA.** The more you integrate your analytical processes into VBA, the more you can take advantage of its many benefits such as looping, record-level testing, and error handling.

Anyone who routinely works with Access knows that several different ways exist to accomplish any given task. Processing data using VBA is no different. Indeed, the beauty of VBA is that its flexibility allows you to perform literally any action in countless ways. That being said, it should be obvious that it would be impossible to cover every possible way to process data using VBA. Therefore, you will focus on using RunSQL statements. This technique will give you some fundamental controls over your processes through VBA and will allow you to start moving more of your analyses behind the scenes.

Processing data with RunSQL statements

In Chapter 6, you learned that the query objects you are accustomed to using are simply visual representations of SQL statements. What you may not know is that you don't necessarily need to create a query object in order to process data. You can process data directly through a RunSQL statement.

The basics of the RunSQL method

If you were designing a macro, you would find RunSQL in the list of macro actions. In technical terms, RunSQL is a method belonging to the DoCmd object. If you have been paying attention you've noticed that up until now, you have been using OpenQuery when working with a query in a macro environment, and `Docmd.OpenQuery` when working with a query through code. In this light, it's important to note the differences between the `RunSQL` method and `OpenQuery` method:

- The `OpenQuery` method executes a saved query, whereas the `RunSQL` method processes a SQL statement without the need for a saved query.

- The `RunSQL` method only allows you to execute action queries (make-table, append, delete, and update), whereas the `OpenQuery` method enables the execution of any type of saved query, including select queries.

- The `OpenQuery` method is ideal for use in a macro environment. The `RunSQL` method, on the other hand, is better suited for dynamic back-end processes performed in VBA.

NOTE Among other reasons, `RunSQL` is better suited for VBA because in a macro environment, the `RunSQL` action limits you to SQL statements that do not exceed 256 characters. This obviously restricts the functionality of `RunSQL` in the macro environment. However, there is no such limitation in the VBA environment.

THE ANATOMY OF RUNSQL STATEMENTS

`DoCmd.RunSQL(SQLStatement, UseTransaction)`
 `RunSQL` **is a method of the** `DoCmd` **object that executes action queries such as append, delete, update, and make-table. This method has the following two arguments:**

- ◆ `SQLStatement` **(required): This is the SQL statement that is to be executed.**

- ◆ `UseTransaction` **(optional): This is a true or false indicator that specifies how Access safeguards your data during the execution of your SQL statement. The default state for this argument is True, which ensures that your SQL statement is tested in a temporary log before final execution. You should rarely set this argument to False.**

For example:

 `DoCmd.RunSQL "Delete * from [MyTable]"` **deletes all records from MyTable.**

Using RunSQL statements

Using RunSQL statements in your code is easy. You simply place each RunSQL statement in your VBA procedure as needed. For instance, the following procedure runs four actions, demonstrating that you can process data without creating one query:

- Makes a table called tblJobCodes
- Inserts a new record into the tblJobCodes table
- Updates the job code "PPL" to "PPL1"
- Deletes the "PPL1" job code

```
Function Look_Ma_No_Queries()

DoCmd.RunSQL "SELECT [Job_Code]INTO [tblJobCodes]FROM [Employee_Master]
GROUP BY [Job_Code]"

DoCmd.RunSQL "INSERT INTO [tblJobCodes] ( [Job_Code] ) SELECT 'PPL' AS
NewCode FROM [Employee_Master] GROUP BY 'PPL'"

DoCmd.RunSQL "UPDATE [tblJobCodes] SET [Job_Code] = 'PPL1' WHERE
[Job_Code]='PPL'"

DoCmd.RunSQL "DELETE * FROM [tblJobCodes] WHERE [Job_Code]='PPL1'"

End Function
```

NOTE You will find this procedure in the sample database within the module called Using_RunSQL. Note that each RunSQL statement should be one line of code. You see the lines broken up here due to layout specifications.

TIP Having trouble creating SQL statements? Here's a handy trick. Create a query in Design view, and then switch to SQL view. Although you will have to adjust the SQL statement a bit, Access will have done most of the work for you.

Advanced techniques using RunSQL statements

Now that you have a firm understanding of what RunSQL statements can do, take a look at some of the advanced techniques that will help enhance your behind-the-scenes processing.

Suppressing warning messages

As you execute your `RunSQL` statements, you will notice that Access throws up the same warning messages you would get if you were to run the same actions with stored queries. You can use the `SetWarnings` method to suppress these messages just as you would in a macro. For example, the following code sets warnings to false, runs the `RunSQL` statement, and then sets warnings back to true:

```
DoCmd.SetWarnings False
DoCmd.RunSQL "DELETE * FROM [tblJobCodes] WHERE [Job_Code]='PPL1'"
DoCmd.SetWarnings True
```

Passing a SQL statement as a variable

One of the biggest challenges in working with the `RunSQL` method is managing and making sense of giant SQL statements. It's difficult to determine what is going on in your code when your `RunSQL` statement runs off the page with more than 1,000 characters in its SQL string. One of the ways to make for easier reading is to pass your SQL statement as a variable. This section demonstrates how passing your SQL statement through a string variable enables you to break up your statement into pieces that are easier to read.

1. Start a procedure and declare a string variable called `MySQL`:

```
Function Passing_SQL_With_Strings()
Dim MySQL As String
```

2. Start assigning the SQL statement to the `MySQL` variable. What you're looking for here is structure, a format that makes the SQL statement easy to read and manage within the VBA editor. The first line starts the string. Each subsequent line is concatenated to the previous line. By the last line, the `MySQL` variable contains the entire SQL string:

```
MySQL = "SELECT TOP 10 Market, Sum(Revenue) AS Rev INTO TopTenList "
MySQL = MySQL & "FROM PvTblFeed "
MySQL = MySQL & "GROUP BY PvTblFeed.Market, PvTblFeed.Customer_Name "
MySQL = MySQL & "ORDER BY Sum(PvTblFeed.Revenue) DESC"
```

3. All that is left to do now is pass the `MySQL` variable to your `RunSQL` statement, as follows:

```
DoCmd.RunSQL MySQL
End Function
```

NOTE Although there are other ways to concatenate this SQL string without the redundancy of typing *"MySQL = MySQL &..."*, this method creates a visual block of code that unmistakably lets the person reviewing the code know that all this goes together.

Passing user-defined parameters from a form to your SQL statement

Even when you are processing data behind the scenes, you can pass user-defined parameters from a form to create dynamic SQL statements. Following are some examples of how you would pass data from a form to your SQL statements.

Passing textual parameters from a form

In this example, you are passing textual criterion from a form. Note that the expression that points to the user-defined parameter on the form must be wrapped in quotes. In addition, because the data type you are passing is textual, the entire expression is wrapped in single quotes.

```
MySQL = "SELECT Market, Customer_Name, EffDate, TransCount "
MySQL = MySQL & "INTO MyResults "
MySQL = MySQL & "FROM MyTable "
MySQL = MySQL & "WHERE Market='" & [Forms]![frmMain].[cboMarket] & "'"
DoCmd.RunSQL MySQL
```

Passing numeric parameters from a form

In this example, you are passing a numeric criterion from a form. Note that the expression that points to the user-defined parameter on the form must be wrapped in quotes.

```
MySQL = "SELECT Market, Customer_Name, EffDate, TransCount "
MySQL = MySQL & "INTO MyResults "
MySQL = MySQL & "FROM MyTable "
MySQL = MySQL & "WHERE TransCount =" & [Forms]![frmMain].[cboCount] & ""
DoCmd.RunSQL MySQL
```

Passing date parameters from a form

In this example, you are passing date criterion from a form. Note that the expression that points to the user-defined parameter on the form must be wrapped in quotes. In addition, because the data type you are passing is a date, the entire expression is wrapped in a pound sign (#).

```
MySQL = "SELECT Market, Customer_Name, EffDate, TransCount "
MySQL = MySQL & "INTO MyResults "
MySQL = MySQL & "FROM MyTable "
MySQL = MySQL & "WHERE EffDate =#" & [Forms]![frmMain].[cboMarket] & "#"

DoCmd.RunSQL MySQL
```

Tricks of the Trade: Troubleshooting SQL Statements with a Message Box

Troubleshooting a SQL statement in VBA can be one of the most frustrating exercises you will undertake, primarily for two reasons. First, you are working in an environment where the SQL statement is broken up into pieces. Although this makes it easier to determine what the SQL statement is doing, it makes debugging problematic because you cannot readily see the statement as a whole. Second, the error messages you get when SQL statements fails are oftentimes vague, leaving you to guess what the problem may be.

For example, the SQL string in Figure 10-28 contains an error. When this procedure is run, the error message shown in Figure 10-29 pops up.

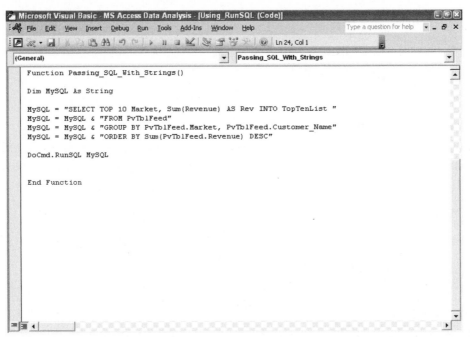

Figure 10-28   The SQL string in this code contains an error. Can you pick it out?

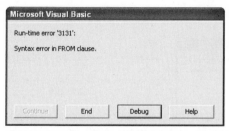

Figure 10-29   The error message you get when the procedure is run provides little help. Nothing seems to be wrong with the FROM clause.

It's obvious that an error lies somewhere, but it's impossible to see it when the SQL string is broken out like this. So how can you see the SQL string in its entirety? Use a message box! Figure 10-30 demonstrates how you can feed the SQL string to a message box before firing the RunSQL statement.

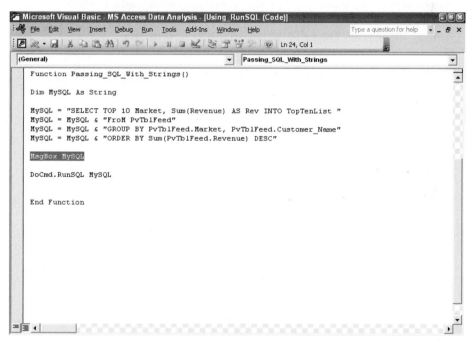

Figure 10-30   Use a message box to read the variable that holds your SQL string. This allows you to see a complete SQL statement and possibly pinpoint the error.

After running the procedure, the message box pops up with the entire SQL statement. How does this help you? Well, the error message stated that the error was in the FROM clause, so you should look there first. If you look closely, you'll see that there is no space between the words *PvTblFeed* and *GROUP BY*.

Missing space

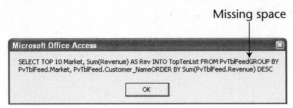

Microsoft Office Access

SELECT TOP 10 Market, Sum(Revenue) AS Rev INTO TopTenList FROM PvTblFeedGROUP BY
PvTblFeed.Market, PvTblFeed.Customer_NameORDER BY Sum(PvTblFeed.Revenue) DESC

OK

Figure 10-31 The message box helped you determine that error was caused by the
fact that there is no space between the words *PvTblFeed and GROUP BY.*

**That's right: One measly space causes the entire SQL statement to fail.
Remember, these lines of code are not separate SQL statements; they are
actually pieces of one SQL statement that have been broken down into parts.
They will be pieced back together when the function is executed. In that light,
you have to consider, and include, all syntax that is necessary to create a valid
SQL statement; including spaces. This is why you always see a space before the
close quotes for each piece of the SQL statement. So the syntax "From
PvTblFeed" should be adjusted to include a space before the close quotes;
"From PvtTbleFeed ". Figure 10-32 shows the fixed procedure.**

Figure 10-32 Using a message box to troubleshoot the SQL statement helped
determine that the error was caused by a missing space after *FROM PvtTblFeed.*

CHAPTER

11

Reporting Your Results Using Excel Automation

In the past few chapters, you learned several ways to automate your analytical processes to achieve higher productivity, controlled analysis, and reproducibility. In this chapter, automation takes on a different meaning. Automation here defines the means of manipulating another application, namely Excel. Why bother automating Excel? Think about all the times you have crunched data in Access only to bring the results into Excel for presentation and distribution. It's a fact of life that Excel is the tool of choice for most business users. Excel provides users with a familiar environment and a flexible platform where inquisitive users can perform their own impromptu calculations right on the spreadsheet. It is not only okay to leverage Excel's powerful features, but it's also very smart to do so.

The Basics of Excel Automation

The idea behind Excel automation is similar to the idea behind automating an analytical process within Access; certain tasks are redundant in nature and can be automated to improve efficiency. For instance, if you send Access data to Excel and build a pivot table on a regular basis, why do it by hand every time? Excel automation can literally take you out of the report building process, creating and saving Excel reports without any human interaction. The difference is that instead of automating the objects within Access, you automate the objects in Excel.

A word on binding Access to Excel

Each program in the Microsoft Office suite comes with its own Object Library. You can think of the *Object Library* as a kind of encyclopedia of all the objects, methods, and properties available in each Office application. Access has its own Object Library, just as all the other Office applications have their own. In order for Access to be able to speak to another Office program such as Excel, you have to bind it to that program. *Binding* is the process of exposing the Object Library for a server application to a client application. In the context of this discussion, Access would be the client application and Excel would be the server application. Two types of binding exist: early binding and late binding.

Early binding

With *early binding*, you explicitly point Access to the Excel Object Library in order to expose Excel's object model during design time, or while programming. Then you use the exposed objects in your code to call a new instance of the application, as follows:

```
Dim XL As Excel.Application      Set XL = New Excel.Application
Dim XL As Excel.Application
Set XL = New Excel.Application
```

Early binding has several advantages:

- Because the objects are exposed at design time, Access can compile your code before execution. This allows your code to run considerably faster than with late binding.

- Because the Object Library is exposed during design time, you have full access to the server application's object model in the Object Browser.

- You have the benefit of using Intellisense. *Intellisense* is the functionality you experience when you type a keyword and a dot (.) or an equals sign (=) and you see a popup list of the methods and properties available to you.

- You automatically have access to the server application's built-in constants.

Late binding

Late binding differs from early binding in that you don't point Access to a specific Object Library; instead, you purposely keep things ambiguous, only using the `CreateObject` function, as follows, to bind to the needed library at runtime, or during program execution:

```
Dim XL As Object
Set XL = CreateObject("Excel.Application")
```

Late binding has one main advantage: it allows your automation procedures to be version-independent. That is, your automation procedure will not fail due to compatibility issues between multiple versions of a component. For example, suppose you decide to use early binding and set a reference to the Excel Object Library on your system. The version of the available library on your system will be equal to your version of Excel. The problem is that if your users have a lower version of Excel on their machine, your automation procedure will fail. You do not have this problem with late binding.

Binding conventions in this book

For the purposes of this book, early binding will be used for a couple of reasons. First, the design-time benefits of early binding, such as Intellisense, are ideal for discovering and experimenting with the methods and properties that come with the Excel Object Library. Second, this block of instruction is in the context of building an automation procedure to report your data analysis, not building an application that will be used by many users. In that light, version issues will not come into play, negating the need for late binding.

Creating your first Excel automation procedure

Start a new module by selecting Insert → Module. Before you start typing any code, you'll have to set a reference to the Excel Object Library by selecting Tools → References. The References dialog box shown in Figure 11-1 activates. This dialog box allows you to set a reference to any of the available Object Libraries you see in the list.

Scroll down until you find the entry "Microsoft Excel *XX* Object Library," where the *XX* is your version of Excel. Place a check in the checkbox next to the entry, as shown in Figure 11-2, and click the OK button.

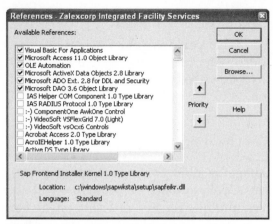

Figure 11-1 Activate the References dialog box.

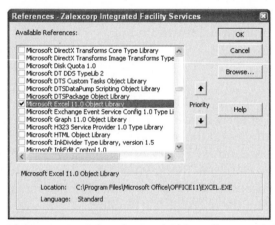

Figure 11-2 Select the Excel Object Library and click the OK button.

NOTE If you don't set a reference to the Excel Object Library, Access will give you a compile error, throwing up the message `Compile error: User-defined type not defined`.

The good news is that once you set a reference to the Excel Object Library in a particular database, it is set for good in that database.

Now that you have referenced the Excel Object Library, you can start writing code. To start, try building a procedure that opens a new Excel workbook and adds a worksheet. Enter the following code into your newly created module:

```
Function MyFirstAutomationCode()

'Step 1: Declare the objects you will work with.
Dim xl As Excel.Application
Dim xlwkbk As Excel.Workbook
Dim xlsheet As Excel.Worksheet

'Step 2: Create a new instance of Excel, start a workbook, and add a worksheet.
Set xl = New Excel.Application
Set xlwkbk = xl.Workbooks.Add
Set xlsheet = xlwkbk.Worksheets.Add

'Step 3: Make the instance of Excel visible.
xl.Visible = True

'Step 4: Clean up memory.
Set xl = Nothing
Set xlwkbk = Nothing
Set xlsheet = Nothing

End Function
```

TIP Notice the line of code that makes the instance of Excel visible (xl.Visible = True). Although this is not necessary, it's generally a good practice to make the instance of Excel visible for a couple of reasons. First, should anything go wrong during the procedure, debugging will be easier if you can see the Excel spreadsheet. Secondly, you can easily close the instance of Excel in debug mode by closing out the Excel window. If the instance is not visible, you will have to kill it by going into the Windows Task Manager and ending the process there.

Congratulations! You have just created your first automation procedure.

Sending Access data to Excel

Now that you have successfully created your first automation procedure, it's time to try something more meaningful: sending Access data to Excel. Transferring your analytical results is the first step in creating an Excel report from your Access analysis.

The process of sending your Access data to Excel can generally be broken down into three main actions. First, you identify the dataset you want to send to Excel and assign it to a recordset object. Next, you open Excel and copy the recordset to a spreadsheet using Excel's CopyFromRecordset method. Finally, because the CopyFromRecordset method does not transfer column headings, you must enumerate through your dataset's column headings and add them to the spreadsheet.

Sending one recordset to Excel

The following procedure sends the PvTblFeed table to a tab called "Pivot Table Feed":

```
Function SendRecordset()

'Step 1: Declare the objects and variables you will work with.
Dim MyRecordset As ADODB.Recordset
Dim xl As Excel.Application
Dim xlwkbk As Excel.Workbook
Dim xlsheet As Excel.Worksheet
Dim C As Integer
Dim I As Integer

'Step 2: Start a new recordset, create a new instance of Excel, start a workbook.
Set MyRecordset = New ADODB.Recordset
Set xl = New Excel.Application
Set xlwkbk = xl.Workbooks.Add

'Step 3: Make the instance of Excel visible.
xl.Visible = True

'Step 4: Assign a dataset to the recordset object.
MyRecordset.Open "PvTblFeed", CurrentProject.Connection, adOpenStatic

'Step 5: Add a new worksheet and name it.
Set xlsheet = xlwkbk.Worksheets.Add
xlsheet.name = "Pivot Table Feed"

'Step 6: Copy the records to the active Excel sheet starting with cell A2 in order to leave
room for the column headings.
With xlsheet
xl.Range("A2").CopyFromRecordset MyRecordset
End With

'Step 7: Enumerate through the fields in the recordset and add column heading names to
the spreadsheet.
C = 1
For I = 0 To MyRecordset.Fields.Count - 1
xl.ActiveSheet.Cells(1, C).Value = MyRecordset.Fields(I).Name
C = C + 1
Next I

'Step 8: Clean up memory.
Set MyRecordset = Nothing
```

```
    Set xl = Nothing
    Set xlwkbk = Nothing
    Set xlsheet = Nothing


End Function
```

Sending two datasets to two different tabs in the same workbook

You will sometimes come across a scenario where you will have to send two or more datasets to Excel into different tabs. This is as easy as repeating parts of the automation procedure for a different recordset. The following code sends the PvTblFeed table to a tab called "Pivot Table Feed," and then sends the MainSummary table to another tab in the same the workbook:

```
Function SendMoreThanOneRecordset()

'Step 1: Declare the objects and variables you will work with.
Dim MyRecordset As ADODB.Recordset
Dim xl As Excel.Application
Dim xlwkbk As Excel.Workbook
Dim xlsheet As Excel.Worksheet
Dim C As Integer
Dim I As Integer

'Step 2: Start a new recordset, create a new instance of Excel, start a workbook.
Set MyRecordset = New ADODB.Recordset
Set xl = New Excel.Application
Set xlwkbk = xl.Workbooks.Add

'Step 3: Make the instance of Excel visible.
xl.Visible = True

'Step 4: Assign a dataset to the recordset object.
MyRecordset.Open "PvTblFeed", CurrentProject.Connection, adOpenStatic

'Step 5: Add a new worksheet and name it.
Set xlsheet = xlwkbk.Worksheets.Add
xlsheet.name = "Pivot Table Feed"

'Step 6: Copy the records to the active Excel sheet starting with cell A2 in order to leave room for the column headings.
With xlsheet
xl.Range("A2").CopyFromRecordset MyRecordset
End With
```

```
'Step 7: Enumerate through the fields in the recordset and add column heading names to
the spreadsheet.
C = 1
For I = 0 To MyRecordset.Fields.Count - 1
xl.ActiveSheet.Cells(1, C).Value = MyRecordset.Fields(I).Name
C = C + 1
Next I

'Step 8: Close the current recordset and repeat steps 4-7 for a new recordset.
MyRecordset.Close
MyRecordset.Open "MainSummary", CurrentProject.Connection, adOpenStatic

Set xlsheet = xlwkbk.Worksheets.Add
xlsheet.name = "Main Summary"

With xlsheet
xl.Range("A2").CopyFromRecordset MyRecordset
End With

C = 1
For I = 0 To MyRecordset.Fields.Count - 1
xl.ActiveSheet.Cells(1, C).Value = MyRecordset.Fields(I).Name
C = C + 1
Next I

'Step 9: Clean up memory.
Set MyRecordset = Nothing
Set xl = Nothing
Set xlwkbk = Nothing
Set xlsheet = Nothing

End Function
```

Tricks of the Trade: Checking for Record Count before Automating Excel

Often, the recordset you send to your spreadsheet will be a query that may or may not return records. Interestingly enough, you will not receive an error when you use the `CopyFromRecordset` method on an empty recordset. That means that it is completely possible to automate Excel, create a workbook, and copy no records to it. This can cause problems later, especially if you further your automation of Excel to include building a pivot table, creating a chart, and so on.

The quick and easy workaround to this potential problem is to check your recordset for a record count before doing anything. If your recordset has zero

records, the procedure will terminate; otherwise, the procedure will continue. The following code demonstrates this concept:

```
'Step 1: Declare the objects and variables you will work with.
Dim MyRecordset As ADODB.Recordset
Dim xl As Excel.Application
Dim xlwkbk As Excel.Workbook
Dim xlsheet As Excel.Worksheet
Dim C As Integer
Dim I As Integer

'Step 2: Start a new recordset.
Set MyRecordset = New ADODB.Recordset
MyRecordset.Open "Employee_Master", CurrentProject.Connection,
adOpenStatic

'Step 3: Check RecordCount property of the recordset.  If less than one, throw up a
message box stating there are no records and then exit the function.
If MyRecordset.RecordCount < 1 Then
    MsgBox ("There are no records to output")
    Set MyRecordset = Nothing
    Exit Function

Else

'Step 4: Continue with your automation code.
```

Advanced Automation Techniques

At this point, you may be asking yourself why you would bother with Excel automation when you can use the `TransferSpreadsheet` method or the `Output` method to send data to Excel. Excel automation goes beyond getting your data to Excel. With Excel automation, you can have Access dynamically add formatting, set print options, add an AutoFilter, create pivot tables, build charts, and the list goes on. How do you learn to do all these things in VBA? You let Excel program for you!

Stealing code from Excel

In Excel, macros are used as a way to record actions that can be played back when needed. When you start recording a macro, Excel automatically generates one or more lines of code for every action you take. After you stop recording, you can open the macro to review, edit, or even copy the generated code. The idea here is that after you send Access data to Excel, you can perform some actions on your data while recording a macro, and then copy the macro-generated code into the Access module where you have the automation procedure. The next time you run the automation procedure, the recorded macro actions will run right from Access.

To illustrate this concept, walk through the following demonstration:

1. In the sample database, execute the `SendRecordset` function in the Excel_Automation_2 module. Once the function finishes running, you should have an Excel spreadsheet that looks similar to the one shown in Figure 11-3.

2. In Excel, select Tools → Macro → RecordNewMacro. This activates the Record Macro dialog box, as shown in Figure 11-4. Name the new macro "MyFirstMacro" and click OK. At this point, Excel is recording every action you take.

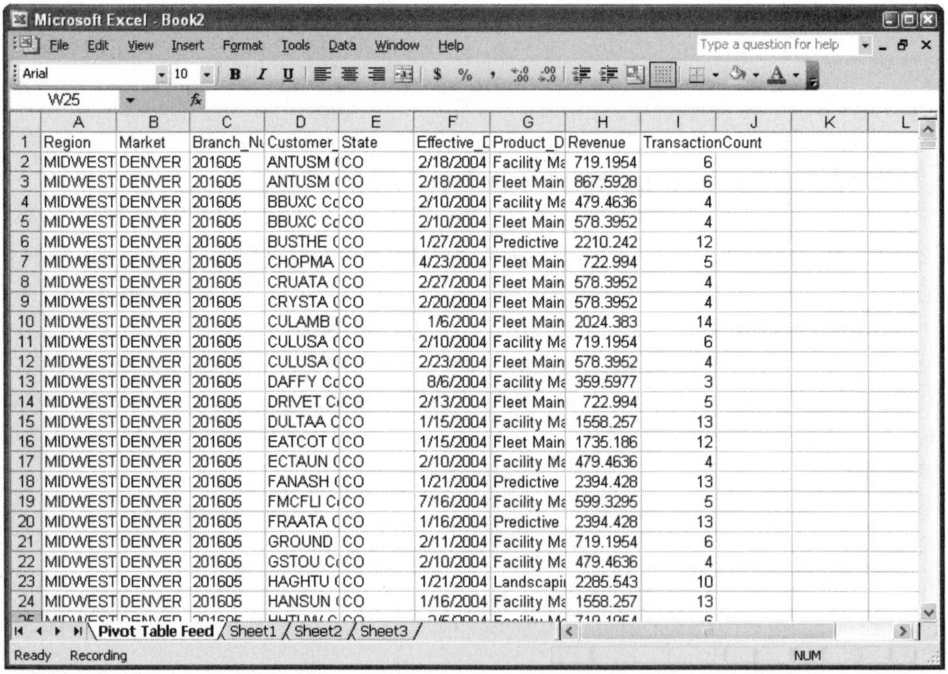

	A	B	C	D	E	F	G	H	I
1	Region	Market	Branch_Nu	Customer_	State	Effective_D	Product_D	Revenue	TransactionCount
2	MIDWEST	DENVER	201605	ANTUSM (	CO	2/18/2004	Facility Ma	719.1954	6
3	MIDWEST	DENVER	201605	ANTUSM (	CO	2/18/2004	Fleet Main	867.5928	6
4	MIDWEST	DENVER	201605	BBUXC Cc	CO	2/10/2004	Facility Ma	479.4636	4
5	MIDWEST	DENVER	201605	BBUXC Cc	CO	2/10/2004	Fleet Main	578.3952	4
6	MIDWEST	DENVER	201605	BUSTHE (	CO	1/27/2004	Predictive	2210.242	12
7	MIDWEST	DENVER	201605	CHOPMA	CO	4/23/2004	Fleet Main	722.994	5
8	MIDWEST	DENVER	201605	CRUATA (	CO	2/27/2004	Fleet Main	578.3952	4
9	MIDWEST	DENVER	201605	CRYSTA (	CO	2/20/2004	Fleet Main	578.3952	4
10	MIDWEST	DENVER	201605	CULAMB (	CO	1/6/2004	Fleet Main	2024.383	14
11	MIDWEST	DENVER	201605	CULUSA (	CO	2/10/2004	Facility Ma	719.1954	6
12	MIDWEST	DENVER	201605	CULUSA (	CO	2/23/2004	Fleet Main	578.3952	4
13	MIDWEST	DENVER	201605	DAFFY Cc	CO	8/6/2004	Facility Ma	359.5977	3
14	MIDWEST	DENVER	201605	DRIVET C	CO	2/13/2004	Fleet Main	722.994	5
15	MIDWEST	DENVER	201605	DULTAA C	CO	1/15/2004	Facility Ma	1558.257	13
16	MIDWEST	DENVER	201605	EATCOT (	CO	1/15/2004	Fleet Main	1735.186	12
17	MIDWEST	DENVER	201605	ECTAUN (	CO	2/10/2004	Facility Ma	479.4636	4
18	MIDWEST	DENVER	201605	FANASH (	CO	1/21/2004	Predictive	2394.428	13
19	MIDWEST	DENVER	201605	FMCFLI C	CO	7/16/2004	Facility Ma	599.3295	5
20	MIDWEST	DENVER	201605	FRAATA (	CO	1/16/2004	Predictive	2394.428	13
21	MIDWEST	DENVER	201605	GROUND	CO	2/11/2004	Facility Ma	719.1954	6
22	MIDWEST	DENVER	201605	GSTOU Cc	CO	2/10/2004	Facility Ma	479.4636	4
23	MIDWEST	DENVER	201605	HAGHTU (	CO	1/21/2004	Landscapi	2285.543	10
24	MIDWEST	DENVER	201605	HANSUN (	CO	1/16/2004	Facility Ma	1558.257	13

Figure 11-3 This is the spreadsheet you start with when you run the `SendRecordset` function.

3. Make the following formatting changes:

    a. Click cell A1.

    b. Select Data → Filter → AutoFilter.

    c. Select cells A1 through I1 and change the background color to gray and the font style to bold.

    d. Select columns A through I, and then select Format → Column → Autofit Selection.

4. Click Cell A1 and save the workbook to your MyDocuments folder.

5. Select Tools → Macro → Stop Recording.

6. Now that you have finished recording the necessary actions, you can copy the macro-generated code out of Excel and into Access. To do so, Select Tools → Macro → "Macros...". This opens the Macro dialog box, as shown in Figure 11-5. Select MyFirstMacro → Edit.

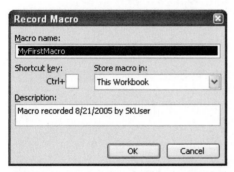

Figure 11-4   Start recording a new macro and call it "MyFirstMacro."

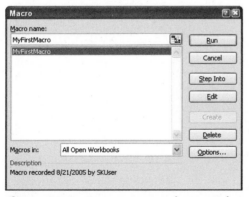

Figure 11-5   Open your newly created macro in Edit mode to copy to the macro-generated code.

7. The code in your macro should look similar to the code shown in Figure 11-6. At this point, all you have to do is select and copy all the code within the Sub procedure (don't include the comments or End Sub).

8. Open the Excel_Automation_2 module in Access and paste the code after the step where you enumerate through the column headings (step 7), as shown in Figure 11-7.

TIP Be sure to paste your macro-generated code in a place within your procedure that makes sense. For example, you don't want to the procedure to encounter this code before the data has been sent to Excel. Generally, Excel-generated code can logically be added directly after the section of code that applies column headings.

Also, notice that in Figure 11-7, there is a clear marker that indicates where the Excel-generated code starts. It's good practice to clearly define the point where you are working with Excel-generated code. This will ensure that you can easily find the section of code in the event you need to replace it, or remove it altogether.

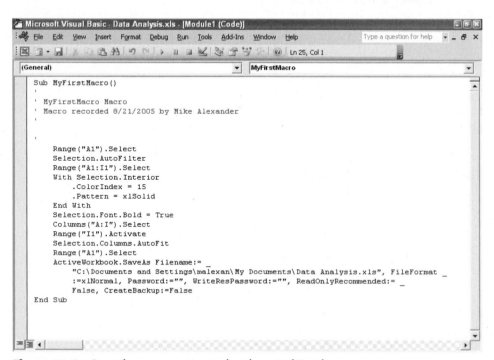

Figure 11-6 Copy the macro-generated code out of Excel.

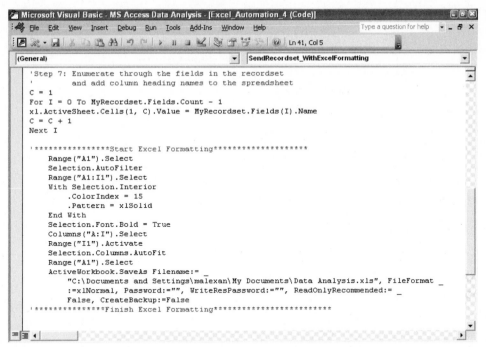

Figure 11-7   Copy the macro-generated code out of Excel and paste it into your Access module.

9. You are almost done! Now add the appropriate application variable name to each foreign object or property in the macro-generated code. In other words, because the objects and properties in the macro-generated code come from the Excel Object Library, you need to let Access know by prefacing each of these with the name you assigned to the Excel application. For example, `Range("A1").Select` would be edited to `xl.Range("A1").Select` because `xl` is the variable name you assigned to the Excel application object. Figure 11-8 is what your code should look like once you have made this change.

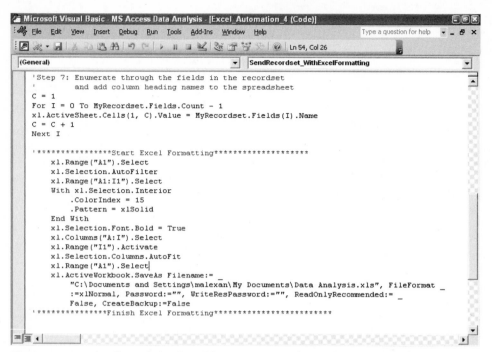

Figure 11-8 Identify each foreign object or property by prefacing it with the variable you assigned to the Excel application object.

NOTE You have to add the application variable name only to objects and properties that are not being used as an object or property of a higher object. Consider the following two lines of code, for example:

```
xl.Columns("A:I").Select
xl.Selection.Columns.AutoFit
```

Notice that when `Columns` is used as a property of the `Selection` object, it is not prefaced with the variable name "xl."

Be warned that skipping step 9 will cause you to get the following seemingly unpredictable runtime errors:

```
Run-time error '1004':   Method 'Range' of object '_Global' failed
Run-time error '91': Object variable or With block variable not set
```

10. Save your module and test it. To test your function, simply place your cursor anywhere inside the function and hit the F5 key on your keyboard.

You have just built your first fully automated Excel report! Keep in mind that this is a simple example. The possibilities are as expansive as Excel itself. For example, you could create a chart, create a pivot table, or apply subtotals. Using this method, you can create a template report in VBA, and then run it whenever you want. You can even add a looping procedure, similar to the one demonstrated in Chapter 10, and automate the same Excel report for every branch, employee, customer, and so on.

> **TIP** Because your automation procedure involves macro-generated code that saves the final Excel file, running the procedure more than once will cause Excel to throw up a message asking if you want to overwrite the previously saved file.
>
> If you want to suppress these messages and automatically overwrite the previously saved files, you can use Excel's `DisplayAlerts` property. The `DisplayAlerts` property is analogous to Access's `SetWarnings` method used to suppress application messages by automatically selecting Yes or OK for the user.
>
> To suppress Excel's alerts, insert the following code before your macro-generated code:
>
> `xl.Application. DisplayAlerts = False`
>
> To turn alerts back on, insert the following code after your macro-generated code:
>
> `xl.Application. DisplayAlerts = True`

Tricks of the Trade: Using Find and Replace to Adjust Your Macro-Generated Code

---

In the preceding walkthrough, you learned there are a set of Excel objects and properties that need to be pointed back to the Excel application object by prefacing them with the name you assigned to the Excel application. For example, `Range("A1").Select` would be edited to `xl.Range("A1").Select` because `xl` is the name you assigned to the Excel application object.

The problem is that this can be quite an ordeal if you have recorded a macro that generated a substantial block of code. It would take a long time to search through the macro-generated code and preface each appropriate object or property. However, there is a set of Excel objects and properties that are used repeatedly in your macro-generated code: `Range`, `ActiveSheet`, `ActiveWorkbook`, `ActiveCell`, `Application`, and `Selection`. The good news is that you can leverage this fact by filtering these objects and properties into the four most commonly used keywords:

continues

```
Range
Selection
Active
Application
```

This is where the find and replace functionality can come in handy. With find and replace, you can find these keywords and preface them all in one fell swoop. To do this, first select all the macro-generated code, and then select Edit → Replace, which activates the Replace dialog box, as shown in Figure 11-9.

As you can see, all you have to do is enter each keyword into the Find What input box and enter the prefaced keyword into the Replace With input box. Again, the four keywords you want to use here are `Range`, `Selection`, `Active`, and `Application`. Keep in mind that depending on your macro-generated code, some of these keywords may not produce any hits, which is okay.

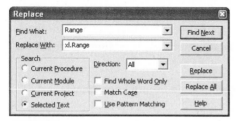

Figure 11-9   Use the find and replace functionality to preface the four most common keywords.

WARNING Notice in Figure 11-9 that there is a search option called Selected Text. This means that any of the find and replace functionality that is applied is limited to the selected text. It is extremely important that you select the macro-generated code and ensure that the Selected Text option is active before you start any find and replace procedures. Otherwise, you could inadvertently change code in other parts of your module.

Bear in mind that these keywords only make up the bulk of the objects and properties that may need to be prefaced in your macro-generated code. There are others that you'll need to preface by hand, the most common of which are

```
Columns
Cells
Rows
```

Why can't you preface these using find and replace? It's a question of object hierarchy. Often, these are used as properties of higher objects, which means you would not need to preface them because the higher object is prefaced. Here's an example:

```
xl.Columns("A:I").Select
xl.Selection.Columns.AutoFit
```

> **Notice that when** `Columns` **is used as a property of the** `Selection`
> **object, it is not prefaced. Prefacing the** `Columns`, `Cells`, **and** `Rows`
> **properties manually will ensure you don't unintentionally cause an error.**

Optimizing macro-generated code

There is no arguing that Excel's macro recorder can prove to be an invaluable
tool when building an automation procedure. The macro-generated code it
provides can not only get you up and running quickly, but it can help you
learn some of Excel's programming fundamentals. The one drawback to using
macro-generated code, however, is that the code itself is rather inefficient. This
is because the macro recorder not only records the functional actions that give
your macro its utility, but it also records mouse moves, mouse clicks, mistakes,
redundant actions, and so forth. This leaves you with a lot of useless code that
has nothing to do with the macro's original purpose. Although the impact of
this superfluous code is typically negligible, larger automation procedures can
take speed and performance hits due to these inefficiencies. In that light, it's
generally a good practice to take some time to clean up and optimize your
macro-generated code.

Remove navigation actions

If you want to enter a formula in a cell within Excel, you have to select that cell
first, and then enter the formula. Indeed, this is true with most actions; you
have to select the cell first, and then perform the action. So as you are recording a macro, you are moving around and clicking each cell on which you need
to perform an action. Meanwhile the macro recorder is generating code for
all that navigation you are doing. However, the fact is that in VBA, you
rarely have to explicitly select a cell before performing an action on it. Therefore, all that code is superfluous and is not needed. Consider the following
macro-generated code:

```
Range("B22:B25").Select
Selection.Interior.ColorIndex = 6
```

In this example, the macro is selecting a range of cells first, and then changing the interior color of all the cells in the range. It's not necessary to select the
range first. This code can be changed to read

```
Range("B22:B25").Interior.ColorIndex = 6
```

The following code shows another version of this type of behavior:

```
Range("A20").Activate
ActiveCell.FormulaR1C1 = "=4+4"
```

In this example, a cell is activated and then a formula is entered into the cell. Again, it is not necessary to select the cell before entering the formula. This code can be changed to read

```
Range("A20").FormulaR1C1 = "=4+4"
```

Navigation code will typically make up a majority of the superfluous entries in your macro-generated code. These are easy to spot and change. Remember these general rules:

- If one line contains the world "Select" and the following line contains "Selection," you should adjust the code.

- If one line contains the word "Activate" and the following line contains "ActiveCell," you should adjust the code.

Delete code that specifies default settings

Certain actions you take in Excel while recording a macro will generate a pre-defined collection of default settings. To demonstrate what this means, open Excel and start recording a macro. Click on any cell, change the font to 12-pitch font, and stop the recording. The code that is generated will look similar to this:

```
Range("A2").Select
With Selection.Font
    .Name = "Arial"
    .Size = 12
    .Strikethrough = False
    .Superscript = False
    .Subscript = False
    .OutlineFont = False
    .Shadow = False
    .Underline = xlUnderlineStyleNone
    .ColorIndex = xlAutomatic
End With
```

Remember that all you did was change the font of one cell, but here you have a litany of properties that reiterate default settings. These default settings are unnecessary and can be removed. This macro can and should be adjusted to read as follows:

```
Range("A2").Font.Size = 12
```

TIP You can easily spot the lines of code that represent default settings because they are usually encapsulated within a `With` statement.

Clean up double takes and mistakes

While you are recording a macro, you will inevitably make missteps and, as a result, redo actions once or twice. As you can imagine, the macro recorder will steadily record these actions, not knowing they are mistakes. To illustrate this, look at the following code:

```
Range("D5").Select
Selection.NumberFormat = "$#,##0.00"
Selection.NumberFormat = "$#,##0"
Range("D4").Select
Range("D5").Select
With Selection.Interior
    .ColorIndex = 6
    .Pattern = xlSolid
End With
Range("D5").Select
Selection.Interior.ColorIndex = 15
```

Believe it or not, only two real actions are being performed here: changing the number format of cell D5, and changing its interior color. So why are there so many lines of code? If you look closely, you will see that number formatting has been applied twice: first with two decimal places and then with no decimal places. In addition, the interior color is being set twice. If you remove these missteps, as follows, you get a more efficient set of code:

```
Range("D5").NumberFormat = "$#,##0"
Range("D5").Interior.ColorIndex = 15
```

TIP When you hit the Undo command while recording a macro, the macro recorder actually erases the lines of code that represent the actions that you are undoing. In that light, make sure you utilize the Undo command before going back to correct your missteps. This will ensure that you don't record mistakes along with good actions.

Disable screen updating temporarily

You will notice that while you are running an Excel macro, your screen flickers and changes as each action is performed. This is because Excel's default behavior is to carry out a screen update with every new action. Unfortunately, screen updating has a negative impact on macros. Because the macro has to wait for the screen to update after every action, macro execution is slowed down. Depending on your system memory, this can have a huge impact on performance.

To resolve this issue, you can temporarily disable screen updating by inserting the following code before your macro-generated code:

```
xl.Application.ScreenUpdating = False
```

To turn screen updating back on, insert the following code after your macro-generated code:

```
xl.Application.ScreenUpdating = True
```

NOTE In the preceding code example, `xl` is the variable name assigned to the Excel application object. This can differ, depending on the variable name you give to the Excel application object.

CHAPTER 12

Query Performance, Database Corruption, and Other Final Thoughts

One of the most important aspects of analyzing data with Access is keeping your database healthy. In this chapter, you learn some of the best practices around building and maintaining your database, ensuring that it runs efficiently and error-free. In addition, this chapter teaches you the best ways to get help in Access when you need a push in the right direction.

Optimizing Query Performance

When you are analyzing a few thousand records, query performance is not an issue. Analytical processes run quickly and smoothly with few problems. However, when you are moving and crunching hundreds of thousands of records, performance becomes a huge issue. There is no getting around the fact that the larger the volume of data, the slower your queries will run. That being said, you can take some steps to optimize query performance, cutting down the time it takes to run your large analytical processes.

Understanding Microsoft Jet's query optimizer

Most relational database programs have a built-in optimizer to ensure efficient performance, even in the face of large volumes of data. Access has the Microsoft Jet query optimizer. Have you ever noticed that when you build a query, close it, then open it again, Access sometimes shuffles your criteria and expressions around? This is evidence of Microsoft Jet's query optimizer.

The query optimizer is charged with the task of establishing a query execution strategy. The query execution strategy is a set of instructions given to the Jet database engine that tells it how to run the query in the quickest, most cost-effective way possible. Jet's query optimizer bases its query execution strategy on the following factors:

- The size of the tables used in the query
- Whether indexes exist in the tables used in the query
- The number of tables and joins used in the query
- The presence and scope of any criteria or expressions used in the query

This execution strategy is created when the query is first run, and recompiled each time you save a query or compact your database. Once a query execution strategy has been established, the Jet database engine simply refers to it each time the query is run, effectively optimizing the execution of the query.

Steps you can take to optimize query performance

You've no doubt heard the phrase "garbage in, garbage out," which refers to the fact that the results you get out of a database are only as good as the data you put in. This concept also applies to Jet's query optimizer. Because Jet's optimization functionality largely depends on the make up and utility of your tables and queries, poorly designed tables and queries can limit the effectiveness of Jet's query optimizer. To that end, the following are actions you can take to help maximize query optimization.

Normalize your database

Many new Access users build one large, flat table and call it a database. This structure seems attractive because you don't have to deal with joins and you have to reference only one table when you build your queries. However, as the volume of data grows in a structure such as this one, query performance will take a nosedive.

When you normalize your database to take on a relational structure, you break up your data into several smaller tables. This has two effects. First, you inherently remove redundant data, giving your query less data to scan. Second, you can query only the tables that contain the information you need, preventing you from scanning your entire database each time you run a query.

Use indexes on appropriate fields

Imagine that you have a filing cabinet that contains 1,000 records that are not alphabetized. How long do you think it would take you to pull out all the records that start with *S*? You would definitely have an easier time pulling out records in an alphabetized filing system. Indexing fields in an Access table is analogous to alphabetizing records in a file cabinet.

When you run a query where you are sorting and filtering on a field that has not been indexed, Access has to scan and read the entire dataset before returning any results. As you can imagine, on large datasets, this can take a very long time. In contrast, queries that sort and filter on fields that have been indexed run much quicker because Access uses the index to check position and restrictions.

You can create an index on a field in a table by going into the table's Design view and adjusting the Indexed property (see Figure 12-1).

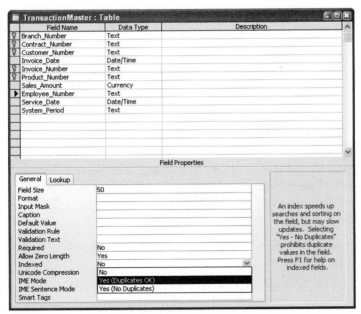

Figure 12-1   Create an index by changing the Indexed property.

> **NOTE** Fields that are tagged as primary keys are already indexed. You can index fields that have duplicate values by setting the Indexed property of the field to Yes (Duplicates OK). Each table in your database can have up to 32 separate indexes.

Now before you go out and start creating an index on every field in your database, there is one caveat to indexing. Although indexes do speed up select queries dramatically, they significantly slow down action queries such as update, delete, and append. This is because when you run an action query on indexed fields, Access has to update each index in addition to changing the actual table. To that end, it's important that you limit the fields that you index. A best practice is to limit your indexes to the following types of fields:

- Fields where you will routinely filter values using criterion
- Fields you anticipate using as joins on other tables
- Fields where you anticipate sorting values regularly

Optimize by improving query design

The following are a few best practices that will help optimize query performance:

- Avoid sorting or filtering fields that are not indexed.
- Avoid building queries that selects "*" from a table—for example, SELECT * FROM MyTable. This forces Access to look up the field names from the system tables every time the query is run.
- When creating a totals query, include only the fields needed to achieve the query's goal. The more fields you include in the GROUP BY clause, the longer the query will take to execute.
- Sometimes you need to include fields in your query design only to set criteria against them. Fields that are not needed in the final results should be set to "not shown." In other words, remove the check from the checkbox in the Show row of the query design grid.
- Avoid using open-ended ranges such as > or <. Instead, use the Between...And statement.
- Use smaller temporary tables in your analytical processes instead of your large core tables. For example, instead of joining two large tables together, consider creating smaller temporary tables that are limited to only the relevant records, and then joining those two. You will often find that your processes will run faster even with the extra steps of creating and deleting temporary tables.
- Use fixed column headings in crosstab queries whenever possible. This way, Access does not have to take the extra step of establishing column headings in your crosstab queries.

- Avoid using calculated fields in subqueries or domain aggregate functions. Subqueries and domain aggregate functions already come with an inherent performance hit. Using calculated fields in them compounds your query's performance loss considerably.

Compact and repair databases regularly

Over time, your database will change simply from the rigors of daily operation. It may increase or decrease the number of tables in your database, you may have added and removed several temporary tables and queries, you may have abnormally closed the database once or twice, and the list goes on. All this action may change your table statistics, leaving your previously compiled queries with inaccurate query execution plans. When you compact and repair your database, you force Access to regenerate table statistics and re-optimize your queries so that they will be recompiled the next time the query is executed. This ensures that Access will run your queries using the most accurate and efficient query execution plans.

TIP You can set your database to automatically compact and repair each time you close it. To do this, activate the Options dialog box by selecting Tools → Options. Click the General tab and place a check next to Compact on Close, and then click the Apply button to confirm the change.

Handling Database Corruption

Corruption is a state where an error occurs in your Access database causing unpredictable behavior or, in worst-case scenarios, rendering your database unusable. To understand why corruption happens, you need to understand how the Jet database engine manages data.

Jet administers your data in a series of blocks, each consisting of 4,096 bytes of data. When you see a table in a database, you see it as a solid object, but it's actually made of blocks of data. Depending on the size of the table, a table can be made of one block of data or many blocks that point to each other. Most corruption is caused by errors that occur when writing to one or more of these blocks. In fact, small-scale corruption happens all the time; you just don't know it because Jet usually resolves these corruption issues during the course of reading and writing data. However, sometimes Jet cannot resolve the issue on its own. In these cases, the database is considered corrupted.

The signs and symptoms of a corrupted database

A database could become corrupted for many reasons. The database may have encountered errors while writing data, table definitions may have been degraded over time, some VBA code or macro may have caused a fatal error, and the list goes on. The point is that a wide range of nebulous issues can cause corruption, and the signs and symptoms of a corrupted database are just as expansive and just as nebulous. You will never see a message explicitly stating that your database is corrupt. So, the question is how do you know if your database has been corrupted?

Databases that fall victim to corruption can generally be separated into two categories: those that you can open and work with, and those that will not open at all.

Watching for corruption in seemingly normal databases

The dangerous thing about corrupted databases that are still usable is that you may never know that you are working with a corrupted database. It can be quite difficult to spot the signs of this type of corruption. That being said, the following are some reasonably clear indicators that strongly suggest corruption:

- You get an error message stating "Invalid field data type" when trying to open a table in either Data view or Design view or when viewing the Relationships window.

- You get an error message stating "Could not find field Description" when trying to compact and repair the database.

- When you try to open a table, a query, a form, a report, or a data access page, you get one of the following messages: "MSAccess can't open the table in datasheet view," "Record is deleted," "Unable to carry out the command," or "There was an error executing the command."

- You get an error message stating "Table 'TempMSysAccessObjects' already exists" when trying to compact and repair the database.

- Nothing happens when you try to open or delete a linked table.

- Access unexpectedly closes and then tries to send an error report.

- You get an error message *falsely* stating that "The changes you requested to the table were not successful because they would create duplicate values in the index, primary key, or relationship."

- #DELETED# starts appearing in your tables.

- Access starts to drop records randomly.

- You get an error message stating "Invalid argument" when clicking on a record.
- All fields for a specific record show `#Error` when you run a query against that record or view it in a form.

Common errors associated with database corruption

A tell-tale sign that a database has become corrupted is when the database will not open at all. The following errors are the most common ones associated with a corrupted database that will not open:

- AOIndex is not an index in this table.
- Could not use; file already in use.
- Enter database password (when none has been set).
- Failure to open/failure to show error.
- Microsoft Access has encountered a problem and needs to close.
- Microsoft Access has encountered a problem and needs to close. We are sorry for the inconvenience.
- Microsoft Jet database engine could not find object MSysDB. Make sure the object exists and that you spell its name correctly and the path name correctly.
- MSysCompactError. Make sure the object exists and that you spell its name correctly and the path name correctly.
- Operation failed; too many indexes. Reduce the number and try again.
- Operation invalid without current index.
- The database 'databasename.mdb' needs to be repaired or isn't a Microsoft Access database file.
- The database has been placed in a state by user <X> on machine <M> that prevents it from being opened or locked.
- The instruction at "0x????????" referenced memory at "0x????????" The memory could not be "written."
- The Microsoft Jet database engine cannot find the input table or query 'MSysAccessObjects'. Make sure it exists and that its name is spelled correctly.
- The Microsoft Jet database engine cannot open the file.
- The Microsoft Jet database engine could not find the object <File name>. Make sure the object exists and that you spell its name and path name correctly.

- The Microsoft Jet database engine could not find the object.

- The Microsoft Jet database engine stopped the process because you and another user are attempting to change the same data at the same time.

- The Visual Basic for Applications project in the database is corrupt.

- This database has been converted from a prior version of Microsoft Access by using the DAO CompactDatabase method instead of the Convert Database command on the Tools menu (Database Utilities submenu). This has left the database in a partially converted state. If you have a copy of the database in its original format, use the Convert Database command on the Tools menu (Database Utilities submenu) to convert it. If the original database is no longer available, create a new database and import your tables and queries to preserve your data. Your other database objects can't be recovered.

- This database is in an unrecognized format. The database may have been created with a later version of Microsoft Access than the one you are using. Upgrade your version of Microsoft Access to the current one, then open this database.

- Unexpected Error 35012.

- Unrecognized database format.

- Visual Basic for Applications Project in This Database Is Corrupt.

- You do not have the necessary permissions to open this object. Please contact your system administrator.

Recovering a corrupted database

If you have determined that your database is indeed corrupt, there are actions you can take to attempt recovery. Keep in mind that your ability to fix a corrupted database depends on the nature and extent of the corruption. The idea is to follow these steps until your issue is resolved:

1. **Make a backup copy of the corrupt database.** Any recovery attempts come with the possibility of permanently disabling the database. You will definitely want a backup in case this happens.

2. **Try working in another environment.** Try opening and using the database on several local machines (especially if you are working with the database through a network). If this resolves your issue, then the problem is probably not a corruption issue. Look for other hardware or software issues.

3. **Delete the .ldb file associated with the database.** When you open an Access database, an .ldb file is created. This file is the mechanism that allows for multi-user operations. Deleting the associated .ldb file will ensure that no rogue instances of the database are left hanging. If you cannot delete the file, use the Windows Task Manager and end all instances of Access and/or any other process that could be logged into the database. In some cases, this action can actually resolve your issue.

4. **Attempt to compact and repair your database.** You can run a compact and repair on your database even if you cannot open it. Open Access without opening a database. Once Access is open, select Tools → Database Utilities → Compact and Repair Database. Select the corrupted database and then select the database you want Access to compact to.

5. **Use the Microsoft Jet Compact Utility.** JetComp is a utility developed by Microsoft that can sometimes correct corruption issues that the built-in compact and repair utility in Access cannot. You can download this free utility from Microsoft's Web site at `http://support` `.microsoft.com/kb/273956`.

6. **Import your database into a fresh .mdb file.** Start a new database and attempt to import your tables, queries, forms, reports, macros, data access pages, and modules from the corrupted database. In most cases, all of your data and code can be salvaged using this method.

7. **Restore the database from a previously backed up version.** If you have a backup of your database, you may want to use it to help restore some of the data you have lost.

8. **Use an Access repair service.** The last resort is to use an Access repair service. These services use specialized software to restore databases, with a success rate close to 99%. This will cost you between $50 and $200, depending on the company you use and the complexity of your issue. You can find a plethora of these services by entering "corrupt Access database" into any of the major search engines.

Preventing database corruption

Unfortunately, there isn't a clear set of warnings alerting you to the fact that your database is on the verge of corruption. By the time you know that you have a corrupted database, it's too late. In that light, remember that preparation is a lot better that desperation. Get into the habit of taking a few simple measures that will minimize the chance of corruption and prepare you in the event of a corrupted database.

Back up your database regularly

Having a backup of your database is like having a spare tire. There is no better safeguard against losing data than having a spare copy of it stored away. When you choose a backup plan, you will want to consider two things: when and where. When should you back up your database? Well, you want to choose a backup schedule that directly relates to your threshold of data loss. For example, if you cannot lose more than one day of data, make a backup of your database every day. If daily backups are excessive, make a weekly backup. Where should you back up your database? You want to choose a location that is safe, accessible, and not in the same folder as your working database.

Compact and repair your database on a regular basis

Certain things happen through the natural course of using a database. For example, the data blocks in the database become fragmented, the table statistics become outmoded, and the database grows in size. Although none of these occurrences directly lead to a corrupt database, they can contribute to one if left unchecked. Many Access users think that the compact and repair utility simply releases disk space, but several important actions are performed with a compact and repair.

The compact and repair database utility does the following:

- Reclaims disk space and ensures the prevention of database bloat.
- Defragments the blocks of data that make up table pages, improving performance and making efficient use of the read ahead cache.
- Resets AutoNumber fields, ensuring that the next value allocated will be one more than the highest value in the remaining records.
- Regenerates table statistics used by the query optimizer to create query execution strategies.
- Flags all queries, indicating a recompile the next time the query is executed.

These actions can play a big part in keeping your database streamlined and efficient. You can set your database to automatically compact and repair each time you close it. To do this, select Tools → Options. This activates the Options dialog box. Click the General tab, place a check next to Compact on Close, and then click the Apply button to confirm the change.

Avoid interruption of service while writing to your database

The most common cause of corruption is interruption while writing to your database. Interrupted write processes can lead to a host of issues from incomplete table definitions to lost indices. In that vein, be sure to avoid any type of abnormal or abrupt termination of Access. Following these general guidelines will help you avoid corruption due to interrupted processes:

- Always wait until all queries, macros, and procedures have completed execution before closing Access.
- Avoid using the Task Manager to shut down Access.
- Never place your Access database on a file server that is regularly shut down or rebooted.
- Avoid power loss while working with your database. If your database is on a file server, make sure the server has protection against power surges or power outages.

Never work with a database from removable media

When you work with an Access database, additional disk space is needed for the LDB file and for the normal database bloat that comes with using Access. If you open an Access database on removable media such as a memory stick or a ZIP disk, you run the risk of corruption due to disk space errors. It's generally a good practice to copy the database to your hard drive, work with the database there, and then copy it back to the removable media when you are done.

Getting Help in Access

As you experiment with new functions and tools in Access, you may often need a little help or a simple push in the right direction. The first place you should look is Access's help system. Now, your humble author will be the first to admit that the help system in Access has its flaws. To a new user, the Access help system may seem like a clunky add-in that returns a perplexing list of topics that has nothing to do with the original topic being searched. The truth is, however, once you learn how to use the Access help system effectively; it is often the fastest and easiest way to get help on a topic. Here are some tips that will help you get the most out of Access's help system.

Location matters when asking for help

You may remember the Help system in Access 97 being a lot more user-friendly and more effective than newer versions of Access. Well, rest assured that you are not just imagining it. The fact is that Microsoft did fundamentally change the mechanics of the Access Help system. In Access 97, when you entered a keyword into the search index, Access did a kind of global search, throwing your search criteria against all the topics within Access. Later versions of Access, however, actually have two Help systems: one providing help on Access features and another on VBA programming topics. Instead of doing a global search with your criteria, Access throws your search criteria only against the help system that is relevant to your current location. This essentially means that the help you get is determined by the area of Access in which you are working. In that vein, if you require help on a topic that involves VBA programming, you will need to be in the VBA Editor while performing your search. On the other hand, if you need help on building a query, it's best to be n the query design view. This will ensure that your keyword search is performed on the correct help system.

Use the table of contents instead of a keyword search

Rather than searching Access Help based on a keyword, you may find it easier to search through the table of contents to find what you need. As you can see in Figure 12-2, you simply click Table of Contents to activate it.

Figure 12-3 shows the tree-view style selection list you can click through to find your needed topic.

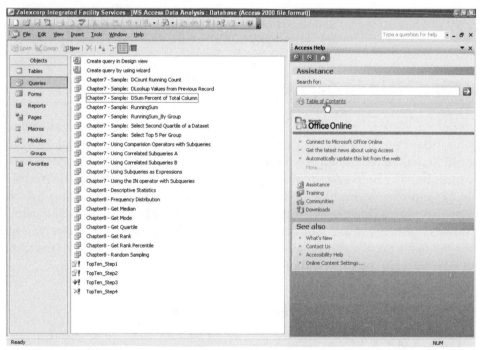

Figure 12-2   Click the Table of Contents hyperlink to open an organized list of topics.

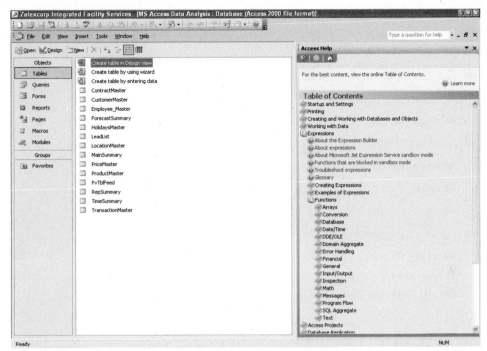

Figure 12-3 You can drill into each topic to see its subtopics. For example, the Functions topic contains subtopics relating to the different function categories.

Online help is better than offline help

When you search for help on a topic, Access checks to see if there is an Internet connection available. If there is, Access returns help results based on online content from Microsoft's site. If no Internet connection is available, Access uses the help files that are locally stored with Microsoft Office. One way to maximize the help you are getting in Access is to use the online help. Online help is generally better than offline help because oftentimes, the content you find with online help is more detailed and includes updated information as well as links to other resources not available offline.

Diversify your knowledgebase with online resources

Familiarize yourself with a handful of Web sites and forums dedicated to Access. These resources can serve as supplemental help, not only providing help on basic Access topics, but also giving you situation-specific tips and tricks. The sites in the following list should get you started. These sites are free to use and are particularly helpful when you need an extra push in the right direction.

- Access topics and general help
  - www.allenbrowne.com
  - www.mvps.org/access/
- Access tutorials and samples
  - www.datapigtechnologies.com
  - www.fontstuff.com
  - www.rogersaccesslibrary.com
- Access discussion groups and forums
  - www.microsoft.com/office/community/en-us/ default.mspx
  - www.utteraccess.com

Data Analyst's Function Reference

Access 2003 has more than 150 built-in functions that perform a wide variety of tasks. This appendix is designed to provide a solid reference to the functions that are most relevant to the realm of data analysis. Several of these functions are covered in detail throughout the chapters in this book.

TIP You can learn more about the functions not covered here by using the Access help system or by visiting the Web site `http://office` `.microsoft.com/en-us/assistance/HP011359591033.aspx`.

This site offers a full list of all the functions available in Access 2003. Keep in mind that some of the functions listed on this site may not be available in Access 2000.

Abs

Purpose

The `Abs` function is a math function that returns a value that represents the absolute value of the number—that is, the magnitude of the number without the positive or negative sign. For example, `Abs(-5)` returns 5.

Arguments

Abs(*Number*)

Number (required). This is the numeric expression you are evaluating. In a query environment, you can use the name of a field to specify that you are evaluating all the row values of that field.

Asc

Purpose

The Asc function is a conversion function used to convert a string to its ASCII code. For example, Asc("A") returns 65 because 65 is the ASCII code for the uppercase letter A. If you pass a whole word to the Asc function, it returns the ASCII code only for the first letter of the word.

Arguments

Asc(*String*)

String (required). This is the string you are evaluating. If the string you are passing to the function contains no characters, the function will fail and produce a runtime error.

Atn

Purpose

The Atn function is a math function that enables you to calculate the arctangent of a number.

Arguments

Atn(*Number*)

Number (required). This is the numeric expression you are evaluating.

Choose

Purpose

The `Choose` function is a program flow function that enables you to return a value from a list of choices based on a given position. For instance, `Choose(3, "Microsoft", "Access", "Data", "Analysis")` returns "Data" because word "Data" is in the third position in the list of values.

Arguments

`Choose(`*`PositionNumber, List of Values Separated by Commas`*`)`

`PositionNumber` (required). This is the numeric expression or field that results in a value between 1 and the number of available choices. If this argument's value is less than 1 or greater than the number of choices in the function, a Null value is returned.

`List of Values Separated by Commas` (required). This is a variant expression that contains a list of one or more values.

Chr

Purpose

The `Chr` function is a conversion function that is used to convert a string to its associated ASCII code. For example, `Chr(65)` returns "A".

Arguments

`Chr(`*`Number`*`)`

`Number` (required). This is the number value that represents an ASCII character code. If the number you are passing to the function is not a valid ASCII character code, the function will fail and produce a runtime error.

Cos

Purpose

The Cos function is a math function that enables you to calculate the cosine of an angle.

Arguments

Cos(*number*)

Number (required). This is the numeric expression that represents an angle in radians.

Date

Purpose

The Date function returns today's date based on your PC's current system date. The Date function is key to performing any analysis that involves a time comparison in relation to today's date. There are no required arguments for this function; to use it, simply enter Date().

DateAdd

Purpose

The DateAdd function returns a date to which a specified interval has been added. In other words, the DateAdd function enables you calculate a date by adding 30 days to it, subtracting 3 weeks from it, adding 4 months to it, or so on. For example

DateAdd("ww",1,#11/30/2004#) adds 1 week, returning 12/7/2004.

DateAdd("m",2,#11/30/2004#) adds 2 months, returning 1/30/2005.

DateAdd("yyyy",-1,#11/30/2004#) subtracts 1 year, returning 11/30/2003.

Arguments

```
DateAdd(Interval, Number, Date)
```

`Interval` (required). This is the interval of time you want to use. The intervals available are:

yyyy (Year)

q (Quarter)

m (Month)

y (Day of year)

d (Day)

w (Weekday)

ww (Week)

h (Hour)

n (Minute)

s (Second)

`Number` (required). This is the number of intervals to add. A positive number returns a date in the future, whereas a negative number returns a date in the past.

`Date` (required). This is the date value with which you are working. In a query environment, you can use the name of a field to specify that you are evaluating all the row values of that field.

DateDiff

Purpose

The `DateDiff` function returns the difference between two dates based on a specified time interval. For example, `DateDiff('yyyy', #5/16/1972#, #5/16/2005#)` returns 33 because there is a difference of 33 years between the two dates.

Arguments

```
DateDiff(Interval, Date1, Date2, FirstDayOfTheWeek, FirstWeekOfTheYear)
```

`Interval` (required). This is the interval of time you want to use. The intervals available are:

`yyyy`	(Year)
`q`	(Quarter)
`m`	(Month)
`y`	(Day of year)
`d`	(Day)
`w`	(Weekday)
`ww`	(Week)
`h`	(Hour)
`n`	(Minute)
`s`	(Second)

`Date1` (required). This is one of the two dates you want to calculate the difference between. In a query environment, you can use the name of a field to specify that you are evaluating all the row values of that field.

`Date2` (required). This is one of the two dates you want to calculate the difference between. In a query environment, you can use the name of a field to specify that you are evaluating all the row values of that field.

`FirstDayOfTheWeek` (optional). This specifies which day you want to count as the first day of the week. Enter 1 in this argument to make the first day Sunday, 2 for Monday, 3 for Tuesday, and so on. If this argument is omitted, the first day is a Sunday by default.

`FirstWeekOfTheYear` (optional). This specifies the first week of the year. In most cases, you would omit this argument. This uses the first week that includes January 1st as the default. However, you can alter this setting by using one of the following values.

0	Use the NLS API setting.
1	Use the first week that includes January 1.
2	Use the first week that has at least four days.
3	Use the first week that has seven days.

DatePart

Purpose

The `DatePart` function enables you to evaluate a date and return a specific interval of time represented in that date. For example, `DatePart("q",#6/4/2004#)` returns 2 (as in second quarter), which is the quarter that is represented in that date.

Arguments

`DatePart(Interval, ValidDate, FirstDayOfTheWeek, FirstWeekOfTheYear)`

`Interval` (required). This is the interval of time you want to use. The intervals available are

yyyy	(Year)
q	(Quarter)
m	(Month)
y	(Day of year)
d	(Day)
w	(Weekday)
ww	(Week)
h	(Hour)
n	(Minute)
s	(Second)

`ValidDate` (required). This is the date value with which you are working. In a query environment, you can use the name of a field to specify that you are evaluating all the row values of that field.

`FirstDayOfTheWeek` (optional). This specifies which day you want to count as the first day of the week. Enter 1 in this argument to make the first day Sunday, 2 for Monday, 3 for Tuesday, and so on. If this argument is omitted, the first day is a Sunday by default.

`FirstWeekOfTheYear` (optional). This specifies the first week of the year. In most cases, you would omit this argument. This uses the first week that includes January 1st as the default. However, you can alter this setting by using one of the following values:

0	Use the NLS API setting.
1	Use the first week that includes January 1.
2	Use the first week that has at least four days.
3	Use the first week that has seven days.

DateSerial

Purpose

The `DateSerial` function enables you to construct a date value by combining given year, month, and day components. This function is perfect for converting disparate strings that, together, represent a date, into an actual date. For example, `DateSerial(2004, 4, 3)` returns April 3, 2004

Arguments

```
DateSerial(Year, Month, Day)
```

`Year` (required). Any number or numeric expression from 100 to 9999.

`Month` (required). Any number or numeric expression.

`Day` (required). Any number or numeric expression.

DateValue

Purpose

The `DateValue` function enables you to convert any string or expression that represents a valid date, time, or both into a date value. For example, `DateValue("October 31, 2004")` returns 10/31/2004.

Arguments

```
DateValue(Expression)
```

`Expression` (required). Any string or valid expression that can represent a valid date, time, or both.

Day

Purpose

The Day function is a conversion function that converts a valid date to a number from 1 to 31, representing the day of the month for a given date. For example, Day(#5/16/1972#) returns 16.

Arguments

Day(*ValidDate*)

ValidDate (required). This is any value that can represent a valid date. In a query environment, you can use the name of a field to specify that you are evaluating all the row values of that field.

DDB

Purpose

The DDB function is a financial function that calculates the depreciation of an asset for a specific period using the double-declining balance method or another specified method.

Arguments

DDB(*Cost*, *Salvage*, *Life*, *Period*, *Factor*)

Cost (required). This is the initial cost of the asset; must be a positive number.

Salvage (required). This is the value of the asset at the end of its useful life; must be a positive number.

Life (required). This is the length of the useful life of the asset.

Period (required). This is the period for which asset depreciation is calculated.

Factor (optional). This is the rate at which the balance declines. The default setting for this argument is the double-declining method (a factor of 2).

Domain Aggregate Functions

Purpose

Domain aggregate functions enable you to extract and aggregate statistical information from an entire dataset (a domain). These functions differ from aggregate queries in that an aggregate query groups data before evaluating the values whereas a domain aggregate function evaluates the values for the entire dataset. There are 12 different domain aggregate functions, but they all have the same arguments.

Arguments

```
("Field Name]","[Dataset Name]", "[Criteria]")
```

Field Name (required). This expression identifies the field containing the data with which you are working. This argument must be in quotes.

Dataset Name (required). This expression identifies the table or query you are working with; also known as the domain. This argument must be in quotes.

Criteria (optional). This expression is used to restrict the range of data on which the domain aggregate function is performed. If omitted, the domain aggregate function is performed against the entire dataset. This argument must be in quotes.

Additional Remarks

The 12 domain aggregate functions are as follows:

DSum. The DSum function returns the total sum value of a specified field in the domain. *DSum("[Sales_Amount]", "[TransactionMaster]")* gives you the total sum of sales amount in the TransactionMaster table.

DAvg. The DAvg function returns the average value of a specified field in the domain. *DAvg("[Sales_Amount]", "[TransactionMaster]")* gives you the average sales amount in the TransactionMaster table.

DCount. The DCount function a returns the total number of records in the domain. *DCount("*", "[TransactionMaster]")* gives you the total number of records in the TransactionMaster table.

DLookup. The DLookup function returns the first value of a specified field that matches the criteria you define within the DLookup function. If you don't supply a criterion, the DLookup function returns a random value in the domain. DLookup functions are particularly useful when you need to retrieve a value from an outside dataset. *DLookUp("[Last_Name]", "[Employee_Master]","[Employee_Number]='42620' ")* returns the value in the Last_Name field of the record where the Employee_Number is '42620'.

DMin, DMax. The DMin and DMax functions return the minimum and maximum values in the domain, respectively. *DMin("[Sales_Amount]", "[TransactionMaster]")* returns the lowest sales amount in the TransactionMaster, whereas *DMin("[Sales_Amount]", "[TransactionMaster]")* returns the highest.

DFirst, DLast. The DFirst and DLast functions return the first and last values in the domain, respectively. *DFirst("[Sales_Amount]", "[TransactionMaster]")* returns the first sales amount in the TransactionMaster whereas *DLast("[Sales_Amount]", "[TransactionMaster]")* returns the last.

DStDev, DStDevP, DVar, DVarP. You can use the DStDev and the DStDevP functions to return the standard deviation across a population sample and a population, respectively. The DVar and the DVarP functions similarly return the variance across a population sample and a population, respectively.

Exp

Purpose

The Exp function is a math function that raises the base of natural logarithms (2.718282) number to a power you specify.

Arguments

Exp(*Number*)

Number (required). This is the numeric expression that is used as the power to raise 2.718282.

FormatCurrency

Purpose

The FormatCurrency function is a conversion function that converts an expression to a currency using the currency symbol defined by your computer's regional settings.

Arguments

FormatCurrency(*Number*, *TrailingDigits*, *LeadingDigits*, *NegativeParens*, *Group*)

Number (required). This is the number value you want to convert. In a query environment, you can use the name of a field to specify that you are evaluating all the row values of that field.

TrailingDigits (optional). This is the number of digits to the right of the decimal you want displayed.

LeadingDigits (optional). This indicates whether a leading zero is displayed for fractional values. The settings for this argument are 1 for True, 0 for False, or 2 to use the computer's regional settings.

NegativeParens (optional). This specifies if negative values should be wrapped in parentheses. The settings for this argument are 1 for True, 0 for False, or 2 to use the computer's regional settings.

Group (optional). This indicates whether or not numbers are grouped using the group delimiter specified in the computer's regional settings. The settings for this argument are 1 for True, 0 for False, or 2 to use the computer's regional settings.

FormatDateTime

Purpose

The FormatDateTime function is a conversion function that converts an expression to a date or time.

Arguments

```
FormatDateTime(Date, NamedFormat)
```

Date (required). This is the date/time expression you want to convert. In a query environment, you can use the name of a field to specify that you are evaluating all the row values of that field.

NamedFormat (optional). This is the format code specifying the date/time format you would like to use. The settings for this argument are as follows:

0	Display date as a short date and time as a long time.
1	Display a date using the long date format specified in your computer's regional settings.
2	Display a date using the short date format specified in your computer's regional settings.
3	Display a time using the time format specified in your computer's regional settings.
4	Display a time using the 24-hour format (hh:mm).

FormatNumber

Purpose

The FormatNumber function is a conversion function that converts a numeric expression to a formatted number.

Arguments

```
FormatNumber(Number, TrailingDigits, LeadingDigits, NegativeParens,
Group)
```

Number (required). This is the number value you want to convert. In a query environment, you can use the name of a field to specify that you are evaluating all the row values of that field.

TrailingDigits (optional). This is the number of digits to the right of the decimal you want displayed.

LeadingDigits (optional). This indicates whether a leading zero is displayed for fractional values. The settings for this argument are 1 for True, 0 for False, or 2 to use the computer's regional settings.

NegativeParens (optional). This specifies if negative values should be wrapped in parentheses. The settings for this argument are 1 for True, 0 for False, or 2 to use the computer's regional settings.

Group (optional). This indicates whether or not numbers are grouped using the group delimiter specified in the computer's regional settings. The settings for this argument are 1 for True, 0 for False, or 2 to use the computer's regional settings.

FormatPercent

Purpose

The FormatPercent function is a conversion function that converts a numeric expression to a formatted percentage with a trailing percent (%) character.

Arguments

```
FormatPercent(Number, TrailingDigits, LeadingDigits, NegativeParens,
Group)
```

Number (required). This is the number value you want to convert. In a query environment, you can use the name of a field to specify that you are evaluating all the row values of that field.

TrailingDigits (optional). This is the number of digits to the right of the decimal you want displayed.

LeadingDigits (optional). This indicates whether a leading zero is displayed for fractional values. The settings for this argument are 1 for True, 0 for False, or 2 to use the computer's regional settings.

NegativeParens (optional). This specifies if negative values should be wrapped in parentheses. The settings for this argument are 1 for True, 0 for False, or 2 to use the computer's regional settings.

Group (optional). This indicates whether or not numbers are grouped using the group delimiter specified in the computer's regional settings. The settings for this argument are 1 for True, 0 for False, or 2 to use the computer's regional settings.

FV

Purpose

The FV function is a financial function that enables you to calculate an annuity's future value. An annuity is a series of fixed cash payments normally made against a loan over a period of time.

Arguments

FV(*Rate*, *PaymentPeriods*, *PaymentAmount*, *PresentValue*, *Type*)

Rate (required). This is the average interest rate per period.

PaymentPeriods (required). This is the total number of payment periods in the annuity.

PaymentAmount (required). This is the payment amount, usually consisting of principal and interest.

PresentValue (optional). This is the present value of future payments. If omitted, 0 is assumed.

Type (optional). This argument specifies when payments are due. A value of 0 means that payments are due at the end of the payment period, and a value of 1 means that payments are due at the beginning of the payment period. If omitted, 0 is assumed.

Hour

Purpose

The Hour function is a conversion function that converts a valid time to a number from 0 to 23, representing the hour of the day. For example, Hour(#9:30:00 PM#) returns 21.

Arguments

Hour(*ValidTime*)

ValidTime (required). This is any combination of values that can represent a valid time. In a query environment, you can use the name of a field to specify that you are evaluating all the row values of that field.

IIf

Purpose

The `IIf` function is a program flow function that enables you to create an `If...Then...Else` statement, returning one value if a condition evaluates to true, and another value if it evaluates to false.

Arguments

`IIf(`*Expression, TrueAnswer, FalseAnswer*`)`

`Expression` (required). This is the expression you want to evaluate.

`TrueAnswer` (required). This is the value to return if the expression is true.

`FalseAnswer` (required). This is the value to return if the expression is false.

InStr

Purpose

The `InStr` function is a text function that searches for a specified string in another string and returns its position number. For example, `InStr("Alexander, Mike","x")` returns 4 because the `"x"` is character number 4 in this string.

Arguments

`InStr(`*Start, SearchString, FindString, Compare*`)`

`Start` (optional). This is the character number to start the search; default is 1.

`SearchString` (required). This is the string to be searched.

`FindString` (required). This is the string to search for.

`Compare` (optional). This specifies the type of string comparison.

Additional Remarks

The Compare argument can have the following values

-1	Performs a comparison using the setting of the Option Compare statement.
0	Performs a binary comparison.
1	Performs a textual comparison.
2	Microsoft Access only. Performs a comparison based on information in your database.

InStrRev

Purpose

The InStrRev function is a text function that searches for a specified string in another string and returns its position number from the end of the string.

Arguments

```
InstrRev(SearchString, FindString, Start, Compare)
```

SearchString (required). This is the string to be searched.

FindString (required). This is the string to search for.

Start (optional). This is the character number to start the search; default is 1.

Compare (optional). This specifies the type of string comparison.

Additional Remarks

The Compare argument can have the following values:

-1	Performs a comparison using the setting of the Option Compare statement.
0	Performs a binary comparison.
1	Performs a textual comparison.
2	Microsoft Access only. Performs a comparison based on information in your database.

IPmt

Purpose

The IPmt function is a financial function that enables you to calculate the interest paid within a specified period during the life of an annuity. An annuity is a series of fixed cash payments normally made against a loan over a period of time.

Arguments

IPmt(*Rate*, *Period*, *PaymentPeriods*, *PresentValue*, *FutureValue*, *Type*)

Rate (required). This is the average interest rate per period.

Period (required). This is the specified payment period in question.

PaymentPeriods (required). This is the total number of payment periods in the annuity.

PresentValue (required). This is the present value of future payments.

FutureValue (optional). This is the future value or final balance on a loan or an investment upon making the last payment. If omitted, 0 is assumed.

Type (optional). This argument specifies when payments are due. A value of 0 means that payments are due at the end of the payment period, and a value of 1 means that payments are due at the beginning of the payment period. If omitted, 0 is assumed.

IRR

Purpose

The IRR function is a financial function that calculates the internal rate of return based on serial cash flow, payments, and receipts.

Arguments

IRR(*IncomeValues, Guess*)

IncomeValues (required). These values make up an array that represents the periodic cash flow values. Within this array, there must be at least one negative number and one positive number.

Guess (optional). This argument enables you to estimate the percent of total investment that will be returned. If this is omitted, 10 percent is used.

IsError

Purpose

The IsError function is an inspection function that determines if an expression evaluates as an error. This function returns a True or False answer.

Arguments

IsError(*Expression*)

Expression (required). This is any value or expression. In a query environment, you can use the name of a field to specify that you are evaluating all the row values of that field.

IsNull

Purpose

The IsNull function is an inspection function that determines if a value contains no valid date. This function returns a True or False answer.

Arguments

```
IsNull(Expression)
```

`Expression` (required). This is any value or expression. In a query environment, you can use the name of a field to specify that you are evaluating all the row values of that field.

IsNumeric

Purpose

The `IsNumeric` function is an inspection function that determines if an expression evaluates as a numeric value. This function returns a True or False answer.

Arguments

```
IsNumeric(Expression)
```

`Expression` (required). This is any value or expression. In a query environment, you can use the name of a field to specify that you are evaluating all the row values of that field.

LCase

Purpose

The `LCase` function converts a string to lowercase letters.

Arguments

```
LCase(String)
```

`String` (required). This is the string to be converted. In a query environment, you can use the name of a field to specify that you are converting all the row values of that field.

Left

Purpose

The Left function returns a specified number of characters starting from the leftmost character of the string. For example, Left("Nowhere", 3) returns "Now".

Arguments

Left(*String*, *NumberOfCharacters*)

String (required). This is the string to be evaluated. In a query environment, you can use the name of a field to specify that you are evaluating all the row values of that field.

NumberofCharacters (required). This is the number of characters you want returned. If this argument is greater than or equal to the number of characters in string, the entire string is returned.

Len

Purpose

The Len function returns a number identifying the number of characters in a given string. This function is quite useful when you need to dynamically determine the length of a string. For instance, Len("Alexander") returns 9.

Arguments

Len(String or Variable)

String or Variable (required). This is the string or variable to be evaluated. In a query environment, you can use the name of a field to specify that you are evaluating all the row values of that field.

Log

Purpose

The Log function is a math function that calculates the natural logarithm of a number.

Arguments

Log(*Number*)

Number (required). This is the numeric expression that is to be evaluated. It must be greater than zero.

LTrim

Purpose

The LTrim function removes the leading spaces from a string. This function comes in handy when cleaning up data received from a mainframe source.

Arguments

LTrim(*String*)

String (required). This is the string you are working with. In a query environment, you can use the name of a field to specify that you are evaluating all the row values of that field.

Mid

Purpose

The Mid function returns a specified number of characters starting from a specified character position. The required arguments for the Mid function are the text you are evaluating, the starting position, and the number of characters you want returned. For example, Mid("Lonely", 2, 3) captures three characters starting from character number 2 in the string, returning "one".

Arguments

Mid(*String*, *StartPosition*, *NumberOfCharacters*)

String (required). This is the string to be evaluated. In a query environment, you can use the name of a field to specify that you are evaluating all the row values of that field.

StartPosition (required). This is the position number of the character you want to start your capture.

NumberofCharacters (required). This is the number of characters you want returned. If this argument is greater than or equal to the number of characters in string, the entire string is returned.

Minute

Purpose

The Minute function converts a valid time to a number from 0 to 59, representing the minute of the hour. For example, Minute(#9:30:00 PM#) returns 30.

Arguments

Minute(*ValidTime*)

ValidTime (required). This is any combination of values that can represent a valid time. In a query environment, you can use the name of a field to specify that you are evaluating all the row values of that field.

MIRR

Purpose

The MIRR function is a financial function that calculates the internal rate of return based on serial cash flow, payments, and receipts that are financed at different rates.

Arguments

MIRR(*IncomeValues*, *FinanceRate*, *ReinvestRate*)

IncomeValues (required). These values make up an array that represents the periodic cash flow values. Within this array, there must be at least one negative number and one positive number.

FinanceRate (required). This is the interest rate paid as the cost of investing. The values of this argument must be represented as decimal values.

ReinvestRate (required). This is the interest rate received on gains from cash reinvestment. The values of this argument must be represented as decimal values.

Month

Purpose

The Month function converts a valid date to a number from 1 to 12, representing the month for a given date. For example, Month(#5/16/1972#) returns 5.

Arguments

Month(*ValidDate*)

ValidDate (required). This is any value that can represent a valid date. In a query environment, you can use the name of a field to specify that you are evaluating all the row values of that field.

MonthName

Purpose

The MonthName function converts a numeric month designation (1 to 12) to a month name. For instance, MonthName(8) returns August. Values less than 1 or greater than 12 will cause an error.

Arguments

MonthName(*NumericMonth*, *Abbreviated*)

NumericMonth (required). This is a number from 1 to 12 that represents a month. 1 represents January, 2 represents February, and so on.

Abbreviated (optional). This specifies whether or not the month is abbreviated. If this argument is omitted, the month is not abbreviated. Enter 1 to return abbreviated months.

Now

Purpose

The Now function returns today's date and time based on your PC's current system date and time. There are no required arguments for this function; to use it, simply enter **Now()**.

NPer

Purpose

The NPer function is a financial function that specifies the number of periods for an annuity based on periodic, fixed payments at a fixed interest rate. An annuity is a series of fixed cash payments normally made against a loan over a period of time.

Arguments

NPer(*Rate*, *PaymentAmount*, *PresentValue*, *FutureValue*, *Type*)

Rate (required). This is the average interest rate per period.

PaymentAmount (required). This is the payment amount, usually consisting of principal and interest.

PresentValue (required). This is the present value of future payments and receipts.

FutureValue (optional). This is the future value or final balance on a loan or an investment upon making the last payment. If omitted, 0 is assumed.

Type (optional). This argument specifies when payments are due. A value of 0 means that payments are due at the end of the payment period, and a value of 1 means that payments are due at the beginning of the payment period. If omitted, 0 is assumed.

NPV

Purpose

The NPV function is a financial function that calculates the net present value or the current value of a future series of payments and receipts based on serial cash flow, payments, receipts, and a discount rate.

Arguments

```
NPV(DiscountRate, IncomeValues)
```

DiscountRate (required). This is the discount rate received over the length of the period. The values of this argument must be represented as decimal values.

IncomeValues (required). These values make up an array that represents the periodic cash flow values. Within this array, there must be at least one negative number and one positive number.

NZ

Purpose

The NZ function enables you to tell Access to recognize Null values as another value, preventing your null values from propagating through an expression.

Arguments

```
NZ(Variant, ValueIfNull)
```

Variant (required). This is the date you are working with.

ValueIfNull (required in the query environment). This is the value you want returned if the Variant is Null.

Partition

Purpose

The `Partition` function is a database function that identifies the particular range in which a number falls and returns a string describing that range. This function is useful when you need to create a quick and easy frequency distribution.

Arguments

```
Partition(Number, Range Start, Range Stop, Interval)
```

`Number` (required). This is the number you are evaluating. In a query environment, you typically use the name of a field to specify that you are evaluating all the row values of that field.

`Range Start` (required). This is a whole number that is to be the start of the overall range of numbers. Note that this number cannot be less than zero.

`Range Stop` (required). This is a whole number that is to be the end of the overall range of numbers. Note that this number cannot be equal to or less than the Range Start.

`Interval` (required). This is a whole number that is to be the span of each range in the series from Range Start to Range Stop. Note that this number cannot be less than one.

Pmt

Purpose

The `Pmt` function is a financial function that calculates the payment for an annuity based on periodic, fixed payments at a fixed interest rate. An annuity is a series of fixed cash payments normally made against a loan over a period of time.

Arguments

```
Pmt(Rate, PaymentPeriods, PresentValue, FutureValue, Type)
```

Rate (required). This is the average interest rate per period.

PaymentPeriods (required). This is the total number of payment periods in the annuity.

PresentValue (required). This is the present value of future payments and receipts.

FutureValue (optional). This is the future value or final balance on a loan or an investment upon making the last payment. If omitted, 0 is assumed.

Type (optional). This argument specifies when payments are due. A value of 0 means that payments are due at the end of the payment period, and a value of 1 means that payments are due at the beginning of the payment period. If omitted, 0 is assumed.

PPmt

Purpose

The PPmt function is a financial function that enables you to calculate the principal payment for a specified period during the life of an annuity. An annuity is a series of fixed cash payments normally made against a loan over a period of time.

Arguments

```
PPmt(Rate, Period, PaymentPeriods, PresentValue, FutureValue, Type)
```

Rate (required). This is the average interest rate per period.

Period (required). This is the specified payment period in question.

PaymentPeriods (required). This is the total number of payment periods in the annuity.

`PresentValue` (required). This is the present value of future payments and receipts.

`FutureValue` (optional). This is the future value or final balance on a loan or an investment upon making the last payment. If omitted, 0 is assumed.

`Type` (optional). This argument specifies when payments are due. A value of 0 means that payments are due at the end of the payment period, and a value of 1 means that payments are due at the beginning of the payment period. If omitted, 0 is assumed.

PV

Purpose

The PV function is a financial function that enables you to calculate an annuity's present value. An annuity is a series of fixed cash payments normally made against a loan over a period of time.

Arguments

`PV(Rate, PaymentPeriods, PaymentAmount, FutureValue, Type)`

`Rate` (required). This is the average interest rate per period.

`PaymentPeriods` (required). This is the total number of payment periods in the annuity.

`PaymentAmount` (required). This is the payment amount, usually consisting of principal and interest.

`FutureValue` (optional). This is the future value or final balance on a loan or an investment upon making the last payment. If omitted, 0 is assumed.

`Type` (optional). This argument specifies when payments are due. A value of 0 means that payments are due at the end of the payment period, and a value of 1 means that payments are due at the beginning of the payment period. If omitted, 0 is assumed.

Rate

Purpose

The Rate function is a financial function that enables you to calculate the interest rate per period for an annuity. An annuity is a series of fixed cash payments normally made against a loan over a period of time.

Arguments

Rate(*Periods*, *PaymentAmount*, *PresentValue*, *FutureValue*, *Type*, *Guess*)

Periods (required). This is the total number of payment periods in the annuity.

PaymentAmount (required). This is the payment amount, usually consisting of principal and interest.

PresentValue (required). This is the present value of future payments and receipts.

FutureValue (optional). This is the future value or final balance on a loan or an investment upon making the last payment. If omitted, 0 is assumed.

Type (optional). This argument specifies when payments are due. A value of 0 means that payments are due at the end of the payment period, and a value of 1 means that payments are due at the beginning of the payment period. If omitted, 0 is assumed.

Guess (optional). This argument enables you to estimate the percent of total investment that will be returned. If this is omitted, 10 percent is used.

Replace

Purpose

The Replace function enables you to replace a specified substring with another substring. This function has the same effect as the "Find and Replace" functionality. For example, Replace("Pear", "P", "B") returns "Bear".

Arguments

Replace(*String, Find, Replace, Start, Count, Compare*)

String (required). This is the full string you are evaluating. In a query environment, you can use the name of a field to specify that you are evaluating all the row values of that field.

Find (required). This is the substring you need to find and replace.

Replace (required). This is the substring used as the replacement.

Start (optional). The position within the substring to begin the search; default is 1.

Count (optional). Number of occurrences to replace; default is all occurrences.

Compare (optional). The kind of comparison to use.

Additional Remarks

The Compare argument can have the following values:

-1	Performs a comparison using the setting of the Option Compare statement.
0	Performs a binary comparison.
1	Performs a textual comparison.
2	Performs a comparison based on information in your database (Microsoft Access only).

Right

Purpose

The Right function returns a specified number of characters starting from the rightmost character of the string. For example, Right("Nowhere", 4) returns "here".

Arguments

```
Right(String, NumberOfCharacters)
```

String (required). This is the string to be evaluated. In a query environment, you can use the name of a field to specify that you are evaluating all the row values of that field.

NumberofCharacters (required). This is the number of characters you want returned. If this argument is greater than or equal to the number of characters in string, the entire string is returned.

Rnd

Purpose

The Rnd function is a math function that generates and returns a random number that is greater than or equal to 0 but less than 1.

Arguments

```
Rnd(Number)
```

Number (optional). This numeric expression determines how the random number is generated. The Rnd function follows these rules:

- If the Number argument is omitted from the function, the next random number in the sequence is generated.

- If the Number argument is less than zero, the same number is generated every time.

- If the Number argument is greater than zero, the next random number in the sequence is generated.

- If the Number argument equals zero, the most recently generated number is returned.

Round

Purpose

The Round function is a math function that enables you to round a number to a specified number of decimal places. For example, Round(456.7276) returns 456.73.

Arguments

Round(*Number*, *DecimalPlaces*)

Number (required). This is the numeric expression you want to evaluate. In a query environment, you typically use the name of a field to specify that you are evaluating all the row values of that field.

DecimalPlaces (optional). This is the number of places to the right of the decimal are included in the rounding. If omitted, the Round function returns an integer with zero decimal places.

RTrim

Purpose

The RTrim function removes the trailing spaces from a string. This function comes in handy when cleaning up data received from a mainframe source.

Arguments

RTrim(*String*)

String (required). This is the string you are working with. In a query environment, you can use the name of a field to specify that you are evaluating all the row values of that field.

Second

Purpose

The Second function converts a valid time to a number from 0 to 59, representing the second of the minute. For example, Second(#9:00:35 PM#) returns 35.

Arguments

Second(*ValidTime*)

ValidTime (required). This is any combination of values that can represent a valid time. In a query environment, you can use the name of a field to specify that you are evaluating all the row values of that field.

Sgn

Purpose

The Sgn function is a math function that returns an integer code associated with the sign of a given number. If the given number is less than zero (has a negative designation), the Sgn function returns –1. If the given number equals zero, the Sgn function returns 0. If the given number is greater than zero (has a positive designation), the Sgn function returns 1.

Arguments

Sgn(*Number*)

Number (required). This is the numeric expression you are evaluating.

Sin

Purpose

The Sin function is a math function that enables you to calculate the sine of an angle.

Arguments

Sin(*Number*)

Number (required). This is any numeric expression that expresses an angle in radians.

SLN

Purpose

The SLN function is a financial function that calculates the straight-line depreciation of an asset for one period.

Arguments

SLN(*Cost, Salvage, Life*)

Cost (required). This is the initial cost of the asset; must be a positive number.

Salvage (required). This is the value of the asset at the end of its useful life; must be a positive number.

Life (required). This is the length of the useful life of the asset.

Space

Purpose

The Space function enables you to create a string with a specified number of spaces to a string. This function comes in handy when you need to clear data in fixed-length strings. For example, you can use the Space function within an expression such as *Space(5) & "Access"*. This would change the string "Access" to " Access".

Arguments

Space(*Number*)

Number (required). This is the number of spaces to include in the string.

SQL Aggregate Functions

Purpose

SQL aggregate functions are the most commonly used functions in Access. These functions perform either mathematical calculations or value evaluations against a given expression. Typically, these functions are used in a query environment where the Expression argument refers to a field in a table where you are evaluating all the row values of that field.

Sum(Expression). Sum calculates the total value of the all the records in the designated field or grouping. This function only works with the following data types: AutoNumber, Currency, Date/Time, and Number.

Avg(Expression). Avg calculates the Average of all the records in the designated field or grouping. This function only works with the following data types: AutoNumber, Currency, Date/Time, and Number.

Count(Expression). Count simply counts the number of entries within the designated field or grouping. This function works with all data types.

StDev(Expression). StDev calculates the standard deviation across all records within the designated field or grouping. This function only works with the following data types: AutoNumber, Currency, Date/Time, and Number.

Var(Expression). Var calculates the amount by which all the values within the designated field or grouping vary from the average value of the group. This function only works with the following data types: AutoNumber, Currency, Date/Time, and Number.

Min(Expression). Min returns the value of the record with the lowest value in the in the designated field or grouping. This function only works with the following data types: AutoNumber, Currency, Date/Time, Number, and Text.

Max(Expression). Max returns the value of the record with the highest value in the in the designated field or grouping. This function only works with the following data types: AutoNumber, Currency, Date/Time, Number, and Text.

First(Expression). First returns the value of the first record in the designated field or grouping. This function works with all data types.

Last(Expression). Last returns the value of the last record in the designated field or grouping. This function works with all data types.

Sqr

Purpose

The `Sqr` function is a math function that calculates the square root of a given number.

Arguments

`Sqr(Number)`

`Number` (required). This is the numeric expression you are evaluating.

Str

Purpose

The `Str` function is a conversion function that converts a numeric value into a string representation of the number. For instance, `Str(2304)` returns " 2304". Note that positive numbers converted with `Str` always have a leading space to represent the positive sign. Negative numbers have a negative sign as the leading character.

Arguments

`Str(Number)`

`Number` (required). This is the number you want to convert to a string. In a query environment, you can use the name of a field to specify that you are evaluating all the row values of that field.

StrConv

Purpose

The `StrConv` function enables you to convert a string to a specified conversion setting such as uppercase, lowercase, or proper case. For example, `StrConv("my text",3)` would be converted to proper case, reading "My Text".

Arguments

```
StrConv(String, ConversionType, LCID)
```

`String` (required). This is the string to be converted. In a query environment, you can use the name of a field to specify that you are converting all the row values of that field.

`ConversionType` (required). The conversion type specifies how to convert the string. The following constants identify the conversion type:

1	Converts the string to uppercase characters.
2	Converts the string to lowercase characters.
3	Converts the first letter of every word in string to uppercase.
64	Converts the string to Unicode using the default system code page.
128	Converts the string from Unicode to the default system code page.

`LCID` (optional). This is the LocaleID you want to use. The system LocaleID is the default.

String

Purpose

The `String` function enables you to return a character string of a certain length. For example, `String(4, "0")` returns "0000".

Arguments

```
String(LengthOfString, StringCharacter)
```

`LengthOfString` (required). This is the number of times you want to repeat the `StringCharacter`.

`StringCharacter` (required). This is the character that will make up your string. If you enter a series of characters, only the first character will be used.

StrReverse

Purpose

The `StrReverse` function returns an expression in reverse order. For instance, `StrReverse("ten")` returns "net". This works with numbers too; `StrReverse(5432)` returns 2345.

Arguments

```
StrReverse(Expression)
```

`Expression` (required). This is the expression that contains the characters you want reversed.

Switch

Purpose

The `Switch` function is a program flow function that enables you to evaluate a list of expressions and return the value associated with the expression determined to be true. To use the `Switch` function, you must provide a minimum of one expression and one value.

Arguments

```
Switch(Expression, Value)
```

`Expression` (required). This is the expression you want to evaluate.

`Value` (required). This is the value to return if the expression is true.

Additional Remarks

To evaluate multiple expressions, simply add another `Expression` and `Value` to the function. For example:

```
Switch(Expression1, Value1, Expression2, Value2, Expression3, Value3)
```

When the Switch function is executed, each expression is evaluated. If an expression evaluates to true, the value that follows that expression is returned. If more than one expression is true, the value for the first true expression is returned.

SYD

Purpose

The SYD function is a financial function that calculates the sum-of-years' digits depreciation of an asset for a specified period.

Arguments

```
SYD(Cost, Salvage, Life, Period)
```

Cost (required). This is the initial cost of the asset; must be a positive number.

Salvage (required). This is the value of the asset at the end of its useful life; must be a positive number.

Life (required). This is the length of the useful life of the asset.

Period (required). This is the period for which asset depreciation is calculated.

Tan

Purpose

The Tan function is a math function that enables you to calculate the tangent of an angle.

Arguments

```
Tan(number)
```

Number (required). This is any numeric expression that expresses an angle in radians.

Time

Purpose

The Time function returns today's time based on your PC's current system time. This function is ideal for time-stamping transactions. There are no required arguments for this function; to use it, simply enter **Time()**.

TimeSerial

Purpose

The TimeSerial function essentially builds a time value based on the given hour, minute, and second components. Keep in mind that this function works on a 24-hour clock, so the expression TimeSerial(18,30,0) returns 6:30:00 PM. This function is perfect for converting disparate strings that represent a time when combined, into an actual time.

Arguments

TimeSerial(*Hour, Minute, Second*)

Hour (required). This is any number or numeric expression that has a value between 0 and 23, inclusive. In a query environment, you can use the name of a field to specify that you are evaluating all the row values of that field; this is true for all the arguments in this function.

Minute (required). This is any number or numeric expression. If the number specified for this argument exceeds the normal range for minutes in an hour, the function increments the hour as appropriate. For instance, TimeSerial(7,90,00) returns 8:30:00 AM.

Second (required). This is any number or numeric expression. If the number specified for this argument exceeds the normal range for seconds in a minute, the function increments the minutes as appropriate. For instance, TimeSerial(7,10, 75) returns 7:11:15 AM.

TimeValue

Purpose

The TimeValue function converts a string representation of a time to an actual time value. For instance, TimeValue("4:20:37 PM") returns 4:20:37 PM. The function also works on a 24-hour clock.

Arguments

```
TimeValue(String)
```

String (required). This is any string or expression that represents a time ranging from 0:00:00 and 23:59:59. The string can be either a 12-hour clock entry or a 24-hour clock entry. In a query environment, you can use the name of a field to specify that you are evaluating all the row values of that field.

Trim

Purpose

The Trim function effectively removes both the leading and trailing spaces from a string. This function comes in handy when cleaning up data received from a mainframe source.

Arguments

```
Trim(String)
```

String (required). This is the string you are working with. In a query environment, you can use the name of a field to specify that you are evaluating all the row values of that field.

TypeName

Purpose

The TypeName function is an inspection function that returns the type information of a variable. For instance, TypeName("Michael") returns "String".

Arguments

TypeName(*Variable*)

Variable (required). This is the variable you want to evaluate. In a query environment, you can use the name of a field to specify that you are evaluating all the row values of that field.

Additional Remarks

The string returned by the TypeName function can be any one of the following:

Object type (an object whose type is *objecttype*)

Byte (a Byte value)

Integer (an Integer type)

Long (a Long integer type)

Single (a Single-precision floating-point number)

Double (a Double-precision floating-point number)

Currency (a Currency value)

Decimal (a Decimal value)

Date (a Date value)

String (a String type)

Boolean (a Boolean value)

Error (an Error value)

Empty (variable has not been initialized)

Null (variable contains no valid data; a Null value)

Object (an object)

Unknown (an object whose type is unknown)

Nothing (an Object variable that does not refer to an object)

UCase

Purpose

The UCase function converts a string to uppercase letters.

Arguments

UCase(*String*)

String (required). This is the string to be converted. In a query environment, you can use the name of a field to specify that you are converting all the row values of that field.

Val

Purpose

The Val function is a conversion function that extracts the numeric part of a string. For instance, Val("5400 Legacy Drive") returns 5400. One caveat to the Val function is that it stops reading the string as soon as it hits a nonnumeric character. Therefore, the number you are extracting needs to be at the beginning of the string.

Arguments

Val(*String*)

String (required). This is the string you want to evaluate. In a query environment, you can use the name of a field to specify that you are evaluating all the row values of that field.

VarType

Purpose

The VarType function is an inspection function that returns the subtype code associated with a variant's character type. For instance, VarType("Michael") returns 8 because this is the subtype code for a string.

Arguments

VarType(*Variant*)

Variant (required). This is the variant you want to evaluate. In a query environment, you can use the name of a field to specify that you are evaluating all the row values of that field.

Additional Remarks

The following is a list of the subtype codes that the VarType function can return:

0	Empty (uninitialized)
1	Null (no valid data)
2	Integer
3	Long integer
4	Single-precision floating-point number
5	Double-precision floating-point number
6	Currency value
7	Date value
8	String
9	Object
10	Error value
11	Boolean value
12	Variant (used only with arrays of variants)
13	A data access object
14	Decimal value
17	Byte value
36	Variants that contain user-defined types
8192	Array

Weekday

Purpose

The Weekday function returns a number from 1 to 7 representing the day of the week for a given date. 1 represents Sunday, 2 represents Monday, and so on. For example, Weekday (#12/31/1997#) returns 4.

Arguments

Weekday(*ValidDate*, *FirstDayOfTheWeek*)

ValidDate (required). This is any value that can represent a valid date. In a query environment, you can use the name of a field to specify that you are evaluating all the row values of that field.

FirstDayOfTheWeek (optional). This specifies which day you want to count as the first day of the week. Enter 1 in this argument to make the first day Sunday, 2 for Monday, 3 for Tuesday, and so on. If this argument is omitted, the first day is a Sunday by default.

WeekdayName

Purpose

The WeekdayName function converts a numeric weekday designation (1 to 7) to a weekday name. For instance, WeekdayName(7) returns Saturday. Values less than 1 or greater than 7 will cause an error.

Arguments

WeekdayName(*WeekdayNumber*, *Abbreviated*, *FirstDayOfTheWeek*)

WeekdayNumber (required). This is a number from 1 to 7 that represents a weekday. 1 represents Sunday, 2 represents Monday, and so on.

Abbreviated (optional). This specifies whether or not the weekday is abbreviated. If this argument is omitted, the weekday is not abbreviated. Enter 1 for this argument to return abbreviated weekdays.

FirstDayOfTheWeek (optional). This specifies which day you want to count as the first day of the week. Enter 1 in this argument to make the first day Sunday, 2 for Monday, 3 for Tuesday, and so on. If this argument is omitted, the first day is a Sunday by default.

Year

Purpose

The Year function returns a whole number representing the year for a given date. For example, Year(#5/16/1972#) returns 1972.

Arguments

Year(*ValidDate*)

ValidDate (required). This is any value that can represent a valid date. In a query environment, you can use the name of a field to specify that you are evaluating all the row values of that field.

Access VBA Fundamentals

If you are new to VBA, you may want to brush up on some of the basics before tackling the latter chapters in this book. The purpose of this appendix is to provide a high-level overview of some of the fundamental concepts and techniques demonstrated in the latter chapters. Bear in mind that because the focus of this book is on data analysis, this appendix provides only an introductory look at VBA. If you are interested in a more in-depth look at programming Access VBA, consider picking up one of the following titles:

Access 2003 Power Programming with VBA (ISBN: 0764525883)

Beginning Access 2000 VBA (ISBN: 0764543830)

Access VBA Programming For Dummies (ISBN: 0764574116)

These books offer a solid introduction to VBA that is ideal for novice Access programmers.

Covering the basics in 10 steps

There is no better way to learn than hands-on experience. So, instead of reading paragraph after paragraph of terms and definitions, in this section you learn some of the basics of VBA in 10 steps!

Step 1: Create a standard module

Have you ever found code on the Internet where you could supposedly copy the code and paste it into Access to do something wonderful, but you didn't know where to paste it? Well, knowing where to put your code is the first step in programming. In Access, VBA code is contained in a *module*. The following are the four types of modules you can use:

- **Standard modules.** This type is the most common, letting you store code that can be used anywhere within your database.

- **Form and report modules.** These types of modules store code that you can only use within the form or report to which they belong.

- **Class modules.** These modules are for those hardcore programmers who want to create and define their own custom objects.

Start a new standard module by selecting Insert → Module. At this point, your screen should look similar to Figure B-1.

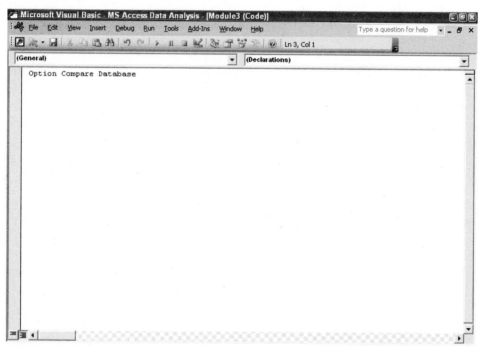

Figure B-1   A module is the container that will hold your code and expose it to other parts of your database.

Step 2: Create a function

A *function* is a set of procedures that returns a value. You can think of a function as a defined task that contains the individual actions that Access needs to perform to reach an answer or goal.

To create a function, go to the first empty line and type **Function MyFirstFunction**.

This creates a new function named MyFirstFunction. After you hit Enter on your keyboard, Access adds a few things to your code. As you can see in Figure B-2, a set of parentheses and the words "End Function" are added automatically.

Step 3: Give your function purpose with a procedure

A function's utility and purpose in life are defined in large part by its procedures. *Procedures* (sometimes called *routines*) are the actions Access will take to accomplish an objective.

Figure B-2   Create a function that will provide the steps for your task.

For your first procedure, you will call a message box. Type **MsgBox** within the function, as follows:

```
Function MyFirstFunction()
MsgBox
End Function
```

After you hit the space bar on your keyboard, a tooltip pops up, shown in Figure B-3, which shows you the valid arguments for MsgBox. This useful functionality, called *Intellisense*, is a kind of cheat sheet that enables you to quickly get a grasp of the methods, properties, and arguments that are involved in the object or function you are working with. Typically, Intellisense is activated when you enter an object or a function, and then follow it with a space, open parenthesis, period, or equal sign.

Finish the MsgBox function by typing **"I am blank years old."** At this point, your function should look like the one shown in Figure B-4.

Figure B-3   Intellisense will prove to be an invaluable tool when working with VBA.

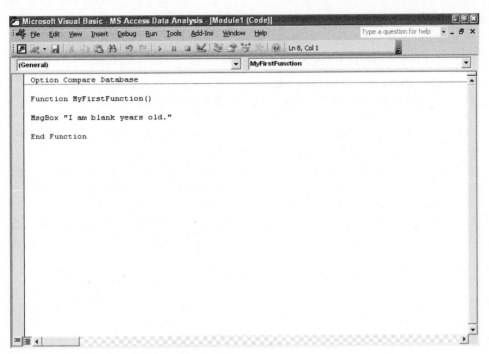

Figure B-4 Your function is ready to play.

Step 4: Test your function

To test your function, simply place your cursor anywhere inside the function and hit the F5 key on your keyboard. If all went well, you should see the message box shown in Figure B-5.

Step 5: Declare a variable

A *variable* is a kind of placeholder for a data type. When you declare a variable, you are telling Access to set aside memory to store a value. The amount of memory that is allocated depends on the data type.

Figure B-5 You have successfully written your first function!

TIP To get a list of the available data types along with the amount of memory that each data type requires, activate Access's Help system and enter *Data Type Summary* in the Search for input box.

Remember that location matters when you are using Access's Help system, so make sure that you are in the VBA Editor while performing this search.

Your next question should be, "How do I know which data type to use?" The data type itself depends on what you are trying to accomplish with the variable. For example, in this scenario, you want to declare a variable that will capture your age. Because age is a number, you will use the Integer data type.

To declare a variable, you must use a Dim statement. Dim, short for dimension, explicitly lets Access know that you are declaring a variable. It is good programming practice to declare all your variables before you start your procedure.

Declare a new variable called MyAge as an Integer data type, as follows:

```
Function MyFirstFunction()
Dim MyAge as Integer
MsgBox "I am blank years old."
End Function
```

Step 6: Assign a value to a variable

Once you have memory set aside for a variable, you can assign a value to it. To assign a value to a variable, simply indicate the value to which it is equal. Here are some examples:

- **MyVariable = 1.** This assigns a 1 to the variable called MyVariable.

- **MyVariable = "Access".** This assigns the word "Access" to MyVariable.

- **MyVariable = [Forms]![MainForm].[TextBox1].** This sets the value of MyVariable to equal the value in the TextBox1 control in the form called MainForm.

- **MyVariable = InputBox("User Input").** This sets the value of MyVariable to equal the value of a user's input using an InputBox.

In this scenario, you will use an InputBox to capture an age from a user, and then pass that age to the MyAge variable. You will then pass the MyAge variable to the message box. You can see the distinct flow of information from a user to an Access message box. Your code should look similar to the code shown here:

```
Function MyFirstFunction()
Dim MyAge as Integer
MyAge = InputBox("Enter your Age")
MsgBox "I am " & MyAge & " years old."
End Function
```

NOTE Note that the MsgBox is broken into three sections separated by ampersands (&):

"I am" (The first two words in the message)

MyAge (The variable that will return your age)

"years old." (The last two words in the message)

Test the function by placing your cursor anywhere inside the function and hitting the F5 key on your keyboard. If you did everything correctly, you should see an input dialog box, as shown in Figure B-6, asking you for your age.

Step 7: Compile your newly created function

You should get into the habit of compiling your code after you create it. Compiling has two major benefits. First, when you compile a procedure, Access checks your code for errors. Second, Access translates your code from the text you can read and understand to a machine language that your computer can understand. To compile your code, select Debug → Compile *xxxx* (where *xxxx* is the name of your project).

Step 8: Save your newly created function

So you have built your first function and you would like to save it. That's easy: simply select File → Save *xxxx* (where *xxxx* is the name of your project).

If your module is new, a dialog box activates asking you to give your module a name. Keep the default name "Module1" and click OK. Close your module and look in the Database window, shown in Figure B-7, to see it in the Modules collection.

Figure B-6 This input box will capture your age and pass it to the MyAge variable.

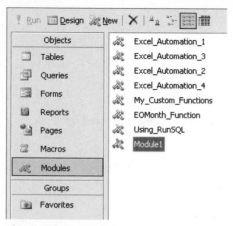

Figure B-7 Once you save a module, you can see it in the Database window in the Modules collection.

Step 9: Run your function in a macro

The benefit of building your VBA procedures in standard modules is that you can run them from anywhere within your database. For example, you can run your newly created function in a macro by simply calling your function using the RunCode macro action.

Create a new macro and add the RunCode macro action. The function name you will be calling is MyFirstFunction(). When your Macro window looks like the one shown in Figure B-8, save the macro and run it.

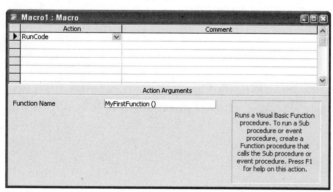

Figure B-8 You can run your VBA procedures as part of a macro process.

Step 10: Run your function from a form

You can also call your functions from a form. Start by creating a new form. You can do this by clicking on the Forms collection in the Database window, as shown in Figure B-9, and then selecting "Create form in Design view."

Next, select View → ToolBox to activate the toolbox shown in Figure B-10. Select the Command Button tool and click anywhere on your form. This places a command button on your form.

NOTE If the Command Button Wizard activates, click Cancel to close. You will not need that wizard for this exercise.

Right-click your newly created command button and select Build Event. This activates the Choose Builder dialog. Select Code Builder, and you are taken to the Form module, as shown in Figure B-11. A form module serves as a container for event procedures managed and executed by the form or its controls.

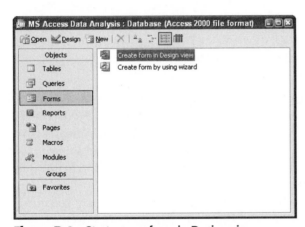

Figure B-9 Start a new form in Design view.

Figure B-10 Add a command button control to your form.

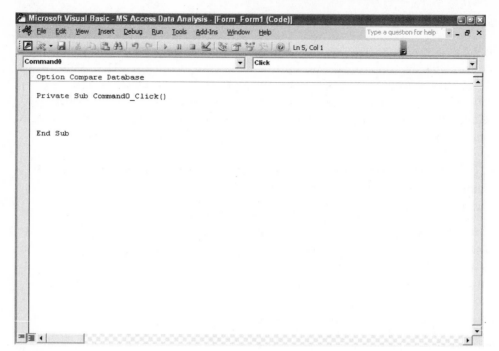

Figure B-11   Create a new event using the Code Builder.

Access is an event-driven environment, which means that procedures are executed with the occurrence of certain events. For example, in Figure B-11, you will notice the procedure's name is Command0_Click(). This means that you are building a procedure for a control called Command0, and this procedure fires when the control is clicked. You can execute your function from here by calling your function, as shown in Figure B-12.

Now you can close the VBA editor and switch to Form view by selecting View → Form View. Click your command button to fire your function.

Let Access teach you VBA

One of the most beneficial functionalities in Access is the ability to convert a macro to VBA code. To do so, click Macros in the Database window and highlight the TopTenB_Child macro, as shown in Figure B-13.

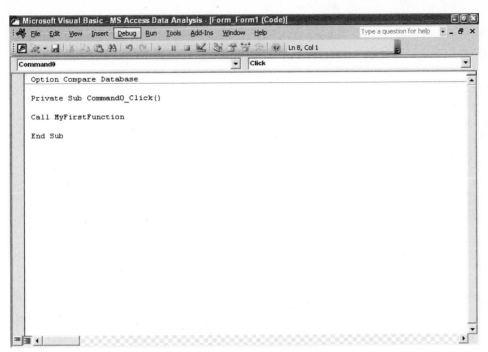

Figure B-12 Call your function from the command button's event procedure.

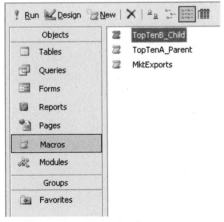

Figure B-13 Highlight the macro you want to convert.

Next, select File → Save As to activate the Save As dialog box. Indicate that you want to save this macro as a module, and then name the module. Figure B-14 demonstrates how to fill out this dialog box.

Next, the dialog box shown in Figure B-15 gives you the options of adding comments and adding error handling to the converted VBA. In this case, you want both, so simply click the Convert button.

Once the conversion is complete, select Modules in the Database window and click the module named Converted Macro- TopTenB_Child, as shown in Figure B-16.

As you can see in Figure B-17, Access has converted all the macro actions in the TopTenB_Child macro to a VBA function, complete with comments and error handling.

Figure B-14 Indicate that you want to save this macro as a module, and then name the module.

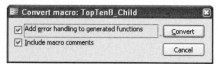

Figure B-15 Tell Access to add comments and include error handling.

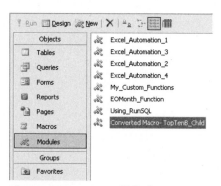

Figure B-16 You will find your converted VBA code within the Modules collection of the Database window.

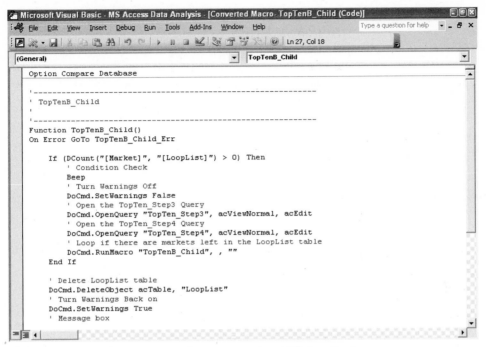

Figure B-17   You have converted your macro to a VBA function!

Keep in mind that this is not just a cool way to get out of writing code; this is a personal tutor! Look at Figure B-17 again. With this one converted macro, you get a first-hand look at how an `If` statement works, how to call queries from code, how to call macros from code, and how to handle errors. You can create a wide variety of macros, and then convert them to VBA to learn about the syntax for each action, and to experiment by adding your own functionality to them. For many Access developers, this was the first step to long programming careers.

Data Analyst's Error Reference

Analyzing data in Access is a trial-and-error endeavor. You will undoubtedly encounter many errors on your path to Access proficiency. The purpose of this appendix is to introduce you to some of the errors you will be likely to come across while working within the context of data analysis.

> **TIP** Did you know that you can generate a complete list of error codes by running a simple VBA procedure? Microsoft shows you how to create a list of Access error messages, complete with the associated error number, in a Knowledge Base article located at `http://support.microsoft.com/?kbid=268721`.

The Top 10 Query Errors

Table C-1 lists the 10 most common errors new users are likely to encounter while working with queries. Ironically, although these are the most common errors in a query environment, they are also the least descriptive. This leaves many new Access users scratching their heads.

Table C-1 Top 10 Query Errors

ERROR	DESCRIPTION
6	Overflow This message usually means that the number you are using is outside the range of the data type you are assigning it to. In other words, the number you are using is either too big or too small for the data type.
7	Out of memory This means that the query or procedure you are running requires more memory than available on your system. Try closing any other applications you have open. You can also try breaking up the query or procedure into steps.
11	Division by zero When you divide a number by zero you get this message.
13	Type mismatch You would typically get this message when you are trying to join two fields with different data types; i.e., Text field and a Number field. Make sure any fields you are joining are the same data type.
16	Expression too complex This typically means that you have too many nested expressions or subqueries in your query. Try breaking up your query into steps.
3060	Wrong data type for parameter `<Parameter Name>`. This means that you are feeding a parameter the wrong type of data.
3068	Not a valid alias name. This means that you have either used a reserved word for your alias name or your alias name contains invalid characters.
3071	This expression is typed incorrectly, or it is too complex to be evaluated. For example, a numeric expression may contain too many complicated elements. Try simplifying the expression by assigning parts of the expression to variables.

ERROR	DESCRIPTION
3073	Operation must use an updateable query.
3326	This Recordset is not updateable.
	These two error messages can be thrown when any of the following applies:
	Your query is using a join to another query: To work around this issue, create a temporary table that you can use instead of the joined query.
	Your query is based on a crosstab query, an aggregate query, a union query, or a subquery that contains aggregate functions: To work around this issue, create a temporary table that you can use instead of the query.
	Your query is based on three or more tables and there is a many-to-one-to-many relationship: To work around this issue, create a temporary table that you can use without the relationship. Your query is based on a table where the Unique Values property is set to Yes: To workaround this issue, Set the Unique Values property of the table to No
	Your query is based on a table on which you do not have Update Data permissions, or is locked by another user: To work around this issue, ensure you have permissions to update the table, and that the table is not in design view or locked by another user
	Your query is based on a table in a database that is open as read-only or is located on a read-only drive: To workaround this issue, obtain write access to the database or drive.
	Your query is based on a linked ODBC table with no unique index or a Paradox table without a primary key: To work around this issue, add a primary key or a unique index to the linked table.
	Your query is based on a SQL pass-through query: To work around this issue, create a temporary table that you can use instead of the query.

Common Parsing Errors

As you start experimenting with different functions and expressions, you will undoubtedly make mistakes. The errors in Table C-2 are parsing errors—that is, errors that are caused by syntax or structure mistakes. These errors are quite descriptive, for the most part telling you what exactly went wrong. If you are new to Access, you should take some time to read some of these errors to get advanced notice about some of the possible mistakes you could make when building your analyses.

Table C-2 Common Parsing Errors to Watch For

ERROR	DESCRIPTION
2420	The expression you entered has an invalid number.
2421	The expression you entered has an invalid date value.
2422	The expression you entered has an invalid string. A string can be up to 2048 characters long, including opening and closing quotation marks.
2423	The expression you entered has an invalid . (dot) or ! operator or invalid parentheses. You may have entered an invalid identifier or typed parentheses following the Null constant.
2424	The expression you entered has a field, control, or property name that <Your Database> can't find.
2425	The expression you entered has a function name that <Your Database> can't find.
2426	The function you entered can't be used in this expression. You may have used a DoEvents, LBound, UBound, Spc, or Tab function in an expression. You may have used an aggregate function, such as Count, in a design grid or in a calculated control or field.
2427	You entered an expression that has no value. The expression may refer to an object that has no value, such as a form, a report, or a label control.
2428	You entered an invalid argument in a domain aggregate function. A field in the string expression may not be in the domain. A field specified in the criteria expression may not be in the domain.
2429	The In operator you entered requires parentheses.
2430	You did not enter the keyword And in the Between...And operator. The correct syntax is as follows: expression [Not] Between value1 And value2
2431	The expression you entered contains invalid syntax. You may have entered a comma without a preceding value or identifier.
2432	The expression you entered contains invalid syntax, or you need to enclose your text data in quotes. You may have entered an invalid comma or omitted quotation marks.
2433	The expression you entered contains invalid syntax. You may have entered an operator, such as the + operator, in an expression without a corresponding operand.
2434	The expression you entered contains invalid syntax. You may have entered an operand without an operator.
2435	The expression you entered has too many closing parentheses.

ERROR	DESCRIPTION
2436	The expression you entered is missing a closing parenthesis, bracket (]), or vertical bar (|).
2437	The expression you entered has invalid vertical bars (|).
2438	The expression you entered contains invalid syntax. You omitted an operand or operator, you entered an invalid character or comma, or you entered text without surrounding it in quotation marks.
2439	The expression you entered has a function containing the wrong number of arguments.
2440	You must enclose `IIf` function arguments in parentheses.
2442	The expression you entered has invalid parentheses. You may have used the parenthesis syntax for an identifier in a query. Use the standard identifier syntax: `Forms![Form]![Control]`.
2443	You can use the `Is` operator only in an expression with Null or Not Null.
2445	The expression you entered is too complex.
2446	There isn't enough memory available to perform this calculation. Close unneeded programs, and try again.
2447	There is an invalid use of the `.` (dot) or `!` operator or invalid parentheses. You may have entered an invalid identifier or typed parentheses following the Null constant.
2448	You can't assign a value to this object. The object may be a control on a read-only form. The object may be on a form that is open in Design view. The value may be too large for this field.
2449	There is an invalid method in an expression. For example, you may have tried to use the Print method with an object other than Report or Debug.
2450	`<Your Database>` can't find the Form `<Form Name>` referred to in a macro expression or Visual Basic code. The form you referenced may be closed or may not exist in this database. `<Your Database>` may have encountered a compile error in a Visual Basic module for the form.
2451	The report name `<Name>` you entered is misspelled or refers to a report that isn't open or doesn't exist.
2452	The expression you entered has an invalid reference to the Parent property. For example, you may be using the Parent property with a control on a main form or report rather than with a control on a subform or subreport.

(continued)

Table C-2 *(continued)*

ERROR	DESCRIPTION
2453	The control name <Name> you entered in your expression is misspelled or refers to a control on a form or report that isn't open or doesn't exist.
2454	The <Object Name> you entered following the ! operator in the expression is invalid. For example, you may have tried to enter an identifier with two control names separated by the ! operator.
2455	You entered an expression that has an invalid reference to the property <Object or Item Name>. The property may not exist or may not apply to the object you specified.

Errors That May Indicate Database Corruption

The errors in Table C-3 are those errors that are commonly associated with database corruption. As you look through these errors, you will notice that many of them are vague or their descriptions point to some other type of problem not related to database corruption. The problem with database corruption is that it can be caused by a wide range of nebulous issues. Therefore, you will rarely see a message explicitly stating that your database is corrupt. However, the errors listed in Table C-3 are key indicators that point to the possibility that your database could be corrupted.

Table C-3 Errors Commonly Associated with Database Corruption

ERROR	DESCRIPTION
2239	The database <Your Database>needs to be repaired or isn't a <Your Database> database file. You may have quit <Your Database> unexpectedly with the database open. To repair the database, click the Repair Database command on the Tools menu (Database Utilities submenu). If the database can't be repaired, the .mdb file is unusable. Restore the database from a backup copy or create a new database.

ERROR	DESCRIPTION
2572	This database is in an unexpected state; <Your Database> can't open it. This database has been converted from a prior version of <Your Database> by using the DAO CompactDatabase method instead of the Convert Database command on the Tools menu (Database Utilities submenu). This has left the database in a partially converted state. If you have a copy of the database in its original format, use the Convert Database command on the Tools menu (Database Utilities submenu) to convert it. If the original database is no longer available, create a new database and import your tables and queries to preserve your data. Your other database objects can't be recovered.
2833	An unexpected error has occurred.
2866	Unexpected data corruption failure.
3011	The Microsoft Jet database engine could not find the object <Object Name>. Make sure the object exists and that you spell its name and the path name correctly.
3019	Operation invalid without a current index.
3033	You do not have the necessary permissions to use the <Object or Item Name> object. Have your system administrator or the person who created this object establish the appropriate permissions for you.
3045	Could not use <Object or Item Name>; file already in use.
3049	Cannot open database <Your Database>. It may not be a database that your application recognizes, or the file may be corrupt.
3051	The Microsoft Jet database engine cannot open the file <File Name>. It is already opened exclusively by another user, or you need permission to view its data.
3078	The Microsoft Jet database engine cannot find the input table or query <Query Name>. Make sure it exists and that its name is spelled correctly.
3197	The Microsoft Jet database engine stopped the process because you and another user are attempting to change the same data at the same time.

(continued)

Table C-3 *(continued)*

ERROR	DESCRIPTION
3340	Query <Query Name> is corrupt.
3343	Unrecognized database format <Path Name>.
3428	A problem occurred in your database. Correct the problem by repairing and compacting the database.
3626	The operation failed. There are too many indexes on table <Table Name>. Delete some of the indexes on the table and try the operation again.
3734	The database has been placed in a state by user <Name> on machine <Name> that prevents it from being opened or locked.
3800	<Object or Item> is not an index in this table.
7801	This database is in an unrecognized format. The database may have been created with a later version of <Your Database> than the one you are using. Upgrade your version of <Your Database> to the current one, then open this database.
29063	The Visual Basic for Applications project in the database is corrupt.
29072	<Your Database> has detected corruption in this file. To try to repair the corruption, first make a backup copy of the file. Then, on the Tools menu, point to Database Utilities and click Compact and Repair Database. If you are currently trying to repair this corruption then you will need to recreate this file or restore it from a previous backup.

Other Access/Jet Errors

Table C-4 lists some of the other Access/Jet errors you can encounter while working with Access.

Table C-4 Access/Jet Errors You May Encounter

ERROR	DESCRIPTION
2001	You canceled the previous operation.
2002	You tried to perform an operation involving a function or feature that was not installed in this version of <Your Database>.
2004	There isn't enough memory to perform this operation. Close unneeded programs and try the operation again.

ERROR	DESCRIPTION
2005	There isn't enough free memory to start `<Your Database>`. Close unneeded programs and try again. For information on freeing memory, search the Microsoft Windows Help index for 'memory, troubleshooting'.
2006	The object Name `<Object Name>` you entered doesn't follow `<Your Database>` object-naming rules.
2007	You already have an open database object named `<Object Name>`. Use a different name for each database object of the same type. If you want this object to replace the original object, close the original object, and then save this object using the same name.
2008	You can't delete the database object `<Object Name>` while it's open. Close the database object, and then delete it.
2009	You can't rename the database object `<Object Name>` while it's open. Close the database object, and then rename it.
2010	You can't delete the database object `<Object Name>` while it's open. Close the database object, and then delete it.
2011	The password you entered is incorrect.
2014	You have given this `<Object or Item Name>` the same name as an existing `<Object or Item Name>` in your database. You can't give a table and a query the same name. Give this object a name that isn't already used by another table or query.
2015	There are no registered wizards of this type. Rerun `<Your Database>` or Microsoft Office Setup to reinstall the wizards. If you want to preserve your security or custom settings, back up the `<Your Database>` workgroup information file.
2016	You can't modify the attributes of System Tables.
2017	Microsoft helps protect this Visual Basic for Applications Project with a password. You must supply the password in the Visual Basic Editor before you can perform this operation.
2018	The data access page name `<Page Name>` you entered is misspelled or refers to a data access page that isn't open or doesn't exist.
2019	The number you used to refer to the data access page is invalid. Use the Count property to count the open data access pages and make sure that the page number is not greater than the number of open data access pages minus one.
2020	The data access page theme name `<Name>` you entered is misspelled or refers to a theme name that doesn't exist.

(continued)

Table C-4 *(continued)*

ERROR	DESCRIPTION
2021	One or more operators in the filter expression is invalid. For a valid list of operators, refer to the help file.
2022	You entered an expression that requires a data access page to be the active window.
2023	The file name you specified for the data access page already exists.
2024	The report snapshot was not created because you don't have enough free disk space for temporary work files. To fix this, free up disk space (for example, empty the Recycle Bin or delete unnecessary files).
2025	The file is not in the correct format for a `<Your Database>` project.
2026	Your computer is missing at least one of the Microsoft Access 97 object libraries. Your converted database will not work until you open this database using Access 97 and then fix any missing references. Press OK to continue saving this database in the Access 97 format with missing references, or press Cancel if you no longer wish to save this database.
2027	This operation is not supported for `<Your Database>` 1.X databases.
2028	`<Your Database>` was unable to close the database object.
2029	Microsoft Office applications cannot suspend while you have documents open from a network location. Exit the applications or close the open documents and try again.
2030	The `<Your Database>` project `<Project Name>` will be opened read-only because one of the following occurred: The file is locked for editing by another user, or the file (or the folder in which it is located) is marked as read-only, or you specified that you wanted to open this file read-only.
2031	You can't convert or enable an MDE file.
2032	Some errors happened during the conversion. No converted database was generated.
2033	Name conflicts with existing module, project, or object library.
2034	Cannot Compile Project.
2035	Cannot Load Project of wrong version.
2036	`<Your Database>` does not support using ADP Projects when running in Runtime Mode.

ERROR	DESCRIPTION
2037	`<Your Database>` could not perform name AutoCorrect during this operation. The 'Log name AutoCorrect' option is set, but the Data and Misc. Objects is not checked out.
2038	The file `<File Name>` cannot be opened because it has been locked by another user.
2039	You cannot convert a workgroup file from Microsoft Access2000 to Access 97. You must create new security settings in Access 97.
2040	`<Your Database>` can't run.
2041	`<Your Database>` couldn't find file `<File Name>`. This file is required for startup.
2042	A system error occurred, or there isn't enough free memory to start `<Your Database>`. Close unneeded programs and try again.
2043	`<Your Database>` can't find the database file `<File Name>`. Make sure you entered the correct path and file name.
2044	You can't exit `<Your Database>` now. If you're running a Visual Basic module that is using OLE or DDE, you may need to interrupt the module.
2045	The command line you used to start `<Your Database>` contains an option that `<Your Database>` doesn't recognize. Exit and restart `<Your Database>` using valid command-line options.
2046	The command or action `<Object or Item Name>` isn't available now. You may be in a read-only database or an unconverted database from an earlier version of `<Your Database>`. The type of object the action applies to isn't currently selected or isn't in the active view. Use only those commands and macro actions that are currently available for this database.
2048	There isn't enough free memory to open the file `<File Name>`. Close unneeded programs and try again.
2049	The Tahoma font is not present. To restore it, please run Detect and Repair from the Help menu.
2050	Enter an OLE/DDE Timeout setting from 0 through 300 seconds.
2051	The object name `<Object or Item Name>` can't be longer than `<Object or Item Name>` characters according to `<Your Database>` object-naming rules.
2052	There isn't enough free memory to update the display. Close unneeded programs and try again.
2053	The command name can't be blank. Please choose a name.

(continued)

Table C-4 *(continued)*

ERROR	DESCRIPTION
2054	`<Your Database>` is unable to load the Visual Basic for Applications dynamic-link library (DLL) Vbe6. Rerun the `<Your Database>` Setup program.
2055	The expression `<Expression Name>` you entered is invalid.
2056	`<Your Database>` can't supply context-sensitive Help.
2057	There isn't enough stack memory left to perform the operation. The operation is too complicated. Try simplifying the operation.
2058	The file `<File Name>` is incompatible. `<Your Database>` needs to be reinstalled. Run Setup to reinstall `<Your Database>`. If you want to preserve your security or custom settings, back up the `<Your Database>` workgroup information file.
2059	`<Your Database>` cannot find the object `<Object Name>`. Make sure the object exists and that you spell its name correctly.
2060	You can't create a field list based on the action query `<Object or Item Name>`. Action queries don't have fields. A form or report must be based on a table, or on a select or crosstab query. Change the RecordSource property for the form or report, or open the action query and change it to a select query.
2061	Enter a zero or greater-than-zero number for this option.
2062	The command name must be shorter than 255 characters.
2063	`<Your Database>` can't create, open, or write to the index file `<File Name>`; the information (.inf) file it uses to keep track of dBASE indexes. The index file may be damaged, or you may not have read/write permission for the network drive you're trying to link to. You can link to the dBASE file without specifying any dBASE indexes, but the existing indexes will not be used with the linked table.
2064	The menu bar value `<Object or Item Name>` is invalid. You supplied an argument to the DoMenuItem method that refers to a menu bar that is invalid. Use an intrinsic constant or numeric value that refers to a valid menu bar value, such as acFormbar.
2065	The name for the menu, command, or subcommand you entered is invalid. You supplied an argument to the DoMenuItem method that refers to a menu name, command, or subcommand that is invalid. Use an intrinsic constant or numeric value that refers to a valid menu, command, or subcommand value, such as acRecordsMenu.
2066	A video adapter resolution of at least 640 x 480 pixels is required to run `<Your Database>`.

ERROR	DESCRIPTION
2067	A menu bar macro can only be run if the menu bar macro name is the setting used by particular properties or options. You tried to run a menu bar macro containing the `AddMenu` action. Set one of the following properties or options to the name of the menu bar macro: The MenuBar property of a form or report. The ShortcutMenuBar property of a form, report, or control. The Menu Bar or Shortcut Menu Bar option in the Startup dialog box. This error also occurs if `<Your Database>` attempts to run a menu bar macro containing an `AddMenu` action that follows an action that makes some other object the active object. For example, the `OpenForm` action.
2068	The selected item is customized and doesn't have context-sensitive Help.
2069	The key or key combination `<Object or Item Name>` in `<Object or Item Name>` has invalid syntax or is not allowed. Use the SendKeys syntax to specify the key or key combinations. For the allowed key or key combinations, click Help.
2070	You already assigned the key or key combination `<Object or Item Name>` in `<Object or Item Name>` to another macro. Only the first key or key combination will be used.
2071	The Docking property can't be set to `<Object or Item Name>` at this time. If you want to set the Docking property to `<Object or Item Name>`, move the toolbar from its current position and try again.
2072	Successfully imported `<Object or Item Name>`.
2073	Successfully exported `<Object or Item Name>`.
2074	This operation is not supported within transactions.
2075	This operation requires an open database.
2076	Successfully linked `<Object or Item Name>`.
2077	This Recordset is not updatable.
2078	Help isn't available due to lack of memory or improper installation of Microsoft Windows or `<Your Database>`.
3355	Syntax error in default value.
3450	Syntax error in query. Incomplete query clause.
3586	Syntax error in partial filter expression on table `<Table Name>`.
2079	Form is read-only, because the Unique Table property is not set.
2080	The toolbar or menu `<Object or Item Name>` already exists. Do you want to replace the existing toolbar or menu?

(continued)

Table C-4 *(continued)*

ERROR	DESCRIPTION
2081	The Create From Macro command only works when a macro is selected in the Database window.
2082	Only fields from the Unique Table can be edited.
2083	The database `<Your Database>` is read-only. You can't save changes made to data or object definitions in this database.
2084	Field `<Object or Item Name>` is based on an expression and can't be edited.
2085	The ODBC Refresh Interval setting must be from 1 through 32,766 seconds.
2086	Recordset requires a form to be updatable.
2087	`<Your Database>` can't display the Add-ins submenu. The Add-ins submenu expression `<Expression Name>` you entered exceeds the 256-character limit. Shorten the macro name or function name expression in the `Menu Add-ins` key of the Windows Registry setting, and then restart `<Your Database>`.
2088	`<Your Database>` can't display the Add-ins submenu `<Object or Item Name>` because a setting you entered in the Windows Registry is missing a macro name or function name expression. Supply the missing expression in the `Menu Add-ins` key of the Windows Registry, and then restart `<Your Database>`.
2089	`<Your Database>` can't display the same menu more than once in a menu bar.
2090	An action within the current global menu's macro group can't change the global menu bar. `<Your Database>` can't display the global menu bar because the macro called when you first set the global menu includes another action that tries to reset the global menu. Check your menu bar macros, and make sure that you set the global menu bar only once.
2091	`<Object or Item>` is an invalid name.
2092	The value you specified for the setting argument in the SetOption method isn't the correct type of Variant for this option. You specified a string when `<Your Database>` expected a number. Check the Options dialog box (Tools menu) to see what type of data is required to set this particular option. For example, the setting for the Default Database Folder option must be a string. To see what type of Variant you passed to the SetOption method, use the VarType function.
2093	The numeric value for the setting argument in the SetOption method doesn't correspond to any list box or option group settings in the Options dialog box. Valid settings are 0 (the first item in the list) through `<Object or Item Name>` (the last item in the list).

ERROR	DESCRIPTION
2094	`<Your Database>` can't find the toolbar `<Toolbar Name>`.You tried to run a macro that includes a `ShowToolbar` action or a Visual Basic procedure that includes a ShowToolbar method. The toolbar name may be misspelled. This action may refer to a custom toolbar that was deleted from or renamed in the current database. This action may refer to a custom toolbar that exists in a different database.
2095	`<Your Database>` can't switch to `<Object or Item Name>`. The Microsoft application you tried to open can't be found or hasn't been installed on your computer.
2096	`<Your Database>` can't open the Microsoft Office application because it can't find the dynamic-link library Mstool32. Run Setup to reinstall `<Your Database>`. If you want to preserve your security or custom settings, back up the `<Your Database>` workgroup information file.
2097	The table you tried to create an import/export specification for was created in an earlier version of `<Your Database>`. Convert this database to the current version of `<Your Database>` by using the Convert Database command (Tools menu, Database Utilities submenu).
2098	The operation could not be completed because the Smart Tag `<Object or Item Name>` is not recognized by your system.
2100	The control or subform control is too large for this location. The number you entered for the Left, Top, Height, or Width property is too large or is a negative number. Reduce the size of the control or subform control, or enter a positive number.
2101	The setting you entered isn't valid for this property. To see the valid settings for this property, search the Help index for the name of the property.
2102	The form name `<Name>` is misspelled or refers to a form that doesn't exist. If the invalid form name is in a macro, an Action Failed dialog box will display the macro name and the macro's arguments after you click OK. Open the Macro window, and enter the correct form name.
2103	The report name `<Name>` you entered in either the property sheet or macro is misspelled or refers to a report that doesn't exist. If the invalid report name is in a macro, an Action Failed dialog box will display the macro name and the macro's arguments after you click OK. Open the Macro window, and enter the correct report name.
2104	You entered the control name `<Control Name>`, which is already in use. You already have a control on the form with this name, or an existing control has its name mapped to this name for Visual Basic. Visual Basic maps spaces in control names to underscores. For example, My Control and My_Control are treated as duplicate names.

(continued)

Table C-4 *(continued)*

ERROR	DESCRIPTION
2105	You can't go to the specified record. You may be at the end of a recordset.
2106	`<Number>` errors occurred when you loaded the form or report. You loaded a form or report that has controls or properties that `<Your Database>` doesn't recognize and will ignore.
2107	The value you entered doesn't meet the validation rule defined for the field or control. To see the validation rule, click Design view, click the appropriate field, and then, if the property sheet isn't open, click the Properties button on the toolbar. Then click the Data tab. To solve this problem, enter a value that meets the validation rule, or press ESC to undo your changes.
2108	You must save the field before you execute the `GoToControl` action, the GoToControl method, or the SetFocus method. You tried to move the focus to another control using the SetFocus method, `GoToControl` action, or the GoToControl method. Set the macro or method to the AfterUpdate property instead of the BeforeUpdate property so it saves the field before changing the focus.
2109	There is no field named `<Name>` in the current record.
2110	`<Your Database>` can't move the focus to the control `<Object or Item Name>`. The control may be a type that can't receive the focus, such as a label. The control's Visible property may be set to No. The control's Enabled property may be set to No.
2111	The changes you made can't be saved. The save operation may have failed due to the temporary locking of the records by another user. Click OK to try again. You may need to click OK several times (or wait until the other user closes the table). Click Cancel if repeated attempts to save your changes fail.
2112	The item on the Clipboard can't be pasted into this control.
2113	The value you entered isn't valid for this field. For example, you may have entered text in a numeric field or a number that is larger than the FieldSize setting permits.
2114	`<Your Database>` doesn't support the format of the file `<File Name>`, or file is too large. Try converting the file to BMP or GIF format.
2115	The macro or function set to the BeforeUpdate or ValidationRule property for this field is preventing `<Your Database>` from saving the data in the field. If this is a macro, open the macro in the Macro window and remove the action that forces a save (for example, GoToControl). If the macro includes a `SetValue` action, set the macro to the AfterUpdate property of the control instead. If this is a function, redefine the function in the Module window.

ERROR	DESCRIPTION
2116	The value in the field or record violates the validation rule for the record or field. For example, you may have changed a validation rule without verifying whether the existing data matches the new validation rule. Click Undo on the Edit menu to restore the previous value, or enter a new value that meets the validation rule for the field.
2117	`<Your Database>` has canceled the Paste operation. The text on the Clipboard is too long to paste into the form. For example, you may have pasted too much text into a label or entered too much text in the ColumnWidths property. Paste smaller sections. For labels, you must paste fewer than 2,048 characters.
2118	You must save the current field before you run the `Requery` action. If you are running a macro from the Database window, save the field first, and then run the macro. If the macro name is the setting of the BeforeUpdate property in a Visual Basic function, set the AfterUpdate property to the name of the macro instead.
2119	The `Requery` action can't be used on the control `<Object or Item Name>`. Certain controls, such as labels and rectangles, can't receive the focus; therefore, you can't apply a `Requery` action to them.
2120	To create a form, report or data access page using this wizard, you must first select the table or query on which the form, report or data access page will be based.
2121	`<Your Database>` can't open the form `<Object or Item Name>`. It contains data that `<Your Database>` doesn't recognize. Re-create the form or, if you maintain backup copies of your database, retrieve a copy of the form.
2122	You can't view a form as a continuous form if it contains a subform, an ActiveX control, or a bound chart. Set the DefaultView property of the form to Single Form, Datasheet, PivotTable, or PivotChart.
2123	The control name you entered doesn't follow `<Your Database>` object-naming rules.
2124	The form name you entered doesn't follow `<Your Database>` object-naming rules.
2125	The setting for the FontSize property must be from 1 through 127.
2126	The setting for the ColumnCount property must be from 1 through 255.
2127	The setting for the BoundColumn property can't be greater than the setting for the ColumnCount property.

(continued)

Table C-4 *(continued)*

ERROR	DESCRIPTION
2128	`<Your Database>` encountered errors while importing `<Object or Item Name>`. For more detailed error information, see the File `<File Name>`.
2129	The setting for the DefaultEditing property must be Allow Edits, Read Only, Data Entry, or Can't Add Records. Enter 1, 2, 3, or 4 for the DefaultEditing property.
2130	The settings for the GridX and GridY properties must be from 1 through 64.
2131	An expression can't be longer than 2,048 characters.
2132	The setting for the DecimalPlaces property must be from 0 through 15, or 255 for Auto (default).
2133	You can't place a form (or report) within itself. Select or enter a different form or report to serve as the subform or subreport.
2134	The setting for the Width property must be from 0 through 22 inches (55.87 cm).
2135	This property is read-only and can't be set.
2136	To set this property, open the form or report in Design view.
2137	You can't use Find or Replace now. The fields are not searchable due to one of the following: The fields are controls (such as buttons or OLE objects). The fields have no data. There are no fields to search.
2138	You can't search the field for the specified value. Resolve the error given in the previous error message before you attempt to search again.
2139	You can't replace the current value of the field with the replacement text. Resolve any errors before making further replacements.
2140	`<Your Database>` can't save the change you made to the record in the Replace operation for the reason given in the previous error message. Click Undo Current Record on the Edit menu, or enter a new value in the field.
2141	`<Your Database>` can't find the text you specified in the Find What box.
2142	The `FindRecord` action requires a Find What argument. You tried to run a macro set to one of the current field's properties, but you left the Find What argument blank. When you click OK, an Action Failed dialog box will display the macro name and the macro's arguments. In the Macro window, enter text or an expression for the Find What argument, and try the Search operation again.

ERROR	DESCRIPTION
2143	You didn't specify search criteria with a `FindRecord` action. In the Macro window, insert a `FindRecord` action before the `FindNext` action.
2144	The setting for the ListRows property must be from 1 through 255.
2145	The ColumnWidths property setting must be a value from 0 through 22 inches (55.87 cm) for each column in a list box or a combo box. If there is more than one column, separate the numbers with either a semicolon or the list separator character. List separator characters are defined in the Regional Settings section of Windows Control Panel.
2146	`<Your Database>` can't save the last change for the reason given in the previous error message. For example, you may have entered a duplicate value in a field with an index that prohibits duplicate values. Click Undo on the Edit menu, or enter a new value in the field.
2147	You must be in Design view to create or delete controls.
2148	The number you used to refer to the form or report section is invalid. Make sure that the number is less than the number of sections in the form or report.
2149	The constant you entered for the control type is invalid. For a list of valid constants you can use to create a control, click Help.
2150	This type of control can't contain other controls.
2151	The parent control can't contain the type of control you selected. For example, you used the CreateControl function to designate an option group as the parent of a text box.
2152	You can set group levels for reports only, not for forms.
2153	You can't specify more than 10 group levels.
2154	You can't call this function when the Sorting and Grouping box is open.
2155	`<Your Database>` has encountered an error in compiling the Visual Basic code. You don't have permission to edit code; inform someone who does have permission about this error.
2156	`<Your Database>` has encountered an error in compiling the Visual Basic code. Do you want to view the error in its context?
2157	The sum of the top margin, the bottom margin, the height of the page header, and the height of the page footer is greater than the length of the page you are printing on.

(continued)

Table C-4 *(continued)*

ERROR	DESCRIPTION
2158	You can use the Print method and the report graphics methods (Circle, Line, PSet, and Scale) only in an event procedure or a macro set to the OnPrint, the OnFormat, or the OnPage event property.
2159	There isn't enough memory to initialize the Print method or one of the report graphics methods (Circle, Line, PSet, Scale). Close unneeded programs and try again to print or preview the report.
2160	`<Your Database>` couldn't create the graphic or text. An error occurred while initializing the Print method or one of the report graphics methods (Circle, Line, PSet, Scale). Close unneeded programs and try again to print or preview the report.
2161	The text or expression you entered doesn't match the type of data you are searching for. Redefine the text or expression, or search in a different field.
2162	A macro set to one of the current field's properties failed because of an error in a `FindRecord` action argument. In the Macro window, change the Search As Formatted argument to Yes. If you want the argument setting to remain No, do all of the following: Select No for the Match Case argument. Select Yes for the Only Current Field argument. Make sure you are searching in a bound control.
2163	The page number you used as an argument for the `GoToPage` action or method doesn't exist in this form.
2164	You can't disable a control while it has the focus.
2165	You can't hide a control that has the focus.
2166	You can't lock a control while it has unsaved changes.
2167	This property is read-only and can't be modified.
2169	You can't save this record at this time. `<Your Database>` may have encountered an error while trying to save a record. If you close this object now, the data changes you made will be lost. Do you want to close the database object anyway?
2170	There isn't enough memory to retrieve data for the list box. Close unneeded programs. Then close and reopen the active form, and click the list box again.
2171	You can't have more than seven nested subforms in a main form. Remove the eighth nested subform.
2172	You can't use a pass-through query or a non-fixed-column crosstab query as a record source for a subform or subreport. Before you bind the subform or subreport to a crosstab query, set the query's ColumnHeadings property.

ERROR	DESCRIPTION
2173	The control <Object or Item Name> the macro is attempting to search can't be searched. Try one of the following: Add a GoToControl action before the FindRecord action. For the FindRecord action, change the Only Current Field action argument from Yes to No. Change the focus to a searchable control.
2174	You can't switch to a different view at this time. Code was executing when you tried to switch views. If you are debugging code, you must end the debugging operation before switching views.
2175	There isn't enough free memory to continue the Search operation. Close unneeded programs. Then try the Search operation again.
2176	The setting for this property is too long. You can enter up to either 255 or 2,048 characters for this property, depending on the data type.
2177	You can't insert a report into a form. A report can be inserted only into a report.
2178	You can't add another section now. The maximum total height for all sections in a report, including the section headers, is 200 inches (508 cm). Remove or reduce the height of at least one section, and then add the new section.
2181	You can't sort on a calculated field in a form. You can sort on a calculated field only in a query. Create a calculated field in a query, sort the field, and then base the form on the query. Because the query must execute before the form opens, the form will open more slowly.
2182	You can't sort on this field.
2183	<Your Database> can't create an object of the type requested. You are trying either to create a form from a report that has been saved as text, or to create a report from a saved form.
2184	The value you used for the TabIndex property isn't valid. The correct values are from 0 through <Object or Item Name>.
2185	You can't reference a property or method for a control unless the control has the focus. Try one of the following: Move the focus to the control before you reference the property. In Visual Basic code, use the SetFocus method. In a macro, use the GoToControl action. Reference or set the property from a macro or event procedure that runs when the GotFocus event for the control occurs.
2186	This property isn't available in Design view. Switch to Form view to access this property, or remove the reference to the property.
2187	This property is available only in Design view.

(continued)

Table C-4 *(continued)*

ERROR	DESCRIPTION
2188	The object you attempted to load from text has an invalid value for the property `<Object or Item Name>` on a `<Object or Item Name>`.
2189	Your code contains a syntax error, or a `<Your Database>` function you need isn't available. If the syntax is correct, check the Control Wizards subkey or the Libraries key in the `<Your Database>` section of the Windows Registry to verify that the entries you need are listed and available. If the entries are correct, you need to correct the `<Your Database>` Utility Add-in or the file acWzlib or this wizard has been disabled. To re-enable this wizard, click About `<Your Database>` on the Help menu, and then click the Disabled Items button to view a list of addins which you can enable. Rerun `<Your Database>` or Microsoft Office Setup to reinstall `<Your Database>`. Before you reinstall, delete the Windows Registry keys for the `<Your Database>` Utility Add-in and acWzlib.
2190	This property has been replaced by a new property; use the new property instead.
2191	You can't set the `<Object or Item Name>` property in print preview or after printing has started. Try setting this property in the OnOpen event.
2192	The bitmap you specified is not in a device-independent bitmap (.dib) format. You tried to set the PictureData property of a form, report, button, or image control.
2193	The left margin, right margin, or both margins are wider than the paper size specified in the Print Setup dialog box.
2194	You can't set the PictureData property in Datasheet view. To see the valid settings for this property, search the Help index for 'PictureData property'.
2195	The section name you entered doesn't follow `<Your Database>` object-naming rules.
2196	`<Your Database>` can't retrieve the value of this property. The property isn't available from the view in which you're running the macro or Visual Basic code, or `<Your Database>` encountered an error while retrieving the value of the property. To see the valid settings for this property, search the Help index for the name of the property.
2197	You can't set a subform control's SourceObject property to a zero-length string if you're displaying the main form in Form view. You can set this property to a zero-length string from Design view, Datasheet view, or Print Preview.

ERROR	DESCRIPTION
2200	The number you entered is invalid.
2201	There was a problem retrieving printer information for the `<Object or Item Name>` on `<Object or Item Name>`. The object may have been sent to a printer that is unavailable.
2202	You must install a printer before you print. To install a printer, point to Settings on the Windows Start menu, click Printers, and then double-click Add Printer. Follow the instructions in the wizard.
2203	The dynamic-link library Commdlg failed: error code '0x`<Object or Item Name>`'. The printer driver for the selected printer may be incorrectly installed.
2204	The default printer driver isn't set up correctly. For information on setting a default printer, search the Microsoft Windows Help index for 'default printer, setting'.
2205	The default printer driver isn't set up correctly. For information on setting a default printer, search the Microsoft Windows Help index for 'default printer, setting'.
2206	The page number you entered is invalid. For example, it may be a negative number or an invalid range, such as 6 to 3.
2207	`<Your Database>` can't print macros. You tried to use the `PrintOut` action or method, but the active object is a macro. If you want to print an object other than a macro, use the `SelectObject` action or method to select the desired object before you run the `PrintOut` action.
2210	`<Your Database>` can't print or preview the page because the page size you selected is larger than 22.75 inches.
2211	`<Your Database>` can't print or preview the Debug window.
2212	`<Your Database>` couldn't print your object. Make sure that the specified printer is available.
2213	There was a problem retrieving printer information for this object. The object may have been sent to a printer that is unavailable.
2214	There was a problem retrieving information from the printer. New printer has not been set.
2215	`<Your Database>` cannot print this PivotTable because its `<Element>` exceed(s) 22.75 inches. Reduce the `<Element>` by making changes to the formatting or included data of the PivotTable view, and then try to print again.
2220	`<Your Database>` can't open the file `<File Name>`.
2221	The text is too long to be edited.

(continued)

Table C-4 *(continued)*

ERROR	DESCRIPTION
2222	This control is read-only and can't be modified.
2223	The file name <Name> is too long. Enter a file name that's 256 characters or less.
2225	<Your Database> couldn't open the Clipboard. The Clipboard isn't responding, probably because another application is using it. Close all other applications and try the operation again.
2226	The Clipboard isn't responding, so <Your Database> can't paste the Clipboard's contents. Another application may be using the Clipboard. There may not be enough free memory for the paste operation. Close all other applications, and then copy and paste again.
2227	The data on the Clipboard is damaged, so <Your Database> can't paste it. There may be an error in the Clipboard, or there may not be enough free memory. Try the operation again.
2229	<Your Database> can't start the OLE server. You tried to use a form, report, or datasheet that contains an OLE object, but the OLE server (the application used to create the object) may not be registered properly. Reinstall the OLE server to register it correctly.
2234	<Your Database> can't paste the OLE object.
2237	The text you entered isn't an item in the list. Select an item from the list, or enter text that matches one of the listed items.
2243	The data in the Clipboard isn't recognizable; <Your Database> can't paste the OLE object.
2244	The file name you specified in the Picture property for a command button or toggle button can't be read. The file you specified may be corrupted. Restore the file from a backup copy or re-create the file. The disk where the file is located may be unreadable.
2245	The file you specified doesn't contain valid icon data. Specify a valid icon file.
2246	<Your Database> can't run the query; the parameter values are too large. The total length of all the values entered for the parameters cannot exceed 1,024 characters.
2260	An error occurred while sending data to the OLE server (the application used to create the object). You may have tried to send too much data. If you're creating a chart and the chart is based on a query, modify the query so that it selects less data. If the chart is based on a table, consider basing it on a query instead so that you can limit the data. You may be using an OLE server that doesn't accept the Clipboard format. You may not be able to start the OLE server because it's not properly registered. Reinstall it to register it. Your computer may be low on memory. Close other application windows to free up memory.

ERROR	DESCRIPTION
2262	This value must be a number.
2263	The number is too large.
2264	`<Your Database>` didn't recognize the unit of measurement. Type a valid unit, such as inches (in) or centimeters (cm).
2265	You must specify a unit of measurement, such as inches (in) or centimeters (cm).
2266	`<Object or Item>` may not be a valid setting for the RowSourceType property, or there was a compile error in the function. For information on valid settings for the RowSourceType property, click Help.
2267	There is not enough disk space to create a temporary buffer file for printing. Free up some disk space to make room for the temporary buffer file.
2269	Some library databases couldn't be loaded because too many were specified. To change library database references, click References on the Tools menu.
2272	The setting for the Update Retry Interval must be from 0 through 1,000 milliseconds.
2273	The setting for Update Retries must be from 0 through 10.
2274	The database `<Your Database>` is already open as a library database.
2275	The string returned by the builder was too long. The result will be truncated.
2276	The custom builder you're using caused an error by changing the focus to a different window while you were using it. Enter a value without using the custom builder.
2277	There was a font initialization error.
2278	`<Your Database>` can't save your changes to this bound OLE object. Either you don't have permission to write to the record in which the object is stored, or the record is locked by another user. Copy the object to the Clipboard (select the object and click).
2279	The value you entered isn't appropriate for the input mask `<Object or Item Name>` specified for this field.
2280	You have added more output formats to the Windows Registry than `<Your Database>` can initialize. Some output formats will not be available. Remove those formats that you never or least often use.

(continued)

Table C-4 *(continued)*

ERROR	DESCRIPTION
2281	The formats that enable you to output data as a Microsoft Excel, rich-text format, MS-DOS text, or HTML file are missing or incorrectly registered in the Windows Registry. Run Setup to reinstall <Your Database> or, if you're familiar with the settings in the Registry, try to correct them yourself. For more information about the Registry, click Help.
2282	The format in which you are attempting to output the current object is not available. Either you are attempting to output the current object to a format that is not valid for its object type, or the formats that enable you to output data as a Microsoft Excel, rich-text format, MS-DOS text, or HTML file are missing from the Windows Registry. Run Setup to reinstall <Your Database> or, if you're familiar with the settings in the Registry, try to correct them yourself. For more information on the Registry, click Help.
2283	The format specification for <Object or Item Name> is invalid. You can't save output data to a file in this format until you correct the setting for the format in the Windows Registry. Run Setup to reinstall <Your Database> or, if you're familiar with the settings in the Registry, try to correct them yourself. For more information on the Registry, click Help.
2284	<Your Database> can't write to the file. The network may not be working. Wait until the network is working, and then try again. You may be out of memory. Close one or more <Your Database> windows, close other applications, and then try again.
2285	<Your Database> can't create the output file. You may be out of disk space on the destination drive. The network may not be working. Wait until the network is working, and then try again. You may be out of memory. Close one or more <Your Database> windows, close other applications, and then try again.
2286	<Your Database> can't close the file. The network may not be working. Wait until the network is working, and then try again. You may be out of memory. Close one or more <Your Database> windows, close other applications, and then try again.
2287	<Your Database> can't open the mail session. Check your mail application to make sure that it's working properly.
2288	<Your Database> can't load the <Object or Item Name> format. The setting for this format in the Windows Registry is incorrect. You can't save the output data to a file in this format until you correct the setting in the Registry. Run Setup to reinstall <Your Database> or, if you're familiar with the settings in the Registry, try to correct them yourself. For more information on the Registry, click Help.

ERROR	DESCRIPTION
2289	`<Your Database>` can't output the module in the requested format.
2290	There were too many message recipients; the message was not sent.
2291	There are too many message attachments; the message was not sent.
2292	The message text is too long, so it was not sent.
2293	`<Your Database>` can't send this e-mail message. Before attempting to send an e-mail message from `<Your Database>`, resolve the problem identified in the previous message, or configure your computer to send and receive e-mail messages.
2294	`<Your Database>` can't attach the object; the message was not sent. The network may not be working. Wait until the network is working, and then try again. You may be out of memory. Close one or more `<Your Database>` windows, close other applications, and then try again.
2295	Unknown message recipient(s); the message was not sent.
2296	The password is invalid; the message wasn't sent.
2297	`<Your Database>` can't open the mail session. You may be out of memory. Close one or more `<Your Database>` windows, close other applications, and then try again. You may also want to check your mail application to ensure that it's working properly.
2298	`<Your Database>` can't start the wizard, builder, or add-in. The library database containing the wizard, builder, or add-in may not be installed. Point to Add-ins on the Tools menu, and then click Add-in Manager to see if the library database is installed. The wizard, builder, or add-in code may not be compiled and `<Your Database>` can't compile it. There may be a syntax error in the code. The key for the add-in in the Windows Registry file may be incorrect.
2299	`<Your Database>` can't open the Zoom box. The `<Your Database>` Utility add-in is missing or was modified. Rerun `<Your Database>` or Microsoft Office Setup to reinstall `<Your Database>` and the `<Your Database>` Utility add-in.
2300	`<Your Database>` can't output because there are too many controls selected that have different styles, such as color and font. Select fewer controls, and then try again.
2301	There are not enough system resources to output the data. Close one or more `<Your Database>` windows and close other applications. Then try to output the data again.

(continued)

Table C-4 *(continued)*

ERROR	DESCRIPTION
2302	`<Your Database>` can't save the output data to the file you've selected. The file may be open. If so, close it, and then save the output data to the file again. If you are using a template, check to make sure the template exists. If the file isn't open, check to make sure that you have enough free disk space. Make sure that the file exists on the path specified. Check to make sure you have permission to write to the specified folder.
2303	`<Your Database>` can't output data now. The network may not be working. Wait until the network is working, and then try again. You may be out of disk space. Free up disk space and try again.
2304	`<Your Database>` can't save output data to the specified file. Make sure that you have enough free disk space on your destination drive.
2305	There are too many columns to output, based on the limitation specified in the output format or by `<Your Database>`.
2306	There are too many rows to output, based on the limitation specified by the output format or by `<Your Database>`.
2307	You haven't selected any data, or the object you've selected is blank.
2308	The file `<File Name>` already exists. Do you want to replace the existing file?
2309	There is an invalid add-in entry for `<Object or Item Name>`. There is an error in the Windows Registry for this add-in. Correct the setting and restart `<Your Database>`. For information on the Registry, click Help.
2311	There isn't enough memory to run the NotInList event procedure.
2312	The shortcut `<Object or Item Name>` must be re-created. The file may be missing, damaged, or in an older format that can't be read.
2313	`<Your Database>` can't find the shortcut databases `<Your Database>` or `<Your Database>`. Re-create the shortcut with the correct locations of the databases.
2314	`<Your Database>` can't find the shortcut database `<Name>`. Re-create the shortcut with the correct location of the database.
2315	The input string is too long.
2316	This table or query can't be opened because it has no visible fields. This can result if the table or query has only system fields, and the Show System Objects option is off. To turn on the Show System Objects option, click Options on the Tools menu, click the View tab, and select the System Objects check box.

ERROR	DESCRIPTION
2317	The database <Your Database> can't be repaired or isn't a <Your Database> database file.
2319	<Your Database> can't import the object <Object Name> while it is open.
2320	<Your Database> can't display the field for which you entered Where in the Total row. Clear the Show check box for that field. If you want this field to appear in the query's results, add it to the design grid twice. For the field that will appear in the query's results, don't specify Where in the Total row, and make sure the Show check box is checked.
2321	You can't set criteria before you add a field or expression to the Field row. Either add a field from the field list to the column and enter an expression, or delete the criteria.
2322	You can't sort on the asterisk (*). Because the asterisk represents all fields in the underlying table or query, you can't sort on it. Add the asterisk to the query design grid, along with the specific fields you want to sort on. Clear the Show check box for the sorting fields, and then specify a sort order.
2323	You can't specify criteria for the asterisk (*). Because the asterisk represents all the fields in the underlying table or query, you can't specify criteria for it. Add the asterisk to the query design grid, along with the field(s) you want to set criteria for, and then enter criteria for the specific fields. In the query design grid, clear the Show check box for the criteria field(s), before you run the query.
2324	You can't calculate totals on the asterisk (*). Because the asterisk represents all the fields in the table, you can't calculate totals on it. Remove the asterisk from the query design grid. Add the fields you want to use to the design grid, and then select the total you want to calculate for specific fields.
2325	The field name you entered exceeds the LinkMasterFields property's 64-character limit. When you use the Relationships command (Tools menu) to define a relationship between the tables underlying a form and subform, <Your Database> links the form and subform automatically and sets the LinkChildFields and LinkMasterFields properties.
2326	You can't specify Group By, Expression, or Where in the Total row for this column. Specify an aggregate function, such as Sum or Count, for the field or expression you designate as the Value in the crosstab query.
2327	You must enter Group By in the Total row for a field that has Column Heading in the Crosstab row. The values derived from the field or expression that you designate as the Column Heading are used to group data in the crosstab query.

(continued)

Table C-4 *(continued)*

ERROR	DESCRIPTION
2328	You can't run an update query on the asterisk (*). Because the asterisk represents all the fields in the table, you can't update it. Remove the asterisk from the query design grid. Add the fields you want to update to the design grid.
2329	To create a crosstab query, you must specify one or more Row Heading(s) options, one Column Heading option, and one Value option.
2330	`<Your Database>` can't represent the join expression `<Object or Item Name>` in Design view. One or more fields may have been deleted or renamed. The name of one or more fields or tables specified in the join expression may be misspelled.
2331	You must enter Group By in the Total row for at least one of the Row Heading options you enter in the Crosstab row.
2332	`<Your Database>` can't match the fields you added using the asterisk (*) in the append query. Because the asterisk represents all the fields in the underlying table or query, you can't append an asterisk to one field or expression, and you can't append a single field or expression to an asterisk. Append an asterisk to an asterisk (for example, a table to a table), or append specific fields.
2333	You must enter the name of the table you are creating or appending records to. You tried to define a make-table or append query without specifying a destination table.
2334	`<Your Database>` can't print `<Object or Item Name>` because it is an action query. Because action queries don't produce a recordset, you can't print a Datasheet view of them. Note that an exclamation point (!) joined to a query icon in the Database window marks an action query. To print a Datasheet view of the records that will be selected by the query, display the query in Design view, click the Datasheet button, and then click the Print button.
2335	You must use the same number of fields when you set the LinkChildFields and LinkMasterFields properties. You entered a different number of fields for one property than you did for the other. If you use the Relationships command (Tools menu) to define a relationship between the tables underlying the form and subform, `<Your Database>` will link the form and subform automatically and then set the LinkChildFields and LinkMasterFields properties.
2337	You can't specify criteria on the same field for which you entered Value in the Crosstab row. You tried to display a crosstab query after entering Value in the Crosstab row and criteria in the Criteria row. If you want this field to supply the cross-tabulated values in the crosstab query, delete the entry in the Criteria row. If you want this to be a criteria field, leave the Crosstab row blank.

ERROR	DESCRIPTION
2338	`<Your Database>` truncated the expression you entered. The expression `<Expression Name>` exceeds the 1,024-character limit for the query design grid.
2339	`<Your Database>` can't create a temporary link. You reached the limit for the number of links in your database. `<Your Database>` needs to create a temporary link in order to import your ODBC table. Remove all unneeded links or tables.
2340	The expression you entered exceeds the 1,024-character limit for the query design grid.
2342	A `RunSQL` action requires an argument consisting of an SQL statement. For example, an action query that appends records starts with INSERT INTO. A data-definition query that creates a table starts with CREATE TABLE.
2343	The value you entered exceeds the Alias property's 64-character limit.
2344	For the TopValues property in the query property sheet, you must enter an integer greater than zero.
2345	For the TopValues property in the query property sheet, you must enter a percentage from 1 through 100.
2346	For the TopValues property in the query property sheet, you must enter a number greater than zero.
2347	`<Your Database>` can't find the file name you entered for the DestinationDB property in an action query's property sheet. You may have misspelled the database file name, or the file may have been deleted or renamed.
2348	You can't leave the Alias property blank.
2349	For the TopValues property in the query property sheet, you must enter a number smaller than 2,147,483,647.
2350	`<Your Database>` can't save the query. The query is a pass-through query and can't be represented as a simple SQL string. Save the query as a named query from the Query Builder. When you close the Query Builder, `<Your Database>` will fill the RecordSource or RowSource property with the saved query name. Make sure the query doesn't have an SQL syntax error.
2351	`<Your Database>` can't represent an implicit VALUES clause in the query design grid. Edit this in SQL view.
2352	You can't modify this query because it has been deleted or renamed by another user.
2353	Bad query parameter `<Parameter Name>`.

(continued)

Table C-4 *(continued)*

ERROR	DESCRIPTION
2360	A field name is missing. You have defined a data type or a description for a field without specifying the field name. Enter a name for the field, or delete the row.
2361	`<Your Database>` can't save this table. There are no fields in this table. Define at least one field by entering a field name and selecting a data type.
2362	You already have a field named `<Name>`.
2363	`<Your Database>` allows only one AutoNumber field per table. Use the Number data type for similar fields.
2364	`<Your Database>` can't open the table in Datasheet view.
2366	`<Your Database>` was unable to save the field ordering. All other changes were saved successfully. Close this database and choose the Repair Database command on the Tools menu (Database Utilities submenu).
2370	Removing or changing the index for this field would require removal of the primary key. If you want to delete the primary key, select that field and click the Primary Key button.
2371	`<Your Database>` can't create a primary key. Your changes weren't saved.
2372	The field name is not valid. Make sure that the name doesn't contain a period (.), exclamation point (!), bracket ([]), leading space, or non-printable character such as a carriage return. If you have pasted the name from another application, try pressing ESC and typing the name again.
2373	The setting for the FieldSize property must be from 0 through 255.
2374	You can't create an index or primary key on more than 10 fields.
2375	You can't paste beyond the end of a table. You have attempted to paste fields beyond the 255th row in a table in Design view.
2376	`<Your Database>` can't create a primary key. You have selected too many fields for a multiple-field primary key.
2377	Once you enter data in a table, you can't change the data type of any field to AutoNumber, even if you haven't yet added data to that field. Add a new field to the table, and define its data type as AutoNumber. `<Your Database>` then enters data in the AutoNumber field automatically, numbering the records consecutively starting with 1.
2378	This table is read-only. Use a different name in the Save As dialog box to save your changes.

ERROR	DESCRIPTION
2379	You can't create a primary key on a field of this data type. You can't define a primary key on fields with an OLE Object data type.
2380	`<Your Database>` can't create a primary key because no fields have been selected. You have selected a row with no fields defined. Place the insertion point somewhere in the row of the field you want to define as the primary key.
2381	`<Your Database>` can't create a primary key because the field doesn't have a name. Name the field, and then define it as a primary key field.
2382	You can't switch to Datasheet view and you can't return to Design view. Another user has opened this table or a query, form, or report that is bound to this table.
2383	`<Your Database>` can't change the data type. There isn't enough disk space or memory.
2384	You can't change one field from an AutoNumber data type and add another AutoNumber field at the same time. Do the following: 1. Delete the AutoNumber field you added, and click Save on the File menu. 2. Add the new AutoNumber field, and save the table again.
2385	Errors were encountered during the save operation.
2386	`<Your Database>` was unable to create the table.
2387	You can't delete the table `<Table Name>`; it is participating in one or more relationships. If you want to delete this table, first delete its relationships in the Relationships window.
2388	You can't change the primary key. This table is the primary table in one or more relationships. If you want to change or remove the primary key, first delete the relationship in the Relationships window.
2389	You can't delete the field `<Object or Item Name>`. It is part of one or more relationships. If you want to delete this field, first delete its relationships in the Relationships window.
2390	You can't change the data type or field size of this field; it is part of one or more relationships. If you want to change the data type of this field, first delete its relationships in the Relationships window.
2391	Field `<Field Name>` doesn't exist in destination table `<Object or Item Name>`. `<Your Database>` was unable to complete the append operation. The destination table must contain the same fields as the table you are pasting from.
2392	You can't set the Unique property of a primary key to No. A primary key, by definition, contains only unique values. If you want to allow nonunique values in this field, remove the primary key definition by setting the Primary property to No.

(continued)

Table C-4 *(continued)*

ERROR	DESCRIPTION
2393	You can't set the IgnoreNulls property of a primary key to Yes. A primary key, by definition, can't allow Null values. If you want Null values in this field, remove the primary key definition by setting the Primary property to No.
2394	The index name is invalid. The index name may be too long (over 64 characters) or contain invalid characters.
2395	Indexes must have names.
2396	<Your Database> can't create an index or primary key. One or more field names are missing. Enter or select at least one field in the Field Name column for each index you name.
2397	You already have an index named <Name>
2398	The primary key has been changed. This table is the primary table in one or more relationships. Changes to the primary key won't be saved.
2399	The setting for the FieldSize property must be from 1 through 8000.
2400	The row you inserted in the grid exceeds the limit of 255 rows (fields) for a table or 1,000 rows (actions) for a macro.
2456	The number you used to refer to the form is invalid. Use the Count property to count the open forms and make sure that the form number is not greater than the number of open forms minus one.
2457	The number you used to refer to the report is invalid. Use the Count property to count the open reports and make sure that the report number is not greater than the number of open reports.
2458	The control number you specified is greater than the number of controls. Use the Count property to count the controls on the form or report and then check that the control number you cite is within the range of existing controls.
2459	You can't refer to the Parent property of a form or report when either is open in Design view.
2460	You can't refer to the RecordsetClone property of a form open in Design view.
2461	Use a section number, not a string, to refer to a form or report section.
2462	The section number you entered is invalid.
2463	Use a number, not a string, to refer to a group level.

ERROR	DESCRIPTION
2464	There is no sorting or grouping field or expression defined for the group level number you used. A valid group level number can be from 0 (for the first field or expression you sort or group on) through 9 (for the tenth). Count the group levels in the report starting with zero.
2465	`<Your Database>` can't find the field `<Field Name>` referred to in your expression. You may have misspelled the field name, or the field may have been renamed or deleted.
2466	The expression you entered has an invalid reference to the Dynaset property. For example, you may have used the Dynaset property with a form that isn't based on a table or query.
2467	The expression you entered refers to an object that is closed or doesn't exist. For example, you may have assigned a form to a Form object variable, closed the form, and then referred to the object variable.
2468	The value you entered for the interval, number, or date argument in the function is invalid. Check the argument to make sure that you entered it correctly.
2469	The expression `<Object or Item Name>` you entered in the form control's ValidationRule property contains the error `<Error>`. `<Your Database>` can't parse the ValidationRule expression you entered. For example, if you enter the expression =MyFunction() in the ValidationRule property, and the function MyFunction doesn't exist, `<Your Database>` displays the following message: Unknown function name in validation rule: 'MyFunction'. To help you create expressions as arguments in Visual Basic, use the Expression Builder. For more information, search the Help index for 'Expression Builder'.
2470	There is a(n) `<Object or Item Name>` in the form control's ValidationRule property. To help you create expressions as arguments in Visual Basic, use the Expression Builder.
2471	The expression you entered as a query parameter produced this error: `<Object or Item Name>`
2472	The LinkMasterFields property setting has produced this error: `<Object or Item Name>`.
2473	The expression `<Object or Item Name>` you entered as the event property setting produced the following error: `<Error>`. The expression may not result in the name of a macro, the name of a user-defined function, or [Event Procedure]. There may have been an error evaluating the function, event, or macro.

(continued)

Table C-4 *(continued)*

ERROR	DESCRIPTION
2474	The expression you entered requires the control to be in the active window. Try one of the following: Open or select a form or report containing the control. Create a new control in the active window, and try the operation again.
2475	You entered an expression that requires a form to be the active window.
2476	You entered an expression that requires a report to be the active window.
2477	You entered an invalid objecttype value <Object or Item Name> in an If TypeOf object Is objecttype condition of an If...Then...Else statement. The objecttype can be any one of the following: BoundObjectFrame, CheckBox, ComboBox, CommandButton, Label, Line, ListBox, UnboundObjectFrame, OptionButton, OptionGroup, PageBreak, Rectangle, Subform, Subreport, TextBox, ToggleButton, ImageControl, or OLEControl.
2478	<Your Database> doesn't allow you to use this method in the current view. Most methods, including the SetFocus and Requery methods, can't be used in form or report Design view.
2479	The event procedure <Procedure Name> can't be a Function procedure; it must be a Sub procedure. If you want to run a Function procedure when an event occurs, try one of the following: Set the event property to the name of a macro containing a RunCode action that runs the Function procedure. Set the event property to =FunctionName().
2480	You referred to a property by a numeric argument that isn't one of the property numbers in the collection. Check the property numbers in the collection.
2481	You can't set a value while a document is in Print Preview.
2482	<Your Database> can't find the name <Name> you entered in the expression. You may have specified a control that wasn't on the current object without specifying the correct form or report context. To refer to a control on another form or report, precede the control name with the name of a collection, usually either Forms or Reports, and the name of the form or report to which the control belongs. For example, Forms![Products]![Units In Stock].
2483	You can't move to a previous control when only one control has had the focus. Use the PreviousControl property only after you've moved the focus to a second control.
2484	There is no active datasheet.

ERROR	DESCRIPTION
2485	`<Your Database>` can't find the macro `<Macro Name>`. The macro (or its macro group) doesn't exist, or the macro is new but hasn't been saved. Note that when you enter the macrogroupname.macroname syntax in an argument, you must specify the name the macro's macro group was last saved under.
2486	You can't carry out this action at the present time. You tried to run a macro or used the DoCmd object in Visual Basic to carry out an action. However, `<Your Database>` is performing another activity that prevents this action from being carried out now. For example, no actions on a form can be carried out while `<Your Database>` is repainting a control or calculating an expression. Carry out the action later.
2487	The Object Type argument for the action or method is blank or invalid. For a `Close, GoToRecord,` or `RepaintObject` action, enter values for both arguments, or leave both blank to perform the action on the active object. For a `DeleteObject, Rename,` or `CopyObject` action, enter values for both arguments, or leave both blank to perform the action on the object currently selected in the Database window. For a `SendObject` or `OutputTo` action, enter values for both arguments, or leave the Object Name argument blank if you want the action performed on the active object of the specified object type. If you're using a method with the DoCmd object, use an intrinsic constant that equates to a valid object type or the corresponding numeric value for the argument name.
2488	You can't use the `ApplyFilter` action on this window. You tried to use the `ApplyFilter` action or method, but you didn't apply the filter to a table, query, form, or report. You may have applied the filter to a form, but the form wasn't open in Form or Datasheet view. You may have applied the filter to a report but didn't use the `ApplyFilter` action in a macro specified by the OnOpen property setting. Use the `SelectObject` action or method to select the table, query, form, or report before applying the filter.
2489	The object `<Object Name>` isn't open. The macro you are running (directly or indirectly) contains a `GoToRecord, RepaintObject,` or `SelectObject` action, but the Object Name argument names an object that is closed. The objectname argument for the GoToRecord, RepaintObject, or SelectObject method names an object that is closed. Use one of the Open actions or methods to open the object so that you can carry out the desired action.

(continued)

Table C-4 *(continued)*

ERROR	DESCRIPTION
2491	The action or method is invalid because the form or report isn't bound to a table or query. You tried to use the `ApplyFilter` action or method. However, the form or report you applied the filter to is not based on a table or query, so the form or report do.
2492	`<Your Database>` can't find the macro `<Macro Name>` in the macro group `<Object or Item Name>`. You used the macrogroupname.macroname syntax to specify a macro. You then tried to run the macro (directly or indirectly), or you used the RunMacro method to run the macro. However, the macro you specified isn't in this macro group. Create the macro in the macro group, specify the correct macro group, or specify the correct macro name.
2493	This action requires an Object Name argument.
2494	The action or method requires a Form Name argument. You tried to use the `OpenForm` action or method, but you left the Form Name argument blank. In the Form Name argument, enter the name of a form in the current database.
2495	The action or method requires a Table Name argument. You tried to use the `OpenTable`, `TransferSpreadsheet`, or `TransferText` action or method, but you left the Table Name argument blank. In the Table Name argument, enter the name of a table that is in the current database.
2496	The action or method requires a Query Name argument. You tried to use the `OpenQuery` action or method, but you left the Query Name argument blank. In the Query Name argument, enter a query name.
2497	The action or method requires a Report Name argument. You tried to use the `OpenReport` action or method, but you left the Report Name argument blank. In the Report Name argument, enter the name of a report.
2498	An expression you entered is the wrong data type for one of the arguments. You tried to run a macro or use a method to carry out an action, but an expression evaluated to the wrong data type. For example, for the Close method you specified a string for the Object Type argument, but this argument can be set only to certain intrinsic constants or their numeric equivalents.
2499	You can't use the `GoToRecord` action or method on an object in Design view. Try one of the following: Switch to Form or Datasheet view for a form. Switch to Datasheet view for a query or table. If you are running a macro or Visual Basic procedure containing an action that opens the object, set the View argument to the correct view before you carry out the `GoToRecord` action.

ERROR	DESCRIPTION
2500	You must enter a number greater than zero for a Repeat Count argument. You tried to use the `RunMacro` action or method, but you entered a value less than zero (or an expression that evaluates to less than zero) in the Repeat Count argument. To run the macro once, leave this argument blank.
2501	The `<Name>` action was canceled. You used a method of the DoCmd object to carry out an action in Visual Basic, but then clicked Cancel in a dialog box. For example, you used the Close method to close a changed form, then clicked Cancel in the dialog box that asks if you want to save the changes you made to the form.
2502	The action or method requires a Macro Name argument. You tried to use the `RunMacro` action or method, but you left the Macro Name argument blank. `<Your Database>` tried to create a custom menu bar for a form or report, but the Menu Macro Name argument of the `AddMenu` action is blank. In the Menu Macro Name argument, enter the name of a macro or macro group that is in the current database.
2503	You can't use this action with the DoCmd object. For a list of the actions that the DoCmd object doesn't support and some alternatives to using these actions, click Help. Any actions that aren't in this list can be used with the DoCmd object.
2504	The action or method requires at least `<Object or Item Name>` argument(s). You tried to run a macro containing an action or used a method or action with the DoCmd object, but you didn't set the required number of arguments. For example, if you use the `MoveSize` action, you must set at least one of the four arguments.
2505	An expression in argument `<Object or Item Name>` has an invalid value. You tried to run a macro or used the DoCmd object in Visual Basic. The argument number above is the position of the argument as it appears in the Macro window, the Action Failed dialog box, or the Object Browser (if you're using the DoCmd object). Try one of the following: Select a setting from the dropdown list box in each argument. Use an intrinsic constant equating to a valid object type. Substitute the correct corresponding expression.
2506	A value you entered for the Transfer Type argument is invalid. An expression in the Transfer Type argument doesn't evaluate to a valid numeric value. Valid values for the Transfer Type argument are as follows: 0, 1, and 2 for the `TransferDatabase` action.

(continued)

Table C-4 *(continued)*

ERROR	DESCRIPTION
2507	The `<Object or Item Name>` type isn't an installed database type or doesn't support the operation you chose. You used the TransferDatabase method, but an expression in the databasetype argument doesn't evaluate to a valid database type for importing, exporting, or linking. For information on valid database types, click Help.
2508	A value you entered for the spreadsheettype argument is invalid. You used the TransferSpreadsheet method, and an expression in the spreadsheettype argument doesn't evaluate to a valid numeric value. Valid values are 0, 2, 3, 4, 5, 6, 7, and 8. Note that 1 is an invalid value; you can't import or export to a Lotus .wks format file.
2509	The setting for the Range argument can't be longer than 255 characters.
2510	The expression you entered in the Specification Name argument exceeds the 64-character limit. Select one of the existing specification names from the argument list box when you use the `TransferText` action in a macro, or enter a name in Visual Basic that follows `<Your Database>` object-naming rules.
2511	The action or method requires a Specification Name argument. You tried to use the `TransferText` action or method and you specified a Transfer Type argument but left the Specification Name argument blank. In the Specification Name argument, enter an existing specification name from the argument list box.
2512	`<Your Database>` can't parse the expression: `<Expression Name>`. Click OK to return to the action argument or conditional expression where this expression appears, and then correct the syntax.
2513	The Macro Name argument can't be longer than 64 characters according to `<Your Database>` object-naming rules.
2514	The action or method requires a Control Name argument. You tried to use the `GoToControl` action or method, but you left the control name blank. In the Control Name argument, enter a control or field name from the active form or datasheet.
2515	`<Your Database>` can't open the macro `<Macro Name>` because it was saved using a different version of `<Your Database>`. Re-create the macro in the current version of `<Your Database>`.
2516	`<Your Database>` can't find the module `<Module Name>`. You tried to use the `OpenModule` action or method, but `<Your Database>` can't find the module you specified in the Module Name argument. Enter a valid module name from the current database.

ERROR	DESCRIPTION
2517	`<Your Database>` can't find the procedure `<Procedure Name>`. You may have used the Run method in Visual Basic but entered an invalid procedure name, or you used the Run method without first opening a database. You tried to use the `OpenModule` action or method, but you used an invalid procedure name.
2519	The database must be open for the SelectObject method to run. You tried to run a function in a library database, and the function contains the SelectObject method.
2520	The action or method requires a Module or Procedure Name argument. You tried to use the `OpenModule` action or method, but you didn't enter a name in either the Module Name or the Procedure Name argument in the Macro window. Enter a valid name in one of these arguments.
2521	You have specified a Transfer Type that doesn't support the HTML Table Name argument. Leave the HTML Table Name argument blank unless you are using the Import HTML or Link HTML Transfer Types.
2522	The action or method requires a File Name argument. You tried to use the `TransferSpreadsheet` or `TransferText` action or method. In the File Name argument, enter a file name.
2523	The value you entered for the show argument is invalid. You used the ShowToolbar method. Valid values for this argument are acToolbarYes, acToolbarWhereApprop, and acToolbarNo, or the corresponding numeric values 0, 1, and 2.
2524	`<Your Database>` can't invoke the application using the `RunApp` action. The path to the application is invalid, or a component of the application is missing. Check the path in Windows Explorer or File Manager.
2525	A macro can call itself a maximum of 20 times. Your macro contains a `RunMacro` action that calls the same macro more than 20 times. Use a condition to stop the macro after it has been run 20 times, or call another macro with the `RunMacro` action.
2526	The `SendKeys` action requires the `<Your Database>` Utility Add-in to be loaded. Rerun `<Your Database>` or Microsoft Office Setup to reinstall `<Your Database>` and the `<Your Database>` Utility Add-in.
2527	Lotus .wks file formats aren't supported in the current version of `<Your Database>`. Convert your .wks file to a more recent format, such as .wk1.
2528	The `RunCommand` macro action argument is missing, or you entered an invalid command ID for the RunCommand method.

(continued)

Table C-4 *(continued)*

ERROR	DESCRIPTION
2529	The Toolbar argument can't be longer than 64 characters.
2530	The SelectObject method can't be used on a report that is currently printing.
2531	Your HTML file does not contain any tabular data that `<Your Database>` can import.
2532	`<Your Database>` can't find the macro or sub procedure `<Procedure Name>`. The specified macro, macro group, or sub procedure doesn't exist. Note that when you enter the macrogroupname.macroname syntax in an argument, you must specify the name the macro's macro group was last saved under. Also, ensure that the referenced macro has been saved, or that the referenced sub procedure expects 0 arguments.
2533	The `ApplyFilter` action requires that either the Filter Name or Where Condition argument is set. You tried to run a macro containing an `ApplyFilter` action, but you didn't set the required arguments.
2534	The action or method requires a data access page Name argument. You tried to use the `OpenDataAccessPage` action or method, but you left the data access page Name argument blank. In the data access page Name argument, enter the name of a data access page in the current database.
2535	The `ApplyFilter` action contains a Filter Name that cannot be applied. The filter name is not a valid argument in the `ApplyFilter` action in Client Server.
2536	Macros are disabled in this database.
2540	The file `<File Name>` you tried to replace is a `<Your Database>` system file that is in use and can't be replaced or deleted.
2541	The contents of the Clipboard have been deleted and can't be pasted. Some applications do not put large objects on the Clipboard. Instead, they put a pointer to the object on the Clipboard. The pointer may vanish before the paste happens.
2542	Specify the database name in the command line so that `<Your Database>` can find the macro.
2543	You can't paste a database object onto itself.

ERROR	DESCRIPTION
2544	`<Your Database>` can't find the `<Object or Item Name>` you referenced in the Object Name argument. The macro you tried to run includes a `SelectObject` action with an invalid name for the Object Name argument. In the Database window, verify the name of the object you want the macro to select. Then open the macro in the Macro window and enter the correct name for the Object Name argument.
2545	The `CopyObject` action requires you to specify a different destination database or a new name to copy from the current database. The macro you are running includes a `CopyObject` action. Open the macro in the Macro window, and select the `CopyObject` action. Enter a destination database or a new name in the appropriate argument box.
2546	Select a database object in the Database window before you run the macro containing the `<Name>` action.
2547	The database `<Your Database>`you tried to delete and replace is read-only and can't be deleted or replaced. Enter a different name for the new database.
2548	`<Your Database>` can't run the Security Wizard because this database is open in exclusive mode. Do you want `<Your Database>` to open the database in shared mode and run the Security Wizard?
2549	`<Your Database>` can't delete `<Object or Item Name>` after compacting it. The compacted database has been named `<Name>`. If you compact a database using the same name, `<Your Database>` creates a new compacted database and then deletes the original database. In this case, however, the original database wasn't deleted because it is read-only. If you can, remove the read-only status, delete the original database, and then rename the new database using the original name. If you can't remove the read-only status, inform your workgroup administrator.
2550	`<Your Database>` can't delete `<Object or Item Name>` after encoding it. The encoded database has been named `<Name>`. If you encode a database using the same name, `<Your Database>` creates a new encoded database, and then deletes the original database. In this case, however, the original database can't be deleted because it is read-only. If you can, remove the read-only status, delete the original database, and then rename the new database using the original name. If you can't remove the read-only status, inform your workgroup administrator.

(continued)

Table C-4   *(continued)*

ERROR	DESCRIPTION
2551	`<Your Database>` can't delete `<Object or Item Name>` after decoding it. The decoded database has been named `<Name>`. If you decode a database using the same name, `<Your Database>` creates a new decoded database, and then deletes the original database. In this case, however, the original database can't be deleted because it is read-only. If you can, remove the read-only status, delete the original database, and then rename the new database using the original name. If you can't remove the read-only status, inform your workgroup administrator.
2552	You can't encode a database that you didn't create or don't own. See the owner of the database or your workgroup administrator.
2553	You can't decode a database that you didn't create or don't own. See the owner of the database or your workgroup administrator.
2554	Can't find the database you specified, or you didn't specify a database at all. Specify a valid database name in the command line, and include a path if necessary.
2556	`<Your Database>` can't run the Security Wizard because the database has had a password set on it. You will have to unset the database password by choosing Tools|Security|Unset Database Password.
2557	The database you tried to convert was either created in or was already converted to the requested version of `<Your Database>`.
2559	`<Your Database>` was unable to refresh the linked Table `<Table Name>` in database `<Name>` during conversion. Try and refresh the links manually by using the Linked Table Manager (Tools menu, Database Utilities submenu).
2560	`<Your Database>` is unable to load the Database Properties.
2561	`<Your Database>` can't display the Database Properties dialog box.
2562	`<Your Database>` is unable to save the Database Properties.
2563	`<Your Database>` can't load a dynamic-link library. Run Setup to reinstall `<Your Database>`. If you want to preserve your security or custom settings, back up the `<Your Database>` workgroup information file. For information on backing up files, search the Microsoft Windows Help index for 'backing up files'.
2564	You can't hide the document `<Object or Item Name>` while it is open. Close the database object first, and then hide it.
2565	You can't unhide the database object `<Object Name>` while it is open. Close the database object first, and then unhide it.

ERROR	DESCRIPTION
2566	\<Your Database\> is unable to set the application's icon to the file \<File Name\>. Make sure the file is a valid icon (.ico) file. If you're using Microsoft Windows, you can also use .bmp files.
2567	\<Your Database\> can't open or convert this previous version database. The database was created in an earlier version of \<Your Database\>. You don't have appropriate security permissions to open or convert databases created in earlier versions.
2568	\<Your Database\> can't undo this operation. An object with the same name already exists. Another user might have created an object named \<Object Name\> after you had performed this operation on an object with the same name.
2569	\<Your Database\> can't delete \<Object or Item Name\> after enabling it. The enabled database has been named \<Name\>. If you enable a database using the same name, \<Your Database\> creates a new enabled database and then deletes the original database. In this case, however, the original database wasn't deleted because it is read-only. If you can, remove the read-only status, delete the original database, and then rename the new database using the original name. If you can't remove the read-only status, inform your workgroup administrator.
2571	You can't modify objects created using an earlier version of \<Your Database\>. To convert this database to the current version of \<Your Database\>, close the database, point to Database Utilities on the Tools menu, and then click Convert Database.
2573	This database is a replica created in a different version of Access. You can only convert this replica by synchronizing with its Design Master. Convert the Design Master of this replica set then synchronize the replica with the Design Master.
2574	You can't create another \<Your Database\> database with the same name and location as an existing database. You carried out the Make MDE File command, but tried to give the new database the same extension as the old one. Accept the default .mde extension for your new MDE database.
2575	You can't create a \<Your Database\> MDE database from a database replica.
2576	This database is a \<Your Database\> 7.0/8.0/9.0 Design Master/Replica. If you click OK, the database you selected will be renamed to \<Name\> and then converted to \<Name\>. Everyone using a replica of this database will have to upgrade to Microsoft Access 2000 after the next synchronization.
2577	The database \<Your Database\> is already open. Close the database before carrying out the Make MDE File command.

(continued)

Table C-4 *(continued)*

ERROR	DESCRIPTION
2578	`<Your Database>` was unable to create an MDE database.
2579	Local forms, reports, macros, and modules in this replica will not be converted. To retain these objects, please be sure to import them into the Design Master from the original replica.
2580	The record source `<Object or Item Name>` specified on this form or report does not exist. You misspelled the name, or it was deleted or renamed in the current database, or it exists in a different database. In the Form or Report's Design view, display the property sheet by clicking the Properties button, and then set the RecordSource property to an existing table or query.
2581	You must define a sort field or expression for the group header or footer in the report you tried to preview or print.
2582	You can't set the GroupInterval property to zero when the GroupOn property is set to Interval. Click Sorting and Grouping on the View menu and try one of the following: Change the GroupInterval property setting to a number higher than zero. Change the GroupOn property setting to Each Value.
2583	The `ApplyFilter` action or method can be carried out only from an Open macro or Open event procedure. You may have tried to run a macro or procedure containing the `ApplyFilter` action or method from a report property other than the OnOpen property. You may have tried to run a macro or event procedure on a report that is already open. To use the `ApplyFilter` action in a report, set the OnOpen property to the name of the macro, close the report, and then reopen it.
2584	You can't use aggregate functions in a page header or footer. The page header or footer of the report you tried to preview contains a calculated control with an aggregate function in its expression. If you want to show the result of an aggregate function in a page header or footer, create a hidden calculated control in an appropriate section of the report. Then create an unbound text box in the page header or footer. If you are running a macro, use the `SetValue` action to set the unbound text box value to the value in the hidden control.
2585	This action can't be carried out while processing a form or report event. A macro specified as the OnOpen, OnClose, OnFormat, OnRetreat, OnPage, or OnPrint property setting contains an invalid action for the property. When you click OK, an Action Failed dialog box will display the name of the macro that failed and its arguments.

ERROR	DESCRIPTION
2586	<Your Database> changed the MoveLayout and NextRecord properties to True from False. The macro or Visual Basic function run by the OnFormat property of one of the sections of the report set both the MoveLayout and NextRecord properties to False. Having both properties set to False can make the report print continuously. Revise the macro or function so that it sets these properties to the values you want.
2587	<Your Database> can't complete the Output operation. The Visual Basic code you entered contains a syntax error or the Output procedures are not available. Make sure there isn't a syntax error in your code. If the syntax is correct, run Setup to reinstall <Your Database>. If you want to preserve your security or custom settings, back up the <Your Database> workgroup information file.
2588	You must select a form to save as a report.
2589	The expression <Expression Name> is invalid. Aggregate functions are only allowed on output fields of the Record Source.
2590	The Var and VarP aggregate functions are not supported in an Access project.
2591	You can't change printer properties in the OnOpen event of a report.
2592	You cannot bind a hierarchical report to a DAO Recordset.
2593	This feature is not available in an MDB.
2594	You cannot Filter By Form when form record source is a recordset object.
2595	<Your Database> cannot set this property when DefaultSize property is set to True.
2596	Printer object is not available on subforms and subreports.
2597	Unable to bind the report to the specified recordset because the shape does not match the sorting and grouping specified on the report.
2598	Recordset property not available for natively bound reports in MDB files.
2600	Verify the new password by retyping it in the Verify box and clicking OK.
2601	You don't have permission to read <Object or Item Name>. To read this object, you must have Read Design permission for it.

(continued)

Table C-4 *(continued)*

ERROR	DESCRIPTION
2602	You don't have permission to modify `<Object or Item Name>`. To modify this object, you must have Modify Design permission for it. If the object is a table, you must also have Delete Data and Update Data permissions for it.
2603	You don't have permission to run `<Object or Item Name>`. To run this object, you must have Open/Run permission for it.
2604	You can't view this object's permissions. To view or change permissions for this object, you must have Administer permission for it.
2605	You can't remove this user account from group `<Object or Item Name>`. You may have tried to remove a user account from the default Users group. `<Your Database>` automatically adds all users to the default Users group. To remove a user account from the Users group, you must first delete the account. You may have tried to remove all users from the Admins group. There must be at least one user in the Admins group.
2606	The object type is invalid.
2607	You don't have permission to cut `<Object or Item Name>`. To cut this object, you must have Modify Design permission for it. If the object is a table, you must also have Delete Data permission for it.
2608	You don't have permission to copy `<Object or Item Name>`. To copy this object, you must have Read Design permission for it. If the object is a table, you must also have Read Data permission for it.
2609	You don't have permission to delete `<Object or Item Name>`. To delete this object, you must have Modify Design permission for it. If the object is a table, you must also have Delete Data permission for it.
2610	You must enter a personal identifier (PID) consisting of at least 4 and no more than 20 characters and digits. `<Your Database>` uses the combination of the user or group name and the PID to identify the user or group. Note that `<Your Database>` hides the PID after you create it, so make sure to write down the exact user or group account name and the PID entries. If you ever have to re-create the account, you must supply the same name and PID entries.
2611	`<Your Database>` can't find the workgroup file `<File Name>`. Would you like to use the default workgroup file?
2612	The account name is invalid. For information about naming conventions, click Help.
2613	You don't have permission to rename `<Object or Item Name>`. To rename a database object, you must have Modify Design permission for the object.

ERROR	DESCRIPTION
2614	You don't have permission to insert this form into another form. To insert a form into another form as a subform, you must have Read Design permission for the form being inserted.
2615	You don't have permission to change the owner of <Object or Item Name>. To change the owner of a database object, you must have Administer permission for it.
2616	You can't change permissions for <Object or Item Name>. To change permissions for this object, you must have Administer permission for it.
2617	You don't have permission to import, export, or link to <Object or Item Name>. To import, export, or link to this object, you must have Read Design and Read Data permissions for it.
2618	You need to have the database open for exclusive use to set or unset the database password. To open the database exclusively, close the database, and then reopen it using the Open command on the File menu. In the Open dialog box, click the arrow to the right of the Open button, and then choose Open Exclusive.
2619	You can't change permissions for <Object or Item Name> in a replica. Permissions may only be changed in the Design Master for the replica set.
2620	The password you entered in the Old Password box is incorrect. Please enter the correct password for this account.
2621	That password isn't valid. You may have used a semicolon.
2622	You can't save <Object or Item Name> because it is read-only. To save, switch to Design View and choose Save As from the File menu.
2623	Saving the database to the previous version of Access will create a new database that contains none of the security information that you have set. Are you sure you want to proceed?
2624	An error has occurred while changing workgroup database.
2625	Workgroup Administrator couldn't create the workgroup information file. Make sure that you have specified a valid path and file name, that you have adequate permissions to create the file, and that you have enough disk space on the destination drive.
2626	Reserved error <Error>; there is no message for this error.
2627	There's not enough disk space.
2628	One of your parameters is invalid.
2629	Could not open workgroup file. This is a directory.

(continued)

Table C-4 *(continued)*

ERROR	DESCRIPTION
2630	The specified path is invalid.
2631	The specified path is too long.
2632	Change Workgroup cannot proceed without your Name, PIN, and a path to the new Workgroup Information File.
2633	`<Your Database>` cannot change the password for the logon account `<Object or Item Name>` because the current connection is using Microsoft Windows NT integrated security.
2634	The new password doesn't match the verify password value.
2635	`<Your Database>` is unable to change the password because the old password doesn't match the password of the currently logged in user.
2636	Workgroup file already exists.
2637	Unable to start SQL Server service. To restart the SQL Server service, double click on the SQL Server System Manager icon in the system tray and click Start/Continue. Once the service is started, point to Connection on the File menu in Access and click OK.
2638	Unable to start SQL Server service. To restart the SQL Server service, double click on the SQL Server System Manager icon in the system tray and click Start/Continue. If the service fails to start, go to the Services console and verify that the MSSQLServer service Log On information is correct. Once the service is started, point to Connection on the File menu in Access and click OK.
2639	`<Your Database>` cannot open `<Object or Item Name>` due to security restrictions. Security settings restrict access to the file because it is not digitally signed.
2646	`<Your Database>` can't create this relationship and enforce referential integrity. Data in the table `<Table Name>` violates referential integrity rules. For example, there may be records relating to an employee in the related table, but no record for the employee in the primary table. Edit the data so that records in the primary table exist for all related records. If you want to create the relationship without following the rules of referential integrity, clear the Enforce Referential Integrity check box.
2648	`<Your Database>` created a one-to-one relationship instead of a one-to-many relationship because there is a unique index on the field(s) specified for the related table. If you want to define a one-to-many relationship between these tables, try one of the following: Delete the one-to-one relationship, and then change the setting of the Indexed property for the foreign key field from No Duplicates to Duplicates OK. Choose different matching fields.

ERROR	DESCRIPTION
2649	`<Your Database>` can't enforce referential integrity for this relationship. Make sure the fields you drag are primary key fields or uniquely indexed and that the unique index or primary key is correctly set. If you want to create the relationship without following the rules of referential integrity, clear the Enforce Referential Integrity check box.
2650	`<Your Database>` can't create this relationship and enforce referential integrity. The fields you chose may have different data types. The fields may have the Number data type but not the same FieldSize property setting. Try one of the following: Select fields with the same data type. Open the tables in Design view, and change the data types and field sizes so that the fields match. If you want to create the relationship without following the rules of referential integrity, clear the Enforce Referential Integrity check box.
2651	You can't create a relationship between fields with the Memo, OLE Object, Yes/No, or Hyperlink data type. You tried to enforce referential integrity for a relationship, but one or more of the fields you chose have the Memo, OLE Object, Yes/No, or Hyperlink data type. Select fields in the grid that don't have these data types, or open the tables in Design view and change data types.
2652	You can't delete a relationship inherited from a linked database.
2680	The form or report includes more OLE objects than `<Your Database>` can display at one time. Delete some of the bound or unbound object frames.
2683	There is no object in this control.
2684	The OLE object is empty. You can't edit a bound object frame if the field in the underlying table doesn't contain an OLE object. Embed or link an OLE object into the bound object frame using the Object command on the Insert menu.
2685	The object doesn't have an OLE object data type. The bound object frame containing the object you tried to edit isn't bound to a field with the OLE object data type. If you want to display an OLE object, set the ControlSource property for the bound object frame to a field with the OLE object data type. Or use a different control, such as a text box, to display the data.
2686	`<Your Database>` is unable to save the `<Object Name>` object. Your computer ran out of disk space while `<Your Database>` was saving the OLE object. For information on freeing disk space, search the Microsoft Windows Help index for 'disk space, freeing'.
2687	There was a problem reading the `<Object Name>` object.

(continued)

Table C-4   *(continued)*

ERROR	DESCRIPTION
2690	A system resource necessary for displaying the <Object Name> object isn't available. Your computer may be low on memory. Close unneeded programs, and try the operation again.
2691	<Your Database> can't communicate with the OLE server. The OLE server may not be registered. To register the OLE server, reinstall it.
2694	The Clipboard isn't available. The Clipboard may be in use by another application, or your computer may be low on memory. If your computer is low on memory, close unneeded programs, and then try the operation again.
2695	<Your Database> is unable to display the converted <Object Name> object. Delete the object in the bound object frame, and then re-create it.
2696	<Your Database> can't read the OLE object. Delete the object in the bound object frame, and then re-create it.
2697	There was a problem loading the <Object Name> object. The object you tried to create or edit is not a valid OLE object. Re-create the object, and then embed or link it again.
2698	The <Object Name> object you tried to create or edit is too large to save. Your database may not contain enough space for the object. Your computer may be out of disk space.
2699	The connection with the OLE server was lost, or the OLE server encountered an error while you were using it. Restart the OLE server, and then try the operation again.
2700	<Your Database> can't find an OLE server or a dynamic-link library (DLL) required for the OLE operation. The OLE server or DLL may not be registered. To register the OLE server or DLL, reinstall it.
2701	The OLE server for the OLE object you tried to create is already open. Switch to the OLE server window and close it. Then try to create or edit the OLE object again.
2702	The <Object Name> object isn't registered. The object may be calling an application that isn't installed. To register the application, reinstall it.
2703	<Your Database> can't read the <Object Name> object because communication was interrupted. If the OLE server application is located on a network server, make sure your computer is connected to it.

ERROR	DESCRIPTION
2704	The <Object Name> object you tried to edit doesn't have any displayable information.
2707	<Your Database> can't open the file containing the OLE object. You may have specified an invalid file name or an invalid unit of data (such as a range of cells from a worksheet) within the file for the OLE object. The file you specified may not be available because it's locked by another user or you don't have permission to use it. Try one of the following: Make sure the file is available and that you used the correct file name. Check the OLE server's documentation for information about the syntax to use when specifying an OLE object's data.
2711	The file name argument in the GetObject function of the Visual Basic procedure you ran is invalid. You may not have entered, or may have misspelled, the file name. The unit of data (such as a range of cells from a worksheet) may not be valid. Try one of the following: Make sure the file is installed on your computer and that you used the correct file name. Check the OLE server's documentation for information about the syntax to use when specifying an OLE object's data.
2713	A problem occurred when <Your Database> tried to access the <Object Name> object. You may have specified an invalid file name or an invalid unit of data (such as a range of cells from a worksheet) within the file for the OLE object. The file you specified may not be available because it's locked by another user or you don't have permission to use it. Try one of the following: Make sure that the file is installed on your computer and that you used the correct file name. Check the OLE server's documentation for information about the syntax to use when specifying an OLE object's data.
2714	The <Object Name> object doesn't support verbs that can be performed on an OLE object, such as play or edit. Check the OLE server's documentation for information on the verbs the OLE object supports, or use the ObjectVerbs property or the ObjectVerbsCount property to find the verbs supported by an OLE object.
2715	The index for the Action or the Verb property for the <Object Name> object is invalid. The setting you entered may be a negative number or may be too large.
2717	The <Object Name> object has no displayable information. You tried to perform an operation on a bound or unbound object frame containing an OLE object, but the OLE object is empty. Use the Object command on the Insert menu to create an OLE object or to embed or link an OLE object from a file that isn't empty.

(continued)

Table C-4 *(continued)*

ERROR	DESCRIPTION
2719	A problem occurred while accessing the <Object Name> object. The OLE server may not be available because it's on a network server and you lost the connection. Try re-establishing the connection. The OLE object may be stored in a linked file, but the file isn't available. Activate the OLE server outside of <Your Database>, and then open the file containing the OLE object to verify that it still exists and can be accessed.
2723	The <Object Name> object doesn't support the attempted operation. The OLE object was changed to a picture, or the link to the object was broken. If you want to perform the operation, delete the OLE object, and then embed or link it again.
2724	One or more dynamic-link libraries required for using OLE objects is an incorrect version. Run Setup to reinstall <Your Database>. If you want to preserve your security or custom settings, back up the <Your Database> workgroup information file. For information on backing up files, search the Microsoft Windows Help index for 'backing up files'.
2725	The OLE server isn't registered. To register the OLE server, reinstall it.
2726	<Your Database> can't perform the OLE operation because it was unable to read the Windows Registry where the OLE server is registered. Reinstall the OLE server, and then try the operation again. If problems continue, reinstall Microsoft Windows and the other applications on your computer. If you reinstall <Your Database>, you may want to back up your <Your Database> workgroup information file first to preserve any custom settings.
2727	<Your Database> can't perform the OLE operation because it was unable to write to the Windows Registry where the OLE server is registered. Reinstall the OLE server, and then try the operation again. If problems continue, reinstall Microsoft Windows and the other applications on your computer. If you reinstall <Your Database>, you may want to back up your <Your Database> workgroup information file first to preserve any custom settings. For information on backing up files, search the Microsoft Windows Help index for 'backing up files'.
2729	The OLE object you tried to edit is busy. Try again later.
2730	There was a problem communicating with the OLE server. Try again later. If you still can't access the object, try one or more of the following: Free up system memory. For information on freeing memory, search the Microsoft Windows Help index for 'memory, troubleshooting'. Reinstall the OLE server to make sure it's registered. Check the OLE server's documentation for information about the syntax to use when specifying an OLE object's data.

ERROR	DESCRIPTION
2731	An error occurred while accessing the OLE server. The OLE server may not be registered. To register the OLE server, reinstall it.
2732	\<Your Database\> can't read the \<Object Name\> object. Communication between \<Your Database\> and the OLE server was interrupted. Make sure your computer is connected to the network server on which the OLE server is located.
2733	The OLE object you tried to edit can't be accessed. You don't have permission to change the object, or another user opened and locked the object.
2734	You can't save the \<Object Name\> object now. The OLE server is running an operation, or another user opened and locked the object. Try to save the object again later.
2735	This disk is write-protected. You can't save the \<Object Name\> object to it.
2737	\<Your Database\> can't find the file containing the linked OLE object you tried to update using the OLE/DDE Links command. You may have misspelled the file name, or the file may have been deleted or renamed. If the file has been moved to a different location, use the OLE/DDE Links command to change the source. Or delete the object, and create a new linked object.
2738	There isn't enough memory to complete the operation. Close unneeded programs and try the operation again.
2739	An error occurred during the operation with an OLE object. The object is in use.
2741	Your computer ran out of disk space while \<Your Database\> was saving the changes you made to the \<Object Name\> object. For information on freeing disk space, search the Microsoft Windows Help index for 'disk space, freeing'.
2742	\<Your Database\> was unable to create more files. Your computer may be low on memory or disk space. Close unneeded programs and try the operation again. For information on freeing memory or disk space, search the Microsoft Windows Help index for 'memory, troubleshooting' or 'disk space, freeing'.
2743	The \<Object Name\> object is stored in a format that is incompatible with the version of OLE on your computer.
2744	\<Your Database\> can't find the OLE server. The setting for the SourceDoc property may be invalid, or the file may have been deleted, renamed, or moved.

(continued)

Table C-4 *(continued)*

ERROR	DESCRIPTION
2745	Share.exe or Vshare.386 is missing from your computer; OLE support needs these files to work correctly. Rerun <Your Database> or Microsoft Office Setup to reinstall <Your Database>, the Share program, and Vshare.386. If you want to preserve your security or custom settings, back up the <Your Database> workgroup information file. Then restore the file to its original location. For information on backing up files, search the Microsoft Windows Help index for 'backing up files'.
2746	You can't switch to Design view because your form contains too many OLE objects. Close other applications, close the form, and then open the form again in Design view. Then delete some of the OLE objects or move them to a different form.
2747	The OLE server can't display the <Object Name> object. There is a problem with the file containing the OLE object, or there isn't enough memory available. Open the OLE server outside of <Your Database>, and then open the OLE object file. If you can do this, then your computer may be low on memory. Close other programs, and then try the operation again.
2748	The Automation object operation isn't available for the <Object Name> object. Check the component's documentation for information on which operations are available for an Automation object.
2749	There isn't enough memory to complete the Automation object operation on the <Object Name> object. Close unneeded programs and try the operation again.
2750	The operation on the <Object Name> object failed. The OLE server may not be registered. To register the OLE server, reinstall it.
2751	The Exit or Update operation failed. You pressed the ESC key (or another key used in the OLE server to stop an operation) while <Your Database> was saving the changes you made to an OLE object in a form or report. Try to exit or update again.
2753	A problem occurred while <Your Database> was communicating with the OLE server or ActiveX Control. Close the OLE server and restart it outside of <Your Database>. Then try the original operation again in <Your Database>.
2754	A problem occurred while <Your Database> was communicating with the OLE server. Try one or more of the following: Make sure you're connected to the network server where the OLE server application is located. Close the OLE server and restart it outside of <Your Database>. Then try the original operation again from within <Your Database>. Reinstall the OLE server to ensure that it's registered.

ERROR	DESCRIPTION
2755	There was a problem referencing a property or method of the object. You tried to run a Visual Basic procedure that references an object property or method. Try one or more of the following: Make sure the component is properly registered. Make sure your computer is connected to the network server where the component is located. Close the component and restart it outside of `<Your Database>`. Then try again to run the procedure in `<Your Database>`.
2756	A problem occurred when `<Your Database>` tried to access the OLE object. Close the `<Your Database>` form or report that displays the OLE object, and close the OLE server. Then reopen the form or report to see if it can display the OLE object.
2757	There was a problem accessing a property or method of the OLE object. Try one or more of the following: Verify that the OLE server is registered correctly by reinstalling it. Make sure your computer is connected to the server on which the OLE server application resides. Close the OLE server and restart it outside of `<Your Database>`. Then try the original operation again from within `<Your Database>`.
2758	There was a problem initializing the dynamic-link library Msole20 when you tried to perform the OLE operation. You may have too many Microsoft applications open. Close Windows applications other than `<Your Database>`, and try the OLE operation again. Your computer may have an older version of the dynamic-link library Msole20, in which case you will need to run Setup to reinstall `<Your Database>`. If you need to reinstall `<Your Database>`, you may want to preserve your security or custom settings by backing up the `<Your Database>` workgroup information file. For information on backing up files, search the Microsoft Windows Help index for 'backing up files'.
2759	The method you tried to invoke on an object failed. You may have specified too many or too few arguments for a property or method of an object. Check the component's documentation for information on the properties and methods it makes available for Automation operations. There may not be enough memory to run the procedure. Close unneeded programs and try to run the procedure again. For more information on freeing memory, search the Microsoft Windows Help index for 'memory, troubleshooting'.
2760	An error occurred while referencing the object. You tried to run a Visual Basic procedure that improperly references a property or method of an object.
2761	There was a problem referencing a property or method of an object. Check the component's documentation for information on the properties and methods it makes available for Automation operations.

(continued)

Table C-4 *(continued)*

ERROR	DESCRIPTION
2762	`<Your Database>` returned an error while referencing a property of an object. Check the component's documentation for information on the properties and methods it makes available for Automation operations.
2763	`<Your Database>` returned the error: `<Error Message>`. Check the component's documentation for information on the properties and methods it makes available for Automation operations.
2764	The object's property or method can't be set. You tried to run a Visual Basic procedure to set a property or apply a method for an object. However, the property or method doesn't support named arguments. Check the component's documentation for information on the properties and methods it makes available to Automation operations.
2765	Visual Basic can't convert the data type of one of the arguments you entered. You tried to run a Visual Basic procedure that executes a method or sets a property of an object. Check the component's documentation for information on the properties and methods it makes available for Automation operations.
2766	The object doesn't contain the Automation object `<Object Name>`. You tried to run a Visual Basic procedure to set a property or method for an object. However, the component doesn't make the property or method available for Automation operations. Check the component's documentation for information on the properties and methods it makes available for Automation operations.
2767	The object doesn't support American English; it was developed using a different language. Use a version of the object developed in Visual Basic that supports the language you are using.
2768	The number you used to reference an element in the array is outside the bounds of the array. For example, the array is from 0 through 10, and you entered a -1 or an 11. Check the component's documentation for information on the properties and methods it makes available for Automation operations.
2769	A property of the Automation object requires or returns a data type that isn't supported by Visual Basic. You tried to run a Visual Basic procedure that references an Automation object's property. However, the value of the property isn't supported by Visual Basic. Check the component's documentation for information on the properties and methods it makes available for Automation operations.
2770	The object you referenced in the Visual Basic procedure as an OLE object isn't an OLE object.

ERROR	DESCRIPTION
2771	The bound or unbound object frame you tried to edit doesn't contain an OLE object. Use the Object command on the Insert menu to add an OLE object to the bound or unbound object frame.
2774	The component doesn't support Automation. You tried to run a Visual Basic procedure that references an Automation object. Check the component's documentation for information on whether it supports Automation.
2775	You specified too many arguments in the Visual Basic procedure, or there isn't enough memory to run the procedure. Specify fewer arguments, or close unneeded programs, and then try to run the procedure again.
2777	The class argument in the CreateObject function of the Visual Basic procedure you're trying to run is invalid. Try one of the following: Make sure the file is installed on your computer and that you used the correct file name. Check the OLE server's documentation for information about the syntax to use when specifying an OLE object's data.
2778	`<Your Database>` tried to create an OLE link, but there was no source document for this object.
2782	You must specify a property or method for the object. You tried to run a Visual Basic procedure that references and sets a property or method for the object. Enter a property or method for the object.
2783	You entered an invalid setting for the Action property. Use one of the `<Your Database>` intrinsic constants for the Action property. For a list of valid settings you can use with the Action property, click Help.
2784	The path you entered for the SourceDoc property setting for a linked OLE object is too long. Move the file to a location with a shorter path.
2785	The OLE server wasn't able to open the object. The OLE server may not be installed. You may have specified an invalid setting for the SourceDoc or SourceItem property in a property sheet, a macro, or a Visual Basic procedure. To see the valid settings for either of these properties, search the Help index for the property topic.
2786	The OLE server doesn't support linking. You tried to run a Visual Basic procedure using the Action property. However, you provided insufficient information to establish a link.
2788	The `<Object Name>` object isn't a linked object. The property you tried to set in Visual Basic applies only to linked objects.
2790	You can't embed an OLE object into a bound or unbound object frame if the OLETypeAllowed property for the bound or unbound object frame is set to Linked. Insert a linked object, or set the OLETypeAllowed property to Embedded or Either, and then embed the object.

(continued)

Table C-4   *(continued)*

ERROR	DESCRIPTION
2791	`<Your Database>` can't link the OLE object or the bound or unbound object frame. The OLETypeAllowed property for the bound or unbound object frame is set to Embedded. Embed the object, or set the OLETypeAllowed property to Linked or Either, and then link the object.
2792	You can't save a locked OLE object.
2793	`<Your Database>` can't perform the operation specified in the Action property of the Visual Basic procedure you're trying to run. The object frame may be locked or disabled. Set the Locked property to No and the Enabled property to Yes.
2794	The ActiveX control you tried to insert isn't registered. For information on registering an ActiveX control, click Help.
2797	This OLE object was created in an earlier version of OLE so it can't be displayed as an icon. For an effect similar to displaying an object as an icon, add an image control to your form, and add the icon for the application to the image control. Then set the image control's OnDblClick property to a Visual Basic procedure that opens the OLE object.
2798	You can't use the Action property to delete a bound OLE object from its underlying table or query. You tried to run a Visual Basic procedure that deletes the object in a bound object frame by setting the Action property to acOLEDelete. Delete the object in a different way, such as with the DAO Delete method in Visual Basic.
2799	The OLE object can't be activated upon receiving the focus. If you selected an OLE object or a chart, and the AutoActivate property for that control is set to GetFocus, the OLE object or chart should be activated automatically when it receives the focus. However, the ActiveX component doesn't support this operation. Check the component's documentation for information on the properties and methods it makes available to Automation operations.
2800	The object is locked, so any changes you make will be discarded when the form is closed. Click Save As on the File menu and save the object under a different name.
2801	The OLE object isn't loaded because the unbound ActiveX control hasn't been initialized.
2802	You can't insert an ActiveX control in a bound or unbound object frame. ActiveX controls are automatically contained in ActiveX control frames.

ERROR	DESCRIPTION
2803	You don't have the license required to use this ActiveX control. You tried to open a form containing an OLE object or an ActiveX control or you tried to create an ActiveX control. To obtain the appropriate license, contact the company that provides the licensed OLE object or ActiveX control.
2804	You can't create an ActiveX control in an unbound object frame. ActiveX controls are automatically contained in ActiveX control frames.
2805	There was an error loading an ActiveX control on one of your forms or reports. Make sure all the controls that you are using are properly registered. For information on registering an ActiveX control, click Help.
2806	`<Your Database>` doesn't support this ActiveX control.
2807	You can't paste this object as the type you specified. Choose another object type.
2808	`<Your Database>` can't find the Active Accessibility dynamic-link library (DLL) OleAcc. Rerun the `<Your Database>` Setup program.
2811	`<Your Database>` is unable to create the data access page.
2812	The path specified was invalid, or may be too long. Please check the path and ensure it is correct.
2813	The file could not be opened. It may currently be in use.
2814	Unable to save the file.
2815	Unable to save the file to an alternate location.
2816	Unable to close the file.
2817	`<Your Database>` is unable to save (or send) the data access page.
2818	`<Your Database>` is unable to retrieve the file: `<File Name>`. Either the file is not available, or you do not have enough disk space to copy the file.
2819	`<Your Database>` is unable to open the data access page.
2820	`<Your Database>` is unable to change the BASE HREF for your document.
2821	File in use.

(continued)

Table C-4 *(continued)*

ERROR	DESCRIPTION
2822	`<Your Database>` encountered an unexpected error while attempting to recover from a failed save (or send). Your data access page may not be in a usable state. Please attempt to save to a different location.
2823	The `<Your Database>` data access page name `<Page Name>` is misspelled or refers to a Page that doesn't exist. If the invalid Page name is in a macro, an Action Failed dialog box will display the macro name and the macro's arguments after you click OK.
2824	You do not have adequate file permissions.
2825	The file does not exist, or you do not have read access to the file.
2827	File read error.
2828	File write error. The disk may be full.
2832	Check file permissions and delete them from their location in your computer's file system.
2835	An attempt to create this file has failed. Please select another location and retry the operation.
2837	There was not enough memory. Please close other applications and try the operation again.
2838	`<Your Database>` is unable to preview the selected theme.
2839	An attempt to create a temporary file has failed. Please confirm that you have adequate disk space on your system drive and try the operation again.
2840	Unable to read the list of supporting files from the data access page.
2842	`<Your Database>` encountered an error after saving (or sending) your data access page.
2845	`<Your Database>` is unable to open the data access page from the mail envelope.
2846	The save destination is full. Please clear space at the destination or save to another location.
2847	Unable to create a folder for the supporting files. You may not have adequate permissions at the save destination.
2848	The maximum path length was exceeded. Please specify a shorter filename, or use a folder that is closer to the root.
2849	There are too many supporting files in your document. Please remove a few supporting files from your document, and try again.

ERROR	DESCRIPTION
2850	You do not have write permission at the save destination.
2851	You are saving to a server that does not support long file names and do not have permission to create a folder. You must have permission to create a folder at the save destination to complete this operation.
2854	<Your Database> was unable to parse the document properties for this data access page. They may be corrupted.
2855	<Your Database> could not delete one or more files related to the page.
2859	Access could not load the e-mail envelope. This could be caused by a network connection problem or a problem with your Office installation.
2860	You cannot insert a bound field to a caption or record navigation section.
2861	<Your Database> is unable to preview the selected web page.
2862	The file you attempted to load was not recognized as HTML. You may have selected the wrong file, or tried to open a database file off of a web server.
2863	Unable to create or load a file due to network or access permission problems.
2864	This file (or a supporting file) is already in use, or has the read-only attribute set.
2865	The disk is write-protected.
2867	Unexpected data I/O failure.
2868	You cannot save this data access page over itself because it is read-only. Please select a different file for the save.
2869	The file does not exist. You do not have adequate permission to modify the data access page link to point to a valid file. Please contact the database administrator.
2870	<Your Database> encountered an error synchronizing the HTML from the Microsoft Script Editor. Please check the HTML for syntax errors and try again.
2871	<Your Database> is unable to create a data access page using the codepage selected in Web Options. The codepage may not be installed on your system. Please install the codepage, or select a different one in Web Options.

(continued)

Table C-4 *(continued)*

ERROR	DESCRIPTION
2873	The file name specified is a long filename, but you have the 'use long file names' web option turned off. Please specify a file name that uses a maximum of eight characters for the name and three characters for the file extension.
2874	Cannot move or paste the groupingfield `<Field Name>` into a section at a higher group level.
2875	Unable to complete the save. The drive or network connection you attempted to save to may no longer be available.
2876	The data definition of this data access page has been corrupted and can't be repaired. You must recreate the page. Save has been disabled.
2877	In a `<Your Database>` database (.mdb), you can't group on a control bound to a field that has a Memo or OLE Object data type. In a `<Your Database>` project (.adp), you can't group on a control bound to a field that has an Image or Text data type.
2878	You cannot add a bound field to a caption or record navigation section.
2879	Caption and record navigation sections cannot contain bound fields.
2880	Can't edit pages that contain framesets.
2881	This web page contains XML namespaces that may conflict with Access namespaces. You should edit the HTML source to ensure that all namespaces have a unique prefix.
2882	The folder that this Web page would use to organize supporting files is already reserved for use in the current location. Please choose a different name or location for this Web page.
2883	A supporting file path for this data access page has been altered outside of Access. Please save this page to a different location and ensure that all supporting files are maintained.
2884	Cannot find the database or some database objects that this page refers to. Update the connection information of the page, or fix the references to the missing database objects.
2885	This page uses a database which is not supported. You will not be able to make data changes until you connect to a supported database
2886	Components necessary for data access pages are not installed.
2887	The path specified is not a valid absolute (non-relative) path or URL. Please enter a valid path.

ERROR	DESCRIPTION
2888	<Your Database> detects some HTML elements between the banner and the section of your data access page. Saving this page in Access will corrupt it. Close the page without saving it, and then edit the page in another HTML editor to remove these elements.
2889	This section cannot be deleted.
2890	You cannot edit this page because it contains frames. The data access page designer cannot edit pages with frames.
2892	You can't move the group filter control to another section. Delete the group filter control from the current section and create it in a different section.
2893	A link to this data access page could not be created because the database cannot be exclusively locked. To create the link later, open the page by selecting 'Edit web page that already exists', and then save.
2894	The link to the data access page specified could not be updated because the database cannot be exclusively locked. To update the link, open this page again when you are the only person using the database.
2895	This page was designed with a version of the Microsoft Office Web Components that is not currently installed on this machine. If you have not been prompted to install those components on this page, please contact the page author for the installation location.
2896	The operation is only valid on a data access page opened in Design View. Please switch the page to Design View and try the operation again.
2897	You have opened a page that was last modified using Access 2000. To be able to edit the page, you must save it using a more recent version of the Microsoft Office Web Components. Do you want Access to convert this page by saving it using a more recent version of the Microsoft Office Web Components?
2898	<Your Database> has created a backup copy of your original page. This page can be used if you want to revert to the Office 2000 Web Components. The backup page name is: <Object or Item Name>
2899	<Your Database> could not create a backup copy of your original page. This page cannot be opened.
2900	<Your Database> could not upgrade the Office Web Components on your page. This page cannot be opened.
2901	Error loading ActiveX control <Object or Item Name> on form or report <Object or Item Name>.

(continued)

Table C-4 *(continued)*

ERROR	DESCRIPTION
2902	Access is unable to save the `<Object Name>` object because it does not support persistence, or your computer may have run out of disk space.
2903	Do you want to set this folder as the default location for data access pages?
2904	You must match each field on the left with a field on the right.
2905	You must choose a linking field for every parameter.
2906	`<Object or Item>` contains no fields that can participate in a relationship.
2907	Do you want to revert to the saved `<Object or Item Name>`?
2908	The Control ID `<Object or Item Name>` is already in use. Specify a different ID for the control.
2909	This relationship is not valid because the fields in the first table do not match the fields in the second table. To repair the relationship, select at least one field from each table.
2910	This connection file refers to a provider not supported by data access pages. Please select a different connection file.
2911	You cannot change the data access page path while it is open. Please close the page and try again.
2912	If you create a data access page in this version of Access, you cannot open it in Design view in Access 2000. If you have installed the Microsoft Office XP Web Components, however, you can open this page in Page view in Access 2000.
2913	Cannot save to a URL address with a bookmark. Please specify a valid path.
2914	`<Your Database>` could not link to a connection file. A connection string will be embedded in the page.
2915	`<Your Database>` is unable to connect to the data source specified in the connection string of this page. The server may not exist on the network, or there may be an error in the connection string information for this page.
2916	You cannot edit HTML pages created using PowerPoint in `<Your Database>`.
2917	Invalid HTML color value.
2918	Unable to read this connection file. Either the file has been damaged or the file format is not valid.

ERROR	DESCRIPTION
2919	You can't place this control in the section you specified.
2920	\<Your Database\> is unable to load the database schema. Save has been disabled. Either repair or reinstall Microsoft Office.
2921	\<Your Database\> cannot open this page because it was created using a newer version of Access. Try opening the page using a newer version of \<Your Database\>.
2922	\<Your Database\> has created a backup copy of your original page. This page can be used if you want to revert to the Office XP Web Components. The backup page name is: \<Object or Item Name\>
3000	Reserved error \<Error\>; there is no message for this error.
3001	Invalid argument.
3002	Could not start session.
3003	Could not start transaction; too many transactions already nested.
3005	\<Object or Item\> is not a valid database name.
3006	Database \<Your Database\> is exclusively locked.
3007	Cannot open library database \<Your Database\>.
3008	The table \<Table Name\> is already opened exclusively by another user, or it is already open through the user interface and cannot be manipulated programmatically.
3009	You tried to lockable \<Table Name\> while opening it, but the table cannot be locked because it is currently in use. Wait a moment, and then try the operation again.
3010	Table \<Table Name\> already exists.
3012	Object \<Object Name\> already exists.
3013	Could not rename installable ISAM file.
3014	Cannot open any more tables.
3015	Index not found.
3016	Field will not fit in record.
3017	The size of a field is too long.
3018	Could not find field.
3020	Update or Cancel Update without Add New or Edit.
3021	No current record.

(continued)

Table C-4 *(continued)*

ERROR	DESCRIPTION
3022	The changes you requested to the table were not successful because they would create duplicate values in the index, primary key, or relationship. Change the data in the field or fields that contain duplicate data, remove the index, or redefine the index to permit duplicate entries and try again.
3024	Could not find file <File Name>.
3025	Cannot open any more files.
3026	Not enough space on disk.
3027	Cannot update. Database or object is read-only.
3028	Cannot start your application. The workgroup information file is missing or opened exclusively by another user.
3029	Not a valid account name or password.
3030	<Object or Item> is not a valid account name.
3031	Not a valid password.
3032	Cannot perform this operation.
3034	You tried to commit or rollback a transaction without first beginning a transaction.
3035	System resource exceeded.
3036	Database has reached maximum size.
3037	Cannot open any more tables or queries.
3038	System resource exceeded.
3039	Could not create index; too many indexes already defined.
3040	Disk I/O error during read.
3041	Cannot open a database created with a previous version of your application.
3042	Out of MS-DOS file handles.
3043	Disk or network error.
3044	<Object or Item> is not a valid path. Make sure that the path name is spelled correctly and that you are connected to the server on which the file resides.
3046	Could not save; currently locked by another user.
3047	Record is too large.

ERROR	DESCRIPTION
3048	Cannot open any more databases.
3050	Could not lock file.
3052	File sharing lock count exceeded. Increase MaxLocksPerFile registry entry.
3053	Too many client tasks.
3054	Too many Memo, OLE, or Hyperlink Object fields.
3055	Not a valid file name.
3056	Could not repair this database.
3057	Operation not supported on linked tables.
3058	Index or primary key cannot contain a Null value.
3059	Operation canceled by user.
3061	Too few parameters. Expected `<Number>`.
3062	Duplicate output alias `<Alias Name>`.
3063	Duplicate output destination `<Field Name>`.
3064	Cannot open action query `<Query Name>`.
3065	Cannot execute a select query.
3066	Query must have at least one destination field.
3067	Query input must contain at least one table or query.
3069	The action query `<Query Name>` cannot be used as a row source.
3070	The Microsoft Jet database engine does not recognize `<Object or Item Name>` as a valid field name or expression.
3074	Cannot repeat table name `<Name>` in FROM clause.
3075	`<Error>` in query expression `<Expression Name>`.
3076	`<Error>` in criteria expression.
3077	`<Error>` in expression.
3079	The specified field `<Field Name>` could refer to more than one table listed in the FROM clause of your SQL statement.
3080	Joined table `<Table Name>` not listed in FROM clause.
3081	Cannot join more than one table with the same name`<Object or Item Name>`.

(continued)

Table C-4 *(continued)*

ERROR	DESCRIPTION
3082	JOIN operation <Object or Item Name> refers to a field that is not in one of the joined tables.
3083	Cannot use internal report query.
3084	Cannot insert data with action query.
3085	Undefined function <Function Name> in expression.
3086	Could not delete from specified tables.
3087	Too many expressions in GROUP BY clause.
3088	Too many expressions in ORDER BY clause.
3089	Too many expressions in DISTINCT output.
3090	Resultant table not allowed to have more than one AutoNumber field.
3091	HAVING <Clause> without grouping or aggregation.
3092	Cannot use HAVING clause in TRANSFORM statement.
3093	ORDER BY <Clause> conflicts with DISTINCT.
3094	ORDER BY <Clause> conflicts with GROUP BY clause.
3095	Cannot have aggregate function in <Expression>.
3096	Cannot have aggregate function in WHERE <Clause>.
3097	Cannot have aggregate function in ORDER BY <Clause>.
3098	Cannot have aggregate function in GROUP BY <Clause>.
3099	Cannot have aggregate function in JOIN operation<Object or Item Name>.
3100	Cannot set field <Field Name> in join key to Null.
3101	The Microsoft Jet database engine cannot find a record in the Table <Table Name> with key matching field(s) <Object or Item Name>.
3102	Circular reference caused by <Object or Item Name>.
3103	Circular reference caused by alias <Object or Item Name> in query definition's SELECT list.
3104	Cannot specify fixed column heading <Object or Item Name> in a crosstab query more than once.
3105	Missing destination field name in SELECT INTO <Statement>.
3106	Missing destination field name in UPDATE <Statement>.

ERROR	DESCRIPTION
3107	Record(s) cannot be added; no insert permission on `<Object or Item Name>`.
3108	Record(s) cannot be edited; no update permission on `<Object or Item Name>`.
3109	Record(s) cannot be deleted; no delete permission on `<Object or Item Name>`.
3110	Could not read definitions; no read definitions permission for table or query `<Query Name>`.
3111	Could not create; no modify design permission for table or query `<Query Name>`.
3112	Record(s) cannot be read; no read permission on `<Object or Item Name>`.
3113	Cannot update `<Object or Item Name>`; field not updateable.
3114	Cannot include Memo, OLE, or Hyperlink Object when you select unique values`<Object or Item Name>`.
3115	Cannot have Memo, OLE, or Hyperlink Object fields in aggregate argument`<Object or Item Name>`.
3116	Cannot have Memo, OLE, or Hyperlink Object fields in criteria`<Object or Item Name>` for aggregate function.
3117	Cannot sort on Memo, OLE, or Hyperlink Object`<Object or Item Name>`.
3118	Cannot join on Memo, OLE, or Hyperlink Object`<Object or Item Name>`.
3119	Cannot group on Memo, OLE, or Hyperlink Object`<Object or Item Name>`.
3120	Cannot group on fields selected with "`<Object or Item Name>`.
3121	Cannot group on fields selected with ".
3122	You tried to execute a query that does not include the specified expression `<Expression Name>` as part of an aggregate function.
3123	Cannot use " in crosstab query.
3124	Cannot input from internal report query`<Object or Item Name>`.
3125	`<Object or Item>` is not a valid name. Make sure that it does not include invalid characters or punctuation and that it is not too long.
3126	Invalid bracketing of name `<Name>`.

(continued)

Table C-4 *(continued)*

ERROR	DESCRIPTION
3127	The INSERT INTO statement contains the following unknown field name: `<Object or Item Name>`. Make sure you have typed the name correctly, and try the operation again.
3128	Specify the table containing the records you want to delete.
3129	Invalid SQL statement; expected 'DELETE', 'INSERT', 'PROCEDURE', 'SELECT', or 'UPDATE'.
3130	Syntax error in DELETE statement.
3131	Syntax error in FROM clause.
3132	Syntax error in GROUP BY clause.
3133	Syntax error in HAVING clause.
3134	Syntax error in INSERT INTO statement.
3135	Syntax error in JOIN operation.
3136	The LEVEL clause includes a reserved word or argument that is misspelled or missing, or the punctuation is incorrect.
3137	Missing semicolon (;) at end of SQL statement.
3138	Syntax error in ORDER BY clause.
3139	Syntax error in PARAMETER clause.
3140	Syntax error in PROCEDURE clause.
3141	The SELECT statement includes a reserved word or an argument name that is misspelled or missing, or the punctuation is incorrect.
3142	Characters found after end of SQL statement.
3143	Syntax error in TRANSFORM statement.
3144	Syntax error in UPDATE statement.
3145	Syntax error in WHERE clause.
3146	ODBC--call failed.
3151	ODBC--connection to `<Object or Item Name>` failed.
3154	ODBC--could not find DLL `<Object or Item Name>`.
3155	ODBC--insert on a linked table `<Table Name>` failed.
3156	ODBC--delete on a linked table `<Table Name>` failed.
3157	ODBC--update on a linked table `<Table Name>` failed.
3158	Could not save record; currently locked by another user.

ERROR	DESCRIPTION
3159	Not a valid bookmark.
3160	Table is not open.
3161	Could not decrypt file.
3162	You tried to assign the Null value to a variable that is not a Variant data type.
3163	The field is too small to accept the amount of data you attempted to add. Try inserting or pasting less data.
3164	Field cannot be updated.
3165	Could not find .inf file.
3166	Cannot locate the requested Xbase memo file.
3167	Record is deleted.
3168	Invalid .inf file.
3169	The Microsoft Jet database engine could not execute the SQL statement because it contains a field that has an invalid data type.
3170	Could not find installable ISAM.
3171	Could not find network path or user name.
3172	Could notParadox.net.
3173	Could not open table 'MSysAccounts' in the workgroup information file.
3174	Could not open table 'MSysGroups' in the workgroup information file.
3175	Date is out of range or is in an invalid format.
3176	Could not open file <File Name>.
3177	Not a valid table name.
3179	Encountered unexpected end of file.
3180	Could not write to file <File Name>.
3181	Invalid range.
3182	Invalid file format.
3183	Not enough space on temporary disk.
3184	Could not execute query; could not find linked table.
3185	SELECT INTO on a remote database tried to produce too many fields.
3186	Could not save; currently locked by user <Name> on machine <Name>.

(continued)

Table C-4 *(continued)*

ERROR	DESCRIPTION
3187	Could not read; currently locked by user `<Name>` on machine `<Name>`.
3188	Could not update; currently locked by another session on this machine.
3189	Table `<Table Name>` is exclusively locked by user '`<Object or Item Name>`' on machine `<Name>`.
3190	Too many fields defined.
3191	Cannot define field more than once.
3192	Could not find output table `<Table Name>`.
3196	The database `<Your Database>`is already in use by another person or process. When the database is available, try the operation again.
3198	Could not start session. Too many sessions already active.
3199	Could not find reference.
3200	The record cannot be deleted or changed because table `<Table Name>` includes related records.
3201	You cannot add or change a record because a related record is required in open table `<Table Name>`.
3202	Could not save; currently locked by another user.
3203	Sub queries cannot be used in the `<Expression>`.
3204	Database already exists.
3205	Too many crosstab column headers`<Object or Item Name>`.
3206	Cannot create a relationship between a field and itself.
3207	Operation not supported on a Paradox table with no primary key.
3208	Invalid Deleted setting in the Xbase key of the Windows Registry.
3210	The connection string is too long.
3211	The database engine could not locktable `<Table Name>` because it is already in use by another person or process.
3212	Could not lock Table `<Table Name>`; currently in use by user `<Name>` on machine `<Name>`.
3213	Invalid Date setting in the Xbase key of the Windows Registry.
3214	Invalid Mark setting in the Xbase key of the Windows Registry.

ERROR	DESCRIPTION
3215	Too many Btrieve tasks.
3216	Parameter `<Parameter Name>` specified where a table name is required.
3217	Parameter `<Parameter Name>` specified where a database name is required.
3218	Could not update; currently locked.
3219	Invalid operation.
3220	Incorrect collating sequence.
3221	Invalid settings in the Btrieve key of the Windows Registry.
3222	Query cannot contain a Database parameter.
3223	`<Object or Item>` is invalid because it is too long, or contains invalid characters.
3224	Cannot read Btrieve data dictionary.
3225	Encountered a record locking deadlock while performing a Btrieve operation.
3226	Errors encountered while using the Btrieve DLL.
3227	Invalid Century setting in the Xbase key of the Windows Registry.
3228	Selected collating sequence not supported by the operating system.
3229	Btrieve--cannot change field.
3230	Out-of-date Paradox lock file.
3231	ODBC--field would be too long; data truncated.
3232	ODBC--could not create table.
3234	ODBC--remote query timeout expired.
3235	ODBC--data type not supported on server.
3238	ODBC--data out of range.
3239	Too many active users.
3240	Btrieve--missing Btrieve engine.
3241	Btrieve--out of resources.
3242	Invalid reference in SELECT statement.
3243	None of the import field names match fields in the appended table.
3244	Cannot import password-protected spreadsheet.

(continued)

Table C-4 *(continued)*

ERROR	DESCRIPTION
3245	Could not parse field names from the first row of the import table.
3246	Operation not supported in transactions.
3247	ODBC--linked table definition has changed.
3248	Invalid NetworkAccess setting in the Windows Registry.
3249	Invalid PageTimeout setting in the Windows Registry.
3250	Could not build key.
3251	Operation is not supported for this type of object.
3252	Cannot open a form whose underlying query contains a user-defined function that attempts to set or get the form's RecordsetClone property.
3254	ODBC--Cannot lock all records.
3256	Index file not found.
3257	Syntax error in WITH OWNERACCESS OPTION declaration.
3258	The SQL statement could not be executed because it contains ambiguous outer joins. To force one of the joins to be performed first, create a separate query that performs the first join and then include that query in your SQL statement.
3259	Invalid field data type.
3260	Could not update; currently locked by user <Name> on machine <Name>.
3261	Table <Table Name> is exclusively locked by user <Name> on machine <Name>.
3262	Could not lock table.
3263	Invalid Database object.
3264	No field defined--cannot append TableDef or Index.
3265	Item not found in this collection.
3266	Cannot append a Field that is already a part of a Fields collection.
3267	Property can be set only when the Field is part of a Recordset object's Fields collection.
3268	Cannot set this property once the object is part of a collection.
3269	Cannot append an Index that is already a part of an Indexes collection.

ERROR	DESCRIPTION
3270	Property not found.
3271	Invalid property value.
3272	Object is not a collection.
3273	Method not applicable for this object.
3274	External table is not in the expected format.
3275	Unexpected error from external database driver`<Object or Item Name>`.
3276	Invalid database object reference.
3277	Cannot have more than 10 fields in an index.
3278	The Microsoft Jet database engine has not been initialized.
3279	The Microsoft Jet database engine has already been initialized.
3280	Cannot delete a field that is part of an index or is needed by the system.
3281	Cannot delete this index or table. It is either the current index or is used in a relationship.
3282	Operation not supported on a table that contains data.
3283	Primary key already exists.
3284	Index already exists.
3285	Invalid index definition.
3286	Format of memo file does not match specified external database format.
3287	Cannot create index on the given field.
3288	Paradox index is not primary.
3289	Syntax error in CONSTRAINT clause.
3290	Syntax error in CREATE TABLE statement.
3291	Syntax error in CREATE INDEX statement.
3292	Syntax error in field definition.
3293	Syntax error in ALTER TABLE statement.
3294	Syntax error in DROP INDEX statement.
3295	Syntax error in DROP TABLE or DROP INDEX.

(continued)

Table C-4 *(continued)*

ERROR	DESCRIPTION
3296	Join expression not supported.
3297	Could not import table or query. No records found, or all records contain errors.
3298	There are several tables with that name. Please specify owner in the format 'owner.table'.
3299	ODBC Specification Conformance Error <Error>. Report this error to the developer of your application.
3300	Cannot create a relationship.
3301	Cannot perform this operation; features in this version are not available in databases with older formats.
3302	Cannot change a rule while the rules for this table are in use.
3303	Cannot delete this field. It is part of one or more relationships.
3304	You must enter a personal identifier (PID) consisting of at least 4 and no more than 20 characters and digits.
3305	Invalid connection string in pass-through query.
3306	You have written a subquery that can return more than one field without using the EXISTS reserved word in the main query's FROM clause. Revise the SELECT statement of the subquery to request only one field.
3307	The number of columns in the two selected tables or queries of a union query do not match.
3308	Invalid TOP argument in select query.
3309	Property value is too large.
3310	This property is not supported for external data sources or for databases created with a previous version of Microsoft Jet.
3311	Property specified already exists.
3312	Validation rules and default values cannot be placed on system or linked tables.
3313	Cannot place this validation expression on this field.
3314	The open field <Field Name> cannot contain a Null value because the Required property for this field is set to True. Enter a value in this field.
3315	Field <Object or Item Name> cannot be a zero-length string.
3317	One or more values are prohibited by the validation rule <Object or Item Name>. set for <Object or Item Name>. Enter a value that the expression for this field can accept.

ERROR	DESCRIPTION
3318	Values specified in a TOP clause are not allowed in delete queries or reports.
3319	Syntax error in union query.
3320	`<Error>` in table-level validation expression.
3321	No database specified in connection string or IN clause.
3322	Crosstab query contains one or more invalid fixed column headings.
3323	The query cannot be used as a row source.
3324	The query is a DDL query and cannot be used as a row source.
3325	Pass-through query with ReturnsRecords property set to True did not return any records.
3327	Field `<Object or Item Name>` is based on an expression and cannot be edited.
3328	Table `<Table Name>` is read-only.
3329	Record in open table `<Table Name>` was deleted by another user.
3330	Record in open table `<Table Name>` is locked by another user.
3331	To make changes to this field, first save the record.
3332	Cannot enter value into blank field on 'one' side of outer join.
3333	Records in open table `<Table Name>` would have no record on the 'one' side.
3334	Can be present only in version 1.0 format.
3335	DeleteOnly called with non-zero cbData.
3336	Btrieve: Invalid IndexDDF option in initialization setting.
3337	Invalid DataCodePage option in initialization setting.
3338	Btrieve: Xtrieve options are not correct in initialization setting.
3339	Btrieve: Invalid IndexDeleteRenumber option in initialization setting.
3341	The current field must match the join key `<Object or Item Name>` in the table that serves as the 'one' side of one-to-many relationship. Enter a record in the 'one' side table with the desired key value, and then make the entry with the desired join key in the 'many-only' table.
3342	Invalid Memo, OLE, or Hyperlink Object in subquery `<Query Name>`.

(continued)

Table C-4 *(continued)*

ERROR	DESCRIPTION
3344	The database engine does not recognize either the field <Field Name> in a validation expression, or the default value in the Table <Table Name>.
3345	Unknown or invalid field reference <Object or Item Name>.
3346	Number of query values and destination fields are not the same.
3347	Cannot add record(s); primary key for table <Table Name> not in recordset.
3348	Cannot add record(s); join key of table <Table Name> not in recordset.
3349	Numeric field overflow.
3350	Object is invalid for operation.
3351	The ORDER BY <Expression> includes fields that are not selected by the query. Only those fields requested in the first query can be included in an ORDER BY expression.
3352	No destination field name in INSERT INTO <Statement>.
3353	Btrieve: Cannot find file Field.ddf.
3354	At most one record can be returned by this subquery.
3356	You attempted to open a database that is already opened exclusively by user <Name> on machine <Name>. Try again when the database is available.
3357	This query is not a properly formed data-definition query.
3358	Cannot open the Microsoft Jet engine workgroup information file.
3359	Pass-through query must contain at least one character.
3360	Query is too complex.
3361	Unions not allowed in a subquery.
3362	Single-row update/delete affected more than one row of a linked table. Unique index contains duplicate values.
3363	Record(s) cannot be added; no corresponding record on the 'one' side.
3364	Cannot use Memo, OLE, or Hyperlink Objectfield <Field Name> in the SELECT clause of a union query.
3365	Property value not valid for REMOTE objects.
3366	Cannot append a relation with no fields defined.

ERROR	DESCRIPTION
3367	Cannot append. An object with that name already exists in the collection.
3368	Relationship must be on the same number of fields with the same data types.
3370	Cannot modify the design of table `<Table Name>`. It is in a read-only database.
3371	Cannot find table or constraint.
3372	No such index `<Object or Item Name>` on Table `<Table Name>`.
3373	Cannot create relationship. Referencedtable `<Table Name>` does not have a primary key.
3374	The specified fields are not uniquely indexed in open table `<Table Name>`.
3375	Table `<Table Name>` already has an index named `<Name>`.
3376	Table `<Table Name>` does not exist.
3377	No such relationship `<Object or Item Name>`. on Table `<Table Name>`.
3378	There is already a relationship named `<Name>` in the current database.
3379	Cannot create relationships to enforce referential integrity. Existing data in Table `<Table Name>` violates referential integrity rules in Table `<Table Name>`.
3380	field `<Field Name>` already exists in Table `<Table Name>`.
3381	There is no field named `<Name>` in Table `<Table Name>`.
3382	Size of field `<Field Name>` is too long.
3383	Cannot delete field `<Field Name>`. It is part of one or more relationships.
3384	Cannot delete a built-in property.
3385	User-defined properties do not support a Null value.
3386	Property `<Object or Item Name>` must be set before using this method.
3387	Cannot find TEMP directory.
3388	Unknown function `<Object or Item Name>` in validation expression or default value on `<Object or Item Name>`.
3389	Query support unavailable.

(continued)

Table C-4 *(continued)*

ERROR	DESCRIPTION
3390	Account name already exists.
3391	An error has occurred. Properties were not saved.
3393	Cannot perform join, group, sort, or indexed restriction. A value being searched or sorted on is too long.
3394	Cannot save property; property is a schema property.
3396	Cannot perform cascading operation. Since related records exist in open table <Table Name>, referential integrity rules would be violated.
3397	Cannot perform cascading operation. There must be a related record in open table <Table Name>.
3398	Cannot perform cascading operation. It would result in a Null key in open table <Table Name>.
3399	Cannot perform cascading operation. It would result in a duplicate key in open table <Table Name>.
3400	Cannot perform cascading operation. It would result in two updates to field <Field Name> in Table <Table Name>.
3401	Cannot perform cascading operation. It would cause field <Field Name> to become Null, which is not allowed.
3402	Cannot perform cascading operation. It would cause field <Field Name> to become a zero-length string, which is not allowed.
3403	Cannot perform cascading operation: <Object or Item Name>.
3404	Cannot perform cascading operation. The value entered is prohibited by the validation rule <Object or Item Name>. set for <Object or Item Name>.
3405	Error <Error> in validation rule.
3406	The expression you are trying to use for the DefaultValue property is invalid because <Object or Item Name>. Use a valid expression to set this property.
3407	The server's MSysConf table exists, but is in an incorrect format. Contact your system administrator.
3408	Too many FastFind Sessions were invoked.
3409	Invalid field definition <Object or Item Name> in definition of index or relationship.
3411	Invalid entry. Cannot perform cascading operation in Table <Table Name> because the value entered is too large for field <Field Name>.

ERROR	DESCRIPTION
3412	Cannot perform cascading update on the table because it is currently in use by another user.
3413	Cannot perform cascading operation on Table `<Table Name>` because it is currently in use by user '`<Object or Item Name>`' on machine `<Name>`.
3414	Cannot perform cascading operation on Table `<Table Name>` because it is currently in use.
3415	Zero-length string is valid only in a Text or Memo field.
3417	An action query cannot be used as a row source.
3418	Cannot open `<Object or Item Name>`. Another user has the table using a different network control file or locking style.
3419	Cannot open this Paradox 4.x or 5.x table because ParadoxNetStyle is set to 3.x in the Windows Registry.
3420	Object invalid or no longer set.
3421	Data type conversion error.
3422	Cannot modify table structure. Another user has the table open.
3423	You cannot use ODBC to import from, export to, or link an external Microsoft Jet or ISAM database table to your database.
3424	Cannot create database because the locale is invalid.
3425	This method or property is not currently available on this Recordset.
3426	This action was cancelled by an associated object.
3427	Error in DAO automation.
3429	Incompatible version of an installable ISAM.
3430	While loading the Microsoft Excel installable ISAM, OLE was unable to initialize.
3431	This is not a Microsoft Excel 5.0 file.
3432	Error opening a Microsoft Excel 5.0 file.
3433	Invalid setting in Excel key of the Engines section of the Windows Registry.
3434	Cannot expand named range.
3435	Cannot delete spreadsheet cells.
3436	Failure creating file.
3437	Spreadsheet is full.

(continued)

Table C-4 *(continued)*

ERROR	DESCRIPTION
3438	The data being exported does not match the format described in the Schema.ini file.
3439	You attempted to link or import a Microsoft Word mail merge file. Although you can export such files, you cannot link or import them.
3440	An attempt was made to import or link an empty text file. To import or link a text file, the file must contain data.
3441	Text file specification field separator matches decimal separator or text delimiter.
3442	In the text file specification <Object or Item Name>, the <Object or Item Name> option is invalid.
3443	The fixed width specification <Object or Item Name> contains no column widths.
3444	In the fixed width specification <Object or Item Name>, column <Object or Item Name> does not specify a width.
3445	Incorrect version of the DLL file <File Name> was found.
3446	Jet VBA file (VBAJET.dll for 16-bit versions, or VBAJET32.dll for 32-bit versions) is missing. Try reinstalling the application that returned the error.
3447	The Jet VBA file (VBAJET.dll for 16-bit versions, or VBAJET32.dll for 32-bit versions) failed to initialize when called. Try reinstalling the application that returned the error.
3448	A call to an OLE system function was not successful. Try reinstalling the application that returned the error.
3449	No country code found in connection string for a linked table.
3451	Illegal reference in query.
3452	You cannot make changes to the design of the database at this replica.
3453	You cannot establish or maintain an enforced relationship between a replicated table and a local table.
3455	Cannot make the database replicable.
3456	Cannot make the <Object Name> object in <Object or Item Name> container replicable.
3457	You cannot set the KeepLocal property for an object that is already replicated.
3458	The KeepLocal property cannot be set on a database; it can be set only on the objects in a database.

ERROR	DESCRIPTION
3459	After a database has been replicated, you cannot remove the replication features from the database.
3460	The operation you attempted conflicts with an existing operation involving this member of the replica set.
3461	The replication property you are attempting to set or delete is read-only and cannot be changed.
3462	Failure to load a DLL.
3463	Cannot find the .dll <Object or Item Name>.
3464	Data type mismatch in criteria expression.
3465	The disk drive you are attempting to access is unreadable.
3468	Access was denied while accessing dropbox folder <Folder Name>.
3469	The disk for dropbox folder <Folder Name> is full.
3470	Disk failure accessing dropbox folder <Folder Name>.
3471	Failure to write to the Synchronizer log file.
3472	Disk full for path <Path Name>.
3473	Disk failure while accessing log File <File Name>.
3474	Cannot open the log File <File Name> for writing.
3475	Sharing violation while attempting to log File <File Name> in Deny Write mode.
3476	Invalid dropbox path <Path Name>.
3477	Dropbox address <Path Name> is syntactically invalid.
3478	The replica is not a partial replica.
3479	Cannot designate a partial replica as the Design Master for the replica set.
3480	The relationship <Object or Item Name> in the partial filter expression is invalid.
3481	The table name <Name> in the partial filter expression is invalid.
3482	The filter expression for the partial replica is invalid.
3483	The password supplied for the dropbox folder <Folder Name> is invalid.
3484	The password used by the Synchronizer to write to a destination dropbox folder is invalid.
3485	The object cannot be replicated because the database is not replicated.

(continued)

Table C-4 *(continued)*

ERROR	DESCRIPTION
3486	You cannot add a second Replication ID AutoNumber field to a table.
3487	The database you are attempting to replicate cannot be converted.
3488	The value specified is not a ReplicaID for any member in the replica set.
3489	The object specified cannot be replicated because it is missing a necessary resource.
3490	Cannot create a new replica because the `<Object or Item Name>` object in `<Object or Item Name>` container could not be replicated.
3491	The database must be opened in exclusive mode before it can be replicated.
3492	The synchronization failed because a design change could not be applied to one of the replicas.
3493	Cannot set the specified Registry parameter for the Synchronizer.
3494	Unable to retrieve the specified Registry parameter for the Synchronizer.
3495	There are no scheduled synchronization's between the two Synchronizers.
3496	Replication Manager cannot find the ExchangeID in the MSysExchangeLog table.
3497	Unable to set a schedule for the Synchronizer.
3499	Cannot retrieve the full path information for a member of the replica set.
3500	You cannot specify two different Synchronizers to manage the same replica.

Index